Lecture Notes in Compute

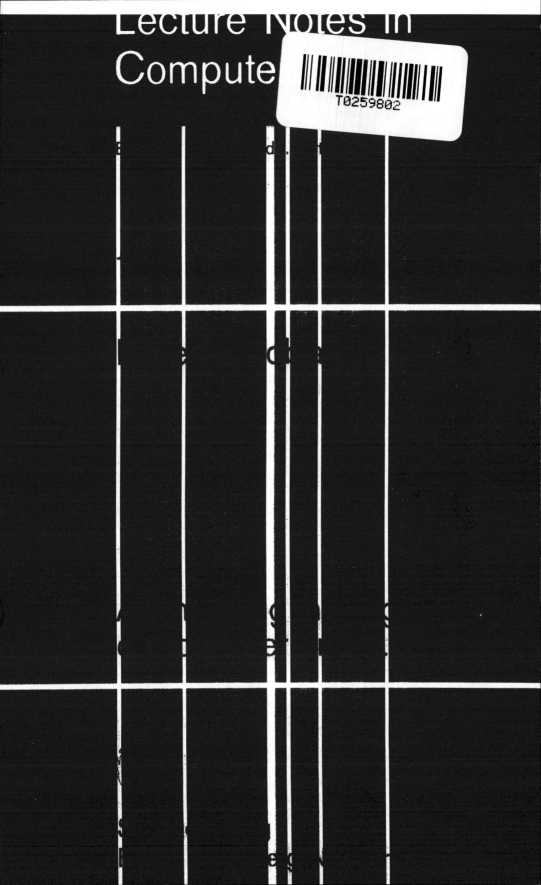

Lecture Notes in Computer Science

Vol. 23: Programming Methodology. 4th Informatik Symposium, IBM Germany Wildbad, September 25–27, 1974. Edited by C. E. Hackl. VI, 501 pages. 1975.

Vol. 24: Parallel Processing. Proceedings 1974. Edited by T. Feng. VI, 433 pages. 1975.

Vol. 25: Category Theory Applied to Computation and Control. Proceedings 1974. Edited by E. G. Manes. X, 245 pages. 1975.

Vol. 26: GI-4. Jahrestagung, Berlin, 9.–12. Oktober 1974. Herausgegeben im Auftrag der GI von D. Siefkes. IX, 748 Seiten. 1975.

Vol. 27: Optimization Techniques. IFIP Technical Conference. Novosibirsk, July 1–7, 1974. (Series: I.F.I.P. TC7 Optimization Conferences.) Edited by G. I. Marchuk. VIII, 507 pages. 1975.

Vol. 28: Mathematical Foundations of Computer Science. 3rd Symposium at Jadwisin near Warsaw, June 17–22, 1974. Edited by A. Blikle. VII, 484 pages. 1975.

Vol. 29: Interval Mathematics. Procedings 1975. Edited by K. Nickel. VI, 331 pages. 1975.

Vol. 30: Software Engineering. An Advanced Course. Edited by F. L. Bauer. (Formerly published 1973 as Lecture Notes in Economics and Mathematical Systems, Vol. 81) XII, 545 pages. 1975.

Vol. 31: S. H. Fuller, Analysis of Drum and Disk Storage Units. IX, 283 pages. 1975.

Vol. 32: Mathematical Foundations of Computer Science 1975. Proceedings 1975. Edited by J. Bečvář. X, 476 pages. 1975.

Vol. 33: Automata Theory and Formal Languages, Kaiserslautern, May 20–23, 1975. Edited by H. Brakhage on behalf of GI. VIII, 292 Seiten. 1975.

Vol. 34: GI – 5. Jahrestagung, Dortmund 8.–10. Oktober 1975. Herausgegeben im Auftrag der GI von J. Mühlbacher. X, 755 Seiten. 1975.

Vol. 35: W. Everling, Exercises in Computer Systems Analysis. (Formerly published 1972 as Lecture Notes in Economics and Mathematical Systems, Vol. 65) VIII, 184 pages. 1975.

Vol. 36: S. A. Greibach, Theory of Program Structures: Schemes, Semantics, Verification. XV, 364 pages. 1975.

Vol. 37: C. Böhm, λ-Calculus and Computer Science Theory. Proceedings 1975. XII, 370 pages. 1975.

Vol. 38: P. Branquart, J.-P. Cardinael, J. Lewi, J.-P. Delescaille, M. Vanbegin. An Optimized Translation Process and Its Application to ALGOL 68. IX, 334 pages. 1976.

Vol. 39: Data Base Systems. Proceedings 1975. Edited by H. Hasselmeier and W. Spruth. VI, 386 pages. 1976.

Vol. 40: Optimization Techniques. Modeling and Optimization in the Service of Man. Part 1. Proceedings 1975. Edited by J. Cea. XIV, 854 pages. 1976.

Vol. 41: Optimization Techniques. Modeling and Optimization in the Service of Man. Part 2. Proceedings 1975. Edited by J. Cea. XIII, 852 pages. 1976.

Vol. 42: James E. Donahue, Complementary Definitions of Programming Language Semantics. VII, 172 pages. 1976.

Vol. 43: E. Specker und V. Strassen, Komplexität von Entscheidungsproblemen. Ein Seminar. V, 217 Seiten. 1976.

Vol. 44: ECI Conference 1976. Proceedings 1976. Edited by K. Samelson. VIII, 322 pages. 1976.

Vol. 45: Mathematical Foundations of Computer Science 1976. Proceedings 1976. Edited by A. Mazurkiewicz. XI, 601 pages. 1976.

Vol. 46: Language Hierarchies and Interfaces. Edited by F. L. Bauer and K. Samelson. X, 428 pages. 1976.

Vol. 47: Methods of Algorithmic Language Implementation. Edited by A. Ershov and C. H. A. Koster. VIII, 351 pages. 1977.

Vol. 48: Theoretical Computer Science, Darmstadt, March 1977. Edited by H. Tzschach, H. Waldschmidt and H. K.-G. Walter on behalf of GI. VIII, 418 pages. 1977.

Vol. 49: Interactive Systems. Proceedings 1976. Edited by A. Blaser and C. Hackl. VI, 380 pages. 1976.

Vol. 50: A. C. Hartmann, A Concurrent Pascal Compiler for Minicomputers. VI, 119 pages. 1977.

Vol. 51: B. S. Garbow, Matrix Eigensystem Routines – Eispack Guide Extension. VIII, 343 pages. 1977.

Vol. 52: Automata, Languages and Programming. Fourth Colloquium, University of Turku, July 1977. Edited by A. Salomaa and M. Steinby. X, 569 pages. 1977.

Vol. 53: Mathematical Foundations of Computer Science. Proceedings 1977. Edited by J. Gruska. XII, 608 pages. 1977.

Vol. 54: Design and Implementation of Programming Languages. Proceedings 1976. Edited by J. H. Williams and D. A. Fisher. X, 496 pages. 1977.

Vol. 55: A. Gerbier, Mes premières constructions de programmes. XII, 256 pages. 1977.

Vol. 56: Fundamentals of Computation Theory. Proceedings 1977. Edited by M. Karpiński. XII, 542 pages. 1977.

Vol. 57: Portability of Numerical Software. Proceedings 1976. Edited by W. Cowell. VIII, 539 pages. 1977.

Vol. 58: M. J. O'Donnell, Computing in Systems Described by Equations. XIV, 111 pages. 1977.

Vol. 59: E. Hill, Jr., A Comparative Study of Very Large Data Bases. X, 140 pages. 1978.

Vol. 60: Operating Systems, An Advanced Course. Edited by R. Bayer, R. M. Graham, and G. Seegmüller. X, 593 pages. 1978.

Vol. 61: The Vienna Development Method: The Meta-Language. Edited by D. Bjørner and C. B. Jones. XVIII, 382 pages. 1978.

Vol. 62: Automata, Languages and Programming. Proceedings 1978. Edited by G. Ausiello and C. Böhm. VIII, 508 pages. 1978.

Vol. 63: Natural Language Communication with Computers. Edited by Leonard Bolc. VI, 292 pages. 1978.

Vol. 64: Mathematical Foundations of Computer Science. Proceedings 1978. Edited by J. Winkowski. X, 551 pages. 1978.

Vol. 65: Information Systems Methodology, Proceedings, 1978. Edited by G. Bracchi and P. C. Lockemann. XII, 696 pages. 1978.

Vol. 66: N. D. Jones and S. S. Muchnick, TEMPO: A Unified Treatment of Binding Time and Parameter Passing Concepts in Programming Languages. IX, 118 pages. 1978.

Vol. 67: Theoretical Computer Science, 4th GI Conference, Aachen, March 1979. Edited by K. Weihrauch. VII, 324 pages. 1979.

Vol. 68: D. Harel, First-Order Dynamic Logic. X, 133 pages. 1979.

Vol. 69: Program Construction. International Summer School. Edited by F. L. Bauer and M. Broy. VII, 651 pages. 1979.

Vol. 70: Semantics of Concurrent Computation. Proceedings 1979. Edited by G. Kahn. VI, 368 pages. 1979.

Vol. 71: Automata, Languages and Programming. Proceedings 1979. Edited by H. A. Maurer. IX, 684 pages. 1979.

Vol. 72: Symbolic and Algebraic Computation. Proceedings 1979. Edited by E. W. Ng. XV, 557 pages. 1979.

Vol. 73: Graph-Grammars and Their Application to Computer Science and Biology. Proceedings 1978. Edited by V. Claus, H. Ehrig and G. Rozenberg. VII, 477 pages. 1979.

Vol. 74: Mathematical Foundations of Computer Science. Proceedings 1979. Edited by J. Bečvář. IX, 580 pages. 1979.

Vol. 75: Mathematical Studies of Information Processing. Proceedings 1978. Edited by E. K. Blum, M. Paul and S. Takasu. VIII, 629 pages. 1979.

Vol. 76: Codes for Boundary-Value Problems in Ordinary Differential Equations. Proceedings 1978. Edited by B. Childs et al. VIII, 388 pages. 1979.

Lecture Notes in Computer Science

Edited by G. Goos and J. Hartmanis

130

Robert Goldblatt

Axiomatising the Logic of Computer Programming

Springer-Verlag
Berlin Heidelberg New York 1982

Author

Robert Goldblatt
Department of Mathematics
Victoria University, Private Bag
Wellington, New Zealand

CR Subject Classifications (1981): 5.21, 5.24

ISBN 3-540-11210-3 Springer-Verlag Berlin Heidelberg New York
ISBN 0-387-11210-3 Springer-Verlag New York Heidelberg Berlin

Library of Congress Cataloging in Publication Data
Goldblatt, Robert. Axiomatising the logic of computer programming. (Lecture notes in computer science; 130) Bibliography: p. Includes index. 1. Programming languages (Electronic computers)– Semantics. 2. Proof theory. I. Title. II. Series.
QA76.7G65 519.4 82-863 ISBN 0-387-11210-3 (U.S.) AACR2

Printing and binding: Beltz Offsetdruck, Hemsbach/Bergstr.
2145/3140-543210

To Helen,

and to Jed and Hannah

PREFACE

This is a small step for Computer Science: a step towards a systematic proof-theory for programming-language semantics. We study a language that is designed to formalise assertions about how programs behave. In this language each program determines a modal connective that has the meaning "*after the program terminates* ...". Such connectives appear in the "algorithmic logic" of A. Salwicki at Warsaw, but the explicit use of techniques from modal logic in this area was initiated more recently by V.R. Pratt at M.I.T., and has become known as "dynamic logic". It is to the latter that the present work is directly related.

Our approach contains a number of distinctive features. Notably, a contrast is made between *external* and *internal* logic : between the operations performed by the programmer in reasoning about program behaviour, and those performed by the computer in evaluating Boolean expressions. The programmer's external propositional logic is the classical two-valued one, while the computer may sometimes leave certain expressions undefined - e.g. if their evaluation fails to terminate. This leads us to a three-valued model of computer logic, based on a "sequential" interpretation of Boolean connectives. (This is not claimed to be the official model, but it is a natural interpretation, and readers interested in others are encouraged to adapt our techniques to cater for them.) The external language includes the internal one (the programmer can talk about the machine, but not conversely), and so the presence of undefined expressions has implications for the programmer's *quantificational* logic. The version used here is a variant of "logic without existence assumptions": it accommodates the possibility that the value of a quantifiable variable may not exist.

The general purpose of this book is to establish a methodological framework for proof-theory and axiomatisation. Within that, our central aim is to analyse the operation of assigning a value to a program variable. This is the most basic of commands, and - although representable as a dynamic form of logical substitution - is the fundamental departure that takes computation theory beyond the traditional province of mathematical logic. In Part I a complete axiomatisation is developed of the class of valid assertions about programs of the following kinds:

assignments	($x := \sigma$)
composites	(compound statements)
conditionals	(*if-then-else*)
iterations	(*while-do*)
alternations	(non-deterministic choice).

This would appear to provide an adequate formalisation of the system used by E.W. Dijkstra in his well-known book *A Discipline of Programming*. Moreover it is known that by using all except the last of these concepts a program can be written to compute each partial recursive function. Hence, by Church's Thesis, this language is *in theory* as powerful as can be: it contains programs for all possible algorithms. But of course in comparison to real programming languages it is extremely limited. Its relationship to the latter is perhaps comparable to the relationship between Turing machines and actual computers. Just as Turing machines are crucial to a theoretical understanding of the nature of algorithms, the above constructs are crucial to a theoretical understanding of the structure of programs (and structured programming).

However, an adequate semantical theory must eventually be applicable to the concepts and devices found in actual programming practise, and so in Part II we begin to move in this direction. We study function declarations, procedure calls, and the syntactic and semantic roles of the indexed variables used to denote components of arrays. This enables us to investigate the various proof rules that have been proposed by C.A.R. Hoare for such notions, and to develop an analysis of the parameter-passing mechanisms of call-by-value, call-by-name, and call-by-reference.

In the more abstract realms of mathematical thought it is sometimes possible for a person to single-handedly exhaust the investigation of a particular topic, and then produce the definitive account of it. Programming-language semantics is not like that. It is an inherently open-ended subject that depends on the perspectives and ideas of many contributors for its development. Its character is as much that of an empirical study as that of an intellectually creative one: it uses mathematics to model real-world phenomena that are produced in response to practical need as much as theoretical principle. An appropriate analogy is with the linguistics of natural languages - no-one would claim to have had the final say about the semantics of English

In such disciplines it is often necessary to produce an exposition of the current state-of-the-art in order to stand back, evaluate, and thereby move on to new understandings. This book should be seen as a stage in such a process. Its object, as the title is intended to convey, is to pursue the problem of proof-theoretically generating *all* the valid assertions about programs in a given language. Its major contributions in this regard can be seen as

(1) the adaptation to quantificational programming logics of the methodology of "Henkin-style" completeness proofs via canonical model constructions; and

(2) the analysis of *while*-commands in terms of an infinitary rule-schema. The techniques and ideas used originate in the mathematical studies of intensional logics that have taken place in the two decades or so since the advent of "Kripke semantics". Thus the work may well be of interest to logicians who are unfamiliar with computer science, as well as to computer scientists who have little background in formal logic. For this reason an initial chapter is provided that gives an informal overview of the necessary conceptual background. But it should be understood that the text does not purport to provide an exposition of the general study of Programming Logics. It is simply an individual contribution to an aspect of that discipline, and as such is not unlike a large research paper. In an appendix to Part I, a survey is given of works by others, but this is little more than an annotated bibliography: its purpose is to lend perspective and context to the present work, and to point the reader in some appropriate directions. By pursuing these references s/he will become aware of the numerous important contributions that have not been cited here.

This typescript has been prepared by Shelley Carlyle, to whom the author is indebted once again for her expertise and cooperation. The cost of preparation was generously subsidised by a grant from the Internal Research Committee of the Victoria University of Wellington.

CONTENTS

Preface v

PART I. FOUNDATIONS 1

Chapter 1 Conceptual Background 2

1. Internal and External Logic 2
2. Correctness and Proof 3
   Adequacy of Rules 12
3. Termination 13
4. Correctness by Refinement 15
5. Modal Logic 17
6. Incompleteness 19
7. Infinitary Rules 22
   The Status of Infinitary Rules 23
8. Extending the Language 25
   Termination 25
   Assignments 26
   Equivalence of Programs 28
   Determinism 29
   The Concept of State 30
9. Undefined Expressions 30
10. The Power of the Language 32
11. Aims and Objects 34

Chapter 2 The Logical Structure of Commands 36

1. Syntax 36
2. Semantics 39
   Models 39
   Satisfaction 42
3. Standard Models 47
   Iteration as a Fixed Point 51
   The Analysis of "*while*" 53
4. Proof Theory 56
   Axioms 57
   Rules of Inference 58
   Theories 65

5. Completeness 71

Canonical Models 76

6. Determinism 87

Weakest Preconditions 90

Test Commands 93

7. Non-Determinism 95

Alternatives 95

Guarded Commands 96

if .... *fi* 97

do .... *od* 104

Chapter 3 Assignments 108

1. The Concept of Data Type 108

Many-sorted Operations 108

Signatures and Algebras 109

2. The Syntax of a Signature 113

3. Semantics 115

Models 115

Rigid Designators 116

Satisfaction 117

Natural Models 122

4. Proof Theory 137

Rich Theories 144

5. Completeness 149

Strong Completeness 163

6. Non-Enumerability of PL 166

7. Axiomatising the Theory of a Data Type 171

The Concept of Data Type Revisited 177

8. Freedom and Substitution 178

Appendix 1 Some Related Studies 183

Engeler's Use of Infinitary Language 183

Algorithmic Logic 186

Constable's Programming Logic 189

Completeness for Hoare-style Rules 190

Dynamic Logic 193

Applications of Temporal Logic 197

Process Logics 199

Kröger's Rules for Loops 203

PART II. APPLICATIONS 205

Chapter 4 Function Declarations 207

1. User-Defined Functions 207

Call-By-Value 209

Side Effects 210

2. Environments and Function Calls 213

3. Standard Models 216

4. Completeness for Simple Calls 219

5. A Proof Rule for Functions 222

6. Call-By-Name 233

7. Non-Recursive Functions 235

Chapter 5 Procedures 238

1. Declarations 238

2. Calling a Procedure 240

3. Hoare's Rule of Substitution 242

Chapter 6 Arrays 251

1. Array Types 251

Index Types 254

The Values of Indexed Variables 255

2. Syntax and Semantics of Arrays 256

Language 256

Models 259

3. Axioms for Arrays 264

4. Call-By-Reference 277

Functions 281

Appendix 2 Syntax in BNF 283

Appendix 3 Axioms 285

Appendix 4 Standard-Model Conditions 289

References 291

List of Symbols 299

Index 302

PART I FOUNDATIONS

It is reasonable to hope that the relationship between computation and mathematical logic will be as fruitful in the next century as that between analysis and physics in the last. The development of this relationship demands a concern for both applications and mathematical elegance.

John McCarthy, 1963.

CHAPTER 1

CONCEPTUAL BACKGROUND

1.1 INTERNAL AND EXTERNAL LOGIC

In the following pages, techniques and ideas from mathematical logic are applied to an aspect of computer science. Our concern is to analyse and formalise the patterns of thought that are used in reasoning about the behaviour of computers and the algorithms that they process. A formal system will be developed on the basis of a distinction between two kinds of logical activity. On the one hand we have the logical operations performed by the computer itself when it calculates the truth-value of certain basic expressions, in order to thereby determine its next action. This will be called *internal* logic. It is, for example, the logic of the expression ε in a command of the form

$$\textit{while}\ \varepsilon\ \textit{do}\ \alpha.$$

External logic, on the other hand, is concerned with the structure of assertions *about* programs and the effects of their execution. When people write programs, they have in mind certain tasks that are to be carried out. Such an intention might be expressed by a programmer in a sentence of the form

(1) *when program* α *terminates,* ψ *will be true,*

or, more generally,

(2) *if the assertion* φ *is true before initiation of program* α,
then the assertion ψ *will be true on its completion.*

For instance, if α is intended to find the remainder r upon division of x by y (where x and y denote natural numbers), then we might express this by taking

φ as

$$0 < y$$

and ψ as

$$\exists q\,(x = q \times y + r) \wedge (r < y),$$

where $\exists q$ is the existential quantifier "for some q" and $\wedge$ is the logical connective "and".

Assertions of the type (1) and (2) belong to external logic, which itself includes, and is intermeshed with, the internal logic. Both aspects are represented within the formal language that will be the object of our investigations. But in addition to this we have an informal *metalanguage* (the language in which this book is written) that is used to make assertions about the formal language (e.g. that certain sentences are provable/imply other sentences/have no models etc.), and so there are all told *three* levels of logical activity. This is in marked contrast to the situation in traditional mathematical logic, where generally we emphasise only two levels - metalanguage and object language, the latter being designed to formally express the properties of conventional algebraic operations. The reason for the extra dimension here is that whereas traditional logic attempts to describe the static properties that these operations have, in the present context we wish to study their dynamic *performance*, in time, by some computing agent. In this introductory chapter we will sketch the historical background to this kind of study, and outline the main conceptual features of the theory to be developed in the chapters to follow.

1.2 CORRECTNESS AND PROOF

How can the programmer be sure that the algorithm he devises actually does what he wants it to do? This is known as the problem of program *correctness*. Consider, for example, the flowchart (3), in which x, y, r are natural-number-valued variables.

(3)

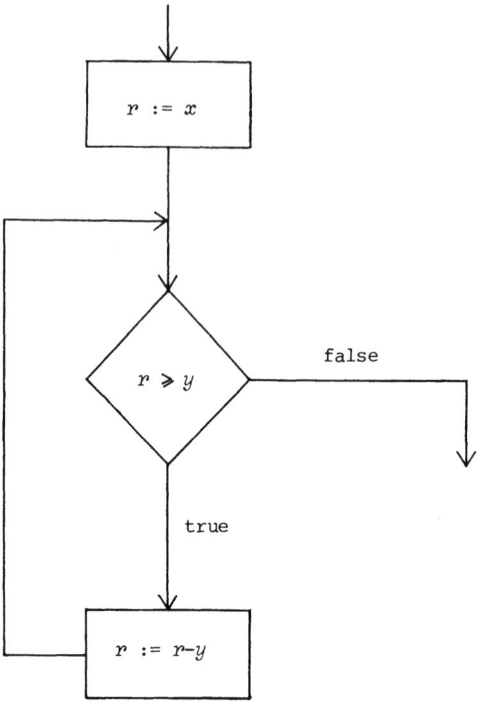

First of all we may ask "what operation does this flowchart perform?" Given an answer, we may then ask for a rigorous mathematical proof that it is the *correct* answer. But then the interrogation could be pushed even deeper, by demanding an explication of the meaning of "rigorous proof".

In fact this flowchart computes the remainder upon division of x by y, and to an experienced computer-scientist this answer may spring off the page almost immediately. We could then inquire as to what aspects of his knowledge and experience allowed him to make this conclusion.

On the other hand, to people unfamiliar with the graphical notation of (3) we would first have to explain what command boxes and decision diamonds are, and perhaps what the symbol := means in an assignment command. Once this has been grasped, it is a matter of their understanding that the particular series of operations specified do indeed lead to the remainder upon division. Of course if they are not sure what "remainder" and "division" mean then we may still have a long way to go towards a proof that is convincing *for them*.

It becomes apparent that the notion of an adequate proof is relative to the person who is trying to grasp it. At the least we can say that a proof, by its nature, consists in a demonstration that a certain fact depends upon, or can be reduced to, certain other facts. The latter may in turn require proving, and so on. But as far as programmers are concerned, we can reasonably claim that in order to be able to carry out their function properly they must understand the characteristic properties of the data types that they write programs for. These structures, initially the integers, the real numbers, and the two-element Boolean algebra, are just the sort of thing that traditional mathematical logic has been developed to analyse. Thus an adequate correctness proof for a program might well consist in the reduction of an assertion to certain facts about data types, with the standard machinery of logic being invoked to provide "proofs" of these later facts.

The kind of standard logical machinery for data types that we have in mind here is called *elementary* ("of elements") or *first-order* logic. Its statements ("well-formed formulae") are built up from an alphabet that comprises

(i) variables $x,y,z,\ldots$ whose values are the individual elements of some data type;

(ii) symbols that denote operations on these elements, e.g. the operations $+$, $\times$, $-$, $\div$ on numbers : the sort of operation that a computer performs;

(iii) symbols for relations between, or properties (predicates) of, individuals, e.g. the relations $=$, $\neq$, $<$, $>$, $\leqslant$, and $\geqslant$: the sort of relations whose truth-values are tested by a computer in applying its internal logic;

(iv) the statement-forming connectives $\wedge$ ("and"), $\vee$ ("or"), $\neg$ ("not"), $\rightarrow$ ("implies"), $\leftrightarrow$ ("if and only if");

(v) the universal quantifier $\forall$ ("for all"), and the existential quantifier $\exists$ ("for some").

The name "first-order" refers to the fact that the variables x, y,... that may be quantified denote basic *elements* of the data type, and not any "higher-order" entities such as sets of elements, sets of sets of elements, etc.

A technique for proving correctness of flowcharts was first developed by R.W. Floyd (1967). (The essential idea appears to have been suggested by von Neumann and Goldstine in 1946 (cf. von Neuman (1963)) and Turing (1949), while a similar notion was independently studied by Naur (1966)). Floyd's method can be understood as follows. A flowchart could be a complex diagram, built up from simpler flowcharts by various constructions, but it will always be assumed to have a unique entry arrow and a unique exit arrow. An *interpretation* of such a flowchart is made by attaching assertions to its entry and exit arrows. The interpretation

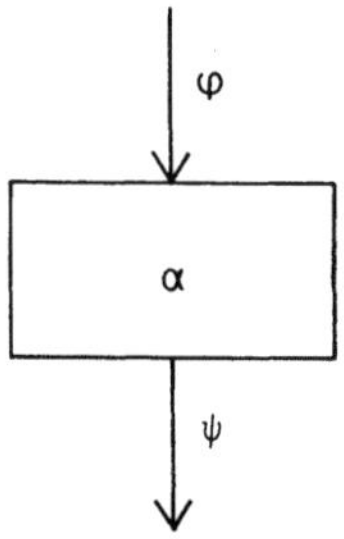

is called *correct* if the assertion ψ is true when the computation process reaches the exit point of flowchart α, provided that φ was true when it reached the entry point to α. Thus correctness of this interpretation amounts to the truth of the statement (2) above. The method then requires the development of rules or conditions for correctness of interpretations, and the correctness of a particular algorithm is given by showing that the desired interpretation obeys these rules. We now consider four such conditions.

I. Rule of Assignment.

The interpretation

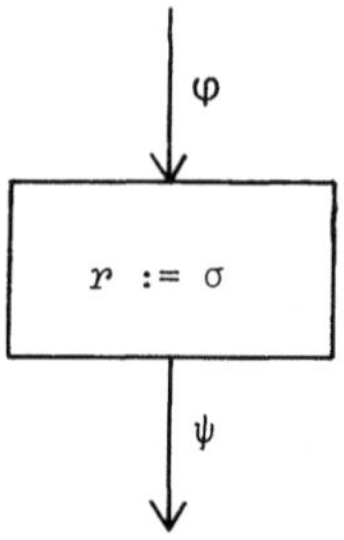

is correct if φ *is the assertion obtained by replacing all free occurrences of* r *in* ψ *by* σ.

The idea behind this rule is that when the assignment has been completed, the variable r has the same value that the expression σ had beforehand, so that any statement that is true of (the value of) r afterwards must have been true of (the value of) σ to begin with. For example, the following is a correct interpretation of an assignment command.

(4)

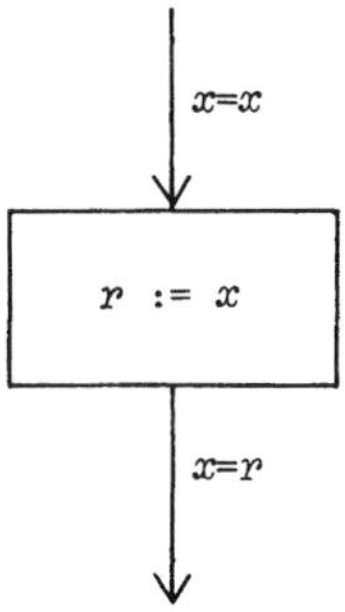

II. Rule of Consequence.

This is a rule that allows us to form a new correct interpretation from a given one. It stipulates that *if*

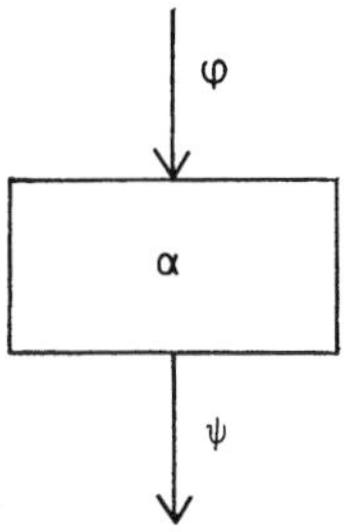

is correct, and moreover

(i) φ' *implies* φ , *and*

(ii) ψ *implies* ψ',

then

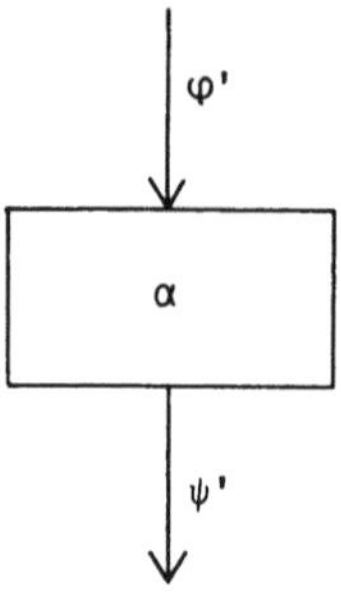

is correct.

This rule is justified by observing that (i) means that if φ' is true then so is φ, while (ii) means that if ψ is true then so is ψ', so that the correctness of the second interpretation does indeed follow from that of the first.

Now the meaning of "implies" tells us that

$$0 < y$$

implies

$$x = x$$

(since $x = x$, being true, is implied by any statement whatever). Furthermore the assertion

$$x = r$$

implies

$$\exists q(x = q \times y + r)$$

(take $q = 0$), and so by applying these facts, and the Rule of Consequence, to interpretation (4) we get

(5)

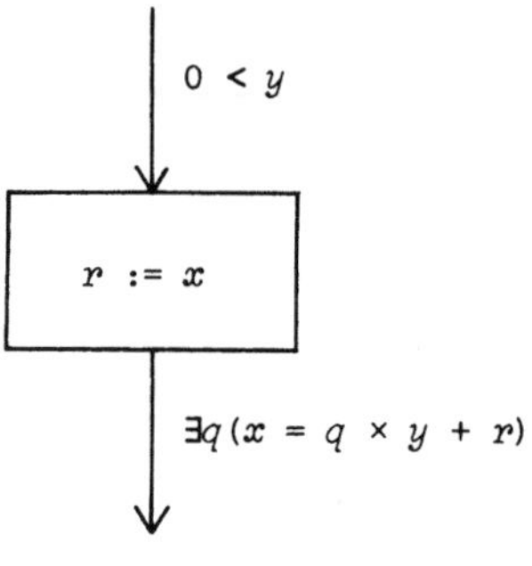

as a correct interpretation. This gives us the first step towards a correctness proof for flowchart (3).

III. Rule of Iteration.

This asserts that *if*

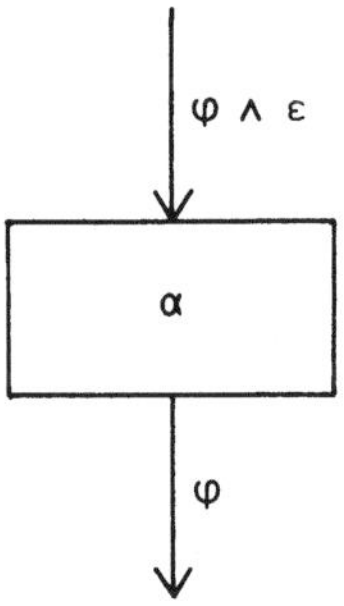

is a correct interpretation, then so too is

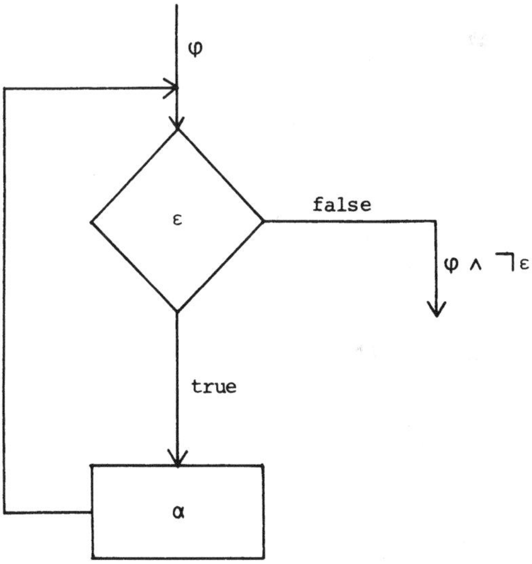

The second of these flowcharts incorporates a loop. Execution involves first testing the "condition" ε. If ε is false then α is omitted. If ε is true then α is executed. This procedure is then repeated over and over until ε is found to be false (hence its negation $\neg\varepsilon$ is true), at which point the process exits from the flowchart. But if φ is true on entry to this diagram, then, by the hypothesis on the first diagram, φ will remain true every time the process loops through α. That is, φ is an *invariant* of the loop, and so finally upon exit φ will be true, along with $\neg\varepsilon$. (This flowchart corresponds to the command *while* ε *do* α).

The Rule of Iteration allows us to derive

(6)

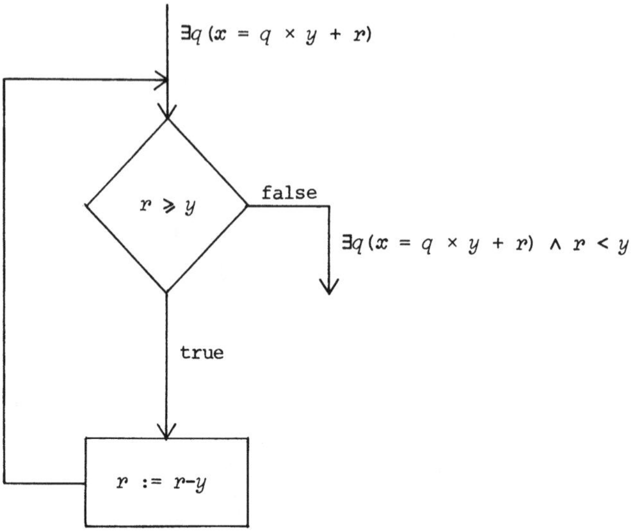

as a correct interpretation from

(7)

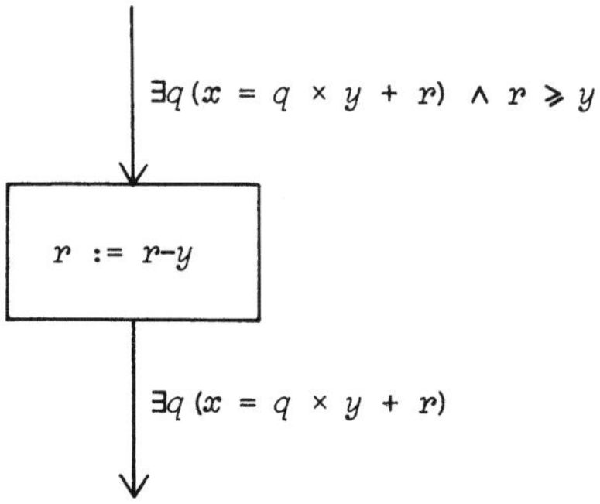

provided that (7) is correct (identifying $\neg(r \geqslant y)$ with $r < y$). But to prove that (7) is indeed correct, observe that if the assertion attached to the entry of (7) is true, then for some number q_o the assertion

$$x = q_o \times y + r \;\wedge\; r \geqslant y$$

is true. Then elementary arithmetical reasoning implies that $(r-y)$ is a well-defined natural number and that the assertion

$$x = (q_o + 1)y + (r-y)$$

is true. Hence the assertion

(8) $$\exists q(x = q \times y + (r-y))$$

is implied by the entry assertion of (7). But the interpretation

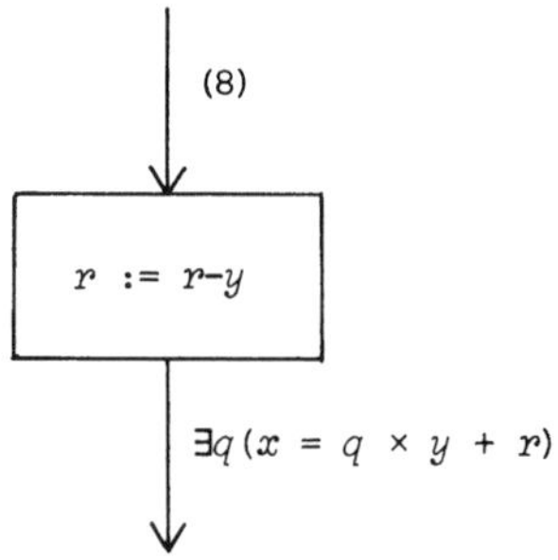

is correct, by the Rule of Assignment, and so this, by the above observations and the Rule of Consequences, yields the correctness of (7).

IV. Rule of Composition.

This applies to a flowchart constructed by juxtaposing two others in sequence. The rule is that *if*

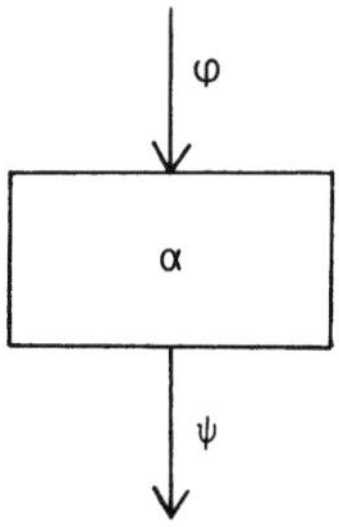

and

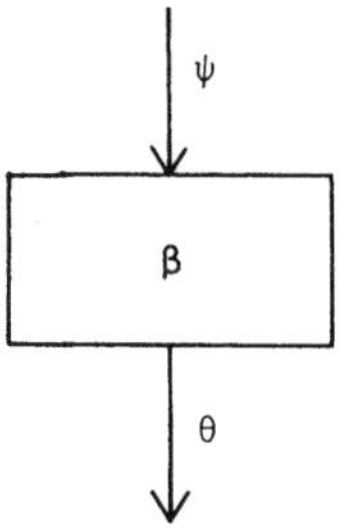

are both correct, then so is

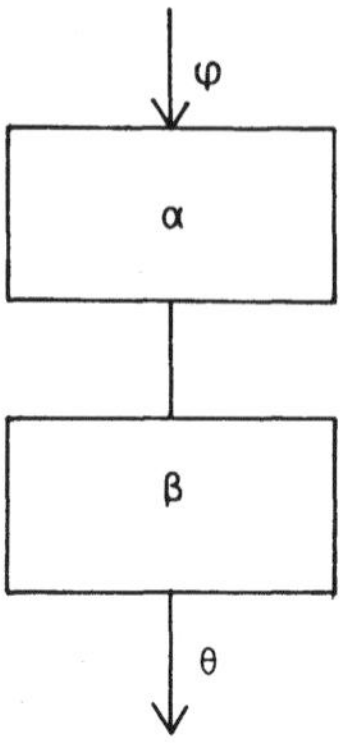

Given the hypothesis of this rule, it is apparent that if φ is true on entry to α, and execution of α is followed immediately by β, then at the end of the whole process, i.e. on exit from β, θ will be true.

Applying the Rule of Composition to diagrams (5) and (6) yields

(9)

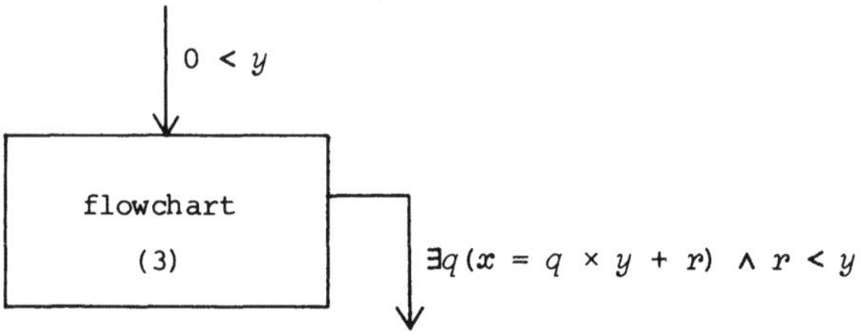

as a correct flowchart interpretation.

ADEQUACY OF RULES

The derivation of interpretation (9) constitutes a "proof" that flowchart (3) computes the remainder upon division of x by y. Reflecting on the principles used in this proof we see that apart from the four rules for flowchart interpretations, all other reasoning (such as the inferring of (8)) can be expressed in the first-order language of the arithmetic of natural numbers. As to the rules themselves, the last three, concerned with operations that construct new interpretations from given ones, were easily justified by consideration of the meanings of the concepts involved. But in order to apply such constructions we have to be given some correct interpretations from the outset, and these are provided by the Rule of Assignment. The latter also was given a heuristic justification, but its status is somewhat different in that it is concerned with syntactic manipulations of statements φ, ψ, and so a proper justification would require an account of how such manipulations influence the truth-values of the statements involved.

Ultimately then our first rule depends upon a rigorous theory of the meaning of entry and exit assertions. For the present we should regard it as a postulate, an assumed principle. By declaring it to be a valid principle we could be said to be giving a description, or even a definition, of what exactly an assignment command is. (This is the point of view taken by Hoare and Wirth (1973) in their axiomatic definition of Pascal). But in that case we must face the question as to whether it is an *adequate* definition, i.e. whether it encapsulates the full meaning of the command ($r := x$), or whether, alternatively, there are valid principles which we might want to use in reasoning about such commands but which are not derivable from the Rule of Assignment.

One of our main tasks in latter chapters will be to develop a semantic analysis of the operation of computations and the meanings of assertions about them. This will lead to a precise mathematical definition of the "meaning" of a command and the truth-value of an assertion. On this basis we will be able to give a rigorous demonstration that the Rule of Assignment is valid, and deal with the question of its adequacy.

1.3 TERMINATION

The attentive reader may feel that the role of the assertion "$0 < y$" in the correctness proof for our remainder-finding algorithm (3) has not been fully exposed. Its insertion (in (5)) was justified by the fact that it implies the statement $x=x$. But as already noted, so does any other assertion, and hence (9) would be a correct interpretation no matter what entry-assertion we took. By taking one that simply *is* true, e.g. $0 = 0$, it follows that what we really have is a proof of the type-(1) assertion

(10) *if* (3) *terminates, then on termination it will be true that* $\exists q(x = q \times y + r) \wedge r < y$.

Now when $0 < y$ is false, i.e. when $y = 0$, division by y, and hence the remainder, is simply undefined. This is quite compatible with (10), because of the crucial presence of the word "if". The point is that when (3) is entered with $y = 0$, then the test condition $r \geqslant y$ becomes $r \geqslant 0$, which is *always* true, as r is a natural-number variable, and so the process loops forever and never reaches the exit. There is no completed computation, and hence no "answer" for the remainder r.

A more rigorous formulation of this non-termination proof can be given by lifting it into the framework of flowchart interpretations, via an argument by reductio ad absurdum. We establish that if termination did occur, then a contradiction would follow. For this it suffices to prove the correctness of an interpretation whose exit-assertion is known to be *false*, and hence cannot be "brought about". For our present example we can formalise the fact that flowchart (3) does not alter the value of y, to obtain from the four rules a proof that the interpretation

(11)

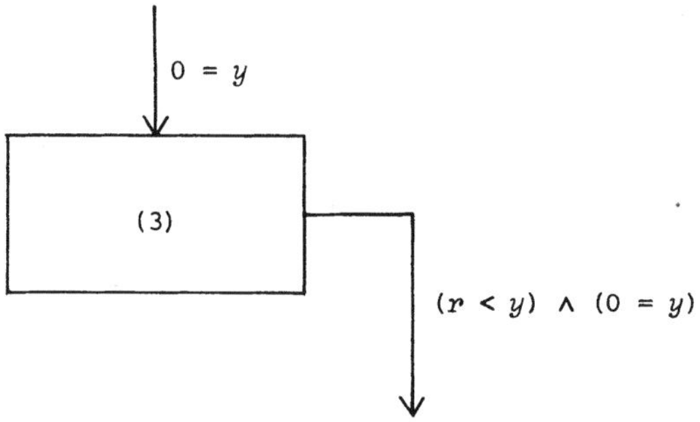

is correct (the details are left to the reader, for whom it is high time an exercise was provided). But the exit condition of (11) is false, since r is a variable over non-negative numbers, so that when the entry condition is true, correctness implies that the exit cannot be reached.

On the other hand if y is positive on entry to (3), computation always does terminate. The reason is that repeated subtraction of y from the value of r must eventually, after a finite number of loops, reduce that value to a number less than y, and so make the test-condition $r \geqslant y$ false (note that by a large enough choice of x we can make the required number of loops as large as we like). This argument can be given a rigorous mathematical form, based on the "well-foundedness" of the

$<$-ordering of the natural numbers. However, unlike non-termination, such an argument cannot be given in terms of our rules for flowchart interpretations, since these establish what happens *if* termination occurs, and do not yield the conclusion *that* it occurs. Termination is a quite seperate issue to correctness, and for this reason statements like (1) and (2) are sometimes called *partial* correctness assertions. *Total* correctness refers to an assertion that a program both terminates and is (partially) correct. (For a survey of various techniques of termination-proof cf. Manna and Waldinger (1978)).

1.4 CORRECTNESS BY REFINEMENT

After Floyd's paper, the next development was the definitive work of C.A.R. Hoare (1969) in adapting the method to programs presented as pieces of linear text. He introduced the symbolism

$$\varphi\{\alpha\}\psi$$

to stand for the partial correctness assertion (2), i.e. "if φ is true before initiation of α, then ψ will be true when α terminates". In this notation, writing

$$\vdash \theta$$

for "θ is provable", the four correctness rules can be given a very concise form, as follows.

I. Rule of Assignment.

$$\vdash \psi^r_\sigma \{r := \sigma\} \psi$$

where ψ^r_σ *is the assertion obtained by replacing all free occurrences of* r *in* ψ *by* σ.

II. Rule of Consequence.

If	$\vdash \varphi\{\alpha\}\psi$
and	$\vdash (\varphi' \rightarrow \varphi)$
and	$\vdash (\psi \rightarrow \psi')$,

then $\vdash \varphi'\{\alpha\}\psi'$

(recall that $\rightarrow$ is the logical connective "implies").

III. Rule of Iteration.

If $\vdash (\varphi \wedge \varepsilon)\{\alpha\}\varphi$

then $\vdash \varphi\{\textit{while } \varepsilon \textit{ do } \alpha\}\ (\varphi \wedge \neg\varepsilon)$.

IV. Rule of Composition.

If $\vdash \varphi\{\alpha\}\psi$ *and* $\vdash \psi\{\beta\}\theta$,

then $\vdash \varphi\{\alpha;\beta\}\theta$

where $\alpha;\beta$, the *composition* of α and β, denotes the command executed by doing α and then following with β immediately afterwards ($\alpha;\beta$ is sometimes called a "compound" command).

Subsequent papers by Hoare and his collaborators introduced rules for other programming concepts, such as the

Conditional Rule:

If $\vdash \varphi \wedge \varepsilon\ \{\alpha\}\ \psi$

and $\vdash \varphi \wedge \neg\varepsilon\ \{\beta\}\ \psi$

then $\vdash \varphi\{\textit{if } \varepsilon \textit{ then } \alpha \textit{ else } \beta\}\psi$.

These studies culminated in an attempt by Hoare and Wirth (1973) to axiomatise a substantial portion of the language Pascal, including rules for operations on array, record, and file types, and procedure and function declarations.

One advantage of this use of linear symbolism is that it provides a way of setting out proofs of correctness assertions that meshes easily with conventional display methods used in formal proof-systems. Hoare's original paper, for example, contains (p.579) a correctness proof for a remainder-finding algorithm that looks just like the sort of proof-sequence that one might find in any standard logic text.

The methodological perspective that has emerged from these axiomatic investigations is that the programmer should be encouraged to develop a correctness proof concurrently with the original development of his algorithm, rather than try to reconstruct one afterwards. A textbook has now been written (Alagic and Arbib (1978)), based on the Hoare-Wirth axioms, that aims to teach the reader how to use Pascal in this way. Its guiding philosophy of program construction, known as *top-down design*, or *step-wise refinement*, is explained by the authors thus (p.2):

> *decompose the over-all problem into precisely specified subproblems, and prove that if each subproblem is solved correctly, and these solutions are fitted together in a specified way, then the original problem will be solved correctly. Repeat this process of "decompose and prove correctness of the decomposition" for the subproblems; and keep repeating this process until reaching subproblems so simple that their solution can be expressed in a few lines of a programming language.*

1.5 MODAL LOGIC

Syntactically speaking, Hoare's notation

(12) $$\varphi\{\alpha\}\psi$$

associates with each program α a *two-placed connective* on statements, i.e. a connective that forms a new statement out of two given ones. More recently, Vaughan Pratt (1976), following a suggestion of R. Moore, has explored the idea of associating a *one-placed* connective with each α, to form assertions

(13) $$[\alpha]\psi,$$

to be read "*after* α *terminates,* ψ *will be true*", i.e. "(1)" (a similar notion has been developed by A. Salwicki (1970) and colleagues in Warsaw).

Now (13) could be *defined* as

$$\mathit{true}\{\alpha\}\psi,$$

where true denotes some universally true assertion (e.g. 0=0), while, conversely, (12) is definable in Pratt's notation as

$$\varphi \rightarrow [\alpha]\psi.$$

Formally the choice of starting point is a matter of convention, but the significance of the introduction of (13) is that the study of one-placed connectives, usually known as *modal* operators, is a well-advanced chapter in mathematical logic. Historically the impetus for developing modal logic was provided by philosophically motivated logicians, studying the expression

$$\Box\,\psi$$

under such interpretations as "it is necessarily true that ψ", "it is believed that/known that/ψ", "it ought to be/could be/will be/has always been/ψ", and so on. There have also been more mathematically inspired readings, such as "it is provable that" (Gödel, 1933), "it is provable in first-order arithmetic that" (cf. Boolos (1979)), and "it is locally the case that" (due to F.W. Lawvere, c.f. Goldblatt (1979, Ch.14)).

Propositional (i.e. quantifier-free) modal logics have been intensively investigated in recent times, using a "relational" semantics due to Saul Kripke (1963a). Their expressive power is now well understood, and sophisticated techniques of model-building are available (cf. Lemmon and Scott (1977), Segerberg (1971), Goldblatt (1976)). The beginnings of a relational semantics for correctness-assertions were given by Hoare and Lauer (1974), and the two theories combined into a propositional modal logic of programs by Fischer and Ladner (1977). The language used by the latter, like that of Pratt, includes modal operators corresponding to such commands as "test φ" (which does not halt if φ is false) and the non-deterministic "do α a finite number of times". Here φ and α are permitted to contain subformulae of arbitrary complexity, including other modal operators, and so such commands are rather powerful. This is indicated by the fact that they can be used to define *while-do* and *if-then-else* (Fischer-Ladner p.290).

In terms of the distinction with which we began this chapter, the sort of commands just described should be seen as part of *external* logic. The test command could only be implemented in general if φ was a Boolean expression, while the non-deterministic one is really a device for reasoning about the behaviour of α (it is similar to the "iteration quantifier" of Salwicki (1970)). But it seems rather unnatural to define standard programming concepts in terms of operations not usually available to the programmer, and so in the logical system presented in this book *while*-commands and conditionals are treated as primitive program-constructors, and all modal operators correspond to commands that are to be found in any high-level programming language. This logical system is a species of "first-order modal logic" (Pratt's school have dubbed their work "dynamic" logic - cf. Harel (1978) - in recognition of its potential application to actions performed by agents other than computers). But readers familiar with the first-order modal systems studied hitherto - such as those in Hughes and Cresswell (1968), Thomason (1970), Gabbay (1976), or Bowen (1979) - should appreciate that the one developed here is different to all of these, and is based on features that seem to be distinctive of computational semantics. This is particularly so of the treatment of Boolean (propositional) variables, the choice of so-called "rigid designators", and the use of undefined expressions.

1.6 INCOMPLETENESS

Let us return to the question of *adequacy* of rules of inference. First of all we need to be more precise about what φ and ψ are to be in the assertion $\varphi\{\alpha\}\psi$. In all of the examples of correctness proofs given by Hoare and Alagic and Arbib, φ and ψ are taken as formulae in the first-order language of the data type involved. This restriction is made quite explicitly by Mitchell Wand (1978) in a demonstration that Hoare's system can be *incomplete* for some structures. Generally, incompleteness of a deductive system means that there are assertions which are true of the intended model(s) of the system but which cannot be derived as theorems of that system. The most celebrated example of this phenomenon is Gödel's Incompleteness Theorem, to the effect that any system for the first-order theory of addition and multiplication of natural numbers must be incomplete (assuming that it is free from contradiction). "Any" here refers to systems whose theorems can be enumerated by an algorithm. Gödel proved in 1931 that for any effective procedure for generating truths of arithmetic, there will always be some such truth that it fails to generate. This had a devastating impact at the time, as it destroyed the project known as "Hilbert's Programme". David Hilbert wanted to demonstrate the consistency of the mathematics of his day by capturing it in a formal proof-system and then showing that the system contained no derivation of any contradictory assertion (like $\varphi \wedge \neg\varphi$). Such an enterprise requires a precise definition of what a proof (derivation) is, and for this Hilbert specified an explicit directly inspectable and mechanically checkable display of finite length. In other words, the property of being a proof had to be algorithmically testable. For such a notion of proof it can be shown that the provable assertions are effectively generable, and so Gödel's result established that the kind of system Hilbert wanted simply did not exist, even for as small a fragment of mathematics as the arithmetic of whole numbers.

From a more positive point of view it can be said that it is due to Gödel's pioneering work that we now have a well-developed theory of computability, including a good deal of knowledge about what can and what cannot be done by algorithms, and how "hard" various procedures are to compute (see Machtey and Young (1978) for a recent report on the state of the art). Today's student of logic, meeting the Incompleteness Theorem for the first time fifty years on, is unlikely to recoil with the shock that Hilbert felt. Without any preconceptions to the contrary, he is more likely to see it as just a fact about the limitations of certain proof procedures - a deep insight into the way things actually are.

Wand's example of incompleteness is based on the data type A depicted in the following diagram.

(14)

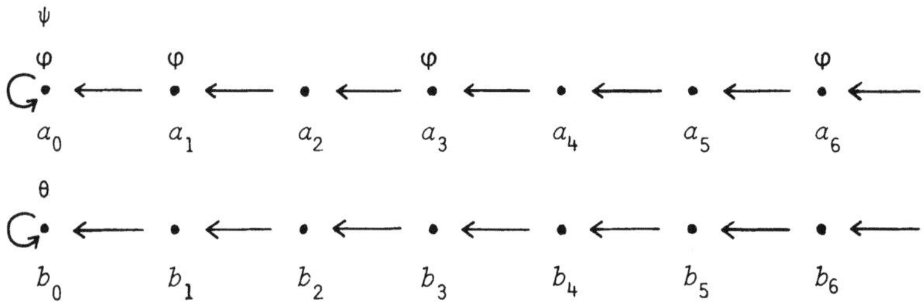

A consists of the set

$$A = \{a_n, b_n : n \in \mathbb{N}\}, \text{ where } \mathbb{N} = \{0,1,2,\ldots\}$$

on which are defined an operation $f : A \to A$ (whose action is indicated by the arrows), and three one-placed predicates φ, ψ, and θ, satisfying

$$f(x_o) = x_o,\quad f(x_{i+1}) = x_i, \qquad \text{for } x = a,b$$

$$\varphi(x) \text{ iff } x = a_{(1/2)k(k+1)} \qquad \text{for some } k \in \mathbb{N}$$

$$\psi(x) \text{ iff } x = a_o$$

$$\theta(x) \text{ iff } x = b_o.$$

The following partial correctness assertion is manifestly true with respect to A.

(15) $$\varphi x\{\mathit{while} \neg\psi x \wedge \neg\theta x \ \mathit{do}\ x := fx\}\psi x.$$

For if φ is initially true of x, so that x denotes an element of the form a_n, and the program in (15) terminates, it will have done so after some finite number of iterations of the operation f, ending at an x-value of which ψ or θ is true. But this value could only be a_o, so ψx is indeed true on termination. (One of the purposes of the semantical theory we are going to develop is to give a systematic analysis and verification of informal arguments like this).

However, (15) cannot be derived by Hoare's rules for correctness assertions, even if we allow as axioms every first-order formula that is true of the structure A. In order to derive (15) we would first have to find a loop invariant for the program, i.e. a formula χ for which

(16) $$\chi \wedge (\neg\psi x \wedge \neg\theta x)\{x := fx\}\chi$$

is provable, yielding

$$\chi\{\mathit{while} \neg\psi x \wedge \neg\theta x \ \mathit{do}\ x := fx\}\chi \wedge (\psi x \vee \theta x)$$

by the Iteration Rule, and then derive

(17) $$\varphi x \rightarrow \chi$$

and

(18) $$\chi \wedge (\psi x \vee \theta x) \rightarrow \psi x$$

in order to finally obtain (15) by the Rule of Consequence. But Wand shows by an elegant model-theoretic argument that there is no formula χ in the first-order language of A such that the assertions (16), (17), and (18) are all true of that structure.

1.7 INFINITARY RULES

Wand's example shows that a particular proof-system is incomplete, but not that there is no possible axiomatisation of the class of true assertions in question. If a derivation of (15) is to be found, it will require some new rule(s) of inference. One way to achieve this is to introduce an *infinitary* rule, i.e. one that employs infinitely many premisses. This seems not inappropriate, in view of the "after some finite number of loops" aspect to reasoning about *while*-commands. We introduce, for each natural number n, a premiss making an assertion about what happens after n loops. The case $n = 0$ is included, and we reserve the name

skip

for the *dummy*, or *empty* command "do nothing" (i.e. "do 0 loops"). *skip* always terminates, leaving everything just as it was, hence the

Dummy Rule

$$\vdash \varphi\{skip\}\varphi.$$

Now for a given command α, we inductively define

$$\alpha^0 = skip$$
$$\alpha^{n+1} = \alpha;\ \alpha^n$$

so that α^n means "do α n times".

Next, consider the assertion

(19n) $$\varphi\{\alpha^n\}(\neg\varepsilon \rightarrow \psi).$$

This states that if φ is true beforehand, then after n executions of α if a situation is reached at which ε is false, ψ will at that point be true. So, suppose we enter the algorithm

while ε *do* α

with φ true. If termination occurs, it will have done so after a finite number, say n, of executions of α, with ε then false. If ($19n$) is true, we may then conclude that ψ holds at this termination point. In other words, the following rule is valid (i.e. yields a true conclusion if the premisses are all true).

(20) $$\text{If } \vdash \varphi\{\alpha^n\}(\neg\varepsilon \rightarrow \psi) \text{ for all } n \in \mathbb{N},$$
$$\text{then } \vdash \varphi\{\mathit{while}\ \varepsilon\ \mathit{do}\ \alpha\}\psi.$$

To apply this rule to Wand's structure A we inductively put

$$f^0x = x$$
$$f^{n+1}x = f(f^nx).$$

Then using the Dummy Rule (for $n = 0$), and the Composition Rule (for the inductive step from n to n+1), we can derive, for each n, and each formula χ, the assertion

($21n$) $$\chi(f^nx)\{(x := fx)^n\}\chi,$$

where $\chi(f^nx)$ is obtained by replacing free x in χ by f^nx.

Now take χ as $(\psi x \vee \theta x) \rightarrow \psi x$, and observe that for this choice the first-order formula

($22n$) $$\varphi x \rightarrow \chi(f^nx)$$

is true of A, hence admissible as an axiom. But then ($21n$), ($22n$), and the Rule of Consequence yield

$$\varphi x\{(x := fx)^n\}((\psi x \vee \theta x) \rightarrow \psi x),$$

for all n. Application of (20) then immediately infers (15).

THE STATUS OF INFINITARY RULES

By allowing the use of inference rules that have infinitely many premisses we have to give up Hilbert's requirements that the notion of a proof be decidable and that theorems be effectively generable. It is known that admission of the well-known "Omega-Rule", which states that

$$\text{if } \vdash \varphi(n) \text{ for all } n \in \mathbb{N}, \text{ then } \vdash \forall x\varphi(x),$$

allows all truths of arithmetic to be derived (even if this rule is only applied when its set of premisses can be algorithmically generated).

But most applications of formal logic to mathematical theories have employed only finitary rules, and seem to presuppose that this is how things must be done. Machtey and Young (1978, p.132), for example, typify the views of many authors in contending that for any "halfway reasonable" theory the provable statements will be effectively enumerable. Whether or not one agrees, it has to be admitted that the point of view is an *assertion*, and it can at least be questioned. In this regard it is pointful to note that Mathematical Logic, as we know it, is a discipline that reached maturity before Computer Science was born and that it was developed to provide a rigorous foundation to *extant* mathematical knowledge. The early foundational studies of this century were concerned to cope with "paradoxes" and "crises" that resulted from the application of little understood methods to new and unfamiliar ideas about infinite sets. Today the practising mathematician understands very well the properties of infinities, and manipulates them with the same confidence with which he treats the finite. But although the use of formal logic played a vital role in bringing this circumstance about, it does not follow that its present techniques will apply to subsequent discoveries, or that new ideas and arguments can be confined to its traditional framework. It is the duty of the logician approaching a new mathematical discipline to acknowledge its actual content and ask the question that Georg Kreisel (1970, p.489) puts thus:

> *"What principles of proof do we recognize as valid once we have understood (or, as one sometimes says, 'accepted') certain given concepts?"*

It seems to this author that the rather facile derivation of (15) by means of the proof principle (20) given above provides an analysis that is a good approximation to the earlier informal argument for the truth of the assertion in question. Our contention is that reasoning about *while*-commands is naturally encapsulated in an infinitary rule, and so such rules are to be used in a system that is designed to formally represent such reasoning. At any rate, as we shall see, we cannot do without them. Faced with the Incompleteness Theorem we have to make a choice. Either we pull down the blinds of Hilbert's Programme and *redefine* a reasonable mathematical theory as one whose theorems are algorithmically generable, or we recognise with Kreisel (p.511, Note 22) that

> *"properly interpreted, Gödel's theorems can be used to support this insight [that proofs are infinite iterations of basic steps], just as they are used to refute Hilbert's* assumption *that finite formal derivations reflect faithfully the structure of mathematical reasoning."*

1.8 EXTENDING THE LANGUAGE

Another way to strengthen Hoare's proof theory would be to relax the limitation on formation of correctness assertions that admits only $\varphi\{\alpha\}\psi$, where φ and ψ are first-order formulae. If the language is based on modal operators then the restriction begins to seem rather artificial, particularly if our system is to be a representation of reasoning *about* programs. At present, for instance, we can formalise certain assertions but not their denials - we admit $[\alpha]\varphi$ but not $\neg[\alpha]\varphi$ - and there are a number of important concepts whose expression requires us to allow modal operators to occur within subformulae of more complex formulae. Here now are some illustrations.

TERMINATION.

Recall the non-termination proof in 1.3 that took the form of showing that if termination did occur then a false assertion would be realised. Thus non-termination of α is expressible as

$$[\alpha]\mathit{false},$$

where false is a constant symbol denoting a universally false statement (e.g. $\neg\mathit{true}$). But then the formula

$$\neg[\alpha]\mathit{false},$$

unavailable in Hoare's notation, expresses "α terminates". Thus

$$\neg\varepsilon \rightarrow \neg[\mathit{while}\ \varepsilon\ \mathit{do}\ \alpha]\mathit{false}$$

formalises the principle that a *while*-command halts if its test condition is false. Indeed in this situation execution of the *while*-command requires no action, so a statement will be true after execution just in case it is true before. Hence

$$\neg\varepsilon \rightarrow ([\mathit{while}\ \varepsilon\ \mathit{do}\ \alpha]\varphi \leftrightarrow \varphi)$$

is valid. We shall modify this slightly below, after making a distinction between internal and external versions of negation.

ASSIGNMENTS.

In the new notion the Rule of Assignment becomes

$$\psi^{r}_{\sigma} \rightarrow [r := \sigma]\psi,$$

but the intuition that suggests that this is valid does the same to

$$[r := \sigma]\psi \rightarrow \psi^{r}_{\sigma}\ ,$$

and hence to

$$\psi^{r}_{\sigma} \leftrightarrow [r := \sigma]\psi$$

(this will be modified below to allow for the possibility that σ has no value). The point is that, intuitively, ψ^{r}_{σ} makes the same assertion about the value of σ that ψ makes about the value of r, and so asserting ψ^{r}_{σ} is tantamount to asserting that "if r were given the same value as σ, then ψ would be true". This is why ψ^{r}_{σ} is to be logically equivalent to $[r := \sigma]\psi$.

In all of our discussion relating to the Rule of Assignment we have not explained what a "free" occurrence of r in ψ is. In first-order logic this just means that the occurrence is not within a subformula of ψ of the form $\forall r\varphi$ or $\exists r\varphi$ (i.e. the occurrence is not within the "scope" of a quantifier). Also, we neglected to say that we only replace r by σ if r is *free for* σ in ψ, which means that no variable occurring in σ becomes "captured" by a quantifier as a result of the substitution. These notions are readily formalised for first-order formulae, and in many books the formal definition is left as a technicality to be filled in by the reader. But in our modal language they assume a new dimension, because of the occurrence of variables within programs. Consider, for example, the intuitively true assertion

$$[x := y+1]\ (x = y+1).$$

If we replace y by x here, we obtain the absurdity

$$[x := x+1]\ (x = x+1).$$

The essential point is that an assignment command changes the value of the variable that appears to the left of the := sign, and acts rather like a quantifier on that variable. Thus all occurrences of x in φ will be treated as bound (i.e. not free) within $[x := \sigma]\varphi$. Also the occurrence of x to the left of := is regarded as bound in this formula, although all occurrences within σ remain free. Thus a legitimate substitution instance of

$$[x := x+1]\ (x > 1)$$

would be

$$[x := 0+1]\ (x > 1)$$

as the second occurrence (only) of x is free. Roughly speaking, the free variables in an expression are those whose function or meaning is not indicated by their syntactic role, but which have to be given a particular value before the whole expression can be said to have a meaning. This suggests that the free occurrences in a program are those that serve only to denote the value of a variable prior to execution, and which do not alter their denotatum as a result of that execution. Thus in

$$(y := y+1\ ;\ x := y)$$

the second occurrence of y should be free, but the other two bound, and in

$$\mathit{while}\ r > y\ \mathit{do}\ (r := r-y)$$

both occurrences of y are free, while r has no free occurrence at all.

It is clear that what is needed is a rigorous definition of "free" and "free for", by induction on the formation of programs, and assertions about them. Such an account is provided in §3.8, but the author is not convinced that it is the whole story (or necessarily the right one). Potentially this is a real stumbling-block, because in classical first-order logic the formula ψ^r_σ plays a crucial role, particularly in dealing with the quantifier $\forall r$ in the Completeness Theorem (see e.g. p.133 of Enderton (1972)). However we get over this difficulty by turning the greater complexity of our language to full advantage: the assertion $[r := \sigma]\psi$ will be explicitly used in places where ψ^r_σ has been traditionally employed. Thus our system constitutes something of a departure even in its treatment of the standard quantifiers.

EQUIVALENCE OF PROGRAMS.

As an instance of

$$\psi^r_\sigma \leftrightarrow [r := \sigma]\psi$$

we have

$$\psi \leftrightarrow [r := r]\psi,$$

reflecting the fact that the command $(r := r)$ changes nothing, and so is "equivalent" to *skip*. But the latter satisfies

$$\psi \leftrightarrow [\mathit{skip}]\psi$$

and so

$$[r := r]\psi \leftrightarrow [\mathit{skip}]\psi$$

is valid. In general, derivability of the schema

$$[\alpha]\psi \leftrightarrow [\beta]\psi$$

formalises the fact that α and β are equivalent programs, i.e. that they halt for the same inputs and bring about the same output situations.

We can also formalise *conditional* equivalences, e.g. that a *while*-command is equivalent to the dummy command when its test expression is false. This becomes

$$\neg\varepsilon \rightarrow ([\textit{while}\ \varepsilon\ \textit{do}\ \alpha]\psi \leftrightarrow [\textit{skip}]\psi).$$

The "fixed-point" semantics for *while*-commands due to Dana Scott is based on the idea that if β denotes

$$\textit{while}\ \varepsilon\ \textit{do}\ \alpha,$$

then β is equivalent to the command

$$\textit{if}\ \varepsilon\ \textit{then}(\alpha;\beta)\ \textit{else}\ \textit{skip}.$$

Our formal theory will both validate and derive the appropriate schema, as above, that corresponds to this equivalence (cf. §2.3).

DETERMINISM.

A program is *deterministic* if its output on termination is uniquely determined by the situation, or "state", that it was in when initiated. Alternatively, a program is non-deterministic if a given input-state can lead to more than one possible terminal state. This may happen if the program is permitted to make a random choice of its next action from a number of possibilities. The point of view we adopt here is the same as that of Dijkstra (1976), namely that we are dealing with a class of things called programs, some of which happen to be deterministic. In the present set-up the deterministic α's are simply characterised as those that validate the assertion

(23) $$[\alpha]\varphi \vee [\alpha]\neg\varphi$$

(or equivalently,

$$\neg[\alpha]\varphi \rightarrow [\alpha]\neg\varphi\ ).$$

To see this, it is best to read [α]φ as "*whenever* α terminates, φ" or "α *always* terminates with φ true". If there is only one possible outcome, it satisfies φ or ¬φ, so that one of the disjuncts of (23) must obtain. But if there are two possible outcomes, one could fail to satisfy φ and the other reject $\neg\varphi$, making both disjuncts false.

Our semantics of programs associates with each α a binary relation between states. If the pair $\langle s,t\rangle$ belongs to this relation, it means that t is one of the possible terminal states when α is initiated in state s. $[\alpha]\varphi$ is true in s just in case φ is true in *all* states to which s is related. In particular $[\alpha]\mathit{false}$ holds iff s has no related terminal states.

The assertion (23) characterises those semantical models in which the α-relation is a *partial function* on the state set, i.e. it relates each s to *at most* one t.

THE CONCEPT OF STATE.

In order to determine the truth-value of an assertion like $(r=x)$ in state s it is necessary to know what the variables r and x are referring to. Thus s must determine a *value* for each variable. In fact it would be possible to *define* a "state" as being a function that makes value-assignments to variables. However it will be more convenient in constructing models to regard states as primitive entities, each of which has a value-assignment associated with it.

A state for us is not the same thing as an instantaneous configuration, or "snapshot", of any particular machine as it processes a particular program, since it may assign values to infinitely many variables and be treated as the initial-state for infinitely many programs. Thus our notion of state is more general than that of the state of a Turing machine or finite automaton. We could have chosen a more neutral word like "situation" or "context" in place of "state", but there seems little harm in following customary usage.

1.9 UNDEFINED EXPRESSIONS

A distinctive feature of our treatment of variables will be to allow them, and hence more complex expressions, to have no value in some situations. This is appropriate in a computing environment for dealing with expressions, such as 0/0, which might be syntactically well-formed but whose evaluation may require an illegal operation, and hence constitute an "error". Another important use concerns *function declarations*, as in languages like Algol and Pascal, that permit the programmer to define his own function by writing a subprogram that calculates its values. In the event that the subprogram fails to terminate, the function-value is undefined : in general function declarations produce partial functions.

The method we adopt for handling undefined expressions is well established in the theory of computation (cf. McCarthy (1963), Manna and McCarthy (1970)), but does not appear to have been axiomatised in this context before. It is similar to what is traditionally known as "free logic" or "logic without existence assumptions" (cf. e.g. Scott (1967)). The basic idea is that each structure A is expanded to $A^+ = A \cup \{\omega\}$, where ω is some entity not in A, and variables of the type of A are taken as ranging over A^+. A variable is assigned ω when it is intended that it be undefined in A. In this way every expression acquires a "formal value", and this allows an inductive definition of the relation "φ holds in state s", which is written

$$\models_s \varphi,$$

for every formula φ. The relation is to obtain only if all variables in φ take values in A relative to s. If φ does not hold in s, we write

$$\not\models_s \varphi.$$

In the definition of $\models_s \varphi$, the range of a quantifier does not include ω, so that $\forall x$ means "for all x in A" and $\exists x$ means "for some x in A" (there is no symbol in our formal language for the "fictitious" entity ω). On this account the classical first-order axiom

$$\forall x\varphi \to \varphi^x_y$$

is not valid, since φ^x_y will not hold, even if $\forall x\varphi$ does, when y is undefined. The axiom must be modified to

$$\forall x\varphi \wedge Dy \to \varphi^x_y$$

where Dy means "y is defined". The formal theory will yield

$$\models_s (y=y) \quad \text{iff} \quad y \text{ is defined in state } s,$$

and so the expression Dy will be identified with (in fact defined as) $y=y$.

For external logic then there are exactly two truth-values:- *holding* and *not-holding* (we eschew the use of "true" and "false" here). But *internally* the computer will react differently according to whether φ is true, false, or undefined. Suppose, for instance, that φ is $(\varepsilon \vee \delta)$, where ε and δ are Boolean expressions, and in state s ε is true but δ is determined by a function declaration involving a subprogram that does not halt when started from s. Then externally $(\varepsilon \vee \delta)$ will be undefined, and hence will not hold in state s. The same applies to $(\delta \vee \varepsilon)$. But consider the commands

(24) *if* $(\varepsilon \vee \delta)$ *then skip, else skip*

(25) *if* $(\delta \vee \varepsilon)$ *then skip, else skip*

Assuming the computer processes expressions from left to right (it will have some preferred direction), then in (24) it will decide that $(\varepsilon \vee \delta)$ is true as it determines that its first disjunct ε is true, and then proceed to execute *skip* and terminate. However in the case of (25), it will attempt to evaluate the undefined δ first, and fail to terminate.

Similarly if ε is false and δ undefined, the computer will treat $(\varepsilon \wedge \delta)$ as false and $(\delta \wedge \varepsilon)$ as undefined. It is at this semantic level that the distinction between internal and external logic is brought out most clearly. Our treatment of logical connectives will follow the classical account externally, while internally we use the "sequential" interpretation of McCarthy (1963). The two interpretations are identical for defined expressions.

1.10 THE POWER OF THE LANGUAGE

Although our language could be called a kind of first-order one, since it has explicit quantification only over elements of structures, it is very much more powerful than non-modal first-order languages, and becomes so as soon as it is able to express the notion of termination. In a sense the modal operators behave like restricted quantifiers over higher order entities ("there exists a terminal state", "φ holds in *all* terminal states", etc.). To see this, let $\alpha_{\mathbb{N}}$ denote the program

$$(x := 0 \ ; \ \mathit{while} \ x \neq y \ \mathit{do} \ x := fx).$$

If 0 denotes the number zero and f the successor function $n \mapsto n+1$, then $\alpha_{\mathbb{N}}$ will always halt (with $x=y$) if x and y are natural-number variables. In other words the assertion

(26) $$\neg[\alpha_{\mathbb{N}}]\mathit{false}$$

is true of the data type $\mathbb{N} = \{0,1,2,\ldots\}$. The reason is that every natural number can be obtained from 0 by a finite number of iterations of the successor function. Indeed this is almost a definition of "natural number", and (26) is a version of the Peano Induction Postulate, which states that any subset of $\mathbb{N}$ containing 0 and closed under the successor function is equal to $\mathbb{N}$. If we conjoin to (26) the statements

$$fx = fy \rightarrow x=y$$

and

$$fx \neq 0$$

we have a remarkably simple version of the Peano Postulates - a single sentence whose only model is $\mathbb{N}$. But it is well known that in non-modal first-order logic there is no such sentence, or even set of sentences. First-order arithmetic has *non-standard* models - structures that have $\mathbb{N}$ as a substructure, satisfy exactly the same first-order sentences as $\mathbb{N}$, but contain elements that are "bigger" than all the numbers in $\mathbb{N}$. If y denotes such an element, then the program $\alpha_{\mathbb{N}}$ will never terminate, since the value of x will go on increasing forever without reaching that of y. Hence (26) will be false with respect to any non-standard model of arithmetic.

This example will be employed in §3.6 to show, with the help of Gödel's Incompleteness Theorem, that our use of infinitary rules about *while*-commands is simply unavoidable: they cannot be replaced by any finitary ones without reducing the class of provable theorems.

1.11 AIMS AND OBJECTS

This Chapter has presented a discursive account of the conceptual background to the formal studies to follow. Our aim is to develop a language for expressing assertions about programs, a mathematical semantics for this language, and an axiomatisation of the resulting class of valid assertions. The path we follow mirrors the "top-down" approach to program-design described in §1.4. In Chapter 2 we analyse Composition, Conditionals, and Iteration - the operations that decompose a program into its subroutines. The fundamental constituents of a complex program are left "blank" at this stage as undefined symbols. In effect this means that we are studying the logical structure of program *schemes*. The only basic expressions dissected here are *Boolean* ones (i.e. the ε in *while* ε ... and *if* ε ...). The treatment of these in computational semantics is quite distinctive: to the extent that they can be true or false they are like the well-formed-formulae of classical propositional logic; to the extent that they denote elements of the data type $\mathbb{B}$ (the two-element Boolean algebra) they are like terms in a first-order language; and to the extent that they are like both they are not quite the same as either.

In Chapter 3 we fill in the blanks by introducing assignment commands, along with quantification over variables that have their values altered by such commands. This completes Part I, and thereby establishes the conceptual framework, techniques, and fundamental results of our study.

Part II applies our methods to the analysis of a number of special notions used in programming languages: procedure and function declarations, array types, and parameter passing mechanisms. The underlying philosophy here is one of "small beginnings". The prospect of producing a single axiom system that derives just the valid assertions about *all* programs in, say, Pascal is a daunting one, and is best approached by a series of individual studies of the many different notions involved. Once each of these is well understood the problem of putting them all together into one structure can be more realistically tackled. A start has been made here: hopefully one that points the way to further progress.

Although the object is to axiomatise the valid assertions, our goal does not simply reside in the set of axioms itself. Rather it is the process of obtaining those axioms that is important (i.e. the medium is the message). We could dismiss the problem in one fell swoop, by introducing the rule

$$\text{if } \varphi \text{ is valid, then } \vdash \varphi,$$

but from that we learn nothing at all. A theorem about *completeness* (i.e. that every valid assertion is a theorem) declares that certain notions have been completely characterised in a certain way. If the proof of this theorem requires us to systematically dismantle those notions and reconstruct them out of more basic and familiar ones, and if the concept of derivability receives a similar structural exegesis, then in studying the theorem we are lead to a much deeper and surer understanding of the intuitive concepts involved. The value then is to be found in knowing, not just *that* there is a completeness theorem, but *how* it works. That is what this book is about.

CHAPTER 2

THE LOGICAL STRUCTURE OF COMMANDS

2.1 SYNTAX

This section presents the formal language of program-schemata, and breaks the definition down into the syntactic categories of *expressions*, *commands*, and *formulae*.

Boolean Expressions.

Let

$$Bvb = \{p_0, p_1, p_2, \ldots.\}$$

be a denumerable set of symbols, which we call *Boolean variables*. The set *Bxp* of *Boolean expressions* is defined inductively as follows:

1. The constant symbol *false* is in *Bxp*,
2. Each Boolean variable $p \in Bvb$ is in *Bxp*,
3. If ε, δ, ∂ are in *Bxp*, then so is $(\varepsilon \supset \delta, \partial)$,
4. If ε, δ are in *Bxp*, then so is $(\varepsilon = \delta)$.

The constant symbol *true* is introduced as a definitional abbreviation for the expression (*false* = *false*).

The word "expression" is being given its conventional computing usage here, which is the same as the use of "term" in first-order logic. An expression has as its value - the thing it denotes - an element of a data type. Boolean expressions denote elements of the truth-value data type

$$\mathbb{B} = \{0, 1\}$$

(where 0 stands for Falsity, 1 for Truth). *false* is an *individual constant*, and names the element 0. *true*, as we shall see, always take the value 1.

The symbol $\supset$ is the logical *conditional* connective, with $(\varepsilon \supset \delta, \partial)$ being read

"if ε then δ, else ∂".

The expression $(\varepsilon = \delta)$ conforms to Pascal notational, whereas in Algol it would be written $(\varepsilon \equiv \delta)$. It (ignoring the question of undefined values) is assigned 1 when ε and δ have the same value, and 0 otherwise. It is syntactically correct to form expressions like

$$((\varepsilon = \delta) = \partial),$$

which is unproblematical when = is given this interpretation as the binary operation of *equivalence* on $\mathbb{B}$, but perhaps less clear if one interprets $(\varepsilon = \delta)$ as the statement "ε equals δ", i.e. as an assertion *about* the structure $\mathbb{B}$. The latter interpretation treats $(\varepsilon = \delta)$ not as a term, but as an *atomic formula* of the language of $\mathbb{B}$. The former interpretation has $(\varepsilon = \delta)$ denote a $\mathbb{B}$-element (just as "$x+y$" may denote an $\mathbb{N}$-element), while in the latter case it is an assertion that either holds of $\mathbb{B}$ or does not (like "$x+y = 3$" for $\mathbb{N}$). The point is that all Boolean expressions are to have *both* roles. The first is their internal role, the second is external. Externally the symbol = in a Boolean expression behaves just as it does in the first-order language of all the data types we study.

We note that each member of *Bxp* is a finite string of symbols, these symbols coming from a denumerable alphabet. Hence there are denumerably many Boolean expressions.

Commands.

Let $\pi_0, \pi_1, \ldots.$ be a denumerable list of symbols, called *program letters*. We define the set *Cmd* of commands by the following inductive closure conditions.

a. *skip* and *abort* are in *Cmd* ;

b. Each program letter π is in *Cmd* ;

c. If α, β are in *Cmd*, then so is $(\alpha;\beta)$;

d. If α, β are in *Cmd*, and ε is in *Bxp*, then $(\varepsilon \Rightarrow \alpha,\beta)$ is in *Cmd* ;

e. If α is in *Cmd*, and ε is in *Bxp*, then $(\varepsilon\#\alpha)$ is in *Cmd*.

The command $(\varepsilon \Rightarrow \alpha,\beta)$ is the conditional (*if* ε *then* α *else* β), while $(\varepsilon\#\alpha)$ denotes the iterative command (*while* ε *do* α). *skip* was defined in §1.7. The command *abort* is described by Dijkstra (1976, p.26) thus:

> *"When evoked, the mechanism named* "abort" *will fail to reach a final state: its attempted activation is interpreted as a symptom of failure".*

On these grounds, the assertion

$$[abort]false$$

is valid, since *abort* never terminates.

Since the "atomic" components of a command are letters π and not "real" instructions, a member of *Cmd* is a symbolic presentation of the *form* of an actual command. In the next chapter, the π's will be replaced by assignments $(x := \sigma)$. Members of *Cmd* other than program letters will be referred to as *structured* commands.

Cmd is denumerably infinite.

Formulae.

The class *Fma* of (well-formed) *formulae* comprises what we have informally called "assertions" and "statements" above. It is defined as follows.

1. Each Boolean expression is a formula, i.e. $Bxp \subseteq Fma$;

2. If φ, ψ are in *Fma*, so is $(\varphi \to \psi)$;

3. If φ is in *Fma*, and α is in *Cmd*, then $[\alpha]\varphi$ is in *Fma*.

Using the logical *implication* connective $\to$, the other standard connectives are defined by the following abbreviations.

Negation: $\neg\varphi$ is $(\varphi \rightarrow \mathit{false})$

Disjunction: $(\varphi \vee \psi)$ is $(\neg\varphi \rightarrow \psi)$

Conjunction: $(\varphi \wedge \psi)$ is $\neg(\varphi \rightarrow \neg\psi)$

Equivalence: $(\varphi \leftrightarrow \psi)$ is $(\varphi \rightarrow \psi) \wedge (\psi \rightarrow \varphi)$

The set *Fma* is denumerable, and so we can enumerate all the formulae in a sequence $\varphi_0, \varphi_1, \varphi_2, \ldots$.

2.2 SEMANTICS

MODELS.

A *model* for the language defined in §2.1 is a structure

$$M = (S, v, [\![\cdot]\!]),$$

where (i) S is a non-empty set, whose members are informally referred to as "states";

(ii) v is an operator that associates with each $s \in S$ a *valuation*, i.e. a function v_s that assigns to each $p \in Bvp$ an element $v_s(p)$ of $\mathbb{B}^+ = \{0, 1, \omega\}$;

(iii) $[\![\cdot]\!]$ is an operator that associates with each $\alpha \in Cmd$ a binary relation $[\![\alpha]\!]$ on S. Thus $[\![\alpha]\!] \subseteq S \times S$.

Boolean Values.

For each $s \in S$, the valuation $v_s : Bvb \rightarrow \mathbb{B}^+$ extends canonically to the whole of *Bxp* by induction on the formation rules for Boolean expressions:

1. $v_s(\mathit{false}) = 0$

2. $$v_s(\varepsilon \supset \delta, \partial) = \begin{cases} \omega & \text{if } v_s(\varepsilon) = \omega \\ v_s(\delta) & \text{if } v_s(\varepsilon) = 1 \\ v_s(\partial) & \text{if } v_s(\varepsilon) = 0 \end{cases}$$

3. If either $v_s(\varepsilon)$ or $v_s(\delta)$ is ω, then $v_s(\varepsilon = \delta)$ is ω; otherwise

$$v_s(\varepsilon = \delta) = \begin{cases} 1 & \text{if } v_s(\varepsilon) = v_s(\delta) \\ 0 & \text{if } v_s(\varepsilon) \neq v_s(\delta). \end{cases}$$

Writing $D\varepsilon$ as an abbreviation for $(\varepsilon = \varepsilon)$, from clause 3 we have

$$v_s(D\varepsilon) = \begin{cases} \omega & \text{if } v_s(\varepsilon) = \omega \\ 1 & \text{if } v_s(\varepsilon) \neq \omega, \end{cases}$$

and hence

$$v_s(\mathit{true}) = v_s(D\mathit{false}) = 1.$$

The interpretation of the connective $\supset$ is the *sequential* one of McCarthy (see McCarthy (1963), Manna and McCarthy (1970)), in which we imagine the computer first evaluating ε and then proceeding to δ or ∂. If ε is undefined (meaning "error", or non-termination of evaluation) then the whole expression is undefined. If evaluation terminates with ε found to have value 1 (meaning ε is true) then δ is evaluated. Otherwise ε is found to be false and ∂ evaluated.

The connective $\supset$ provides similar sequential interpretations of the standard logical connectives if we define

not-ε	as	$(\varepsilon = \mathit{false})$	(hence *not-false* is *true*)
ε *implies* δ	as	$(\varepsilon \supset \delta, \mathit{true})$	
ε *or* δ	as	$(\varepsilon \supset \mathit{true}, \delta)$	
ε *and* δ	as	$(\varepsilon \supset \delta, \mathit{false})$	
ε *iff* δ	as	$(\varepsilon \supset \delta, (\delta \supset \mathit{false}, \mathit{true}))$.	

As operations on $\mathbf{B}^+$ these have "truth-tables"

	not
1	0
0	1
ω	ω

implies	1	0	ω
1	1	0	ω
0	1	1	1
ω	ω	ω	ω

or	1	0	ω
1	1	1	1
0	1	0	ω
ω	ω	ω	ω

and	1	0	ω
1	1	0	ω
0	0	0	0
ω	ω	ω	ω

iff	1	0	ω
1	1	0	ω
0	0	1	ω
ω	ω	ω	ω

These tables summarize the workings of the internal propositional logic. When restricted to {0,1} they are the classical truth-tables for the connectives concerned. But notice that the internal equivalence (ε *iff* δ) has exactly the same interpretation as ($\varepsilon = \delta$), as was indicated in 2.1 (note also that *not*-ε could have been defined as ($\varepsilon \supset$ *false*,*true*)), and thus we could have used $\supset$ to define =. However we prefer to treat the latter as a primitive symbol, to emphasise both its fundamental importance to the theory and the fact that its interpretation as the equality relation in $\mathbb{B}$ is exactly the same as its interpretation as this relation in any other data type.

In general a function f of the form

$$A_1 \times \ldots\ldots \times A_n \rightarrow A_{n+1}$$

can be extended canonically to one of the form

$$A_1^+ \times \ldots\ldots \times A_n^+ \rightarrow A_{n+1}^+$$

by putting $f(x_1, \ldots, x_n) = \omega$ whenever $x_i = \omega$ for some i. The intuitive principle here is that a function's value is regarded as undefined if any of its arguments is undefined. This will be the typical manner in which we treat operations on data types, e.g. the operations +, × on $\mathbb{N}$.

Now the equality relation on A, i.e. the relation

$$E_A = \{\langle a,a\rangle : a \in A\}$$

can be represented by its *characteristic function*

$$f_A : A \times A \rightarrow \mathbb{B}$$

given by

$$f_A(a,b) = \begin{cases} 1 & \text{if} \quad a = b \\ 0 & \text{if} \quad a \neq b \end{cases}$$

In the case that $A = \mathbb{B}$, this characteristic function extends in the above canonical fashion to become the operation on $\mathbb{B}^+$ given by the table for *iff*. But notice that the operations on $\mathbb{B}^+$ corresponding to *and*, *implies*, and *or* are not the canonical extensions of the corresponding truth-functions on $\mathbb{B}$, because of the special sequential method of evaluating connectives. The role of $\mathbb{B}$ in the theory is very special indeed and there are good reasons for analysing it in detail before introducing other data types.

The proof of the following result, by induction on the formation-rules for *Bxp*, is left as an exercise for the reader.

2.2.1 THEOREM. *If* $v_s(\varepsilon) = v_s(\delta)$, *then* $v_s(\partial) = v_s(\partial')$ *where* ∂' *is any Boolean expression obtained from* ∂ *by replacing* ε *in one or more (not necessarily all) places by* δ. ■

SATISFACTION.

We can now define the relation "φ *holds* (or is *satisfied*) in M at s", which is symbolised

$$M \models_s \varphi$$

(the prefix M may be dropped when it is clear which model is being referred to). The definition is by induction on the formation of $\varphi \in Fma$.

1. If $\varphi \in Bxp$, then

$$M \models_s \varphi \quad \text{iff} \quad v_s(\varphi) = 1$$

2. $M \models_s (\varphi \rightarrow \psi)$ iff $M \models_s \varphi$ implies $M \models_s \psi$

3. $M \models_s [\alpha]\varphi$ iff for all $t \in S$ such that $s [\![\alpha]\!] t$,

$$M \models_t \varphi.$$

It follows from these clauses that

$M \models_s \mathit{true}$;

$M \not\models_s \mathit{false}$, i.e. not $M \models_s \mathit{false}$;

$M \models_s \neg\varphi$ iff $M \not\models_s \varphi$;

$M \models_s \varphi \vee \psi$ iff $M \models_s \varphi$ or $M \models_s \psi$;

$M \models_s \varphi \wedge \psi$ iff $M \models_s \varphi$ and $M \models_s \psi$;

$M \models_s (\varphi \leftrightarrow \psi)$ iff ($M \models_s \varphi$ if and only if $M \models_s \psi$).

Consequently we have

$$M \models_s [\alpha]\mathit{false}$$

just in case there is no t such that $s [\![\alpha]\!] t$, so that holding of $[\alpha]\mathit{false}$ formally expresses non-termination of α.

A formula φ is said to be *valid* in M, in symbols $M \models \varphi$, if we have $M \models_s \varphi$ for *all* $s \in S$. Other locutions for "$M \models \varphi$" are "M is a model *of* φ", and "M is a φ-model". φ is valid, per se, if it is valid in all models.

2.2.2 EXERCISES.

(1) The following are valid

$[\alpha](\varphi \to \psi) \to ([\alpha]\varphi \to [\alpha]\psi)$

$([\alpha]\varphi \wedge [\alpha]\psi) \leftrightarrow [\alpha](\varphi \wedge \psi)$

$([\alpha]\varphi \vee [\alpha]\psi) \to [\alpha](\varphi \vee \psi)$

(2) If $M \models \varphi$ then $M \models [\alpha]\varphi$.

(3) If $M \models (\varphi \to \psi)$ then $M \models ([\alpha]\varphi \to [\alpha]\psi)$.

(4) If $[\![\alpha]\!]$ is a *functional* relation, i.e.

$$s [\![\alpha]\!] t \text{ and } s [\![\alpha]\!] u \text{ implies } t=u,$$

then

$$([\alpha]\varphi \rightarrow [\alpha]\psi) \rightarrow [\alpha](\varphi \rightarrow \psi),$$

$$[\alpha](\varphi \vee \psi) \rightarrow ([\alpha]\varphi \vee [\alpha]\psi), \quad \text{and}$$

$$[\alpha]\varphi \vee [\alpha]\neg\varphi$$

are all valid in M. ■

Now an *n-ary relation* R on a set A, i.e. a subset R of A^n, can be identified with its characteristic function $A^n \rightarrow \mathbb{B}$ and then canonically extended to a function of the form $(A^+)^n \rightarrow \mathbb{B}^+$. In particular we can take n=1 and R=A, i.e. regard A as a one-placed relation on A, and extend to a function $d_A : A^+ \rightarrow \mathbb{B}^+$ having

$$d_A(a) = \begin{cases} \omega & \text{if } a = \omega \\ 1 & \text{if } a \in A. \end{cases}$$

d_A represents the subset of "defined" elements of A^+ (i.e. the members of A). Since in general

$$d_A(v_s(\varepsilon)) = v_s(D\varepsilon),$$

we may read $D\varepsilon$ as "ε is defined". Indeed

$$M \models_s D\varepsilon \quad \text{iff} \quad v_s(\varepsilon) \neq \omega.$$

Occassionally we informally say "ε is undefined in s" to mean that $v_s(\varepsilon) = \omega$.

Although $D\varepsilon$, as a Boolean expression, is part of the syntax of internal logic, its interpretation as "ε is defined" is an external matter. The computer cannot answer the question "is ε defined?" by evaluating $D\varepsilon$, since the latter is itself undefined when ε is, and so in that case a command like (*while* $D\varepsilon$ *do* α) will fail to terminate.

There is another extension of the standard equality relation, symbolised $\equiv$, that has been extensively employed by authors like Manna and Vuilemin (1973), who specify (p.274n.) that "*$a \equiv b$ is true if a and b are undefined, but is false if only one of them is undefined.*" This is an *external* relation, meaning that a and b have the same (possibly undefined) value, and so $(\varepsilon \equiv \delta)$ should be treated as a formula that is not a Boolean expression, with the semantic analysis

$$M \models_s (\varepsilon \equiv \delta) \quad \text{iff} \quad v_s(\varepsilon) = v_s(\delta).$$

Thus $(\varepsilon \equiv \delta)$ holds in s when ε and δ are both undefined. But then we see that $(\varepsilon \equiv \delta)$ can be *defined* as

$$(D\varepsilon \vee D\delta) \rightarrow (\varepsilon = \delta),$$

which in turn makes

$$(\varepsilon = \delta) \leftrightarrow ((\varepsilon \equiv \delta) \wedge D\varepsilon \wedge D\delta)$$

valid.

Other standard relations on $\mathbb{B}$ that are available in programming languages are $\leqslant$, $<$, and $\neq$. These can be introduced in Boolean expressions by definitional abbreviations, writing

$$(\varepsilon \neq \delta) \quad \text{for} \quad \mathit{not}(\varepsilon = \delta)$$

$$(\varepsilon \leqslant \delta) \quad \text{for} \quad (\varepsilon \supset \delta, D\delta)$$

$$(\varepsilon < \delta) \quad \text{for} \quad (\varepsilon \leqslant \delta)\,\mathit{and}\,(\varepsilon \neq \delta)$$

Such expressions are then given $\mathbb{B}^+$-values according to the following tables, which show them to be canonical extensions of the corresponding relations on $\mathbb{B}$.

$\neq$	1	0	ω
1	0	1	ω
0	1	0	ω
ω	ω	ω	ω

$\leqslant$	1	0	ω
1	1	0	ω
0	1	1	ω
ω	ω	ω	ω

$<$	1	0	ω
1	0	0	ω
0	1	0	ω
ω	ω	ω	ω

Notice that $(\varepsilon \neq \delta)$ cannot be identified with the formula $\neg(\varepsilon = \delta)$, since the latter will hold (because $(\varepsilon = \delta)$ does not) when either ε or δ is undefined, whereas $(\varepsilon \neq \delta)$ can only hold (have value 1) when ε and δ are both defined. Similarly $\neg\varepsilon$ and not-ε differ in that

$$M \models_s \mathit{not}\text{-}\varepsilon \quad \text{iff} \quad v_s(\varepsilon) = 0$$

while

$$M \models_s \neg\varepsilon \quad \text{iff} \quad v_s(\varepsilon) \neq 1.$$

2.2.3 EXERCISES.

(1) Show that the following are valid.

$\varepsilon \rightarrow D\varepsilon$

$D\varepsilon \leftrightarrow DD\varepsilon$

$D(\varepsilon = \delta) \leftrightarrow D\varepsilon \wedge D\delta$

$\mathit{not}\text{-}\varepsilon \rightarrow D\varepsilon$

$(\varepsilon \dagger \delta) \rightarrow D\varepsilon \wedge D\delta$, for $\dagger \in \{\leqslant, <, \neq, \mathit{and}, \wedge\}$

$(\varepsilon \dagger \delta) \rightarrow D\varepsilon$, for $\dagger \in \{\mathit{implies}, \mathit{or}\}$

$(\varepsilon = \delta) \rightarrow (\varepsilon \leftrightarrow \delta)$

$(\varepsilon = \delta) \leftrightarrow (D\varepsilon \wedge D\delta \wedge (\varepsilon \leftrightarrow \delta))$

$D\mathit{true} \wedge D\mathit{false}$

$(\varepsilon = \mathit{true}) \leftrightarrow \varepsilon$

$D\varepsilon \rightarrow ((\varepsilon = \mathit{true}) = \varepsilon)$

true

$D\varepsilon \leftrightarrow (\varepsilon \ \mathit{or} \ \mathit{not}\text{-}\varepsilon)$

$D\varepsilon \leftrightarrow (\varepsilon \vee \mathit{not}\text{-}\varepsilon)$

$\mathit{not}\text{-}\varepsilon \leftrightarrow (\varepsilon \supset \mathit{false}, \mathit{true})$

$\mathit{not}\text{-}\varepsilon \leftrightarrow (D\varepsilon \wedge \neg\varepsilon)$

$\neg\varepsilon \leftrightarrow (D\varepsilon \rightarrow \mathit{not}\text{-}\varepsilon)$

$\neg\mathit{not}\text{-}D\varepsilon$

$(\varepsilon \ \mathit{implies} \ \delta) \leftrightarrow (D\varepsilon \wedge (\varepsilon \rightarrow \delta))$

$(\varepsilon \rightarrow \delta) \leftrightarrow (D\varepsilon \rightarrow \varepsilon \ \mathit{implies} \ \delta)$

$(\varepsilon \ \mathit{or} \ \delta) \leftrightarrow (D\varepsilon \wedge (\varepsilon \vee \delta))$

$(\varepsilon \ \mathit{and} \ \delta) \leftrightarrow (\varepsilon \wedge \delta)$

$(\varepsilon \supset \delta, \partial) \leftrightarrow (\varepsilon \wedge \delta) \vee (\mathit{not}\text{-}\varepsilon \wedge \partial)$

$(\varepsilon \supset \delta, \partial) \leftrightarrow ((\varepsilon \ \mathit{and} \ \delta) \ \mathit{or} \ (\mathit{not}\text{-}\varepsilon \ \mathit{and} \ \partial))$

$D(\varepsilon \supset \delta, \partial) \leftrightarrow (\varepsilon \wedge D\delta) \vee (\mathit{not}\text{-}\varepsilon \wedge D\partial)$

$(\varepsilon < \delta) \leftrightarrow (\varepsilon = \mathit{false}) \wedge (\delta = \mathit{true})$

$(\varepsilon < \delta) \leftrightarrow (\mathit{not}\text{-}\varepsilon) \ \mathit{and} \ \delta$

$(\varepsilon < \delta) \leftrightarrow (\varepsilon \leqslant \delta) \wedge \neg(\varepsilon = \delta)$

$(\varepsilon \leqslant \delta) \leftrightarrow (\varepsilon < \delta) \vee (\varepsilon = \delta)$

$$(\varepsilon \leqslant \delta) \leftrightarrow (\varepsilon < \delta) \text{ or } (\varepsilon = \delta)$$

2. Explain why the following are *not* valid

$$(\varepsilon = \mathit{true}) \text{ iff } \varepsilon$$

$$D\varepsilon = (\varepsilon = \varepsilon)$$

$$D\varepsilon \text{ iff } (\varepsilon \text{ or not-}\varepsilon)$$

$$(\varepsilon \supset \delta, \partial) = ((\varepsilon \text{ and } \delta) \text{ or } (\text{not-}\varepsilon \text{ and } \partial))$$

2.3 STANDARD MODELS

Thus far the relation $[\![\alpha]\!]$ on a model has not been constrained in any way. But we wish it to convey the *meaning* of α, so that if, for example, we have

$$s [\![\beta;\gamma]\!] t,$$

then the model ought to convey that t has been reached from s by performing β and then γ. So there should be some $u \in S$ with $s [\![\beta]\!] u$ and $u [\![\gamma]\!] t$. A model in which the properties of the relations $[\![\alpha]\!]$ reflect the intended meanings of commands will be called *standard*, and as new concepts are introduced we will give their associated criteria for the definition of "standardness" of models. To this end we need some notation about relations $R \subseteq S\times S$. As is customary we use "sRt" and "$<s,t> \in R$" interchangeably, and instead of "sRu and uPt" we often write "$sRuPt$".

Equality: $E_S = \{<s,s> : s \in S\}$

Restrictions: $\varphi]R = \{<s,t> : sRt \text{ and } \models_s \varphi\}$

$$[\![\varphi]\alpha]\!] = \varphi] [\![\alpha]\!]$$

$$R[\varphi = \{<s,t> : sRt \text{ and } \models_t \varphi\}$$

$$[\![\alpha[\varphi]\!] = [\![\alpha]\!] [\varphi$$

Composition: $PoR = \{<s,t> : \text{for some } u,\ sRuPt\}$

Iteration: $R^{0} = E_S$

$R^{n+1} = R^{n} \circ R$

Closure: $R^{\infty} = \bigcup_{n \in \mathbb{N}} R^{n}$

2.3.1 EXERCISES.

(1) $sR^{n}t$ iff there exist $s_0, \ldots, s_n$ with $s = s_0$, $t = s_n$, and $s_i R s_{i+1}$ whenever $0 \leqslant i < n$.

(2) Let $[\alpha]^{0}\varphi = \varphi$

$[\alpha]^{n+1}\varphi = [\alpha]([\alpha]^{n}\varphi)$.

Then for all $n \in \mathbb{N}$,

$$M \models_s [\alpha]^{n}\varphi \text{ iff } s [\![\alpha]\!] t \text{ implies } \models_t \varphi.$$ ∎

A model M for the language of §2.1 is called *standard* if it satisfies the following conditions:

a. $[\![\mathit{skip}]\!] = E_S$,

i.e. $s [\![\mathit{skip}]\!] t$ iff $s=t$;

b. $[\![\mathit{abort}]\!] = \emptyset$,

i.e. $s [\![\mathit{abort}]\!] t$ is false for all s,t;

c. $[\![\alpha;\beta]\!] = [\![\beta]\!] \circ [\![\alpha]\!]$,

i.e. $s [\![\alpha;\beta]\!] t$ iff for some u, $s [\![\alpha]\!] u [\![\beta]\!] t$

d. $[\![\varepsilon \Rightarrow \alpha,\beta]\!] = [\![\varepsilon]\alpha]\!] \cup [\![\mathit{not}\text{-}\varepsilon]\beta]\!]$,

i.e. $s [\![\varepsilon \Rightarrow \alpha,\beta]\!] t$ iff either $v_s(\varepsilon) = 1$ and $s [\![\alpha]\!] t$

or $v_s(\varepsilon) = 0$ and $s [\![\beta]\!] t$

(N.B. $v_s(\mathit{not}\text{-}\varepsilon) = 1$ iff $v_s(\varepsilon) = 0$);

e. $[\![\varepsilon\#\alpha]\!] = [\![\varepsilon]\alpha]\!]^{\infty} \lceil \mathit{not}\text{-}\varepsilon$,

i.e. $s [\![\varepsilon\#\alpha]\!] t$ iff $s [\![\varepsilon]\alpha]\!]^{\infty}$ and $\models_t \mathit{not}\text{-}\varepsilon$

iff for some $n \in \mathbb{N}$, $s [\![\varepsilon]\alpha]\!]^n t$

and $v_t(\varepsilon) = 0$

iff for some n, and some $s_0, \ldots, s_n$ we

have $s = s_0$, $t = s_n$, with $s_i [\![\alpha]\!] s_{i+1}$

and $v_{s_i}(\varepsilon) = 1$ whenever $0 \leqslant i < n$,

and $v_t(\varepsilon) = 0$.

(In the case $n=0$, the right-hand side of this last condition simplifies (because $0 \leqslant i < n$ is false) to

$$s = t \text{ and } v_s(\varepsilon) = 0 \;).$$

Our claim is that conditions a - e capture the intended meaning of the commands involved. Notice that in regard to termination, if $s [\![\varepsilon \Rightarrow \alpha,\beta]\!] t$, then $v_s(\varepsilon) \neq \omega$, and so there can be no termination of $(\varepsilon \Rightarrow \alpha,\beta)$ from s in a standard model if ε is undefined there. Similarly if $s [\![\varepsilon\#\alpha]\!] t$ for some t, then either $v_s(\mathit{not}\text{-}\varepsilon) = 1$ and so $v_s(\varepsilon) = 0$ (when $n=0$), or else $v_s(\varepsilon) = 1$, and so in any case ε is defined at s.

One important way to obtain a standard model, given S and v, would be to choose $[\![\pi]\!]$ in some fashion for program letters π, and then inductively *define* $[\![\alpha]\!]$ for structured commands α by the conditions a - e. This construction will be used for the Completeness Theorem of §2.5 below.

2.3.2 EXERCISES.

Show that the following are valid in any standard model

$[\mathit{abort}]\mathit{false}$

$[\mathit{abort}]\varphi$

$[\mathit{skip}]\varphi \leftrightarrow \varphi$

$\neg[\mathit{skip}]\mathit{false}$

$[\alpha\ \beta]\varphi \leftrightarrow [\alpha][\beta]\varphi$

$[\alpha]^n\varphi \leftrightarrow [\alpha^n]\varphi$ (cf. §1.7, and Ex. 2.3.1(2))

$[\alpha]\mathit{false} \rightarrow [\alpha;\beta]\mathit{false}$

$[\varepsilon \Rightarrow \alpha\ \beta]\varphi \leftrightarrow ((\varepsilon \rightarrow [\alpha]\varphi) \wedge (\mathit{not}\text{-}\varepsilon \rightarrow [\beta]\varphi))$

$[\varepsilon \Rightarrow \alpha\ \beta]\varphi \leftrightarrow (\neg D\varepsilon \vee (\varepsilon \wedge [\alpha]\varphi) \vee (\mathit{not}\text{-}\varepsilon \wedge [\beta]\varphi))$

$\neg D\varepsilon \rightarrow [\varepsilon \Rightarrow \alpha,\beta]\mathit{false}$

$\neg D\varepsilon \rightarrow [\varepsilon\#\alpha]\mathit{false}$

$[\varepsilon\#\alpha]\mathit{not}\text{-}\varepsilon$

$\mathit{not}\text{-}\varepsilon \rightarrow \neg[\varepsilon\#\alpha]\mathit{false}$

$\mathit{not}\text{-}\varepsilon \rightarrow (\varphi \leftrightarrow [\varepsilon\#\alpha]\varphi)$

$\neg\varepsilon \rightarrow (\varphi \rightarrow [\varepsilon\#\alpha]\varphi)$ ■

The notation $\models \varphi$ will be reserved to mean that formula φ is valid in all *standard* models.

Returning now to Hoare's deduction rules for correctness assertions, we can show that the Consequence, Iteration, Composition, Conditional, and Dummy rules, as given in Chapter 1, are valid in any standard model. But they are also valid in any model that has $[\![\alpha]\!] = \emptyset$ for all α, i.e. a model in which α is always equivalent to *abort*! This is because a correctness assertion has the form $\varphi \rightarrow [\alpha]\psi$, and $[\alpha]\psi$ is valid in a model having $[\![\alpha]\!] = \emptyset$. In general, validity of each of Hoare's rules requires only "half" of the appropriate standard-model condition, as each of the following results show.

2.3.3 EXERCISES.

In any model M,

1. If $[\![\mathit{skip}]\!] \subseteq E_S$, then $M \models \varphi \rightarrow [\mathit{skip}]\varphi$.

2. If $[\![\alpha;\beta]\!] \subseteq [\![\beta]\!] \circ [\![\alpha]\!]$,

   with $M \models \varphi \rightarrow [\alpha]\psi$

   and $M \models \psi \rightarrow [\beta]\theta$,

   then $M \models \varphi \rightarrow [\alpha;\beta]\theta$.

3. If $[\![\varepsilon \Rightarrow \alpha,\beta]\!] \subseteq [\![\varepsilon]\alpha]\!] \cup [\![\mathit{not}\text{-}\varepsilon]\beta]\!]$,

with $M \models \varphi \wedge \varepsilon \rightarrow [\alpha]\psi$

and $M \models \varphi \wedge \mathit{not}\text{-}\varepsilon \rightarrow [\beta]\psi$,

then $M \models \varphi \rightarrow [\varepsilon \Rightarrow \alpha,\beta]\psi$.

4. If $[\![\varepsilon\#\alpha]\!] \subseteq [\![\varepsilon]\alpha]\!]^{\infty} \lceil \mathit{not}\text{-}\varepsilon$,

and $M \models \varphi \wedge \varepsilon \rightarrow [\alpha]\varphi$,

then $M \models \varphi \rightarrow [\varepsilon\#\alpha](\varphi \wedge \mathit{not}\text{-}\varepsilon)$.

5. If $\varphi \rightarrow [\alpha]\psi$, $\varphi' \rightarrow \varphi$, and $\psi \rightarrow \psi'$ are all valid in M, then so is $\varphi' \rightarrow [\alpha]\psi'$. ∎

The point here is that in, for instance, the 4th exercise we need to know that

$$\mathit{if}\ s\ [\![\varepsilon\#\alpha]\!]\ t,\ \text{then}\ s\ [\![\varepsilon]\alpha]\!]^{\infty}\ t\ \text{and}\ \models_t \mathit{not}\text{-}\varepsilon,$$

but not conversely. The details of these exercises are strongly recommended to the reader's own verification.

ITERATION AS A FIXED POINT.

In §1.8 we mentioned the desired equivalence of the commands $\varepsilon\#\alpha$ and

$$(\varepsilon \Rightarrow (\alpha;\ \varepsilon\#\alpha),\mathit{skip}).$$

In fact in any standard model the schema

$$[\varepsilon\#\alpha]\varphi \leftrightarrow [\varepsilon \Rightarrow (\alpha;\ \varepsilon\#\alpha),\mathit{skip}]\varphi$$

is valid. This is immediate from the following result.

2.3.4 THEOREM. *In a standard model,*

$$[\![\varepsilon\#\alpha]\!] = \varepsilon\rceil ([\![\varepsilon\#\alpha]\!] \circ [\![\alpha]\!]) \cup \mathit{not}\text{-}\varepsilon \rceil [\![\mathit{skip}]\!]$$

Proof.

Suppose $s [\![\varepsilon\#\alpha]\!] t$, so that for some $n \in \mathbb{N}$, $s [\![\varepsilon\rceil\alpha]\!]^n t$ and $\models_t \mathit{not}\text{-}\varepsilon$. If $n=0$, we have $s=t$ and so $s(\mathit{not}\text{-}\varepsilon \rceil [\![\mathit{skip}]\!])t$. Otherwise $s [\![\varepsilon\rceil\alpha]\!]^{n-1} \circ [\![\varepsilon\rceil\alpha]\!] t$, so that for some u, $s [\![\varepsilon\rceil\alpha]\!] u [\![\varepsilon\rceil\alpha]\!]^{n-1} t$. But then $u [\![\varepsilon\rceil\alpha]\!]^{\infty} t$, and so $u [\![\varepsilon\#\alpha]\!] t$. But then we have $s [\![\alpha]\!] u [\![\varepsilon\#\alpha]\!] t$ and $\models_s \varepsilon$, which gives $s(\varepsilon\rceil [\![\varepsilon\#\alpha]\!] \circ [\![\alpha]\!]) t$.

Conversely, if $\langle s,t\rangle$ belongs to the relation on the right in the statement of the Theorem, there are two possibilities:

Case 1. $s [\![\mathit{skip}]\!] t$ and $\models_s \mathit{not}\text{-}\varepsilon$. Then $s=t$, so $s [\![\varepsilon\rceil\alpha]\!]^0 t$ and $\models_t \mathit{not}\text{-}\varepsilon$, giving $s [\![\varepsilon\#\alpha]\!] t$.

Case 2. $\models_s \varepsilon$, and for some u, $s [\![\alpha]\!] u$ and $u [\![\varepsilon\#\alpha]\!] t$. Then for some n, $u [\![\varepsilon\rceil\alpha]\!]^n t$ and $\models_t \mathit{not}\text{-}\varepsilon$. But $s [\![\varepsilon\rceil\alpha]\!] u$, so $s [\![\varepsilon\rceil\alpha]\!]^{n+1} t$, giving $s [\![\varepsilon\#\alpha]\!] t$ again. ■

2.3.5 COROLLARY. *The schema*

$$\varepsilon \rightarrow ([\varepsilon\#\alpha]\varphi \leftrightarrow [\alpha][\varepsilon\#\alpha]\varphi)$$

is valid in any standard model.

Proof.

If $\models_s \varepsilon$, then by the Theorem we have for any t that

$$s [\![\varepsilon\#\alpha]\!] t \quad \text{iff} \quad s [\![\varepsilon\#\alpha]\!] \circ [\![\alpha]\!] t.$$

From this it follows that for any φ

$$\models_s [\varepsilon\#\alpha]\varphi \quad \text{iff} \quad \models_s [\alpha][\varepsilon\#\alpha]\varphi$$ ■

The proof of 2.3.4 shows in effect that the formidable equation

$$[\![\varepsilon\rceil\alpha]\!]^{\infty} \lceil \mathit{not}\text{-}\varepsilon = \varepsilon\rceil ([\![\varepsilon\rceil\alpha]\!]^{\infty} \lceil \mathit{not}\text{-}\varepsilon \circ [\![\alpha]\!]) \cup \mathit{not}\text{-}\varepsilon\rceil E_S$$

is true of *any* model, and this simplifies to the desired result by the standard-model conditions for *skip* and (ε#α). More generally, given a command α then from any relation R on S we can define a new relation $F_\alpha(R)$ by putting

$$F_\alpha(R) = \varepsilon\rceil(R \circ [\![\alpha]\!]) \cup \mathit{not}\text{-}\varepsilon\rceil E_S.$$

The previous equation shows that the relation $[\![\varepsilon\rceil\alpha]\!]^\infty \lceil \mathit{not}\text{-}\varepsilon$ is a *fixed point* of the operator F_α, which means that it is a solution to the equation

$$R = F_\alpha(R).$$

We can actually characterise $[\![\varepsilon\rceil\alpha]\!]^\infty \lceil \mathit{not}\text{-}\varepsilon$ in these terms as the *least* such fixed point. For $R \subseteq S{\times}S$ it turns out that

$$R = F_\alpha(R) \text{ implies } [\![\varepsilon\rceil\alpha]\!]^\infty \lceil \mathit{not}\text{-}\varepsilon \subseteq R,$$

and so

$$[\![\varepsilon\rceil\alpha]\!]^\infty \lceil \mathit{not}\text{-}\varepsilon = \bigcap \{R : R = F_\alpha(R)\}.$$

In the Scott-Strachey denotational semantics for programming languages (cf. e.g. Scott and Strachey (1971), Stoy (1977)), the meaning of a *while*-command is *defined* as the least fixed point of an operator of the form of F_α.

THE ANALYSIS OF "*while*".

As our Exercises have indicated, the formulae $[\alpha;\beta]\varphi$ and $[\varepsilon \Rightarrow \alpha,\beta]\varphi$ are equivalent in standard models to

$$[\alpha][\beta]\varphi$$

and

$$(\varepsilon \rightarrow [\alpha]\varphi) \wedge (\mathit{not}\text{-}\varepsilon \rightarrow [\beta]\varphi)$$

respectively. Thus we can eliminate modal operators corresponding to composites and conditionals in favour of modalities associated with their component commands.

If ; and $\Rightarrow$ were the only command-forming operators in our language then any formula could thereby be replaced by one in which the only modal operators were [*skip*], [*abort*], and $[\pi]$ for program letters π. As soon as Iteration is introduced however, this reduction is no longer possible. The best we can do is "reduce" $[\varepsilon\#\alpha]\varphi$ to an infinite set of formulae involving $[\alpha]$.

Given $\varepsilon \in Exp$, $\alpha \in Cmd$, and $\varphi \in Fma$, a series $\varphi_0(\varepsilon,\alpha), \ldots, \varphi_n(\varepsilon,\alpha), \ldots$ is inductively defined by letting

$$\varphi_0(\varepsilon,\alpha) \text{ be } (\mathit{not}\text{-}\varepsilon \rightarrow \varphi)$$

and

$$\varphi_{n+1}(\varepsilon,\alpha) \text{ be } (\varepsilon \rightarrow [\alpha]\varphi_n(\varepsilon,\alpha)).$$

2.3.6 THEOREM. *In any model, for any $n \in \mathbb{N}$,*

$$\models_s \varphi_n(\varepsilon,\alpha) \quad \textit{iff} \quad (s\, [\![\, \varepsilon]\alpha\,]\!]^n\, t \ \textit{ and } \ \models_t \mathit{not}\text{-}\varepsilon) \ \textit{implies} \models_t \varphi.$$

Proof.

The result is proven for all s, by induction on n.

When $n=0$, we have to show that

$$\models_s \varphi_0(\varepsilon,\alpha) \quad \text{iff} \quad (s=t \text{ and } \models_t \mathit{not}\text{-}\varepsilon) \text{ implies } \models_t \varphi,$$

i.e. that

$$\models_s \mathit{not}\text{-}\varepsilon \rightarrow \varphi \quad \text{iff} \quad \models_s \mathit{not}\text{-}\varepsilon \text{ implies } \models_s \varphi,$$

which is true by the semantic clause for $\rightarrow$.

Now assume the result for n. Let $\models_s \varphi_{n+1}(\varepsilon,\alpha)$. Then if $s\, [\![\, \varepsilon]\alpha\,]\!]^{n+1}\, t$ and $\models_t \mathit{not}\text{-}\varepsilon$, for some u, $s\, [\![\, \varepsilon]\alpha\,]\!]\, u\, [\![\, \varepsilon]\alpha\,]\!]^n\, t$. But then $\models_s \varepsilon$ and $s\, [\![\, \alpha\,]\!]\, u$, so from the definition of $\varphi_{n+1}(\varepsilon,\alpha)$ we see that $\models_u \varphi_n(\varepsilon,\alpha)$. The induction hypothesis on n then applies to u and t, to give $\models_t \varphi$ as desired. On the other hand, if $\not\models_s \varphi_{n+1}(\varepsilon,\alpha)$ then $\models_s \varepsilon$ and $\not\models_s [\alpha]\varphi_n(\varepsilon,\alpha)$, so for some u, $s\, [\![\, \alpha\,]\!]\, u$ and $\not\models_u \varphi_n(\varepsilon,\alpha)$.

By the induction hypothesis then there exists a t with $u [\![\varepsilon]\alpha]\!]^n t$ and $\models_t$ *not*-ε, but $\not\models_t \varphi$. Since $s [\![\varepsilon]\alpha]\!] u$, we have $s [\![\varepsilon]\alpha]\!]^{n+1} t$, which establishes the Theorem.

∎

2.3.7 COROLLARY. *In a standard model,*

$$\models_s [\varepsilon\#\alpha]\varphi \quad \textit{iff} \quad \textit{for all } n \in \mathbb{N} \ \models_s \varphi_n(\varepsilon,\alpha).$$

Proof.

Suppose $\models_s [\varepsilon\#\alpha]\varphi$. For any n, if $s [\![\varepsilon]\alpha]\!]^n t$ and $\models_t$ *not*-ε we have $s [\![\varepsilon\#\alpha]\!] t$ by the standard-model condition, and therefore $\models_t \varphi$. Hence by the Theorem, $\models_s \varphi_n(\varepsilon,\alpha)$.

Conversely, if $\not\models_s [\varepsilon\#\alpha]\varphi$ then for some t we have $s [\![\varepsilon\#\alpha]\!] t$ and $\not\models_t \varphi$. As the model is standard there must then be an $n \in \mathbb{N}$ with $s [\![\varepsilon]\alpha]\!]^n t$ and $\models_t$ *not*-ε. Hence by the Theorem $\not\models_s \varphi_n(\varepsilon,\alpha)$. ∎

The result of this Corollary can be extended somewhat. Thus if $[\beta][\varepsilon\#\alpha]\varphi$ holds at s then so does $[\beta]\varphi_n(\varepsilon,\alpha)$ for all n, and conversely. Similarly $(\psi \to [\varepsilon\#\alpha]\varphi)$ holds at s iff $(\psi \to \varphi_n(\varepsilon,\alpha))$ holds there for all n. To obtain a general result along these lines, we subsume them under the notion of an *admissible form* which, roughly, is a symbolism of the form

$$\psi_1 \to [\beta_1](\psi_2 \to \ldots\ldots (\psi_m \to [\beta_m]\#) \ \ldots.)$$

(in which some ψ_i's and β_j's may be left out). This is not actually a formula, because of the single occurrence of the symbol #, but it becomes one as soon as this occurrence is replaced by a genuine member of *Fma*.

To make all of this precise, the class *Afm* of admissible forms is defined inductively as follows:

1. $\# \in Afm$
2. If $\Phi \in Afm$ and $\beta \in Cmd$, then $[\beta]\Phi \in Afm$
3. If $\Phi \in Afm$ and $\psi \in Fma$, then $(\psi \to \Phi) \in Afm$.

Each $\Phi \in Afm$ has a unique (and innermost) occurrence of the symbol #, and it is not part of a modal operator. We denote by $\Phi(\varphi)$ the member of *Fma* obtained by replacing this occurrence of # by $\varphi \in Fma$. It is easy to see that

$$([\beta]\Phi)(\varphi) \text{ is } [\beta](\Phi(\varphi))$$

and

$$(\psi \to \Phi)(\varphi) \text{ is } \psi \to (\Phi(\varphi))$$

and so we do not have to be fastidious about bracketing here.

We leave it to the reader to prove the following result, by induction over the formation rules for admissible forms.

2.3.8 THEOREM. *In a standard model, for any* $\Phi \in Afm$,

$$\models_s \Phi([\varepsilon\#\alpha]\varphi) \text{ iff for all } n \models_s \Phi(\varphi_n(\varepsilon,\alpha)). \qquad \blacksquare$$

2.4 PROOF THEORY.

The purpose of our proof theory is to provide a syntactic characterisation of the property

$$\models \varphi$$

of validity in all standard models. We wish to define a predicate

$$\vdash \varphi,$$

to read "φ is *deducible*", and show that it is identical with $\models$, i.e. that

$$\vdash \varphi \text{ iff } \models \varphi.$$

By a "syntactic characterisation" of $\models$ we mean that the deducibility predicate $\vdash$ is to be defined inductively by operations on formulae that depend only on their syntactic structure, as given in the formation rules for *Fma*, and not on any reference to semantic notions of truth, validity, holding-in-a-state etc.

By a *logical system* we shall mean a set Λ of formulae that has a distinguished subset, called the set of Λ-*axioms*, and that is closed under certain *rules of inference*. The members of Λ are generally called the *theorems* of Λ, and we usually write

$$\vdash_{\Lambda} \varphi$$

to mean that $\varphi \in \Lambda$ (and $\nvdash_{\Lambda} \varphi$ for $\varphi \notin \Lambda$).

AXIOMS

Tautologies

A1 $\varphi \rightarrow (\psi \rightarrow \varphi)$

A2 $(\varphi \rightarrow (\psi \rightarrow \theta)) \rightarrow ((\varphi \rightarrow \psi) \rightarrow (\varphi \rightarrow \theta))$

A3 $\neg\neg\varphi \rightarrow \varphi$

Termination

A4 $[\alpha](\varphi \rightarrow \psi) \rightarrow ([\alpha]\varphi \rightarrow [\alpha]\psi)$

Structured Commands

A5 $[\mathit{skip}]\varphi \leftrightarrow \varphi$

A6 $[\mathit{abort}]\mathit{false}$

A7 $[\alpha;\beta]\varphi \leftrightarrow [\alpha][\beta]\varphi$

A8 $[\varepsilon \Rightarrow \alpha,\beta]\varphi \leftrightarrow ((\varepsilon \rightarrow [\alpha]\varphi) \wedge (\mathit{not}\text{-}\varepsilon \rightarrow [\beta]\varphi))$

A9 $\mathit{not}\text{-}\varepsilon \rightarrow \neg[\varepsilon\#\alpha]\mathit{false}$

A10 $[\varepsilon\#\alpha]\varphi \rightarrow (\varepsilon \rightarrow [\alpha][\varepsilon\#\alpha]\varphi)$

Boolean Expressions

A11 $(\varepsilon = \delta) \rightarrow (\partial \rightarrow \partial')$, where ∂' differs from ∂ only in having δ in one or more places where ∂ has ε

A12 true

A13 $D\varepsilon \leftrightarrow (\varepsilon \vee \mathit{not}\text{-}\varepsilon)$

A14 $\varepsilon \to (\varepsilon = \mathit{true})$

A15 $(\varepsilon \supset \delta,\partial) \leftrightarrow ((\varepsilon \wedge \delta) \vee (\mathit{not}\text{-}\varepsilon \wedge \partial))$

A16 $D(\varepsilon \supset \delta,\partial) \leftrightarrow ((\varepsilon \wedge D\delta) \vee (\mathit{not}\text{-}\varepsilon \wedge D\partial))$

A17 $D(\varepsilon = \delta) \leftrightarrow (D\varepsilon \wedge D\delta)$

Each of these "axioms" is really an axiom *schema* in which ε, φ, ψ, α, β etc. are *meta-variables* ranging over *Bxp*, *Cmd*, and *Fma*. Thus, for example, each of infinitely many choices of α, φ, ψ gives an actual formula of the form of A4. Hence A4 denotes the set of all formulae of that form, and we may speak of *instances* or *members* of A4.

All instances of A1 - A17 are valid in standard models (cf. 2.2.1, 2.2.2, 2.2.3, 2.3.2, 2.3.5).

RULES OF INFERENCE

Detachment (Modus Ponens)

MP: *From* $(\varphi \to \psi)$ *and* φ, *infer* ψ

Termination

TR: *From* φ *infer* $[\alpha]\varphi$

Omega-Iteration

OI: *From* $\Phi(\varphi_n(\varepsilon,\alpha))$ *for all* $n \in \mathbb{N}$, *infer* $\Phi([\varepsilon\#\alpha]\varphi)$.

These rules preserve the property of validity in a standard model in passing from their set of premisses to the conclusion.

The presence of the infinitary rule OI requires us to adopt a more abstract approach to deducibility than is traditional in finitary logic. Usually the notion "φ is deducible" is defined as follows:

> there exists a *proof-sequence* for φ, i.e. a sequence $\varphi_0, \varphi_1, \ldots, \varphi_m$ of formulae such that $\varphi_m = \varphi$ and, for all $i \leqslant n$, φ_i is either an axiom or follows from earlier members of the sequence by a rule of inference.

An alternative formulation is:

> φ belongs to the smallest subset of *Fma* that contains all axioms and is closed under the rules of inference.

Here the "smallest" set with a certain property means the intersection of all sets having that property - provided that the intersection itself has the property, which *will* be the case for the kind of closure conditions we are using.

These two types of formulation lead to the same set of theorems. But when infinitary rules are allowed, proof sequences become infinite in length, and so we would have to take m as in the first formulation to be an infinite ordinal number and invoke all the technical machinery of the arithmetic of order-types. For this reason the second formulation becomes much more attractive, relying as it does only on the most elementary set theory and being no more complicated at all for infinitary rules than it is for finitary ones.

A *logical system*, or *logic*, will now be formally defined as a set $\Lambda \subseteq Fma$ that contains all instances of the axiom-schemata A1 - A17, and is closed under the rules MP, TR, and OI, i.e. satisfies

(1) $\varphi, (\varphi \rightarrow \psi) \in \Lambda$ only if $\psi \in \Lambda$,

(2) $\varphi \in \Lambda$ only if $[\alpha]\varphi \in \Lambda$,

(3) $\{\Phi(\varphi_n(\varepsilon,\alpha)) : n \in \mathbb{N}\} \subseteq \Lambda$ only if $\Phi([\varepsilon\#\alpha]\varphi) \in \Lambda$,

for all $\varphi, \psi \in Fma$, $\alpha \in Cmd$, $\varepsilon \in Bxp$, and $\Phi \in Afm$.

Propositional Calculus

By the *propositional calculus*, PC, we mean the smallest subset of *Fma* that contains all instances of A1, A2, and A3, and is closed under the rule MP. This set, contained in Λ, consists of all formulae that have the structure of *tautologies*. It is assumed that the reader is familiar with this notion and with the classical theory of the propositional calculus. We often put "by PC" to indicate that a result is provided by this theory.

2.4.1 THEOREM.

(1) *Rule of* Terminal Implication:

$$\text{TI: } \textit{If } \vdash_\Lambda \varphi \to \psi \textit{ then } \vdash_\Lambda [\alpha]\varphi \to [\alpha]\psi.$$

(2) *If* $\vdash_\Lambda (\varphi \leftrightarrow \psi)$ *then* $\vdash_\Lambda [\alpha]\varphi \leftrightarrow [\alpha]\psi$.

(3) $\vdash_\Lambda [\alpha](\varphi \wedge \psi) \leftrightarrow [\alpha]\varphi \wedge [\alpha]\psi$.

(4) $\vdash_\Lambda [\alpha]\varphi \vee [\alpha]\psi \to [\alpha](\varphi \vee \psi)$.

(5) $\vdash_\Lambda [\alpha]^n\varphi \leftrightarrow [\alpha^n]\varphi$.

(6) $\vdash_\Lambda [\alpha]\mathit{false} \to [\alpha]\varphi$.

(7) $\vdash_\Lambda [\mathit{abort}]\varphi$.

(8) $\vdash_\Lambda \neg[\alpha]\mathit{false} \to ([\alpha]\neg\varphi \to \neg[\alpha]\varphi)$.

Proof.

(1) If $\vdash_\Lambda \varphi \to \psi$ then $\vdash_\Lambda [\alpha](\varphi \to \psi)$ by TR, and the result follows by A4 and MP.

(2) By TI and PC.

(3) From PC, by TI, we have

$$\vdash_\Lambda [\alpha](\varphi \wedge \psi) \to [\alpha]\varphi$$

and $$\vdash_\Lambda [\alpha](\varphi \wedge \psi) \to [\alpha]\psi,$$

which by PC give $\vdash_\Lambda [\alpha](\varphi \wedge \psi) \to [\alpha]\varphi \wedge [\alpha]\psi$. On the other hand,

PC and TI give

$$\vdash_\Lambda [\alpha]\varphi \to [\alpha](\psi \to \varphi \wedge \psi),$$

which by A4 and PC leads to

$$\vdash_\Lambda [\alpha]\varphi \to ([\alpha]\psi \to [\alpha](\varphi \wedge \psi)),$$

and hence $\vdash_\Lambda [\alpha]\varphi \wedge [\alpha]\psi \to [\alpha](\varphi \wedge \psi)$ by PC again.

(4) Using TI, we have $[\alpha]\varphi \to [\alpha](\varphi \vee \psi)$ and $[\alpha]\psi \to [\alpha](\varphi \vee \psi)$ as Λ-theorems, from which the result follows by PC.

(5) Use A5, A7, (2), and induction on n.

(6) By TI, as $\vdash_{PC} \mathit{false} \to \varphi$.

(7) By A6 and (6).

(8) By A4, $\vdash_\Lambda [\alpha](\varphi \to \mathit{false}) \to ([\alpha]\varphi \to [\alpha]\mathit{false})$, hence by PC, and the definition of $\neg$, $\vdash_\Lambda [\alpha]\neg\varphi \to (\neg[\alpha]\mathit{false} \to \neg[\alpha]\varphi)$. The rest is PC.

■

2.4.2 THEOREM.

(1) $\vdash_\Lambda \mathit{not}\text{-}\varepsilon \to \neg\varepsilon$.

(2) $\vdash_\Lambda \varepsilon \to D\varepsilon$.

(3) $\vdash_\Lambda \mathit{not}\text{-}\varepsilon \to D\varepsilon$.

(4) $\vdash_\Lambda \varepsilon = \delta \to D\varepsilon \wedge D\delta$.

(5) $\vdash_\Lambda \varepsilon = \delta \to \delta = \varepsilon$.

(6) $\vdash_\Lambda \varepsilon = \delta \to (\varepsilon = \partial \to \delta = \partial)$.

(7) $\vdash_\Lambda \varepsilon = \delta \to (\delta = \partial \to \varepsilon = \partial)$.

(8) $\vdash_\Lambda \mathit{not}\text{-}\varepsilon \to (\mathit{not}\text{-}\delta \to (\varepsilon = \delta))$.

(9) $\vdash_\Lambda \varepsilon \wedge \delta \to (\varepsilon = \delta)$.

(10) $\vdash_\Lambda \neg D\varepsilon \to [\varepsilon \Rightarrow \alpha,\beta]\varphi$.

(11) $\vdash_\Lambda (\varepsilon = \delta) \to (\partial \leftrightarrow \partial')$, *where* ∂ *and* ∂' *are as in* A11.

Proof.

(1) $(\varepsilon = \mathit{false}) \to (\varepsilon \to \mathit{false})$ is an instance of A11.

(2) Since $\vdash_{PC} \varepsilon \to (\varepsilon \vee \mathit{not}\text{-}\varepsilon)$, apply A13.

(3) Similar to (2).

(4) By (2), $\vdash_\Lambda \varepsilon = \delta \to D(\varepsilon = \delta)$. Then use A17.

(5) From A11, $\vdash_\Lambda \varepsilon = \delta \to (\varepsilon = \varepsilon \to \delta = \varepsilon)$.
But by (4), $\vdash_\Lambda \varepsilon = \delta \to \varepsilon = \varepsilon$, and so PC gives the result.

(6) By A11.

(7) A11, part (5), and PC.

(8) By A11, $\vdash_\Lambda \mathit{false} = \varepsilon \to (\mathit{false} = \delta \to \varepsilon = \delta)$. Hence by part (5) and PC,

$$\vdash_\Lambda \varepsilon = \mathit{false} \to (\delta = \mathit{false} \to \varepsilon = \delta).$$

(9) By A14,

$$\vdash_\Lambda \varepsilon \wedge \delta \to (\varepsilon = \mathit{true}) \wedge (\delta = \mathit{true}),$$

while (5) and (6) yield, with PC,

$$\vdash_\Lambda (\varepsilon = \mathit{true}) \wedge (\delta = \mathit{true}) \to \varepsilon = \delta.$$

(10) We have

$$\vdash_{PC} \neg\varepsilon \wedge \neg \mathit{not}\text{-}\varepsilon \to (\varepsilon \to [\alpha]\varphi) \wedge (\mathit{not}\text{-}\varepsilon \to [\beta]\varphi)$$

But by (2) and (3), $\vdash_\Lambda \neg D\varepsilon \to \neg\varepsilon \wedge \neg \mathit{not}\text{-}\varepsilon$. Hence by A8 and PC, (10) follows.

(11) $\vdash_\Lambda (\delta = \varepsilon) \rightarrow (\partial' \rightarrow \partial)$, since this is itself an instance of A11. Hence by part (5), $\vdash_\Lambda (\varepsilon = \delta) \rightarrow (\partial' \rightarrow \partial)$. Together with A11, PC then gives the desired result. ■

2.4.3 THEOREM.

(1) *Hoare's* Iteration Rule:

If $\vdash_\Lambda \psi \wedge \varepsilon \rightarrow [\alpha]\psi,$

then $\vdash_\Lambda \psi \rightarrow [\varepsilon\#\alpha](\psi \wedge \mathit{not}\text{-}\varepsilon).$

(2) $\vdash_\Lambda [\varepsilon\#\alpha]\mathit{not}\text{-}\varepsilon.$

(3) $\vdash_\Lambda \neg\varepsilon \rightarrow (\varphi \rightarrow [\varepsilon\#\alpha]\varphi).$

(4) $\vdash_\Lambda \mathit{not}\text{-}\varepsilon \rightarrow (\varphi \leftrightarrow [\varepsilon\#\alpha]\varphi).$

(5) $\vdash_\Lambda \Phi([\varepsilon\#\alpha]\varphi) \rightarrow \Phi(\varphi_n(\varepsilon,\alpha)).$

Proof.

(1) Let $\varphi = (\psi \wedge \mathit{not}\text{-}\varepsilon)$. We show by induction on n that

$$\vdash_\Lambda \psi \rightarrow \varphi_n(\varepsilon,\alpha).$$

The desired conclusion is then given by the rule OI for the admissible form $(\psi \rightarrow \#)$. For the case n=0, observe that

$$\psi \rightarrow (\mathit{not}\text{-}\varepsilon \rightarrow \varphi)$$

is a tautology.

Assuming the result for n, application of TI (2.4.1(1)) gives

$$\vdash_\Lambda [\alpha]\psi \rightarrow [\alpha]\varphi_n(\varepsilon,\alpha).$$

But PC applied to the hypothesis of Hoare's Rule gives $\vdash_\Lambda \psi \rightarrow (\varepsilon \rightarrow [\alpha]\psi)$, and so we then obtain

$$\vdash_\Lambda \psi \to (\varepsilon \to [\alpha]\varphi_n(\varepsilon,\alpha)),$$

i.e. $\vdash_\Lambda \psi \to \varphi_{n+1}(\varepsilon,\alpha)$ as desired.

(2) By A12 and TR, $\vdash_\Lambda [\alpha]\mathit{true}$, hence by PC

$$\vdash_\Lambda \mathit{true} \wedge \varepsilon \to [\alpha]\mathit{true}.$$

Hoare's Rule then gives

$$\vdash_\Lambda \mathit{true} \to [\varepsilon\#\alpha](\mathit{true} \wedge \mathit{not}\text{-}\varepsilon).$$

But then $[\varepsilon\#\alpha]\mathit{not}\text{-}\varepsilon$ follows by A12, 2.4.1(3) and PC.

(3) Since $\neg\varepsilon \wedge \varphi \wedge \varepsilon \to [\alpha](\neg\varepsilon \wedge \varphi)$ is a tautology, by Hoare's Rule we get

$$\vdash_\Lambda \neg\varepsilon \wedge \varphi \to [\varepsilon\#\alpha](\neg\varepsilon \wedge \varphi \wedge \mathit{not}\text{-}\varepsilon),$$

from which (3) follows by 2.4.1(3) and PC.

(4) By (3) and 2.4.2(1),

$$\vdash_\Lambda \mathit{not}\text{-}\varepsilon \to (\varphi \to [\varepsilon\#\alpha]\varphi). \qquad \text{(i)}$$

But as another instance of (3) we have

$$\vdash_\Lambda \neg\varepsilon \to (\neg\varphi \to [\varepsilon\#\alpha]\neg\varphi),$$

which by 2.4.2(1), A4, and the definition of $\neg$ leads to

$$\vdash_\Lambda \mathit{not}\text{-}\varepsilon \to (\neg\varphi \to ([\varepsilon\#\alpha]\varphi \to [\varepsilon\#\alpha]\mathit{false})).$$

Then using A9 and PC,

$$\vdash_\Lambda \mathit{not}\text{-}\varepsilon \to ([\varepsilon\#\alpha]\varphi \to (\neg\varphi \to \neg\mathit{not}\text{-}\varepsilon)),$$

hence by PC

$$\vdash_\Lambda \mathit{not}\text{-}\varepsilon \to ([\varepsilon\#\alpha]\varphi \to (\mathit{not}\text{-}\varepsilon \to \varphi)),$$

which reduces by PC to

$$\vdash_{\Lambda} \textit{not-}\varepsilon \rightarrow ([\varepsilon\#\alpha]\varphi \rightarrow \varphi). \tag{ii}$$

(i) and (ii) then yield (4).

(5) We prove the result for all n, by induction. If it holds for a particular admissible form Φ, then it holds for the form $[\beta]\Phi$ by the rule TI (2.4.1(1)), and for the form $(\psi \rightarrow \Phi)$ by PC. Hence it suffices to prove it when Φ is #, i.e. to show that

$$\vdash_{\Lambda} [\varepsilon\#\alpha]\varphi \rightarrow \varphi_n(\varepsilon,\alpha).$$

But for n=0, that

$$\vdash_{\Lambda} [\varepsilon\#\alpha]\varphi \rightarrow (\textit{not-}\varepsilon \rightarrow \varphi)$$

follows immediately by PC from part (4) of this theorem as just proven.

Assuming, inductively, the result for n, by applying TI we get

$$\vdash_{\Lambda} [\alpha][\varepsilon\#\alpha]\varphi \rightarrow [\alpha]\varphi_n(\varepsilon,\alpha),$$

which by A10 yields

$$\vdash_{\Lambda} [\varepsilon\#\alpha]\varphi \rightarrow (\varepsilon \rightarrow [\alpha]\varphi_n(\varepsilon,\alpha)).$$

But this is the desired result for n+1. ■

The intersection of any collection of logics is itself a logic. Hence there exists a *smallest* logical system, which we call PL ("Program Logic"). The major goal of this chapter is to prove that

$$\vdash_{PL} \varphi \quad \text{iff} \quad \models \varphi,$$

i.e. the PL-theorems are exactly those formulae valid in all standard models.

THEORIES

A *Λ-theory*, for a logic Λ, is any subset Γ of *Fma* that contains Λ, i.e. $\Lambda \subseteq \Gamma$, and is closed under the two rules MP and OI, i.e. satisfies

$$\varphi,\ (\varphi \to \psi) \in \Gamma \quad \text{only if} \quad \psi \in \Gamma,$$

and
$$\{\Phi(\varphi_n(\varepsilon,\alpha)) : n \in \mathbb{N}\} \subseteq \Gamma \quad \text{only if} \quad \Phi([\varepsilon\#\alpha]\varphi) \in \Gamma.$$

The intersection of any collection of Λ-theories is a Λ-theory, and so there is a smallest Λ-theory - namely Λ itself.

If $\Sigma \cup \{\varphi\} \subseteq Fma$, we define φ to be Λ-*deducible from* Σ, in symbols

$$\Sigma \vdash_\Lambda \varphi,$$

if φ belongs to every Λ-theory that contains Σ. Again in symbols,

$$\Sigma \vdash_\Lambda \varphi \quad \text{iff} \quad \varphi \in \bigcap \{\Gamma \subseteq Fma : \Sigma \subseteq \Gamma \text{ and } \Gamma \text{ is a } \Lambda\text{-theory}\}.$$

Thus the set $\{\varphi : \Sigma \vdash_\Lambda \varphi\}$ is the intersection of all Λ-theories that contain Σ, and hence is a Λ-theory itself - the smallest one containing Σ. In particular we have $\emptyset \vdash_\Lambda \varphi$ iff $\vdash_\Lambda \varphi$.

We write $\Sigma \nvdash_\Lambda \varphi$ if "$\Sigma \vdash_\Lambda \varphi$" is false.

2.4.4 THEOREM.

(1) *If* $\varphi \in \Sigma$ *then* $\Sigma \vdash_\Lambda \varphi$.

(2) *If* $\Sigma \vdash_\Lambda \varphi$ *and* $\Sigma \subseteq \Delta \subseteq Fma$, *then* $\Delta \vdash_\Lambda \varphi$.

(3) *If* $\vdash_\Lambda \varphi$ *then* $\Sigma \vdash_\Lambda \varphi$.

(4) *If* $\Sigma \vdash_\Lambda \varphi$ *and* $\Sigma \vdash_\Lambda \varphi \to \psi$, *then* $\Sigma \vdash_\Lambda \psi$.

(5) *If* $\Sigma \vdash_\Lambda \Phi(\varphi_n(\varepsilon,\alpha))$ *for all* n, *then* $\Sigma \vdash_\Lambda \Phi([\varepsilon\#\alpha]\varphi)$.

Proof.

(1) and (2) are straightforward. (3) - (5) amount to the result that $\{\varphi : \Sigma \vdash_\Lambda \varphi\}$ is a Λ-theory. ∎

A set $\Sigma \subseteq Fma$ is *Λ-consistent* if $\Sigma \nvdash_\Lambda$ *false*. Since (*false* $\rightarrow \varphi$) is a PC-theorem, this is equivalent (by 2.4.4(4)) to the requirement that $\Sigma \nvdash_\Lambda \varphi$ for at least one formula φ.

2.4.5 EXERCISES.

(1) Σ is Λ-consistent iff there is no $\varphi \in Fma$ for which $\Sigma \vdash_\Lambda \varphi$ and $\Sigma \vdash_\Lambda \neg\varphi$.

(2) If M is a standard model, then

$$\Lambda_M = \{\varphi : M \models \varphi\}$$

is a logic.

(3) If M is standard then for each state s in M, $\{\varphi : M \models_s \varphi\}$ is a Λ_M-theory, where Λ_M is defined in the previous exercise. ■

The difference between a logic and one of its theories parallels, as the last two exercises indicate, the difference between the set of formulae valid in a model and the set of formulae that hold at some state in that model. This analogy is exploited below. It also explains the absence of the Termination Rule from the definition of "Λ-theory". For if φ holds at s it does not follow of course that $[\alpha]\varphi$ does.

2.4.6 THEOREM. *If Γ is a Λ-theory, then*

(1) *true* $\in \Gamma$;

(2) Γ *is* deductively closed, *i.e.* $\Gamma \vdash_\Lambda \varphi$ *only if* $\varphi \in \Gamma$;

(3) *If* $\vdash_\Lambda \varphi \rightarrow \psi$ *and* $\varphi \in \Gamma$, *then* $\psi \in \Gamma$;

(4) Γ *is Λ-consistent iff false* $\notin \Gamma$ *iff* $\Gamma \neq Fma$;

(5) $\varphi \wedge \psi \in \Gamma$ *iff* $\varphi \in \Gamma$ *and* $\psi \in \Gamma$;

(6) *If* $\varphi \in \Gamma$ *or* $\psi \in \Gamma$, *then* $\varphi \vee \psi \in \Gamma$;

(7) $\Phi([\varepsilon\#\alpha]\varphi) \in \Gamma$ *iff* $\{\Phi(\varphi_n(\varepsilon,\alpha)) : n \in \mathbb{N}\} \subseteq \Gamma$.

Proof.

(1) By A12, $\vdash_\Lambda$ *true*. But $\Lambda \subseteq \Gamma$.

(2) If $\Gamma \vdash_\Lambda \varphi$ then φ belongs to every Λ-theory containing Γ. But Γ is a Λ-theory containing Γ, so $\varphi \in \Gamma$.

(3) If $\vdash_\Lambda (\varphi \to \psi)$, then $(\varphi \to \psi) \in \Gamma$. But Γ is closed under MP.

(4) From (2) and 2.4.4(1), $\Gamma \vdash_\Lambda \varphi$ if and only if $\varphi \in \Gamma$. (4) then follows from the above definition, and associated observation, of Λ-consistency.

(5) Use the closure of Γ under MP, part (2), and the fact that $\vdash_\Lambda \varphi \wedge \psi \to \varphi$, $\vdash_\Lambda \varphi \wedge \psi \to \psi$, and $\vdash_\Lambda \varphi \to (\psi \to \varphi \wedge \psi)$.

(6) By the fact that $\vdash_\Lambda \varphi \to \varphi \vee \psi$ and $\vdash_\Lambda \psi \to \varphi \vee \psi$.

(7) By the closure of Γ under OI and the result 2.4.3(5), viz

$$\vdash_\Lambda \Phi([\varepsilon\#\alpha]\varphi) \to \Phi(\varphi_n(\varepsilon,\alpha)). \qquad \blacksquare$$

2.4.7 THE DEDUCTION THEOREM.

$$\Sigma \cup \{\varphi\} \vdash_\Lambda \psi \quad \textit{iff} \quad \Sigma \vdash_\Lambda (\varphi \to \psi).$$

Proof.

If $\Sigma \vdash_\Lambda (\varphi \to \psi)$ then by Theorem 2.4.4, parts (1) and (2), both φ and $(\varphi \to \psi)$ are Λ-deducible from $\Sigma \cup \{\varphi\}$. Hence by 2.4.4(4), $\Sigma \vdash_\Lambda \psi$.

Conversely, suppose $\Sigma \cup \{\varphi\} \vdash_\Lambda \psi$. Let

$$\Gamma = \{\theta : \Sigma \vdash_\Lambda (\varphi \to \theta)\}.$$

We wish to show that $\psi \in \Gamma$. By our hypothesis it will suffice then to show that Γ

is a Λ-theory containing $\Sigma \cup \{\varphi\}$.

Now if $\chi \in \Sigma$ or $\vdash_\Lambda \chi$, we have $\Sigma \vdash_\Lambda \chi$. Since $\chi \to (\varphi \to \chi)$ is a tautology, it is Λ-deducible from Σ (2.4.4(3)), and this leads to $\Sigma \vdash_\Lambda (\varphi \to \chi)$, and hence $\chi \in \Gamma$. Similarly, since $(\varphi \to \varphi)$ is a tautology we get $\varphi \in \Gamma$. Altogether then, $\Sigma \cup \{\varphi\} \cup \Lambda \subseteq \Gamma$, and it remains only to show Γ is closed under MP and OI.

MP: If $(\theta \to \chi)$, $\theta \in \Gamma$, then since

$$(\varphi \to (\theta \to \chi)) \to ((\varphi \to \theta) \to (\varphi \to \chi))$$

is an instance of A2, the definition of Γ implies, by 2.4.4(4), that

$$\Sigma \vdash_\Lambda \varphi \to \chi,$$

and so $\chi \in \Gamma$.

OI: Suppose $\{\Phi(\chi_n(\varepsilon,\alpha)) : n \in \mathbb{N}\} \subseteq \Gamma$,
for some $\Phi \in Afm$, $\chi \in Fma$, $\varepsilon \in Bxp$, and $\alpha \in Cmd$. Then,

$$\Sigma \vdash_\Lambda \varphi \to \Phi(\chi_n(\varepsilon,\alpha)) \quad \text{for all } n \in \mathbb{N}.$$

But then applying 2.4.4(5) to the admissible form $(\varphi \to \Phi)$ gives

$$\Sigma \vdash_\Lambda \varphi \to \Phi([\varepsilon\#\alpha]\chi),$$

and so

$$\Phi([\varepsilon\#\alpha]\chi) \in \Gamma. \qquad ■$$

2.4.8 COROLLARY.

(1) $\Sigma \cup \{\varphi\}$ *is Λ-consistent iff* $\Sigma \nvdash_\Lambda \neg\varphi$.

(2) $\Sigma \cup \{\neg\varphi\}$ *is Λ-consistent iff* $\Sigma \nvdash_\Lambda \varphi$.

Proof.

(1) By the Deduction Theorem,

$$\Sigma \cup \{\varphi\} \text{ is } \Lambda\text{-consistent iff } \Sigma \nvdash_\Lambda (\varphi \to \mathit{false}).$$

(2) From (1), since $\Sigma \vdash_\Lambda \varphi$ iff $\Sigma \vdash_\Lambda \neg\neg\varphi$, as $\varphi \leftrightarrow \neg\neg\varphi$ is a tautology.

■

2.4.9 THE α-DEDUCTION LEMMA.

If $\Sigma \vdash_\Lambda \varphi$, *then* $\{[\alpha]\psi : \psi \in \Sigma\} \vdash_\Lambda [\alpha]\varphi$.

Proof.

Suppose $\Sigma \vdash_\Lambda \varphi$, and let Γ be any Λ-theory containing $\{[\alpha]\psi : \psi \in \Sigma\}$. Put

$$\Delta = \{\psi : [\alpha]\psi \in \Gamma\}.$$

Our aim is to show that $[\alpha]\varphi \in \Gamma$, i.e. that $\varphi \in \Delta$. By our hypothesis then it suffices to prove that Δ is a Λ-theory containing Σ.

But if $\psi \in \Sigma$, $[\alpha]\psi \in \Gamma$ by hypothesis on Γ, so $\psi \in \Delta$ by definition of Δ. Hence $\Sigma \subseteq \Delta$. If $\vdash_\Lambda \psi$, then by TR $\vdash_\Lambda [\alpha]\psi$, so $[\alpha]\psi$ belongs to the Λ-theory Γ, whence $\psi \in \Delta$. Thus $\Lambda \subseteq \Delta$, and it remains to show that Δ is closed under MP and OI.

MP: If $(\psi \to \theta)$, $\psi \in \Delta$, then $[\alpha](\psi \to \theta)$, $[\alpha]\psi \in \Gamma$. But then by axiom A4,

$$\vdash_\Lambda [\alpha](\psi \to \theta) \to ([\alpha]\psi \to [\alpha]\theta).$$

Hence we get (2.4.6(3)) $[\alpha]\theta \in \Gamma$, so that $\theta \in \Delta$.

OI: If $\{\Phi(\psi_n(\varepsilon,\beta)) : n \in \mathbb{N}\} \subseteq \Delta$, then

$$\{[\alpha]\Phi(\psi_n(\varepsilon,\beta)) : n \in \mathbb{N}\} \subseteq \Gamma.$$

But then applying the OI-closure of Γ to the admissible form $[\alpha]\Phi$, we get $[\alpha]\Phi([\varepsilon\#\beta]\psi) \in \Gamma$, hence $\Phi([\varepsilon\#\beta]\psi) \in \Delta$. ■

2.4.10 COROLLARY. *If* Γ *is a* Λ*-theory, then* $[\alpha]\varphi \in \Gamma$ *iff* $\Gamma(\alpha) \vdash_\Lambda \varphi$, *where* $\Gamma(\alpha) = \{\psi : [\alpha]\psi \in \Gamma\}$.

Proof.

If $[\alpha]\varphi \in \Gamma$, then $\varphi \in \Gamma(\alpha)$, hence $\Gamma(\alpha) \vdash_\Lambda \varphi$.

Conversely, if $\Gamma(\alpha) \vdash_\Lambda \varphi$ then, by the Theorem, $[\alpha]\varphi$ is Λ-deducible from the set

$$\{[\alpha]\psi : \psi \in \Gamma(\alpha)\} = \{[\alpha]\psi : [\alpha]\psi \in \Gamma\} \subseteq \Gamma,$$

and so (2.4.4(2)) $\Gamma \vdash_\Lambda [\alpha]\varphi$. Since Γ is Λ-deductively closed (2.4.6(2)), $[\alpha]\varphi \in \Gamma$.

■

2.5 COMPLETENESS

If M is a Λ-*model*, i.e. has

$$M \models \varphi \text{ for all } \varphi \in \Lambda,$$

then each state s in M determines the set

$$\Gamma_s = \{\varphi : M \models_s \varphi\}$$

as an extension of Λ that is closed under MP. If M is *standard*, then Γ_s will also be closed under OI (2.3.8) and so will be a Λ-theory that is consistent (since *false* does not hold at s). But since in general either φ or $\neg\varphi$ holds at s, Γ_s satisfies the special property

$$\varphi \in \Gamma \textit{ or } \neg\varphi \in \Gamma, \textit{ for all } \varphi \in \mathit{Fma}.$$

A *maximal* Λ-*theory* is, by definition, a *consistent* Λ-theory Γ satisfying this last condition. Such a Γ is properly contained in no Λ-theory other than the inconsistent theory *Fma* (why?).

Now vis-a-vis the semantics of our formal language, the state s can be identified with the maximal theory Γ_s, since to know what holds in s is precisely to know what belongs to Γ_s. This motivates the construction of a "canonical" model for Λ based on the set

$$S_\Lambda = \{\Gamma \subseteq \mathit{Fma} : \Gamma \text{ is a maximal } \Lambda\text{-theory}\}.$$

2.5.1 THEOREM. *If Γ is a maximal Λ-theory,*

(1) $false \notin \Gamma$;

(2) *exactly one of* φ *and* $\neg\varphi$ *belongs to* Γ, *for all* φ;

(3) $(\varphi \to \psi) \in \Gamma$ *iff* $\varphi \in \Gamma$ *implies* $\psi \in \Gamma$;

(4) $(\varphi \vee \psi) \in \Gamma$ *iff* $\varphi \in \Gamma$ *or* $\psi \in \Gamma$;

(5) $(\varphi \leftrightarrow \psi) \in \Gamma$ *iff* $(\varphi \in \Gamma$ *iff* $\psi \in \Gamma)$;

(6) Exactly *one of* $\neg D\varepsilon$, ε, *and* $not\text{-}\varepsilon$ *belongs to* Γ, *for all* $\varepsilon \in Bxp$.

Proof.

(1) Γ is Λ-consistent.

(2) If both φ and $(\varphi \to false)$ belonged to Γ, by MP we would have $false \in \Gamma$, contrary to (1).

(3) From left to right is just the MP-closure of Γ. Conversely, suppose $\varphi \in \Gamma$ implies $\psi \in \Gamma$. If in fact $\varphi \in \Gamma$, then by hypothesis $\psi \in \Gamma$. But the tautology $\psi \to (\varphi \to \psi)$ belongs to Γ, whence by MP, $(\varphi \to \psi) \in \Gamma$. On the other hand, if $\varphi \notin \Gamma$ then, as Γ is maximal, $\neg\varphi \in \Gamma$. Similarly then, via the tautology $\neg\varphi \to (\varphi \to \psi)$, we again get $(\varphi \to \psi) \in \Gamma$.

(4) Suppose $\varphi \vee \psi = (\neg\varphi \to \psi) \in \Gamma$. Then either $\varphi \in \Gamma$, or else $\neg\varphi \in \Gamma$ and so by MP $\psi \in \Gamma$. The converse is 2.4.6(6).

(5) From part (3), using 2.4.6(5) to show that

$$(\varphi \leftrightarrow \psi) \in \Gamma \quad \text{iff} \quad (\varphi \to \psi),\ (\psi \to \varphi) \in \Gamma.$$

(6) If $\neg D\varepsilon \notin \Gamma$, then $D\varepsilon \in \Gamma$, so by A13 $(\varepsilon \vee not\text{-}\varepsilon) \in \Gamma$. Hence part (4) gives $\varepsilon \in \Gamma$ or $not\text{-}\varepsilon \in \Gamma$. So at least one of the three is in Γ.

But if $\neg D\varepsilon \in \Gamma$, $D\varepsilon \notin \Gamma$ by part (2). But $\vdash_\Lambda \varepsilon \to D\varepsilon$ (2.4.2(2)), so by the MP-closure of Γ, $\varepsilon \notin \Gamma$. Similarly, as $\vdash_\Lambda not\text{-}\varepsilon \to D\varepsilon$ (2.4.2(3)), $not\text{-}\varepsilon \notin \Gamma$.

If, on the other hand, $\varepsilon \in \Gamma$, then $D\varepsilon \in \Gamma$ by 2.4.2(2) and so $\neg D\varepsilon \notin \Gamma$.

Also $\neg\varepsilon \in \Gamma$ by part (2), so as $\vdash_\Lambda \mathit{not}\text{-}\varepsilon \to \neg\varepsilon$ (2.4.2(1)), $\mathit{not}\ \varepsilon \notin \Gamma$.

Finally, if $\mathit{not}\text{-}\varepsilon \in \Gamma$, then by 2.4.2(1) and 2.4.2(3), $\neg\varepsilon \in \Gamma$ and $D\varepsilon \in \Gamma$, so $\varepsilon \notin \Gamma$ and $\neg D\varepsilon \notin \Gamma$. ■

Our next result establishes that in characterising the deducibility relation we can confine our attention to maximal theories.

2.5.2 THEOREM.

(1) $\Sigma \vdash_\Lambda \varphi$ *iff for all* $\Gamma \in S_\Lambda$ *such that* $\Sigma \subseteq \Gamma$, $\varphi \in \Gamma$.

(2) $\vdash_\Lambda \varphi$ *iff for all* $\Gamma \in S_\Lambda$, $\varphi \in \Gamma$.

Proof.

(1) From left to right is immediate from the definition of "$\Sigma \vdash_\Lambda \varphi$".

For the converse, suppose that $\Sigma \nvdash_\Lambda \varphi$. We have to show that $\varphi \notin \Gamma$ for some $\Gamma \in S_\Lambda$ with $\Sigma \subseteq \Gamma$. To do this we construct such a Γ that contains $\Sigma \cup \{\neg\varphi\}$.

Let $\varphi_0, \varphi_1, \varphi_2, \ldots.$ be an enumeration of the whole (denumerable) set *Fma* of formulae. We use this enumeration to define an increasing sequence $\Gamma_0 \subseteq \Gamma_1 \subseteq \ldots.$ of sets of formulae, starting with

$$\Gamma_0 = \Sigma \cup \{\neg\varphi\}.$$

Assuming inductively that Γ_n has been defined, Γ_{n+1} is defined according to the following possibilities.

Case 1: If $\Gamma_n \vdash_\Lambda \varphi_n$, put $\Gamma_{n+1} = \Gamma_n \cup \{\varphi_n\}$;

Otherwise (i.e. if $\Gamma_n \nvdash_\Lambda \varphi_n$),

Case 2: If φ_n is *not* of the form $\Phi([\varepsilon\#\alpha]\psi)$, put $\Gamma_{n+1} = \Gamma_n \cup \{\neg\varphi_n\}$;

and otherwise

Case 3: If φ_n *is* of the form $\Phi([\varepsilon\#\alpha]\psi)$, let

$$\Gamma_{n+1} = \Gamma_n \cup \{\neg\Phi(\psi_j(\varepsilon,\alpha)), \neg\varphi_n\},$$

where j is chosen as the least (to be explicit) number such that

$$\Gamma_n \nvdash_\Lambda \Phi(\psi_j(\varepsilon,\alpha))$$

(such a j exists by Theorem 2.4.4(5)).

This completes the definition of Γ_{n+1}.

Next we put $\Gamma = \bigcup\{\Gamma_n : n \in \mathbb{N}\}$.

To complete the result we have to show that Γ is a maximal Λ-theory. For, since $\neg\varphi \in \Gamma_0 \subseteq \Gamma$, this will ensure $\varphi \notin \Gamma$.

Lemma 1. *For all $n \in \mathbb{N}$, Γ_n is Λ-consistent.*

Proof.

By induction on n. When $n=0$, consistency of $\Gamma_0 = \Sigma \cup \{\neg\varphi\}$ follows from 2.4.8(2), since $\Sigma \nvdash_\Lambda \varphi$.

Assume inductively that Γ_n is Λ-consistent, and consider the three possibilities for Γ_{n+1}

Case 1: If $\Gamma_n \vdash_\Lambda \varphi_n$, the inductive assumption that Γ_n is Λ-consistent implies (Ex. 2.4.5(1)) that $\Gamma_n \nvdash_\Lambda \neg\varphi_n$, and so (2.4.8(1))

$$\Gamma_n \cup \{\varphi_n\} = \Gamma_{n+1} \text{ is } \Lambda\text{-consistent.}$$

Case 2: If $\Gamma_{n+1} = \Gamma_n \cup \{\neg\varphi_n\}$ were not Λ-consistent we would have $\Gamma_n \vdash_\Lambda \varphi_n$, by 2.4.8(2), contrary to the definition of this case.

Case 3: If $\Gamma_{n+1} = \Gamma_n \cup \{\neg\Phi(\psi_j(\varepsilon,\alpha))\} \cup \{\neg\varphi_n\}$ were not Λ-consistent then we would have

$$\Gamma_n \cup \{\neg\Phi(\psi_j(\varepsilon,\alpha))\} \vdash_\Lambda \varphi_n.$$

(where $\varphi_n = \Phi([\varepsilon\#\alpha]\psi)$). But

$$\varphi_n \to \Phi(\psi_j(\varepsilon,\alpha))$$

is a Λ-theorem (2.4.3(5)), so it follows that

$$\Gamma_n \cup \{\neg\Phi(\psi_j(\varepsilon,\alpha))\} \vdash_\Lambda \Phi(\psi_j(\varepsilon,\alpha)),$$

which makes $\Gamma_n \cup \{\neg\Phi(\psi_j(\varepsilon,\alpha))\}$ inconsistent.

Hence $\Gamma_n \vdash_\Lambda \Phi(\psi_j(\varepsilon,\alpha))$ (2.4.8(2)). But this is in contradiction with the definition of j. This completes the proof of Lemma 1. ■

Lemma 2. *Exactly one of ψ and $\neg\psi$ belongs to Γ, for any $\psi \in Fma$.*

Proof.

Any ψ is φ_n for some n. But either $\varphi_n \in \Gamma_{n+1} \subseteq \Gamma$ (Case 1), or else $\neg\varphi_n \in \Gamma_{n+1}$ (Cases 2 and 3). So at least one of ψ, $\neg\psi$ is in Γ. But if both are, then for some m, ψ, $\neg\psi \in \Gamma_m$, making Γ_m Λ-inconsistent - in contradiction with Lemma 1. Hence Lemma 2 holds. ■

Lemma 3. *Γ is closed under* MP *and* OI.

Proof.

MP: Let θ, $(\theta \to \psi) \in \Gamma$. If $\psi \notin \Gamma$ then $\neg\psi \in \Gamma$, by Lemma 1, and so

$$\{\theta, (\theta \to \psi), \neg\psi\} \subseteq \Gamma_m, \quad \text{for some } m.$$

But, from the tautology $(\theta \to \psi) \to (\neg\psi \to \neg\theta)$, this would imply that Γ_m was not Λ-consistent, again contradicting Lemma 1. Hence $\psi \in \Gamma$.

OI: Suppose $\{\Phi(\psi_k(\varepsilon,\alpha)) : k \in \mathbb{N}\} \subseteq \Gamma$.
Let $\Phi([\varepsilon\#\alpha]\psi) = \varphi_n$. Then if $\varphi_n \notin \Gamma$, $\Gamma_n \nvdash_\Lambda \varphi_n$ (or else $\varphi_n \in \Gamma_{n+1}$). But then by Case 3 of the definition of Γ_{n+1}, $\neg\Phi(\psi_j(\varepsilon,\alpha)) \in \Gamma$ for some j. Hence by Lemma 2, $\Phi(\psi_j(\varepsilon,\alpha)) \notin \Gamma$, contrary to hypothesis. We conclude $\varphi_n \in \Gamma$, completing the proof of Lemma 3. ■

To finish, finally, the proof of the main result, observe that if $\vdash_\Lambda \varphi_n$ then $\Gamma_n \vdash_\Lambda \varphi_n$, whence $\varphi_n \in \Gamma_{n+1}$. Thus Γ contains Λ, which by Lemma 3 makes Γ a Λ-theory. But then Γ must be Λ-consistent, for if *false* $\in \Gamma$ (2.4.6(4)) we would have *false* $\in \Gamma_n$ for some n, contrary to Lemma 1. Thus by Lemma 2, Γ is a maximal Λ-theory as desired. and this completes the proof of part (1).

(2) Put $\Sigma = \emptyset$ in (1). ∎

2.5.3 COROLLARY.

$$\vdash_\Lambda \neg D\varepsilon \rightarrow [\varepsilon\#\alpha]\varphi$$

Proof.

Let Γ be any member of S_Λ. If $\neg D\varepsilon \in \Gamma$, then we know that $\varepsilon \notin \Gamma$ and *not*-$\varepsilon \notin \Gamma$, by 2.5.1(1). But then (*not*-$\varepsilon \rightarrow \psi$) and $(\varepsilon \rightarrow \psi)$ are in Γ for any ψ (2.5.1(3)), which makes $\varphi_n(\varepsilon,\alpha) \in \Gamma$ for all $n \in \mathbb{N}$. Hence by OI, $[\varepsilon\#\alpha]\varphi \in \Gamma$. Therefore by 2.5.1(3) $(\neg D\varepsilon \rightarrow [\varepsilon\#\alpha]\varphi) \in \Gamma$. Since this holds for all $\Gamma \in S_\Lambda$, Theorem 2.5.2 gives the desired result. ∎

CANONICAL MODELS

The *canonical model* for a logic Λ is the structure

$$M_\Lambda = (S_\Lambda,\ v,\ [\![\cdot]\!]),$$

based on the set S_Λ of maximal Λ-theories, that has

(i) for each $p \in Bvb$ and $\Gamma \in S_\Lambda$,

$$v_\Gamma(p) = \begin{cases} 1 & \text{if } p \in \Gamma \\ 0 & \text{if } not\text{-}p \in \Gamma \\ \omega & \text{if } \neg Dp \in \Gamma \end{cases}$$

(by 2.5.1(6) $v_\Gamma(p)$ is well-defined).

(ii) the relation $[\![\alpha]\!]$ on S_Λ is defined inductively by putting

$$\Gamma [\![\pi]\!] \Delta \quad \text{iff} \quad \{\psi \in \mathit{Fma} : [\pi]\psi \in \Gamma\} \subseteq \Delta,$$

for program letters π, and then for a structured command α defining $[\![\alpha]\!]$ by the appropriate standard-model condition for α (cf. §2.3).

Thus M_Λ is a standard model *by definition*.

The key to our axiomatisation problem is the

FUNDAMENTAL THEOREM FOR Λ. *For any* $\varphi \in \mathit{Fma}$, *and any* $\Gamma \in S_\Lambda$,

$$M_\Lambda \models_\Gamma \varphi \quad \textit{iff} \quad \varphi \in \Gamma. \qquad \blacksquare$$

Holding the proof of this Theorem in abeyance for a while, we proceed to show how it yields a solution to our problem.

COMPLETENESS THEOREM FOR Λ.

$$\vdash_\Lambda \varphi \quad \textit{iff} \quad M_\Lambda \models \varphi$$

Proof.

By the Fundamental Theorem, "$M_\Lambda \models \varphi$" is equivalent to "for all $\Gamma \in S_\Lambda$, $\varphi \in \Gamma$". But by Theorem 2.5.2, part (2), this in turn is equivalent to "$\vdash_\Lambda \varphi$".

$\blacksquare$

COMPLETENESS THEOREM FOR PL.

$$\vdash_{PL} \varphi \quad \textit{iff} \quad \varphi \textit{ is valid in every standard model.}$$

Proof.

Recall that PL is, by definition, the smallest (i.e. intersection) of all logics.

Now if M is any standard model, then the set $\{\varphi : M \models \varphi\}$ is a logic, as noted in Exercise 2.4.5(2), and so contains the smallest logic. Thus all PL-theorems are valid in M.

Conversely, if φ is valid in all standard models, then in particular φ is valid in M_{PL}. Hence, by the previous result, $\vdash_{PL} \varphi$. ∎

As we follow the process of step-wise refinement in later chapters, new formula-and-program-constructing devices will be added to the language, for which corresponding new axioms will be introduced, and corresponding standard-model conditions given. In each case, to prove the Completeness Theorem for the new notions of "logic" and "smallest logic" we will have to do two things:

(i) extend the definition of M_Λ to incorporate the new standard-model criteria,

and (ii) extend the Fundamental Theorem to cover the new kinds of formula.

Completeness will then follow just as above.

This actually provides a systematic method for obtaining an axiomatisation of the class of valid formulae, for a given notion of validity. For, we take as axioms just those valid schemata that are needed to prove the Fundamental Theorem. And it is by attempting to construct such a proof that we discover what the necessary schemata are. This is how the process of axiomatisation produces a detailed analysis of the semantic concepts involved.

The Fundamental Theorem actually yields more information than the results stated above: it leads to a *Strong Completeness Theorem* for Λ. Theorems of this latter kind typically have the form

Every consistent set of formulae is satisfiable.

In the present context, if Σ is Λ-consistent, then by 2.5.2(1) there is a maximal

Λ-theory Γ that contains Σ. Then by the Fundamental Theorem, Σ is *simultaneously satisfied* (i.e. all members of Σ hold) at the state Γ in the canonical Λ-model. In particular, for PL we get the following Strong Completeness Theorem:

Every PL-*consistent set is simultaneously satisfied at a state of some standard model.*

A notable feature of our analysis is of course the use of the *infinitary* rule OI. But in fact for the propositional language of this chapter this rule is not essential, in that the PL-theorems would still be generated by Hoare's Iteration Rule in its place. This fact, announced in Goldblatt (1979i), is proven in detail (for a slightly simplified semantics) in Goldblatt (1981), where it is also shown that the property of validity in all standard models is decidable. The difference between the system with OI and that with only Hoare's rule is that, whereas the two have the same theorems, and hence the same consistent formulae, the latter has more consistent *sets* of formulae than the former and is not strongly complete. Hence the canonical-model method does not work for it in the way it does here. The reason for our use of OI at this stage is that this chapter is really the first phase in a structured completeness theorem for the quantificational languages of Chapter 3. For such languages, the use of infinitary rules is essential, as will be explained in §3.6.

We now proceed to the proof of the Fundamental Theorem, beginning with the case of Boolean expressions.

2.5.4 THEOREM. *In* M_Λ, *for any* $\varepsilon \in Bxp$ *we have*

$$v_\Gamma(\varepsilon) = \begin{cases} 1 & \text{if } \varepsilon \in \Gamma \\ 0 & \text{if } not\text{-}\varepsilon \in \Gamma \\ \omega & \text{if } \neg D\varepsilon \in \Gamma. \end{cases}$$

Proof.

(Since exactly one of ε, *not*-ε, and $\neg D\varepsilon$ is in Γ, this result immediately implies that obtained by replacing "if" by "iff" in each of the three cases).

1. For the expression *false*, we have $v_\Gamma(\textit{false}) = 0$ by definition. But *not*-*false* is *true*, and *true* $\in \Gamma$ by A12.

2. For $\varepsilon \in Bvb$ the result holds by definition.

3. Assume, inductively, the result for ε, δ, and ∂, and consider $(\varepsilon \supset \delta,\partial)$. There are three cases.

(3a). If $(\varepsilon \supset \delta,\partial) \in \Gamma$ then by A15 and properties of maximal theories (2.5.1, 2.4.6), either $\varepsilon,\delta \in \Gamma$ or else *not*-$\varepsilon,\partial \in \Gamma$. Hence by the induction hypothesis either $v_\Gamma(\varepsilon) = v_\Gamma(\delta) = 1$, or else $v_\Gamma(\textit{not}\text{-}\varepsilon) = 1$ (i.e. $v_\Gamma(\varepsilon) = 0$) and $v_\Gamma(\partial) = 1$. In either case, $v_\Gamma(\varepsilon \supset \delta,\partial) = 1$.

(3b). If *not*-$(\varepsilon \supset \delta,\partial) \in \Gamma$ then $(\varepsilon \supset \delta,\partial) \notin \Gamma$, hence from A15 neither $(\varepsilon \wedge \delta) \in \Gamma$ nor $(\textit{not}\text{-}\varepsilon \wedge \partial) \in \Gamma$ are possible. But from 2.4.2(3) we get $D(\varepsilon \supset \delta,\partial) \in \Gamma$ and so, using A16, either $(\varepsilon \wedge D\delta) \in \Gamma$ or $(\textit{not}\text{-}\varepsilon \wedge D\partial) \in \Gamma$.

In the first of these alternatives, we have ε, $D\delta \in \Gamma$, and so $\neg D\delta \notin \Gamma$, and $\delta \notin \Gamma$ (or else $\varepsilon \wedge \delta \in \Gamma$, contrary to our earlier conclusion). Hence we must have *not*-$\delta \in \Gamma$. The induction hypothesis then gives $v_\Gamma(\varepsilon) = 1$ and $v_\Gamma(\delta) = 0$, which makes $v_\Gamma(\varepsilon \supset \delta,\partial) = 0$.

Similarly, for the other alternative we find that *not*-ε, $\partial \in \Gamma$, so $v_\Gamma(\varepsilon) = 0$ and $v_\Gamma(\varepsilon \supset \delta,\partial) = v_\Gamma(\partial) = 0$.

(3c). If $\neg D(\varepsilon \supset \delta,\partial) \in \Gamma$ then, using A16, neither $(\varepsilon \wedge D\delta)$ nor $(\textit{not}\text{-}\varepsilon \wedge D\partial)$ belong to Γ. Then either (i) $\neg D\varepsilon \in \Gamma$, whence $v_\Gamma(\varepsilon) = \omega$ by the induction hypothesis; or (ii) $\varepsilon \in \Gamma$, hence $D\delta \notin \Gamma$ (or else $\varepsilon \wedge D\delta \in \Gamma$), so $\neg D\delta \in \Gamma$ and altogether $v_\Gamma(\varepsilon) = 1$ and $v_\Gamma(\delta) = \omega$; or finally (iii) *not*-$\varepsilon \in \Gamma$, so $D\partial \notin \Gamma$, giving $v_\Gamma(\varepsilon) = 0$ and $v_\Gamma(\partial) = \omega$.

In all of (i), (ii), (iii) we have $v_\Gamma(\varepsilon \supset \delta,\partial) = \omega$. Thus the Theorem holds for $(\varepsilon \supset \delta,\partial)$.

4. Assume the result for ε and δ, and consider $(\varepsilon = \delta)$.

(4a). If $(\varepsilon = \delta) \in \Gamma$, then by 2.4.2(4), $D\varepsilon \in \Gamma$, and so either $\varepsilon \in \Gamma$ or *not*-$\varepsilon \in \Gamma$. But by 2.4.2(11), each of

$$(\varepsilon = \delta) \rightarrow (\varepsilon \leftrightarrow \delta)$$

$$(\varepsilon = \delta) \rightarrow (\mathit{not}\text{-}\varepsilon \leftrightarrow \mathit{not}\text{-}\delta)$$

are Λ-theorems, and so both $(\varepsilon \leftrightarrow \delta)$ and $(\mathit{not}\text{-}\varepsilon \leftrightarrow \mathit{not}\text{-}\delta)$ belong to Γ. But then either $\varepsilon, \delta \in \Gamma$ or *not*-ε, *not*-$\delta \in \Gamma$, giving by the induction hypothesis either $v_\Gamma(\varepsilon) = v_\Gamma(\delta) = 1$, or $v_\Gamma(\varepsilon) = v_\Gamma(\delta) = 0$, both of which make $v_\Gamma(\varepsilon = \delta)$ equal to 1.

(4b). If *not*-$(\varepsilon = \delta) \in \Gamma$ then (2.4.2(3)) $D(\varepsilon = \delta) \in \Gamma$, and by A17 $D\varepsilon$, $D\delta \in \Gamma$, so that neither of $v_\Gamma(\varepsilon)$ nor $v_\Gamma(\delta)$ is ω. Thus $v_\Gamma(\varepsilon = \delta) \neq \omega$. But $(\varepsilon = \delta) \notin \Gamma$, and so by the Λ-theorems

$$\varepsilon \wedge \delta \rightarrow (\varepsilon = \delta) \qquad \text{and}$$

$$\mathit{not}\text{-}\varepsilon \rightarrow (\mathit{not}\text{-}\delta \rightarrow (\varepsilon = \delta)).$$

(cf. 2.4.2), (i) we cannot have $\varepsilon, \delta \in \Gamma$ and

(ii) we cannot have *not*-ε, *not*-$\delta \in \Gamma$.

But since $D\varepsilon \in \Gamma$,

(iii) either $\varepsilon \in \Gamma$ or *not*-$\varepsilon \in \Gamma$.

Similarly, (iv) either $\delta \in \Gamma$ or *not*-$\delta \in \Gamma$.

These requirements imply that either ε, *not*-$\delta \in \Gamma$ or else *not*-ε, $\delta \in \Gamma$. But in either case, the induction hypothesis gives $v_\Gamma(\varepsilon) \neq v_\Gamma(\delta)$, which means that $v_\Gamma(\varepsilon = \delta)$ is 0.

(4c). If $\neg D(\varepsilon = \delta) \in \Gamma$, then by A17 $D\varepsilon \wedge D\delta \notin \Gamma$, so either $D\varepsilon \notin \Gamma$, whence $v_\Gamma(\varepsilon) = \omega$, or $D\delta \notin \Gamma$, whence $v_\Gamma(\delta) = \omega$. Thus $v_\Gamma(\varepsilon = \delta) = \omega$.

4a - 4c establish the Theorem for $\varepsilon = \delta$, and hence complete the inductive proof for all Boolean expressions. ■

2.5.5 COROLLARY. *For any* $\varepsilon \in Bxp$,

$$M_\Lambda \models_\Gamma \varepsilon \quad \textit{iff} \quad \varepsilon \in \Gamma$$

Proof.

$$M_\Lambda \models_\Gamma \varepsilon \quad \text{iff} \quad v_\Gamma(\varepsilon) = 1. \qquad \blacksquare$$

2.5.5 is the Fundamental Theorem for Boolean expressions. For formulae that involve modal operators we need some further preliminaries.

2.5.6 FIRST α-LEMMA. *In* M_Λ, *for all* $\Gamma, \Delta \in S_\Lambda$ *we have*

$$\Gamma [\![\alpha]\!] \Delta \quad \textit{only if} \quad \{\varphi : [\alpha]\varphi \in \Gamma\} \subseteq \Delta$$

Proof.

By induction on the formation of α

a. If α is *skip*, then $\Gamma [\![\textit{skip}]\!] \Delta$ means that $\Gamma = \Delta$. But then if $[\textit{skip}]\varphi \in \Gamma$, by axiom A6 $\varphi \in \Gamma$. Hence the result holds for *skip*.

If α is *abort*, then the result is true (vacuously), since $\Gamma [\![\textit{abort}]\!] \Delta$ is false.

b. The result holds if α is π (a program letter), by definition of $[\![\pi]\!]$ in M_Λ.

c. Assume the result for α and β, in order to show inductively that it holds for $(\alpha;\beta)$.

If $\Gamma [\![\alpha;\beta]\!] \Delta$ then by definition of M_Λ, we have $\Gamma [\![\alpha]\!] \Delta' [\![\beta]\!] \Delta$ for some $\Delta' \in S_\Lambda$. But then if $[\alpha;\beta]\varphi \in \Gamma$, A7 implies that $[\alpha][\beta]\varphi \in \Gamma$. The induction hypothesis on α then gives $[\beta]\varphi \in \Delta'$. From this, by the hypothesis on β, it follows that $\varphi \in \Delta$ as required.

d. Assume the result for α and β, in order to prove it for $(\varepsilon \rightarrow \alpha,\beta)$.

If $\Gamma [\![\varepsilon \rightarrow \alpha,\beta]\!] \Delta$, then either

(i) $v_\Gamma(\varepsilon) = 1$ and $\Gamma [\![\alpha]\!] \Delta$

or (ii) $v_\Gamma(\varepsilon) = 0$ and $\Gamma [\![\beta]\!] \Delta$.

Now if $[\varepsilon \Rightarrow \alpha,\beta]\varphi \in \Gamma$, then using A8 we deduce that both $(\varepsilon \rightarrow [\alpha]\varphi)$ and $(\mathit{not}\text{-}\varepsilon \rightarrow [\beta]\varphi)$ belong to Γ. But if case (i) obtains we have $\varepsilon \in \Gamma$ (2.5.4 etc.), so that $[\alpha]\varphi \in \Gamma$. But also $\Gamma [\![\alpha]\!] \Delta$, so the hypothesis on α gives $\varphi \in \Delta$. Similarly in case (ii) we get $\Gamma [\![\beta]\!] \Delta$, with $\mathit{not}\text{-}\varepsilon \in \Gamma$ and therefore $[\beta]\varphi \in \Gamma$, whence by the hypothesis on β, again $\varphi \in \Delta$.

e. Suppose the Lemma holds for α. Then to prove it holds for $(\varepsilon\#\alpha)$ we need a preliminary result:

Sublemma. *For all* $\Gamma, \Delta \in S_\Lambda$, *if*

$\Gamma [\![\varepsilon]\alpha]\!]^n \Delta$ *and* $\models_\Delta \mathit{not}\text{-}\varepsilon$, *then* $\varphi_n(\varepsilon,\alpha) \in \Gamma$ *only if* $\varphi \in \Delta$.

Proof.

By induction on n.

If $n=0$, we have $\Gamma = \Delta$ and so $\models_\Gamma \mathit{not}\text{-}\varepsilon$, whence $\mathit{not}\text{-}\varepsilon \in \Gamma$ by 2.5.5. But then if $\varphi_0(\varepsilon,\alpha)$, i.e. $(\mathit{not}\text{-}\varepsilon \rightarrow \varphi)$, belongs to Γ, MP-closure of the latter gives $\varphi \in \Gamma$.

Now assume the Sublemma holds for n. Then if $\Gamma [\![\varepsilon]\alpha]\!]^{n+1} \Delta$ and $\models_\Delta \mathit{not}\text{-}\varepsilon$, for some Δ' we have $\Gamma [\![\varepsilon]\alpha]\!] \Delta' [\![\varepsilon]\alpha]\!]^n \Delta$. But then $v_\Gamma(\varepsilon) = 1$ and $\Gamma [\![\alpha]\!] \Delta'$. Thus if $\varphi_{n+1}(\varepsilon,\alpha)$, i.e. $\varepsilon \rightarrow [\alpha]\varphi_n$, belongs to Γ, since $\varepsilon \in \Gamma$ (2.5.5) we get $[\alpha]\varphi_n \in \Gamma$. The main hypothesis on α for the α-Lemma then implies $\varphi_n \in \Delta'$. From this, by the inductive hypothesis on n for the Sublemma, we infer $\varphi \in \Delta$. This shows that the Sublemma holds for n+1, and hence completes its inductive proof. ■

Returning now to the main result for $\varepsilon\#\alpha$, if $\Gamma [\![\varepsilon\#\alpha]\!] \Delta$ in M_Λ, then for some n we have $\Gamma [\![\varepsilon]\alpha]\!]^n \Delta$ and $\models_\Delta \mathit{not}\text{-}\varepsilon$. But then if $[\varepsilon\#\alpha]\varphi \in \Delta$, since

$$[\varepsilon\#\alpha]\varphi \rightarrow \varphi_n(\varepsilon,\alpha)$$

is a Λ-theorem by 2.4.3(5), we have $\varphi_n(\varepsilon,\alpha) \in \Gamma$ and so by the Sublemma $\varphi \in \Delta$.

This completes the inductive case (e), and so completes the proof of the First α-Lemma. ■

2.5.7 SECOND α-LEMMA. *For all formulae* φ,

if $M_\Lambda \models_\Gamma \varphi$ *implies* $\varphi \in \Gamma$ *for all* $\Gamma \in S_\Lambda$,

then $M_\Lambda \models_\Gamma [\alpha]\varphi$ *implies* $[\alpha]\varphi \in \Gamma$ *for all* $\Gamma \in S_\Lambda$.

Proof. By induction

a. If α is *skip*, then $\models_\Gamma [skip]\varphi$ only if $\models_\Gamma \varphi$, since M_Λ is standard. The hypothesis on φ then gives $\varphi \in \Gamma$, whence by A5 $[skip]\varphi \in \Gamma$.

If α is *abort*, then for any φ we have $\models_\Gamma [abort]\varphi$. But $[abort]\varphi$ is a Λ-theorem, by 2.4.1(7), and so belongs to Γ.

b. Let α be a program letter π, and suppose $\models_\Gamma [\pi]\varphi$. Let $\Gamma(\pi) = \{\psi : [\pi]\psi \in \Gamma\}$. Then if $\Gamma(\pi) \subseteq \Delta \in S_\Lambda$, $\Gamma [\![\pi]\!] \Delta$ in M_Λ and so $\models_\Delta \varphi$. The hypothesis on φ then gives $\varphi \in \Delta$. This shows that φ belongs to every maximal Λ-theory containing $\Gamma(\pi)$, and hence, by 2.5.2, that $\Gamma(\pi) \vdash_\Lambda \varphi$. Corollary 2.4.10 then gives $[\pi]\varphi \in \Gamma$.

c. Assume the result for α and β, in order to prove it for $(\alpha;\beta)$.

Given the hypothesis on φ, the assumption on β gives that

$$\models_\Gamma [\beta]\varphi \text{ implies } [\beta]\varphi \in \Gamma, \text{ for all } \Gamma.$$

But then applying the assumed result for α to the formula $[\beta]\varphi$ (the Lemma states "For all formulae ....") we have that

$$\models_\Lambda [\alpha][\beta]\varphi \text{ implies } [\alpha][\beta]\varphi \in \Gamma, \text{ for all } \Gamma.$$

Thus in the standard model M_Λ, if $\models_\Gamma [\alpha;\beta]\varphi$, then $\models_\Gamma [\alpha][\beta]\varphi$ and so $[\alpha][\beta]\varphi \in \Gamma$, which by A7 implies that $[\alpha;\beta]\varphi \in \Gamma$.

d. Assume the result for α and β. Let $\models_\Gamma [\varepsilon \Rightarrow \alpha,\beta]\varphi$. Then the formulae $(\varepsilon \rightarrow [\alpha]\varphi)$ and $(not\text{-}\varepsilon \rightarrow [\beta]\varphi)$ both hold at Γ in M_Λ.

Thus, if $\varepsilon \in \Gamma$ then $\models_\Gamma \varepsilon$, and so $\models_\Gamma [\alpha]\varphi$, whence by the assumption on α,

$[\alpha]\varphi \in \Gamma$. Therefore (2.5.1(3)), $(\varepsilon \to [\alpha]\varphi) \in \Gamma$.

Similarly, the assumption on β yields a proof that $(\mathit{not}\text{-}\varepsilon \to [\beta]\varphi) \in \Gamma$. Using A8 we then conclude that $[\varepsilon \Rightarrow \alpha,\beta]\varphi \in \Gamma$.

This establishes the result for $(\varepsilon \Rightarrow \alpha,\beta)$.

e. Assume the result for α. To prove it for $(\varepsilon\#\alpha)$ we need, as in the proof of this case for the First α-Lemma, a preliminary result.

Given the hypothesis on φ, we show the following.

Sublemma. *For all* $\Gamma \in S_\Lambda$,

$$M_\Lambda \models_\Gamma \varphi_n(\varepsilon,\alpha) \quad \textit{implies} \quad \varphi_n(\varepsilon,\alpha) \in \Gamma.$$

Proof.

Let $\varphi_0(\varepsilon,\alpha)$, i.e. $(\mathit{not}\text{-}\varepsilon \to \varphi)$, hold at Γ. Then if $\mathit{not}\text{-}\varepsilon \in \Gamma$, $\models_\Gamma \mathit{not}\text{-}\varepsilon$ and hence $\models_\Gamma \varphi$, whence $\varphi \in \Gamma$ by the hypothesis on φ. This shows that $(\mathit{not}\text{-}\varepsilon \to \varphi) \in \Gamma$, and establishes the Sublemma for the case $n=0$.

Assume then that it holds for n, and let $\models_\Gamma \varphi_{n+1}(\varepsilon,\alpha)$, i.e. $\models_\Gamma \varepsilon \to [\alpha]\varphi_n(\varepsilon,\alpha)$. If $\varepsilon \in \Gamma$, we have $\models_\Gamma \varepsilon$ and so $\models_\Gamma [\alpha]\varphi_n(\varepsilon,\alpha)$. But then by the hypothesis on α for the main result, and the assumption on n for the Sublemma, $[\alpha]\varphi_n(\varepsilon,\alpha) \in \Gamma$. This establishes the Sublemma for $n+1$. Hence by induction it holds for all $n \in \mathbb{N}$. ∎

Returning to the main result for $(\varepsilon\#\alpha)$, if $\models_\Gamma [\varepsilon\#\alpha]\varphi$ then for any $n \in \mathbb{N}$, $\models_\Gamma \varphi_n(\varepsilon,\alpha)$ and so, by the Sublemma, $\varphi_n(\varepsilon,\alpha) \in \Gamma$. Since Γ is closed under OI, $[\varepsilon\#\alpha]\varphi \in \Gamma$. This completes the inductive case (e), and thus completes the proof of the Second α-Lemma. ∎

At last we are ready to give the proof of the Fundamental Theorem, i.e.

$$M_\Lambda \models \varphi \quad \text{iff} \quad \varphi \in \Lambda.$$

We proceed inductively:

1. For $\varphi \in \mathit{Bxp}$ the result is 2.5.5.

2. Assuming the result holds for φ and ψ, the semantic clause for $\rightarrow$ and the fact (2.5.1(3)) that

$$(\varphi \rightarrow \psi) \in \Gamma \quad \text{iff} \quad (\varphi \in \Gamma \quad \text{implies} \quad \psi \in \Gamma)$$

allow us to conclude that it holds for the formula $(\varphi \rightarrow \psi)$.

3. Assume the result for φ, and let $\alpha \in \mathit{Cmd}$. Then if $\models_\Gamma [\alpha]\varphi$, the Second α-Lemma gives $[\alpha]\varphi \in \Gamma$. Conversely, let $[\alpha]\varphi \in \Gamma$. Then if $\Gamma [\![\alpha]\!] \Delta$, we get $\varphi \in \Delta$ by the First α-Lemma, and so $\models_\Delta \varphi$ by the assumption on φ. This shows that $\models_\Gamma [\alpha]\varphi$, and so establishes the result for the formula $[\alpha]\varphi$.

This completes the proof of the Fundamental Theorem. ■

2.5.8 EXERCISES. The following formulae and rules are valid in all standard models, and so by the Completeness Theorem are PL-deducible. Give *proof-theoretic* demonstrations of this.

$\neg[\alpha]\mathit{false} \rightarrow ([\alpha]\neg\varphi \rightarrow \neg[\alpha]\varphi)$

$\varepsilon \rightarrow ([\alpha][\varepsilon\#\alpha]\varphi \rightarrow [\varepsilon\#\alpha]\varphi)$

$[\varepsilon\#\alpha]\varphi \leftrightarrow [\varepsilon \Rightarrow (\alpha;\ \varepsilon\#\alpha),\ \mathit{skip}]\varphi$

$\varepsilon \rightarrow ([\varepsilon\#\alpha]\varphi \rightarrow [\alpha^n](\mathit{not}\text{-}\varepsilon \rightarrow \varphi))$

$[\alpha^n](\mathit{not}\text{-}\varepsilon \rightarrow \varphi) \rightarrow \varphi_n(\varepsilon,\alpha)$

$\varepsilon \leftrightarrow \mathit{not}\text{-}\mathit{not}\text{-}\varepsilon$

$D\varepsilon \leftrightarrow D\mathit{not}\text{-}\varepsilon$

$(\varepsilon = \mathit{true}) \rightarrow \varepsilon$

$\mathit{not}\text{-}(\mathit{true} = \mathit{false})$

From $\Phi(\varphi_n(\varepsilon,\alpha))$ for all n, infer $\Phi([\varepsilon\#\alpha](\varphi \wedge \mathit{not}\text{-}\varepsilon))$

From $\Phi([\alpha]^n(\mathit{not}\text{-}\varepsilon \rightarrow \varphi))$ for all n, infer $\Phi([\varepsilon\#\alpha](\varphi \wedge \mathit{not}\text{-}\varepsilon))$

From $\Phi([\alpha]^n\varepsilon)$ for all n, infer $\Phi([\varepsilon\#\alpha]\mathit{false})$.

■

2.6 DETERMINISM

A deterministic command is one whose initial state determines a unique final state - if termination occurs. Such a command α may be modelled semantically by a partial function f_α on the state set S. f_α is defined at $s \in S$ just in case α terminates when initiated at s, with $f_\alpha(s)$ being the terminal state reached after that initiation. This is the approach taken in the Scott-Strachey denotational semantics.

In our present set-up determinism amounts simply to the requirement that the relation $[\![\alpha]\!]$ on S be *functional*, i.e. that

$$\text{if } s [\![\alpha]\!] t \text{ and } s [\![\alpha]\!] u, \text{ then } t = u,$$

and this property is captured by the axiom

AD_α : $[\alpha]\varphi \vee [\alpha]\neg\varphi$.

2.6.1 THEOREM. *If* $[\![\alpha]\!]$ *is functional in a model* M, *then for any* φ,

$$M \models [\alpha]\varphi \vee [\alpha]\neg\varphi.$$

Proof.

If $\not\models_s [\alpha]\varphi \vee [\alpha]\neg\varphi$ then $\not\models_s [\alpha]\varphi$ and $\not\models_s [\alpha]\neg\varphi$, so there must exist a t with $s [\![\alpha]\!] t$ and $\not\models_t \varphi$, and a u with $s [\![\alpha]\!] u$ and $\not\models_u \neg\varphi$. But then $t \neq u$, which contradicts the functionality of $[\![\alpha]\!]$. ■

2.6.2 THEOREM. *For a particular* α, suppose that

$$\vdash_\Lambda [\alpha]\varphi \vee [\alpha]\neg\varphi, \textit{ for all } \varphi \in Fma.$$

Then in M_Λ $[\![\alpha]\!]$ *is a functional relation.*

Proof.

Suppose $\Gamma [\![\alpha]\!] \Delta$ and $\Gamma [\![\alpha]\!] \Delta'$ in M_Λ. Then if $\varphi \in \Delta$, $\neg\varphi \notin \Delta$, and so by the First α-Lemma (2.5.6) $[\alpha]\neg\varphi \notin \Gamma$. But from the hypothesis, $[\alpha]\varphi \vee [\alpha]\neg\varphi \in \Gamma$, and so we must have $[\alpha]\varphi \in \Gamma$. The First α-Lemma again then gives $\varphi \in \Delta'$. Hence $\Delta \subseteq \Delta'$. Since Δ is a *maximal* theory, it follows that $\Delta = \Delta'$ as desired (alternatively the symmetry of the argument yields also $\Delta' \subseteq \Delta$.) ∎

Combining these two Theorems with the Completeness Theorem for Λ gives an axiomatisation of the class of sentences valid in all models that treat α deterministically: it is the smallest logic that contains all instances of AD_α. But the role of AD_α in M_Λ can be made even more explicit, for we have in this model that

$$f_\alpha(\Gamma) = \Gamma(\alpha) = \{\varphi : [\alpha]\varphi \in \Gamma\}.$$

The point is that *in general* $\Gamma(\alpha)$ is a Λ-theory: if $\vdash_\Lambda \varphi$ then by the rule TR, $[\alpha]\varphi \in \Gamma$ and so $\varphi \in \Gamma(\alpha)$; the axiom A4 guarantees that $\Gamma(\alpha)$ is closed under MP; and for OI we have that if $\{\Phi(\varphi_n(\varepsilon,\beta)) : n \in \mathbb{N}\} \subseteq \Gamma(\alpha)$ then $\{[\alpha]\Phi\, \varphi_n(\varepsilon,\beta)) : n \in \mathbb{N}\} \subseteq \Gamma$, and so by OI applied to the admissible form $[\alpha]\Phi$, $[\alpha]\Phi([\varepsilon\#\beta]\varphi) \in \Gamma$, whence $\Phi([\varepsilon\#\beta]\varphi) \in \Gamma(\alpha)$.

But in the presence of AD_α, we have the additional property that

$$\varphi \in \Gamma(\alpha) \quad \text{or} \quad \neg\varphi \in \Gamma(\alpha), \quad \text{for all } \varphi,$$

so that $\Gamma(\alpha)$ can have no *consistent* proper extensions. Since the First α-Lemma tells us that

$$\Gamma [\![\alpha]\!] \Delta \quad \text{only if} \quad \Gamma(\alpha) \subseteq \Delta,$$

with AD_α present we have

$$\Gamma [\![\alpha]\!] \Delta \quad \text{only if} \quad \Gamma(\alpha) = \Delta.$$

But $\Gamma(\alpha)$ will now be a *maximal* Λ-theory if, and only if, it is consistent, i.e. iff *false* $\notin \Gamma(\alpha)$. Thus $\Gamma(\alpha) \in S_\Lambda$ iff $[\alpha]$*false* $\notin \Gamma$, and so f_α will be defined, and be $\Gamma(\alpha)$, precisely for those Γ that contain

AT_α : $\neg[\alpha]$*false*,

the formula that expresses termination.

2.6.3 THEOREM. *Let* $\neg[\alpha]\mathit{false} \in \Gamma \in S_\Lambda$. *Then in* M_Λ *there exists a* $\Delta \in S_\Lambda$ *with* $\Gamma [\![\alpha]\!] \Delta$.

Proof.

By the Fundamental Theorem, $\not\models_\Gamma [\alpha]\mathit{false}$. ∎

Thus AD_α and AT_α together axiomatise validity in the class of models in which $[\![\alpha]\!]$ represents a *totally* defined function.

2.6.4 EXERCISES.

(1) Show that a logic contains each of the following schemata iff it contains all of the others (hence any of them would do as an axiom of determinism)

$$[\alpha]\varphi \vee [\alpha]\neg\varphi$$

$$\neg[\alpha]\varphi \rightarrow [\alpha]\neg\varphi$$

$$[\alpha](\varphi \vee \psi) \rightarrow [\alpha]\varphi \vee [\alpha]\psi$$

$$[\alpha](\varphi \rightarrow \psi) \rightarrow [\alpha](\varphi \rightarrow \psi).$$

(2) Show that $\vdash_\Lambda \neg[\alpha]\mathit{false}$ iff Λ contains the schema

$$[\alpha]\neg\varphi \rightarrow \neg[\alpha]\varphi.$$

(3) Show that the schema

$$[\alpha]\neg\varphi \leftrightarrow \neg[\alpha]\varphi$$

gives an alternative axiomatisation of the notion "α is deterministic and always terminates".

(4) *skip* and *abort* are deterministic in standard models, i.e.

$$\vdash_\Lambda AD_{\mathit{skip}} \quad \text{and} \quad \vdash_\Lambda AD_{\mathit{abort}}.$$

(5) $\vdash_\Lambda AT_{\mathit{skip}}$, $\vdash_\Lambda \neg AT_{\mathit{abort}}$.

(6) Let L be a collection of program letters that are deterministic in a *standard* model M, i.e. $[\![\pi]\!]$ is functional in M for all $\pi \in L$. Show that any program $\alpha \in Cmd$ whose program letters all come from L is deterministic in M.

(7) Show that for any logic that includes the schema AD_α for all α, the rule OI can be simplified to

$$\textit{From } \psi \to [\beta]\varphi_n(\varepsilon,\alpha) \textit{ for all } n, \textit{ infer } \psi \to [\beta][\varepsilon\#\alpha]\varphi.$$

WEAKEST PRECONDITIONS

The semantical theory developed by E.W. Dijkstra in his book *A Discipline of Programming* (1976), henceforth referred to as ADP, is based on the notion of the *weakest precondition* for a program α that corresponds to a "post-condition" φ. This will be denoted $wp(\alpha,\varphi)$, and is defined (ADP, p.16) as

> *"the condition that characterises the set of all initial states such that activation will certainly result in a properly terminating happening leaving the system in a final state satisfying a given post-condition".*

Thus it appears that the condition $wp(\alpha,\varphi)$ is satisfied by a state s just in case

(i) α terminates when initiated in s,

$$\text{i.e. } \models_s \neg[\alpha]\mathit{false},$$

and (ii) when α does terminate φ holds,

$$\text{i.e. } \models_s [\alpha]\varphi,$$

and so we may *define* $wp(\alpha,\varphi)$ in our present language to be the formula

$$\neg[\alpha]\mathit{false} \wedge [\alpha]\varphi$$

2.6.5 EXERCISES.

For any model M,

(1) $M \models wp(\alpha,\mathit{false}) \leftrightarrow \mathit{false}$;

(2) If $M \models \varphi \rightarrow \psi$, then $M \models wp(\alpha,\varphi) \rightarrow wp(\alpha,\psi)$;

(3) $M \models wp(\alpha,\varphi) \wedge wp(\alpha,\psi) \leftrightarrow wp(\alpha, \varphi \wedge \psi)$;

(4) $M \models wp(\alpha,\varphi) \vee wp(\alpha,\psi) \rightarrow wp(\alpha, \varphi \vee \psi)$;

(5) If $[\![\alpha]\!]$ is functional in M, then

$$M \models wp(\alpha,\varphi) \vee wp(\alpha,\psi) \leftrightarrow wp(\alpha, \varphi \vee \psi).$$

(6) $M \models wp(\alpha,\mathit{true})$ iff $M \models \neg[\alpha]\mathit{false}$. ∎

Exercises (1) - (4) above correspond to Properties 1 - 4 of ADP pp.18-19, while (5) is Property 4'. In particular they apply to the model M_Λ for any logic Λ, and so by the Completeness Theorem for Λ we can replace "$M \models$" in each case by "$\vdash_\Lambda$", with the proviso in (5) that Λ contains the schema AD_α. Syntactic proofs of these facts are not difficult and are recommended as exercises.

Dijkstra also develops the notion of a weakest *liberal* precondition, $wlp(\alpha,\varphi)$, which is described thus (ADP p.21):

> *"it only guarantees that the system won't produce the wrong result, i.e. will not reach a final state not satisfying φ, but non-termination is left as an alternative".*

It appears then that $wlp(\alpha,\varphi)$ is identical to our formula $[\alpha]\varphi$, and this is substantiated by the identification (ADP pp.21-22) of

(i) $wp(\alpha,\varphi)$ with $(wlp(\alpha,\varphi))$ and $wp(\alpha,\mathit{true})$ (cf. Ex. 2.6.5(6));

(ii) $wlp(\alpha,\mathit{true})$ with true; and

(iii) $(wlp(\alpha,\mathit{false})$ and $wp(\alpha,\mathit{true}))$ with false.

2.6.6 EXERCISES.

(1) Translate the properties (a) - (abc) of ADP pp.21-22 into formulae of our present language, and prove their Λ-deducibility.

(2) $\vdash_\Lambda wp(\mathit{skip},\varphi) \leftrightarrow \varphi$

(3) $\vdash_\Lambda wp(\mathit{abort},\varphi) \leftrightarrow \mathit{false}$

(4) $\vdash_\Lambda wp(\alpha, wp(\beta,\varphi)) \rightarrow wp(\alpha;\beta, \varphi)$ ∎

Exercises (2) and (3) above correspond to Dijkstra's definitions of $wp(\mathit{skip},\varphi)$ as φ and $wp(\mathit{abort},\varphi)$ as false (his definitions are being represented as logical equivalences here). However he also defines $wp(\alpha;\beta, \varphi)$ to be $wp(\alpha, wp(\beta,\varphi))$, which would entail the validity of the converse to (4). But this we can obtain only under a strong limitation on α.

2.6.7 THEOREM. *If* $[\![\alpha]\!]$ *is functional in* M, *and* M *is standard, then*

$$M \models wp(\alpha;\beta, \varphi) \rightarrow wp(\alpha, wp(\beta,\varphi))$$

Proof.

If $\models_s \neg[\alpha;\beta]\mathit{false} \wedge [\alpha;\beta]\varphi$, then we have $\models_s \neg[\alpha][\beta]\mathit{false}$ and $\models_s [\alpha][\beta]\varphi$. Functionality of $[\![\alpha]\!]$ then gives $\models_s [\alpha]\neg[\beta]\mathit{false}$, hence we have

$$\models_s [\alpha](\neg[\beta]\mathit{false} \wedge [\beta]\varphi). \qquad \text{(i)}$$

But if $(\alpha;\beta)$ terminates from s, then α must do so as well, whence

$$\models_s \neg[\alpha]\mathit{false} \qquad \text{(ii)}$$

Then (i) and (ii) give $\models_s wp(\alpha, wp(\beta,\varphi))$. ∎

The identification of $wp(\alpha,\varphi)$ with $(\neg[\alpha]\mathit{false} \wedge [\alpha]\varphi)$ appears only to be appropriate in the context of deterministic programs. In the next section (2.7) we will adduce further evidence for this, and attempt to explain why it is so.

TEST COMMANDS.

The language of dynamic logic (Pratt 1976) includes commands that will test an expression for its truth-value and halt just in case the expression is true. (As noted earlier, Pratt allows such commands to test any formula, so in general for non-Boolean formulae they are devices of external logic that cannot be implemented by an actual computer.) The command that tests φ will be denoted $\varphi?$ Its semantics is

$$s \, [\![\varphi?]\!] \, t \quad \text{iff} \quad \models_s \varphi \quad \text{and} \quad s=t,$$

corresponding to the axiom-schema

$$[\varphi?]\psi \leftrightarrow (\varphi \rightarrow \psi)$$

(which yields $[\varphi?]\mathit{false} \leftrightarrow \neg\varphi$ by taking ψ as false).

In our present language we can *define* the command $\varepsilon?$, for a Boolean expression ε, to be

$$(\varepsilon \Rightarrow \mathit{skip},\ \mathit{abort}),$$

since in a standard model we have

$$s \, [\![\varepsilon \Rightarrow \mathit{skip},\ \mathit{abort}]\!] \, t \quad \text{iff} \quad \text{either} \quad \models_s \varepsilon \quad \text{and} \quad s \, [\![\mathit{skip}]\!] \, t$$

$$\text{or} \quad \models_s \mathit{not}\text{-}\varepsilon \quad \text{and} \quad s \, [\![\mathit{abort}]\!] \, t,$$

which simplifies, because $[\![\mathit{abort}]\!] = \emptyset$, to

$$s \, [\![\varepsilon \Rightarrow \mathit{skip},\mathit{abort}]\!] \, t \quad \text{iff} \quad \models_s \varepsilon \quad \text{and} \quad s=t.$$

Now we have

$$\vdash_\Lambda \textit{not-}\varepsilon \rightarrow [\textit{abort}]\varphi,$$

(since $\vdash_\Lambda [\textit{abort}]\varphi$), and so using A5 and PC we deduce that

$$\vdash_\Lambda (\varepsilon \rightarrow \varphi) \leftrightarrow (\varepsilon \rightarrow [\textit{skip}]\varphi) \wedge (\textit{not-}\varepsilon \rightarrow [\textit{abort}]\varphi).$$

From this, by A8, we obtain

$$\vdash_\Lambda (\varepsilon \rightarrow \varphi) \leftrightarrow [\varepsilon?]\varphi .$$

2.6.8 EXERCISES.

(1) $\varepsilon?$ is deterministic, i.e. $\vdash_\Lambda [\varepsilon?]\varphi \vee [\varepsilon?]\neg\varphi$.

(2) $\vdash_\Lambda \textit{wp}(\varepsilon?,\varphi) \leftrightarrow \varepsilon \wedge \varphi$.

(3) $\vdash_\Lambda [\textit{skip}]\varphi \leftrightarrow [\textit{true}?]\varphi$.

(4) $\vdash_\Lambda [\textit{abort}]\varphi \leftrightarrow [\textit{false}?]\varphi$.

(5) $\vdash_\Lambda [\textit{true}?;\alpha]\varphi \leftrightarrow [\alpha]\varphi$.

(6) $\vdash_\Lambda [\textit{false}?;\alpha]\varphi \leftrightarrow [\textit{abort}]\varphi$.

(7) $\vdash_\Lambda [\varepsilon?;\alpha]\varphi \leftrightarrow (\varepsilon \rightarrow [\alpha]\varphi)$.

(8) $\vdash_\Lambda [\varepsilon?;\alpha]\varphi \leftrightarrow [\varepsilon \Rightarrow \alpha,\textit{abort}]\varphi$.

(9) $\vdash_\Lambda [\alpha]\varphi \rightarrow [\varepsilon?;\alpha]\varphi$.

(10) $\vdash_\Lambda \neg[\varepsilon?;\alpha]\textit{false} \leftrightarrow \varepsilon \wedge \neg[\alpha]\textit{false}$.

(11) $\vdash_\Lambda [\varepsilon?;\delta?]\varphi \leftrightarrow [\varepsilon \textit{ and } \delta?]\varphi$.

2.7 NON-DETERMINISM

ALTERNATIVES

We now expand the language defined in §2.1 by adding to the formation rules for *Cmd* the clause

$$\text{if } \alpha,\beta \in \mathit{Cmd}, \text{ then } (\alpha|\beta) \in \mathit{Cmd}.$$

This new type of member of *Cmd* is called an *alternative* command, and is executed by doing either α or β. Thus in general it is non-deterministic. Its standard-model condition is

$$[\![\alpha|\beta]\!] = [\![\alpha]\!] \cup [\![\beta]\!],$$

i.e.

$$s [\![\alpha|\beta]\!] t \quad \text{iff} \quad s [\![\alpha]\!] t \text{ or } s [\![\beta]\!] t,$$

and the corresponding axiom-schema is

A18 $\qquad [\alpha|\beta]\varphi \leftrightarrow [\alpha]\varphi \wedge [\beta]\varphi.$

2.7.1 EXERCISE.

If $[\![\alpha|\beta]\!] = [\![\alpha]\!] \cup [\![\beta]\!]$ in M, then M validates A18. ∎

To develop an axiomatisation of this new concept with respect to standard models, we extend the definition of M_Λ by *defining* $[\![\alpha|\beta]\!]$ inductively to be $[\![\alpha]\!] \cup [\![\beta]\!]$ on S_Λ, so that the canonical Λ-model is still a standard one. In order then to prove the Fundamental Theorem for the enlarged class of formulae we have only to deal with one new case:- that of formulae of the type $[\alpha|\beta]\varphi$. For this it suffices to extend the two α-Lemmata 2.5.6 and 2.5.7 to cover alternative commands: we show that if Λ contains all instances of A18 then in M_Λ,

I. $\Gamma \llbracket \alpha|\beta \rrbracket \Delta$ *only if* $\{\varphi : [\alpha|\beta]\varphi \in \Gamma\} \subseteq \Delta$,

and

II. *if* $M_\Lambda \models_\Gamma \varphi$ *implies* $\varphi \in \Gamma$ *for all* Γ,

then $M_\Lambda \models_\Gamma [\alpha|\beta]\varphi$ *implies* $[\alpha|\beta]\varphi \in \Gamma$ *for all* Γ.

Proof of I.

We assume inductively that the analogue of I holds for α and for β. If $\Gamma \llbracket \alpha|\beta \rrbracket \Delta$ then either $\Gamma \llbracket \alpha \rrbracket \Delta$ or $\Gamma \llbracket \beta \rrbracket \Delta$. But if $[\alpha|\beta]\varphi \in \Gamma$ then using A18 we get $[\alpha]\varphi \in \Gamma$ and $[\beta]\varphi \in \Gamma$. Thus if $\Gamma \llbracket \alpha \rrbracket \Delta$, the inductive hypothesis on α gives $\varphi \in \Delta$. Alternatively we use the hypothesis on β to get our desideratum $\varphi \in \Delta$.

■

Proof of II.

If $\models_\Gamma [\alpha|\beta]\varphi$ then (cf. 2.7.1) $\models_\Gamma [\alpha]\varphi$ and $\models_\Gamma [\beta]\varphi$. Assuming inductively that the analogue of II holds for α and for β, we may then conclude from the hypothesis on φ that $[\alpha]\varphi \in \Gamma$ and $[\beta]\varphi \in \Gamma$, whence $([\alpha]\varphi \wedge [\beta]\varphi) \in \Gamma$. A18 then gives $[\alpha|\beta]\varphi \in \Gamma$. ■

2.7.2 EXERCISE.

In a standard model,

$$\llbracket \varepsilon \Rightarrow \alpha,\beta \rrbracket = \llbracket (\varepsilon?;\alpha) \,|\, (\mathit{not}\text{-}\varepsilon?;\beta) \rrbracket$$

$$= \llbracket \varepsilon \Rightarrow \alpha,\mathit{abort} | \mathit{not}\text{-}\varepsilon \Rightarrow \beta,\mathit{abort} \rrbracket \,. \qquad ■$$

GUARDED COMMANDS

Non-determinism in the system of Dijkstra's *A Discipline of Programming* is based on a device called the *guarded command*, a symbolism of the form

$$\varepsilon \rightarrow \alpha,$$

in which the Boolean expression ε is called the *guard*. Dijkstra explains (p.33):

> *"The idea is that the statement following the arrow will only be executed provided initially the corresponding guard is true. The guard enables us to prevent execution of a statement under those initial circumstances under which execution would be undesirable or, if partial operations are involved, impossible.*
>
> *The truth of the guard is a necessary condition for the execution of the guarded command as a whole; it is, of course, not sufficient because in some way or another, it must potentially be "its turn". That is why a guarded command is not considered as a statement: a statement is irrevocably executed when its turn has arrived, the guarded command can be used as a building block for a statement".*

(Dijkstra's "statement" is synonymous with our "command").

There are two kinds of "statement" that are built out of guarded commands: the *if* ... *fi* and the *do* ... *od*.

if ... *fi*.

This is a command that is symbolised

$$\textit{if}\ \varepsilon_0 \to \alpha_1 \mid \varepsilon_2 \to \alpha_2 \mid \ldots\ldots \mid \varepsilon_n \to \alpha_n\ \textit{fi},$$

about whose execution the following description (ADP pp.33-34) is given:

> *"One of the guarded commands whose guard is true is selected and its statement activated. ... It is assumed that all guards are defined; if not, i.e. if the evaluation of a guard may lead to a not properly terminating activity, then the whole construct is allowed to fail to terminate properly. ... In general our construct will give rise to non-determinancy, viz, for each initial state for which more than one guard is true, because it is left undefined which of the corresponding statements will be selected for activation. ... If the initial state is such that none of the guards are true we are faced with an initial state for which none of the alternatives and therefore neither the construct as a whole does cater. Activation in such an initial state will lead to abortion..."*

This whole description can be summarised in the model-condition (given for the case n=2 for expository clarity)

$$s \,[\![\, \textit{if}\ \varepsilon \to \alpha \,|\, \delta \to \beta\ \textit{fi} \,]\!]\, t \quad \text{iff}$$

(i) $\models_s D\varepsilon$ and $\models_s D\delta$, and

(ii) either $\models_s \varepsilon$ and $s \,[\![\, \alpha \,]\!]\, t$

or $\models_s \delta$ and $s \,[\![\, \beta \,]\!]\, t$.

Condition (i) corresponds to the requirement that *all* guards be defined for termination to be possible, and is equivalent to

$$\models_s (D\varepsilon \textit{ and } D\delta),$$

and hence in standard models to

$$s \,[\![\, (D\varepsilon \textit{ and } D\delta)? \,]\!]\, s.$$

The other requirements are covered by (ii). But notice that the conjunction of $\models_s \varepsilon$ and $s \,[\![\, \alpha \,]\!]\, t$ is equivalent in standard models to

$$s \,[\![\, \varepsilon?;\alpha \,]\!]\, t.$$

Thus the *if* ... *fi* command can be *defined* in our language as

$$(D\varepsilon \textit{ and } D\delta)? \ ; \ (\varepsilon?;\alpha \,|\, \delta?;\beta).$$

In place of $(D\varepsilon \textit{ and } D\delta)?$ we could use here the command $(D\varepsilon?;D\delta?)$ (cf. Exercise 2.6.7(11)).

2.7.3 EXERCISES.

In a standard model:

(1) $[\![\, \alpha|\beta \,]\!] = [\![\, \textit{if true} \to \alpha \,|\, \textit{true} \to \beta\ \textit{fi} \,]\!]$

$= [\![\, (\textit{true}?;\alpha) \,|\, (\textit{true}?;\beta) \,]\!]$.

(2) $[\![\, \varepsilon \Rightarrow \alpha,\beta \,]\!] = [\![\, \textit{if}\ \varepsilon \to \alpha \,|\, \textit{not-}\varepsilon \to \beta\ \textit{fi} \,]\!]$. ∎

2.7.4 THEOREM. *Let Λ be any logic containing the schema* A18. *Then the following are Λ-theorems, where* DIF *abbreviates* $(\mathit{if}\ \varepsilon \to \alpha|\delta \to \beta\ \mathit{fi})$ *as defined above, and* IF *abbreviates*

$$(\varepsilon?;\alpha \mid \delta?;\beta)$$

(so that DIF *is* $(D\varepsilon \text{ and } D\delta?);\text{IF}$*).*

(1) $[\text{DIF}]\varphi \leftrightarrow (D\varepsilon \text{ and } D\delta \to (\varepsilon \to [\alpha]\varphi) \wedge (\delta \to [\beta]\varphi))$.

(2) $[\alpha]\varphi \wedge [\beta]\varphi \to [\text{DIF}]\varphi$.

(3) $\neg[\text{DIF}]\mathit{false} \leftrightarrow (D\varepsilon \text{ and } D\delta) \wedge ((\varepsilon \wedge \neg[\alpha]\mathit{false}) \vee (\delta \wedge \neg[\beta]\mathit{false}))$.

(4) $(D\varepsilon \text{ and } D\delta) \wedge (\varepsilon \vee \delta) \wedge (\varepsilon \to wp(\alpha,\varphi)) \wedge (\delta \to wp(\beta,\varphi)) \to wp(\text{DIF},\varphi)$.

(5) $[\text{IF}]\varphi \leftrightarrow (\varepsilon \to [\alpha]\varphi) \wedge (\delta \to [\beta]\varphi)$.

(6) $[\text{DIF}]\varphi \leftrightarrow (D\varepsilon \text{ and } D\delta \to [\text{IF}]\varphi)$.

(7) $D\varepsilon \text{ and } D\delta \to ([\text{DIF}]\varphi \leftrightarrow [\text{IF}]\varphi)$.

(8) $[\alpha]\varphi \wedge [\beta]\varphi \to [\text{IF}]\varphi$.

(9) $\neg[\text{IF}]\mathit{false} \leftrightarrow (\varepsilon \wedge \neg[\alpha]\mathit{false}) \vee (\delta \wedge \neg[\beta]\mathit{false})$.

(10) $(\varepsilon \vee \delta) \wedge \neg[\alpha]\mathit{false} \wedge \neg[\beta]\mathit{false} \to \neg[\text{IF}]\mathit{false}$.

(11) $(\varepsilon \vee \delta) \wedge wp(\alpha,\varphi) \wedge wp(\beta,\varphi) \to wp(\text{IF},\varphi)$.

(12) $(\varepsilon \vee \delta) \wedge (\varepsilon \to wp(\alpha,\varphi)) \wedge (\delta \to wp(\beta,\varphi)) \to wp(\text{IF},\varphi)$.

Proof.

By the Completeness Theorem for Λ, since (1) - (12) are all valid in standard models. (Syntactic proofs are accessible and readers are urged to construct them for themselves.) ∎

Dijkstra's formal definition of the weakest precondition for *if ... fi* indicates that he identifies the command with what we have called IF here. But his definition is based on the assumption that all guards are defined. He writes (ADP p.34): "*If this is not the case, the expression should be prefixed ... by the additional requirement that the initial state lies in the domain of all the guards*". This requirement is represented here by the Boolean expression ($D\varepsilon$ *and* $D\delta$), which when true renders IF and DIF equivalent (cf. 2.7.4(7) above).

Thus far our analysis seems to be in accord with Dijkstra's intentions. However his definition of *wp*(IF,φ) (ADP p.34) amounts in our terms to the requirement that both 2.7.4(12) *and* its converse be valid, i.e. that *wp*(IF,φ) be identifiable with the antecedent of 2.7.4(12), and this converse is not valid in general. To see this, let ε, δ, and φ all be *true*, α be *skip*, and β be *abort*. Using 2.6.7(5) and our axioms for *skip*, *abort*, and |, we get

$$\vdash_{\Lambda} [true?;skip \mid true?;abort]\varphi \leftrightarrow \varphi,$$

and so in this example (which is taken from Harel (1978)), the consequent of 2.7.4(12) is logically equivalent to *true* and valid in all standard models, while the antecedent proves to be equivalent to *false* (since *wp*(*abort*,*true*) is - cf. 2.6.6(3)), and so holds at no state in any standard model. This same example shows that the converse of 2.7.4(4) is not valid either.

It seems that our formalisation of *wp*(IF,φ) as $(\neg[\text{IF}]false \wedge [\text{IF}]\varphi)$ produces a condition weaker than Dijkstra's weakest precondition for IF. The problem here lies with our interpretation of *termination*. To locate the problem quite bluntly, consider the program-form

$$(\alpha \mid abort)$$

which in a standard model has

$$[\![\alpha \mid abort]\!] = [\![\alpha]\!] \cup [\![abort]\!] = [\![\alpha]\!],$$

giving α and (α|*abort*) the same "meaning". If α terminates, so then will α|*abort*. For instance it is an easy matter, using A5 and A18, to show that

$$\vdash_{\Lambda} \neg[skip \mid abort]false.$$

But this obscures the fact that if we execute (*skip*|*abort*) by choosing the *abort* alternative then no final state will actually be reached. We have an instance of what Plotkin (1976) describes as "non-determinism masking non-termination".

The point here is that if $[\alpha]$ means "after α terminates", i.e. "after *every* terminating execution of α", then $\neg[\alpha]\mathit{false}$ means "there is a (i.e. at least one) terminating execution of α", and this is quite compatible with there being other executions of the same α from the same initial state which do not terminate (as with *skip*|*abort*). But this is not the termination property expressed by the notion of weakest precondition, which was quoted above to be that "activation will *certainly* result in a properly terminating happening". This seems to be saying that *any* execution of α must lead to a final state.

Let us denote by $t(\alpha)$ the assertion that execution of α always terminates. Then as a new attempt to represent the weakest-precondition concept we denote by $wp_t(\alpha,\varphi)$ the assertion

$$t(\alpha) \wedge [\alpha]\varphi.$$

Now assuming inductively that $t(\alpha)$ and $t(\beta)$ have been defined, we can define $t(\mathrm{IF})$ as

$$(\varepsilon \vee \delta) \wedge (\varepsilon \rightarrow t(\alpha)) \wedge (\delta \rightarrow t(\beta)),$$

which states that one of the guards is true, and (since in executing IF we are free to choose any true guard) all true guards are associated with commands that always terminate. But then given (2.7.4(5)) that

$$\vdash_\Lambda [\mathrm{IF}]\varphi \leftrightarrow (\varepsilon \rightarrow [\alpha]\varphi) \wedge (\delta \rightarrow [\beta]\varphi),$$

it requires only PC to derive

$$\vdash_\Lambda wp_t(\mathrm{IF},\varphi) \leftrightarrow (\varepsilon \vee \delta) \wedge (\varepsilon \rightarrow wp_t(\alpha,\varphi)) \wedge (\delta \rightarrow wp_t(\beta,\varphi)).$$

But from this, still using only PC, we obtain the following Hoare-style rule, which is Dijkstra's "basic theorem for the alternative construct" (ADP p.37):

If $\vdash_\Lambda \psi \to \varepsilon \vee \delta$

and $\vdash_\Lambda \psi \wedge \varepsilon \to wp_t(\alpha,\varphi)$

and $\vdash_\Lambda \psi \wedge \delta \to wp_t(\beta,\varphi)$,

then $\vdash_\Lambda \psi \to wp_t(\mathrm{IF},\varphi)$.

2.7.5 EXERCISES.

(1) Show that this "basic theorem" still holds with our wp in place of wp_t.

(2) Define $t(\mathrm{DIF})$ to be $(D\varepsilon$ *and* $D\delta) \wedge t(\mathrm{IF})$. Show that

(a) $\vdash_\Lambda wp_t(\mathrm{DIF}) \leftrightarrow (D\varepsilon$ *and* $D\delta) \wedge wp_t(\mathrm{IF})$;

(b) If $\vdash_\Lambda \psi \to (D\varepsilon$ *and* $D\delta) \wedge (\varepsilon \vee \delta)$

and $\vdash_\Lambda \psi \wedge \varepsilon \to wp_t(\alpha,\varphi)$

and $\vdash_\Lambda \psi \wedge \delta \to wp_t(\beta,\varphi)$,

then $\vdash_\Lambda \psi \to wp_t(\mathrm{DIF},\varphi)$. ■

The definability of $\Rightarrow$ in terms of a DIF-type command (Exercise 2.7.3(2)) suggests that we take $t(\varepsilon \Rightarrow \alpha,\beta)$ as

$$(\varepsilon \vee not\text{-}\varepsilon) \wedge (\varepsilon \to t(\alpha)) \wedge (not\text{-}\varepsilon \to t(\beta)).$$

(We can leave off $(D\varepsilon$ *and* $Dnot\text{-}\varepsilon)$, since $\vdash_\Lambda (\varepsilon \vee not\text{-}\varepsilon) \to D\varepsilon$ *and* $Dnot\text{-}\varepsilon)$. But since $\vdash_\Lambda \varepsilon \to (not\text{-}\varepsilon \to \theta)$ and $\vdash_\Lambda not\text{-}\varepsilon \to (\varepsilon \to \theta)$, the suggested formula is provably (using PC) equivalent to

$$(\varepsilon \wedge t(\alpha)) \vee (not\text{-}\varepsilon \wedge t(\beta)),$$

which certainly accords with one's intuition about what it takes for $(\varepsilon \Rightarrow \alpha,\beta)$ to always terminate. From this we find that

$$\vdash_\Lambda wp_t((\varepsilon \Rightarrow \alpha,\beta),\varphi) \leftrightarrow (\varepsilon \wedge wp_t(\alpha,\varphi)) \vee (not\text{-}\varepsilon \wedge wp_t(\beta,\varphi)).$$

The "basic theorem" for DIF (i.e. Exercise 2.7.5(2b) above), together with A13, then leads to the following rule:

$$\begin{array}{ll} \textit{If} & \vdash_{\Lambda} \psi \rightarrow D\varepsilon \\ \textit{and} & \vdash_{\Lambda} \psi \wedge \varepsilon \rightarrow wp_{\mathcal{t}}(\alpha,\varphi) \\ \textit{and} & \vdash_{\Lambda} \psi \wedge \textit{not-}\varepsilon \rightarrow wp_{\mathcal{t}}(\beta,\varphi), \\ \textit{then} & \vdash_{\Lambda} \psi \rightarrow wp_{\mathcal{t}}((\varepsilon \Rightarrow \alpha,\beta),\varphi). \end{array}$$

(compare this to Hoare's Conditional Rule in Chapter 1).

Returning finally to *composite* commands, observe that since execution of $(\alpha;\beta)$ requires doing α and then β, to guarantee termination we need α to always terminate, and β to always terminate thereafter. Hence we define $\mathcal{t}(\alpha;\beta)$ as

$$\mathcal{t}(\alpha) \wedge [\alpha]\mathcal{t}(\beta).$$

2.7.6 THEOREM.

$$\vdash_{\Lambda} wp_{\mathcal{t}}(\alpha;\beta,\varphi) \leftrightarrow wp_{\mathcal{t}}(\alpha, wp_{\mathcal{t}}(\beta,\varphi)).$$

Proof.

$wp_{\mathcal{t}}(\alpha, wp_{\mathcal{t}}(\beta,\varphi))$ is the formula

$$\mathcal{t}(\alpha) \wedge [\alpha](\mathcal{t}(\beta) \wedge [\beta]\varphi)$$

which is Λ-provably equivalent, by 2.4.1(3), to

$$\mathcal{t}(\alpha) \wedge [\alpha]\mathcal{t}(\beta) \wedge [\alpha][\beta]\varphi,$$

and hence, by A7, to

$$\mathcal{t}(\alpha;\beta) \wedge [\alpha;\beta]\varphi \qquad \blacksquare$$

2.7.7 EXERCISES.

If $\vdash_\Lambda t(\alpha) \leftrightarrow \neg[\alpha]\mathit{false}$

and $\vdash_\Lambda t(\beta) \leftrightarrow \neg[\beta]\mathit{false}$,

then

(1) $\vdash_\Lambda t(\varepsilon \Rightarrow \alpha,\beta) \leftrightarrow \neg[\varepsilon \Rightarrow \alpha,\beta]\mathit{false}$

and $\vdash_\Lambda wp_t((\varepsilon \Rightarrow \alpha,\beta),\varphi) \leftrightarrow wp((\varepsilon \Rightarrow \alpha,\beta),\varphi)$,

(2) If Λ contains the determinism schema AD_α for α, then

$\vdash_\Lambda t(\alpha;\beta) \leftrightarrow \neg[\alpha;\beta]\mathit{false}$

and $\vdash_\Lambda wp_t(\alpha;\beta,\varphi) \leftrightarrow wp(\alpha;\beta,\varphi)$. ■

The last exercise, and Theorem 2.7.6, should be viewed in the light of Theorem 2.6.7 and the observations leading up to the latter.

do ... od.

About the execution of the command

$$do\ \varepsilon \rightarrow \alpha \mid \delta \rightarrow \beta\ od,$$

which is abbreviated to DO, Dijkstra has the following to say (ADP p.35):

> *"... we allow the state in which no guards are true to lead to proper termination .... the activity is not allowed to terminate as long as one of the guards is true. That is, upon activation the guards are inspected. The activity terminates if there are no true guards; if there are true guards one of the corresponding statements is activated and upon its termination the implementation starts all over again inspecting the guards."*

It appears that what is being described here is the command

$$\mathit{while}\ (\varepsilon\ \mathit{or}\ \delta)\ do\ (\mathit{if}\ \varepsilon \rightarrow \alpha \mid \delta \rightarrow \beta\ \mathit{fi}),$$

i.e. $(\varepsilon\ \mathit{or}\ \delta)$ # DIF,

and this will be taken as the definition of DO for the present language. Notice that we are using the *internal* disjunction *or* here, so that DO will halt at state s just in case $v_s(\mathit{not}\text{-}(\varepsilon\ \mathit{or}\ \delta)) = 1$, i.e. $v_s(\varepsilon) = v_s(\delta) = 0$.

Now Dijkstra's basic result about DO, the "Fundamental Invariance Theorem for Loops" (ADP pp.38-39), is, in our notation, that if

$$\varphi \wedge (\varepsilon\ \mathit{or}\ \delta) \rightarrow wp_t(\mathrm{DIF},\varphi)$$

is valid, then so is

$$\varphi \wedge wp_t(\mathrm{DO},\mathit{true}) \rightarrow wp_t(\mathrm{DO},\ \varphi \wedge \mathit{not}\text{-}(\varepsilon\ \mathit{or}\ \delta)).$$

This is similar to Hoare's Iteration Rule, given our definition of DO in terms of #. $wp_t(\mathrm{DO},\mathit{true})$ is equivalent to the assertion $t(\mathrm{DO})$ that DO always terminates, since $[\mathrm{DO}]\mathit{true}$ is universally valid. Moreover we can strengthen the result a little by replacing $wp_t(\mathrm{DIF},\varphi)$ by the "liberal" precondition $[\mathrm{DIF}]\varphi$. For, from

$$\varphi \wedge (\varepsilon\ \mathit{or}\ \delta) \rightarrow [\mathrm{DIF}]\varphi$$

we derive

$$\varphi \rightarrow [\mathrm{DO}](\varphi \wedge \mathit{not}\text{-}(\varepsilon\ \mathit{or}\ \delta))$$

by Hoare's rule, and hence by PC we get

$$\varphi \wedge t(\mathrm{DO}) \rightarrow t(\mathrm{DO}) \wedge [\mathrm{DO}](\varphi \wedge \mathit{not}\text{-}(\varepsilon\ \mathit{or}\ \delta))$$

as desired.

It is not possible to define $t(\mathrm{DO})$ as a single formula involving $t(\mathrm{DIF})$, for the same reasons that $[\varepsilon\#\alpha]\varphi$ cannot be reduced in general to a single formula involving $[\alpha]\varphi$. Dijkstra's approach here is to inductively define $H_k(\varphi)$ as "*the weakest precondition such that the do ... od construct will terminate after at most k selections of a guarded command, leaving the system in a final state satisfying the post-condition* φ" (ADP p.35). He then puts

$$wp(\mathrm{DO},\varphi) = (\exists k > 0 : H_k(\varphi)).$$

His definition of the H_k's is essentially

$$H_0(\varphi) = \varphi \wedge (\mathit{not}\text{-}(\varepsilon\ \mathit{or}\ \delta))$$

$$H_{k+1}(\varphi) = \mathit{wp}(\mathrm{DIF}, H_k(\varphi)) \vee H_0(\varphi),$$

but in our present terms a more refined approach is possible. We define a formula $t_k(\mathrm{DO})$ which intuitively means "execution of DO always halts after at most k iterations of DIF". Inductively we put

$$t_0(\mathrm{DO}) = \mathit{not}\text{-}(\varepsilon\ \mathit{or}\ \delta)$$

$$\begin{aligned} t_{k+1}(\mathrm{DO}) &= D(\varepsilon\ \mathit{or}\ \delta) \wedge (\varepsilon\ \mathit{or}\ \delta \to \mathit{wp}_t(\mathrm{DIF}, t_k(\mathrm{DO}))) \\ &= D(\varepsilon\ \mathit{or}\ \delta) \wedge (\varepsilon\ \mathit{or}\ \delta \to t(\mathrm{DIF}) \wedge [\mathrm{DIF}]t_k(\mathrm{DO})). \end{aligned}$$

We can then define $H_k(\varphi)$ as

$$t_k(\mathrm{DO}) \wedge [\mathrm{DO}]\varphi$$

2.7.8 EXERCISES.

(1) Let $t(\alpha) = \neg[\alpha]\mathit{false}$. Then in a standard model,

$\models_s t_k(\mathrm{DO})$ iff (i) for some t, and some $j < k$,
$s [\![\varepsilon\ \mathit{or}\ \delta]\mathrm{DIF}]\!]^j\, t$ and $\models_t \mathit{not}\text{-}(\varepsilon\ \mathit{or}\ \delta)$,

and (ii) if $s [\![\varepsilon\ \mathit{or}\ \delta]\mathrm{DIF}]\!]^k\, u$, then $\models_u \mathit{not}\text{-}(\varepsilon\ \mathit{or}\ \delta)$.

(2) Give a derivation (proof-theoretic and/or model-theoretic), based on our present definition of $H_k(\varphi)$, of the following analogue of Dijkstra's definition.

$$\vdash_\Lambda H_0(\varphi) \leftrightarrow \varphi \wedge \mathit{not}\text{-}(\varepsilon\ \mathit{or}\ \delta)$$

$$\vdash_\Lambda H_{k+1}(\varphi) \leftrightarrow (\mathit{wp}_t(\mathrm{DIF}, H_k(\varphi)) \vee H_0(\varphi)).$$ ■

Since our semantics gives the same meaning to such programs as (*skip*|*abort*) and *skip*, it is not finally adequate to discuss non-determinism properly. A possible way forward might be to add $\mathcal{t}(-)$ as a primitive connective to our language, with the semantics

$$\models_s \mathcal{t}(\alpha) \quad \text{iff} \quad \alpha \text{ always terminates when initiated in } s.$$

This would require a model-theoretic notion of a "terminating execution" of α. Pratt (1979) has suggested interpreting α in M not as a binary relation but as a collection of sequences s_0, s_1, s_2, ... of states. Such a sequence is to be thought of as being generated by the process of executing α from s_0. Non-termination corresponds to the generation of an infinite sequence. Some progress on the axiomatisation of this idea has been made by Harel, Kozen, and Parikh (1980) (cf. the Appendix to Part I).

A development of the kind just suggested should be regarded as belonging to a latter phase of our top-down approach to computational semantics, and it would presumably have to be built on the sort of techniques developed in this chapter. For the present we have still to account for more basic types of the commands that occur in standard programming languages. The next chapter examines the most basic of them all.

CHAPTER 3

ASSIGNMENTS

3.1 THE CONCEPT OF DATA TYPE

MANY-SORTED OPERATIONS

A data type is more than just a collection of bits of data. Its specification may require reference to a number of collections, and, most importantly, to certain operations on them. In general a data type supports an algebraic structure. The actual definition of "data-type" that we adopt is that expounded by the ADJ group (J.A. Gougen, J.W. Thatcher, E.G. Wagner, and J.B. Wright), namely "many-sorted algebra" (cf. ADJ (1977)).

Now an abstract *algebra* is generally understood to be a set A that carries a collection of finitary operations of various "arity". An *n-ary* operation on A is a function from A^n to A, i.e. one of the form

$$\underbrace{A \times A \times \ldots\ldots \times A}_{n \text{ times}} \to A$$

Since A^0 is $\{\emptyset\}$, a one-element set, an operation $f : \{\emptyset\} \to A$ of arity 0 (also called a *nullary* operation) can be identified with a unique element - viz. $f(\emptyset)$ - of A. Such an operation is called a *constant* of the algebra.

The operations dealt with in computer science often require their various arguments (inputs) and values (outputs) to come from several different domains. In other words, they are *many-sorted*. Thus the conditional *if - then - else* when used as in Algol to form arithmetical expressions like

$$\textit{if } x > 0 \textit{ then } x + 1 \textit{ else } 3$$

is interpreted as the operation

$$cond: \mathbb{B} \times \mathbb{N} \times \mathbb{N} \to \mathbb{N}$$

that has $cond(1,m,n) = m$ and $cond(0,m,n) = n$. To take a second example, a relation (predicate) $R \subseteq A^n$ may be represented as an operation of the form

$$A^n \to \mathbb{B}$$

(its characteristic function). This was the approach we took to relations like $\leqslant$ and $=$ on $\mathbb{B}$ in §2.2, and it corresponds naturally to the way a computer evaluates an expression such as $R(a_1, \ldots, a_n)$ in commands like

$$\textit{while } R(a_1, \ldots, a_n) \textit{ do } \alpha.$$

This kind of representation applies also to relations *between* data types. For instance the set membership relation *in*, which in Pascal creates expressions like "x *in* B", corresponds to the operation

$$e : A \times P(A) \to \mathbb{B},$$

where $P(A)$ is the *powerset* $\{B : B \subseteq A\}$ of A, defined by

$$e(a,B) = \begin{cases} 1 & \text{if } a \in B \\ 0 & \text{if } a \notin B \end{cases}$$

SIGNATURES AND ALGEBRAS

If Z is a set, then Z^* denotes the set of all finite sequences (strings) that are made up of elements of Z. The string $\mu_1\mu_2 \ldots \mu_n$ is said to be of *length* n. Included in Z^* is the *empty string*, of length 0, which is denoted λ.

An Z-*sorted signature* is a collection O of sets $O_{\nu,\mu}$ for $\nu \in Z^*$ and $\mu \in Z$. A member of Z is called a *sort*, while a member of $O_{\nu,\mu}$ is called an *operation symbol* of arity ν and sort μ. A member of $O_{\lambda,\mu}$ is an *individual constant symbol* of sort μ. (N.B. it is permitted that $O_{\nu,\mu} = \emptyset$).

If $\{A_\mu : \mu \in Z\}$ is a collection of sets indexed by Z, then for each $\nu \in Z^*$ we define a set A_ν by putting

$$A_\lambda = \{\emptyset\}$$

and

$$A_{\mu_1 \dots \mu_n} = A_{\mu_1} \times \dots \times A_{\mu_n}$$

An *O-algebra* is a structure A comprising

(i) a collection $\{A_\mu : \mu \in Z\}$ of sets indexed by Z, A_μ being the *carrier of* A *of sort* μ;

with

(ii) for each ν, μ, and each $f \in O_{\nu,\mu}$, a function

$$f_A : A_\nu \to A_\mu,$$

called the operation of A *named by* f.

In particular a constant symbol $c \in O_{\lambda,\mu}$ names a nullary operation, and hence an element c_A of A_μ. The operations (elements) named by constant symbols are called the *constants* of the algebra A.

3.1.1 EXAMPLES.

(1) The data-type $\mathbb{B} = \{0,1\}$ is a *one-sorted* algebra. With $Z = \{Bool\}$, its signature may be taken to have

$$O_{\lambda,Bool} = \{false\},$$

$$O_{Bool\ Bool,Bool} = \{=\},$$

$$O_{Bool\ Bool\ Bool,Bool} = \{\supset\},$$

and $O_{\nu,\mu} = \emptyset$ otherwise.

(2) The data type $\mathbb{N} = \{0,1,2,.....\}$ can be regarded as *two*-sorted, with

$$Z = \{Nat, Bool\}$$

$$O_{\lambda,Nat} = \{0,1,2,.....\}$$

$$O_{Nat\ Nat,Nat} = \{+,\times\}$$

$$O_{Nat\ Nat,Bool} = \{<, \leqslant, =\}$$

$$O_{Bool\ Nat\ Nat,Nat} = \{\mathit{if\text{-}then\text{-}else}\}$$

etc. ■

The data types actually used in computing are rather special kinds of many-sorted algebras. Often they are finite, and while they can be infinite (e.g. $\mathbb{N}$) they are never more than *denumerably* so. The reason is, as Hoare (1972, p.93) observes, that "*each value of the type must be constructible by a finite number of computer operations, and must be representable in a finite amount of store. Arbitrary real numbers, functions with infinite domains, and other classes of non-denumerable cardinality can never be represented as stored data within a computer...*".

Another feature of data types, and one that will be incorporated in our formalism, is that we can only write programs about things we can refer to, and so data have to be *nameable* in the programming language. Thus elements of $\mathbb{N}$ are referred to either by their constant names $0,1,2,....$, or by expressions like $(2+3)\times 4$ that involve constants and operation symbols. To formalise this naming process, we define for a given Z-sorted signature O the collection $\{Con_\mu(O) : \mu \in Z\}$, where $Con_\mu(O)$ is the set of *constant expressions of O of sort* μ, to be the smallest collection of sets that satisfies

(i) $O_{\lambda,\mu} \subseteq Con_\mu(O)$;

(ii) if $f \in O_{\mu_1..\mu_n,\mu}$ and $\sigma_i \in Con_{\mu_i}(O)$ for $1 \leqslant i \leqslant n$,

then $f(\sigma_1,...,\sigma_n) \in Con_\mu(O)$.

We then put $Con(O) = \bigcup\{Con_\mu(O) : \mu \in Z\}$ (see the Appendix of Goguen, Thatcher, and Wagner (1978) for an analysis of this inductive definition).

If A is an $\mathcal{O}$-algebra, then each $\sigma \in Con_\mu(\mathcal{O})$ *names* an element σ_A of A_μ. If σ is a constant symbol $c \in \mathcal{O}_{\lambda,\mu}$, then σ_A is the constant c_A. If σ is of the form $\delta(\sigma_1,\ldots,\sigma_n)$, as in case (ii) above, we inductively put

$$\sigma_A = \delta_A((\sigma_1)_A, \ldots, (\sigma_n)_A)$$

(thus we define σ_A by induction on the *length* of an expression when considered as a string of symbols).

Our requirement on nameability in a data type can be put thus:

every $a \in A_\mu$ *is named by some* $\sigma \in Con_\mu(\mathcal{O})$
(i.e. is σ_A for some σ).

This condition can be expressed algebraically in terms of the notion of *subalgebra*. If A and B are $\mathcal{O}$-algebras, then B is a subalgebra of A if

(i) $B_\mu \subseteq A_\mu$ for all $\mu \in Z$

and (ii) for each $\delta \in \mathcal{O}_{\nu,\mu}$, δ_B is the restriction of δ_A to B_ν.

Condition (ii) here implies that $c_B = c_A$ whenever $c \in \mathcal{O}_{\lambda,\mu}$, so that the B-constants of sort μ are precisely the A-constants of that sort.

Any $\mathcal{O}$-algebra A has at least one subalgebra - itself. A is called $\mathcal{O}$*-minimal* if it has no other subalgebras. But A always has a *smallest* subalgebra, $A^\downarrow$, which is informally specified as the closure of the set of all A-constants under the operations of A. To put it another way, the members of $A^\downarrow$ are just those elements that can be constructed from A-constants by a finite number of A-operations. More precisely, putting

$$A_\mu^\downarrow = \{\sigma_A : \sigma \in Con_\mu(\mathcal{O})\}$$

gives $\{A_\mu^\downarrow : \mu \in Z\}$ as a subalgebra of A that lies inside any other subalgebra of A. Hence A will be minimal just in case $A^\downarrow = A$, and so requiring that everything in A be nameable by a constant expression of $\mathcal{O}$ is equivalent to requiring that A be a minimal $\mathcal{O}$-algebra.

Minimality of an algebra is a signature-dependent notion: any $\mathcal{O}$-algebra A

can be made to have all elements nameable by expanding $\mathcal{O}$ by simply adding enough new "names". A new signature $\mathcal{O}^{A}$ is formed by putting

$$\mathcal{O}^{A}_{\nu,\mu} = \mathcal{O}_{\nu,\mu} \quad \text{for} \quad \nu \neq \lambda$$

and

$$\mathcal{O}^{A}_{\lambda,\mu} = \mathcal{O}_{\lambda,\mu} \cup \{c_a : a \in A_\mu\}.$$

By taking $(c_a)_A = a$, A is "expanded" to become a minimal $\mathcal{O}^{A}$-algebra.

We will have more to say about the definition of "data type" in §3.7.

3.2 THE SYNTAX OF A SIGNATURE

Let Z be a countable set, and $\mathcal{O}$ an Z-sorted signature that has each $\mathcal{O}_{\nu,\mu}$ countable. For each $\mu \in Z$ let X_μ be a *denumerable* set of symbols, called *individual variables of sort* μ. Then $X = \{X_\mu : \mu \in Z\}$ will be called an *Z-sorted system of variables*, and the triple $L = (Z,\mathcal{O},X)$ is a *language*. From such an alphabet we generate the syntactic categories $Bxp(L)$, $Axp(L)$, $Cmd(L)$, $Fma(L)$ of Boolean expressions, algebraic expressions, commands, and formulae of L, respectively. In the case of algebraic expressions we have

$$Axp(L) = \bigcup\{Axp_\mu(L) : \mu \in Z\},$$

where $Axp_\mu(L)$ is the set of *algebraic expressions of sort* μ. These expressions are intended to denote members of A_μ in any $\mathcal{O}$-algebra A. The inductive formation rules are as follows.

(i) $X_\mu \subseteq Axp_\mu(L)$;

(ii) $\mathcal{O}_{\lambda,\mu} \subseteq Axp_\mu(L)$;

(iii) If $f \in \mathcal{O}_{\mu_1\ldots\mu_n,\mu}$ and $\sigma_i \in Axp_{\mu_i}(L)$ for $1 \leq i \leq n$, then $f(\sigma_1, \ldots, \sigma_n) \in Axp_\mu(L)$;

(iv) If $\varepsilon \in Bxp(L)$, and $\sigma,\tau \in Axp_\mu(L)$, then $(\varepsilon \supset \sigma,\tau) \in Axp_\mu(L)$.

The clause (iv) invokes the set $Bxp(L)$, which is itself defined by the four rules that defined Bxp at the beginning of §2.1, with the additional rule

if $\sigma,\tau \in Axp_\mu(L)$ for some μ, then $(\sigma=\tau) \in Bxp(L)$.

Thus Boolean expressions may contain algebraic ones within them, and vice versa. The categories $Bxp(L)$ and $Axp(L)$ are therefore generated *simultaneously* by induction. In proofs and definitions we will as usual base the induction on the *length* of the expression concerned.

To define $Cmd(L)$ we keep the rules for *skip*, *abort*, ;, ⇒, #, and |, as before, and add the following

if either $x \in X_\mu$ and $\sigma \in Axp_\mu(L)$ for some μ, or else
$x \in Bvb$ and $\sigma \in Bxp(L)$, then $(x := \sigma) \in Cmd(L)$.

$(x := \sigma)$ is the *assignment* command "set x to σ". Assignments are now our "atomic" commands, in place of the program letters π.

Finally, $Fma(L)$ is defined by the rules:

1. $Bxp(L) \subseteq Fma(L)$;
2. If $\varphi,\psi \in Fma(L)$ then $(\varphi \to \psi) \in Fma(L)$;
3. If $\varphi \in Fma(L)$ and $\alpha \in Cmd(L)$ then $[\alpha]\varphi \in Fma(L)$;
4. If $\varphi \in Fma(L)$, and, for some μ, $x \in X_\mu$, then $\forall x\varphi \in Fma(L)$.

We denote by VarT the set of all variables that occur in T, where T may be an expression, a command, or a formula, and put $Var\Omega = \bigcup\{Var\mathrm{T} : \mathrm{T} \in \Omega\}$. Occassionally we write x_μ to indicate that the variable in question is of sort μ.

A *first-order* formula is, by definition, one that has no subformula of the form $[\alpha]\varphi$.

In view of the restrictions on Z and O it is demonstrable that the sets $Bxp(L)$, $Axp(L)$, $Cmd(L)$, and $Fma(L)$ are all *denumerable*.

As usual, $\exists x\varphi$ abbreviates the formula $\neg\forall x \neg\varphi$.

Although the language just described contains only a few of the main features of realistic high-level programming languages, it is far from trivial. Apart from the fact that it appears to be expressive enough to formalise the system of Dijkstra's *A Discipline of Programming*, there is the significant theoretical point that any partial recursive function on $\mathbb{N}$ can be computed by a program built out of *skip* and assignment commands by using only conditionals $\Rightarrow$, composites ;, and iterations #. By Church's Thesis this means that any algorithm can, after suitable coding, be performed by some such program. For a detailed discussion of this result, which is due to C. Bohm and G. Jacopini, see Chapter 3 of Clark and Cowell (1976).

3.3 SEMANTICS

MODELS

A *model* for a language $L = (Z, O, X)$ is a structure

$$M = (A,\ S,\ v,\ [\![\cdot]\!]),$$

where

(i) A is an O-algebra, the *base* of M;

(ii) S is a set (of states as before);

(iii) v is an operator that associates with each $s \in S$ an A-*valuation*, i.e. a function v_s that assigns

(a) to each $p \in Bvb(L)$ an element $v_s(p)$ of $\mathbb{B}^+$,

and (b) to each $x \in X_\mu$ an element $v_s(x)$ of A_μ^+;

(iv) $[\![\cdot]\!]$ associated with each $\alpha \in Cmd(L)$ a relation $[\![\alpha]\!] \subseteq S \times S$.

Given such a model M, we may expand L to the language $L^A = (Z, O^A, X)$, generated by the signature O^A, as defined in §3.1, that has names for all A-elements. Then each A-valuation v_s extends to assign values to all expressions in $Bxp(L^A) \cup Axp(L^A)$ as follows.

a. If $\varepsilon \in Bxp(L^A)$ then $v_s(\varepsilon) \in \mathbb{B}^+$ is defined exactly as in §2.2. The only new kind of Boolean expression is $(\sigma=\tau)$ when σ and τ are algebraic. But given, inductively, the values of σ and τ in s, the interpretation of the equality symbol = is just as before.

b. For $\sigma \in Axp_\mu(L^A)$, we proceed inductively to define $v_s(\sigma) \in A^+_\mu$:

(i) for $x \in X_\mu$, $v_s(x)$ is given by the model M;

(ii) if $c \in O^A_{\lambda,\mu}$, then $v_s(c) = c_A$, the A_μ-element named by c;

(iii) if $f \in O^A_{\nu,\mu}$, where ν is $\mu_1 \ldots \mu_n$, and $\sigma_i \in Axp_{\mu_i}(L^A)$ for $1 \leqslant i \leqslant n$, then

1. if $v_s(\sigma_i) = \omega$ for some i, then $v_s(f(\sigma_1, \ldots, \sigma_n)) = \omega$, and otherwise

2. $v_s(f(\sigma_1, \ldots, \sigma_n)) = f_A(v_s(\sigma_1), \ldots, v_s(\sigma_n))$, where $f_A : A_\nu \to A_\mu$ is the A-operation named by f.

(iv)

$$v_s(\varepsilon \supset \sigma,\tau) = \begin{cases} \omega & \text{if } v_s(\varepsilon) = \omega \\ v_s(\sigma) & \text{if } v_s(\varepsilon) = 1 \\ v_s(\tau) & \text{if } v_s(\varepsilon) = 0. \end{cases}$$

(Note that we ambiguously use the same symbol ω to denote the "undefined" member of A^+ for all sets A).

RIGID DESIGNATORS

By an inductive proof, using parts (ii) and (iii) of the definition of $v_s(\sigma)$ just given, it follows that if $\sigma \in Con_\mu(O^A)$, i.e. σ is a constant A-expression, then $v_s(\sigma)$ is σ_A, the A_μ-element named by σ (as defined in §3.1). Thus $v_s(\sigma)$ does not depend on s when σ is constant. In general a symbol whose value is the same with respect to all states is known as a *rigid designator*. In many of the first-order modal systems that have been studied (cf. Kripke (1963b), Thomason (1970), Gabbay (1976) etc.), operation and relation symbols have state-dependent interpretations, while individual variables are rigid. The study of systems in which variables have context-dependent values (cf. e.g. Hughes and Cresswell (1968), Chapter 11) has been in the main motivated philosophically by a concern with the notion of "individual concept". An example of this notion is "the number of citizens of New Zealand". This expression certainly refers to a number, but the particular member of $\mathbb{N}$ that it denotes varies from time to time.

For computational semantics it is most natural to treat operation symbols as rigid, since they refer to fixed operations on given data types. But the notion of a variable changing its value from state to state is of the essence of what we mean by "state" in the first place (cf. the concept of "natural model" below). Of course it is possible in a given model M that $v_s(x) = v_t(x)$ for all $s,t \in S$. In that case M is said to *treat x as a constant*, since as far as M is concerned x denotes a fixed A-element and so behaves like a member of $O_{\lambda,\mu}$. This type of variable behaviour will play a pivotal role in the canonical model construction to follow in §3.5.

SATISFACTION

To define the relation

$$M \models_s \varphi$$

for all $\varphi \in Fma(L^A)$ we have only to deal with one new case - when φ has the form $\forall x\psi$. To this end we first review the classical semantics of *first-order* formulae, i.e. those with no occurrence of a modal operator $[\alpha]$.

First-order satisfaction requires the assignment of values to the "unquantified" variables of a formula. For this we use the notion of an A-*valuation*, as presented in clause (iii) of the definition of L-model above. The set of all A-valuations will be denoted S_A. We define a relation

$$A^+ \models \varphi[s],$$

to be read "φ is satisfied in A by the valuation $s \in S_A$". Intuitively this means that φ makes a true assertion about A when each unquantified variable x of φ is taken as denoting the individual $s(x)$. The +-superscript refers to the fact that the function s may have $s(\sigma) = \omega$ for certain expressions σ. The inductive definition of satisfaction is as follows.

$$A^+ \models \varphi[s] \quad \text{iff} \quad s(\varphi) = 1, \text{ for } \varphi \in Bxp(L^A)$$

$$A^+ \models \varphi \to \psi[s] \quad \text{iff} \quad A^+ \models \varphi[s] \text{ implies } A^+ \models \psi[s]$$

$$A^+ \models \forall x_\mu \varphi[s] \quad \text{iff} \quad \text{for all } a \in A_\mu,$$

$$A^+ \models \varphi[s(x_\mu/a)]$$

where $s(x_\mu/a)$ is that valuation $t \in S_A$ defined by

$$t(y) = \begin{cases} s(y) & \text{if } y \neq x_\mu \\ a & \text{if } y = x_\mu . \end{cases}$$

(Notice that in this definition the range of the quantifier $\forall x_\mu$ is A_μ and not A_μ^+.)

We say that A *satisfies* φ, in symbols $A^+ \models \varphi$, if φ is satisfied by every valuation $s \in S_A$. In fact satisfaction of φ by s proves to depend only on the values that s assigns to variables that have a *free* occurrence in φ - where by a free occurrence of x in φ we mean one that is not part of a subformula of φ of the form $\forall x\psi$. Hence satisfaction does not depend on any particular s when φ is a first-order *sentence*, i.e. has no free variables (cf. the Exercises below). Moreover, the truly classical theory does not allow variables to be undefined, but is based on *total* valuations, which are those that never assign ω to any variable. We use the notation

$$A \models \varphi$$

to mean that φ is satisfied by every total valuation $s \in S_A$. This is the classical conception of "A is a model of φ" or "φ is true in A".

3.3.1 EXERCISES.

(1) If $s(x) = t(x)$ whenever x occurs free in φ, then

$$A^+ \models \varphi[s] \quad \text{iff} \quad A^+ \models \varphi[t].$$

(2) If φ is a sentence and $A^+ \models \varphi[s]$ for some $s \in S_A$, then $A^+ \models \varphi$, and so $A \models \varphi$.

■

3.3.2 THEOREM.

(1) *If $x_1, \ldots, x_n$ are all of the free variables of first-order φ, then*

$$A \models \varphi \quad \textit{iff} \quad A^+ \models Dx_1 \wedge \ldots \wedge Dx_n \rightarrow \varphi.$$

(2) *If φ is a sentence,*

$$A \models \varphi \quad \textit{iff} \quad A^+ \models \varphi.$$

Proof.

(1) If s fails to satisfy φ, for some *total* s, then $s(x_i) \neq \omega$ so that s satisfies $Dx_1 \wedge \ldots \wedge Dx_n$, and so fails to satisfy $(Dx_1 \wedge \ldots \wedge Dx_n \rightarrow \varphi)$. Conversely, if this last formula is not satisfied by an $s \in S_A$, then this s fails to satisfy φ but assigns to all of $x_1, \ldots, x_n$ a value other than ω. Hence we can construct a *total* valuation s' that agrees with s on the free variables of φ. But then by 3.3.1(1), s' does not satisfy φ.

(2) For the reader. ■

If g and h are abstract functions defined on the same domain G, then we write

$$g =_b h$$

to mean that g and h agree except (possibly) at b, i.e. that

$$\text{for all } b' \in G, \text{ if } b' \neq b \text{ then } g(b') = h(b').$$

Thus the function $s(x_\mu/a)$ defined above can be characterised as that valuation having $s =_x s(x_\mu/a)$ and $s(x_\mu/a)(x) = a$. In a general model we write

$$s(x/a)t$$

where $s,t \in S$, to mean that v_t is $v_s(x/a)$, i.e. $v_s =_x v_t$ and $v_t(x) = a$ (possibly a is ω here). Then the definition of the relation $M \models_s \varphi$ proceeds as in §2.1 for $\varphi \in Bxp(L^A)$ and the inductive cases for $(\varphi \rightarrow \psi)$ and $[\alpha]\varphi$. The new clause, for $\varphi \in Fma(L^A)$ and $x \in X_\mu$ is

$$M \models_s \forall x\varphi \quad \text{iff} \quad \text{for all } a \in A_\mu, \text{ if } s(x/a)t \text{ then } M \models_t \varphi.$$

3.3.3 EXERCISES.

(1) $M \models \forall x Dx$

(2) $M \models \forall x(\varphi \rightarrow \psi) \rightarrow (\forall x\varphi \rightarrow \forall x\psi)$

(3) If $M \models \varphi$, then $M \models \forall x\varphi$

(4) If $M \models (Dx \rightarrow \varphi)$ then $M \models \forall x\varphi$

(5) Suppose $\Sigma \cup \{\varphi\} \subseteq Fma(L^A)$, and for all $s \in S$,

$$M \models_s \varphi \quad \text{iff} \quad \text{for all } \psi \in \Sigma \quad M \models_s \psi.$$

Then for all $s \in S$,

$$M \models_s \forall x\varphi \quad \text{iff} \quad \text{for all } \psi \in \Sigma \quad M \models_s \forall x\psi.$$ ∎

Of course if the quantifier $\forall x$ is really to mean "for all members of A_μ", then a state t having $s(x/a)t$, as referred to in the semantic clause, must be available in M for each $a \in A_\mu$. We say that a model M *has enough states* if it satisfies the requirement for all $\mu \in Z$, $x \in X_\mu$, $s \in S$, and $a \in A_\mu$, there exists a $t \in S$ with $s(x/a)t$.

3.3.4 EXERCISE.

If M has enough states, and φ is first-order, then

(1) $M \models_s \varphi$ iff $A^+ \models \varphi[v_s]$;

(2) If $A^+ \models \varphi$ then $M \models \varphi$;

(3) If φ is a sentence and $M \models_s \varphi$ for some s, then $A^+ \models \varphi$ and hence $A \models \varphi$.

■

We now extend our substitution-notation by writing $s(x/\sigma)t$ to mean that $s(x/v_s(\sigma))t$. In particular this entails that $s(x/c_a)t$ if and only if $s(x/a)t$.

An A-based L-model M is *standard* if it is an L^A-model, i.e. $[\![\alpha]\!]$ is defined in M for all $\alpha \in Cmd(L^A)$, and, in addition to the standard-model conditions for *skip*, *abort*, ;, $\Rightarrow$, #, and $|$, it satisfies for each assignment $(x := \sigma) \in Cmd(L^A)$ the two conditions

(i) if $v_s(\sigma) \neq \omega$, then there is a $t \in S$ with $s[\![x := \sigma]\!]t$; and

(ii) if $s[\![x := \sigma]\!]t$ then $v_s(\sigma) \neq \omega$ and $s(x/\sigma)t$.

This amounts to requiring that execution of $(x := \sigma)$ serves to assign to x the initial value $v_s(\sigma)$ of σ, causing no *side effects* (i.e. changes to the values of other variables), with the command terminating if and only if the initial value of σ is defined.

By taking σ as the constant c_a, for $a \in A_\mu$, we see that these two conditions together imply that *a standard model always has enough states*, and so gives the correct interpretation of universal quantifiers.

NATURAL MODELS

The *natural model* over an $\mathcal{O}$-algebra A is the structure

$$M_A = (A, S_A, v^A, [\![\cdot]\!]),$$

where

(i) the M_A-states are the A-valuations $s \in S_A$;

(ii) for each $s \in S_A$ and variable x (in Bvb or X_μ);

$$v_s^A(x) = s(x);$$

(iii) $[\![\alpha]\!]$ is defined inductively by putting

$$s [\![x := \sigma]\!] t \quad \text{iff} \quad s(\sigma) \neq \omega \text{ and } t = s(x/s(\sigma))$$

for assignments, and then defining $[\![\alpha]\!]$ by the appropriate standard-model condition when α is a structured command.

Since the members of S_A comprise all possible ways of making assignments to variables, and since v_s^A is just s, it is apparent that M_A is a *standard* model. Moreover, in this model the relation $[\![x := \sigma]\!]$ is functional, and determines a function with domain

$$\{s : s(\sigma) \neq \omega\}.$$

Thus M_A validates the formulae

$$\neg[x := \sigma]\mathit{false} \leftrightarrow D\sigma$$

and

$$[x := \sigma]\varphi \vee [x := \sigma]\neg\varphi.$$

But although every standard model validates these formulae (cf. Theorem 3.3.8(3) below), functionality is not part of the definition of "standardness" of assignment-execution. Indeed since states are allowed to be abstract points in S, there is nothing to prevent the sort of duplication that has $s [\![x := \sigma]\!] t$ and $s [\![x := \sigma]\!] u$ with $t \neq u$. But in that case we will have $v_t = v_u$ $(= v_s(x/v_s(\sigma)))$, with t and u

semantically indistinguishable (cf. 3.3.8(2)).

3.3.5 EXERCISES.

(1) If φ is first-order,

$$M_A \models \varphi \quad \text{iff} \quad A^+ \models \varphi.$$

(2) If φ is a first-order *sentence*,

$$M_A \models \varphi \quad \text{iff} \quad A \models \varphi. \qquad \blacksquare$$

Notice that if M is any A-based model, each state s of M has its valuation v_s as a state of M_A, with the value assigned by v^A to x in the M_A-state v_s being $v_s(x)$ - which is the value assigned to x at the M-state s.

3.3.6 EXERCISES.

(1) For any L^A-expression σ,

$$v^A_{v_s}(\sigma) = v_s(\sigma).$$

(2) For $\varepsilon \in Bxp(L^A)$,

$$M \models_s \varepsilon \quad \text{iff} \quad M_A \models_{v_s} \varepsilon.$$

(3) $s(x/\sigma)t$ in M iff $v_s(x/\sigma)v_t$ in M_A. $\blacksquare$

3.3.7 THEOREM.

If M is a standard model with base A, then for all $\alpha \in Cmd(L^A)$,

(1) $s [\![\alpha]\!] t$ *in M implies* $v_s [\![\alpha]\!] v_t$ *in* M_A;

and

(2) v_s ⟦ α ⟧ u *in* M_A *implies that* s ⟦ α ⟧ t *in* M *for some* M*-state* t *having* $v_t = u$.

Proof.

(1) By induction on the formation of α.

a. If α is the assignment $(x := \sigma)$ and s ⟦ α ⟧ t, then by the second standard-model condition on α, $v_s(\sigma) \neq \omega$ and $s(x/\sigma)t$, i.e. $v_s =_x v_t$ and $v_t(x) = v_s(\sigma)$. But then, by definition, v_s ⟦ α ⟧ v_t in M_A.

b. The cases that α is *skip* or *abort* are left to the reader.

c. Assume the result for α and β, in order to prove it for (α;β).

If s ⟦ α;β ⟧ t, then for some u in M we have s ⟦ α ⟧ u ⟦ β ⟧ t. The induction hypothesis then gives v_s ⟦ α ⟧ v_u ⟦ β ⟧ v_t, and hence v_s ⟦ α;β ⟧ v_t, in M_A.

d. Assume the result for α and β, and consider (ε ⇒ α,β).

If s ⟦ ε ⇒ α,β ⟧ t, then either $M \models_s \varepsilon$ and s ⟦ α ⟧ t, or else $M \models_s$ *not*-ε and s ⟦ β ⟧ t. In the first case, by Exercise 3.3.6(2) and the hypothesis on α we have $M_A \models_{v_s} \varepsilon$ and v_s ⟦ α ⟧ v_t. Similarly, in the second case we get $M_A \models_{v_s}$ *not*-ε and v_s ⟦ β ⟧ v_t. In any case, v_s ⟦ ε ⇒ α,β ⟧ v_t.

e. Assume the result for α, in order to prove it for (ε#α).

If s ⟦ ε#α ⟧ t, then for some $n \in \mathbb{N}$, there exist M-states $s_0, \ldots, s_n$ having $s_0 = s$, $s_n = t$, $\models_{s_n}$ *not*-ε and for $0 \leq i < n$, s_i ⟦ α ⟧ s_{i+1} and $\models_{s_i} \varepsilon$. But then by the induction hypothesis and 3.3.6(2), in M_A *not*-ε holds at v_t, and for $0 \leq i < n$, ε holds at v_{s_i} and v_{s_i} ⟦ α ⟧ $v_{s_{i+1}}$. Hence v_s ⟦ ε]α ⟧^{n} v_t. Thus v_s ⟦ ε#α ⟧ v_t.

f. If the result holds for α and β, and s ⟦ α|β ⟧ t, then s ⟦ α ⟧ t or s ⟦ β ⟧ t. Thus v_s ⟦ α ⟧ v_t or v_s ⟦ β ⟧ v_t, giving v_s ⟦ α|β ⟧ v_t. Hence the result holds for (α|β).

(2) Again we proceed by induction.

a. Let α be $(x := \sigma)$. Then if $v_s [\![\alpha]\!] u$ in M_A, we have $v_s(\sigma) \neq \omega$, $u =_x v_s$, and $u(x) = v_s(\sigma)$. But by the first standard-model condition on α, there is an M-state t with $s [\![x := \sigma]\!] t$ in M, and so by the second standard-model condition $s(x/\sigma)t$, i.e. $v_t =_x v_s$ and $v_t(x) = v_s(\sigma)$. But then the functions v_t and u are identical.

b. The result holds vacuously when α is *abort*, since $v_s [\![\textit{abort}]\!] u$ is false in general.

If $v_s [\![\textit{skip}]\!] u$, then $v_s = u$, so taking $t=s$ gives $s [\![\textit{skip}]\!] t$ and $v_t = u$ as desired.

c. Assume the result for α and β. Then if $v_s [\![\alpha;\beta]\!] u$, there exists an M_A-state u' for which $v_s [\![\alpha]\!] u' [\![\beta]\!] u$. By the hypothesis on α then, there is an M-state t' having $s [\![\alpha]\!] t'$ and $v_{t'} = u'$. But then $v_{t'} [\![\beta]\!] u$, so by the hypothesis on β there is an M-state t with $t' [\![\beta]\!] t$, making $s [\![\alpha;\beta]\!] t$, and $v_t = u$.

d. The inductive case for $(\varepsilon \Rightarrow \alpha,\beta)$ is left to the reader.

e. Assume the result for α. Then if $v_s [\![\varepsilon\#\alpha]\!] u$, in M_A, *not*-ε holds at u and for some n there exist states $u_0, \ldots, u_n$ having $u_0 = v_s$, $u_n = u$, with ε holding at u_i and $u_i [\![\alpha]\!] u_{i+1}$ whenever $0 \leqslant i < n$.

We then proceed to construct a sequence $s_0, \ldots, s_n$ such that in M we have $s_0 = s$ and $s_i [\![\alpha]\!] s_{i+1}$ and $v_{s_{i+1}} = u_{i+1}$ whenever $0 \leqslant i < n$. Since then $v_{s_0} = u_0$, this will imply that $v_{s_i} = u_i$ whenever $0 \leqslant i \leqslant n$, so that by 3.3.6(2) it will follow that in M we have *not*-ε holding at s_n while ε holds at s_i whenever $0 \leqslant i < n$. But this makes $s [\![\varepsilon\#\alpha]\!] s_n$ and so, as $v_{s_n} = u_n = u$, establishes the result for the command $(\varepsilon\#\alpha)$.

To define the s_i's, we begin by putting $s_0 = s$, so that $v_{s_0} = u_0$. Then assuming that for some i such that $0 \leqslant i < n$ we have obtained s_i satisfying $v_{s_i} = u_i$, it follows that in M_A we have $v_{s_i} [\![\alpha]\!] u_{i+1}$, and so by the induction hypothesis on

α, there is an M-state t having $s_i \llbracket \alpha \rrbracket t$ and $v_t = u_{i+1}$. We put $s_{i+1} = t$. This inductively generates the sequence $s_0, \ldots, s_n$ with the desired properties.

f. The case of $(\alpha|\beta)$ is left to the reader. ■

3.3.8 THEOREM

If M *is a standard* A*-based model, then for any* $\varphi \in Fma(L^A)$:

(1) $M \models_s \varphi$ *iff* $M_A \models_{v_s} \varphi$, *for any* M*-state* s;

(2) *If* $v_s = v_t$, *then* $M \models_s \varphi$ *iff* $M \models_t \varphi$;

(3) *If* $M_A \models \varphi$ *then* $M \models \varphi$.

Proof.

(2) and (3) are straightforward consequences of (1), and so we prove only the latter, proceeding by induction on the formation of φ.

1. If $\varphi \in Bxp(L^A)$, the result is Exercise 3.3.6(2).

2. The inductive case for $\rightarrow$ is left to the reader.

3. Assume that (1) holds for φ, in order to prove it for $[\alpha]\varphi$.

If $M \not\models_s [\alpha]\varphi$ then for some t such that $s \llbracket \alpha \rrbracket t$ we have $M \not\models_t \varphi$. By 3.3.7(1) we then have $v_s \llbracket \alpha \rrbracket v_t$ in M_A, and by the hypothesis on φ we have $M_A \models_{v_t} \varphi$. Hence $M_A \not\models_{v_s} [\alpha]\varphi$.

Conversely, if $M_A \not\models_{v_s} [\alpha]\varphi$, then for some M_A-state u we have $v_s \llbracket \alpha \rrbracket u$ and $M_A \not\models_u \varphi$. But then by 3.3.7(2) there is a state t in M with $s \llbracket \alpha \rrbracket t$ and $v_t = u$. The hypothesis on φ then gives $M \not\models_t \varphi$, so that $M \not\models_s [\alpha]\varphi$.

4. Assume the result for φ and consider $\forall x\varphi$, where $x \in X_\mu$.

If $M \not\models_s \forall x\varphi$, then for some $a \in A_\mu$ and some M-state t we have $s(x/a)t$ and $M \not\models_t \varphi$. The hypothesis on φ then gives $M_A \not\models_{v_t} \varphi$. But in M_A we have $v_s(x/a)v_t$

(cf. 3.3.6(3)), and so $M_A \nvDash_{v_s} \forall x\varphi$.

Conversely, if $M_A \nvDash_{v_s} \forall x\varphi$, then for some $a \in A_\mu$ there is an M_A-state u such that $v_s(x/a)u$ and $M_A \nvDash_u \varphi$. But then in M_A, $v_s \llbracket x := c_a \rrbracket u$ and so by 3.3.7(2) there is an M-state t having $s \llbracket x := c_a \rrbracket t$ and $v_t = u$. By the hypothesis on φ then, $M \nvDash_t \varphi$. But since M is standard we have $s(x/c_a)t$, i.e. $s(x/a)t$, and so $M \nvDash_s \forall x\varphi$. ∎

Part (3) of this last Theorem has the important consequence that to show that a formula is valid in all standard models it suffices to establish its validity in natural ones.

3.3.9 THEOREM.

In a standard model M, if $x \in X_\mu$:

(1) $M \vDash_s \forall x\varphi$ *iff for all* $a \in A_\mu$ $M \vDash_s [x := c_a]\varphi$

(2) $M \vDash_s [\alpha]\varphi$ *iff* $v_s \llbracket \alpha \rrbracket v_t$ *in* M_A *implies* $M \vDash_t \varphi$.

Proof.

(1) Let $M \vDash_s \forall x\varphi$. Then since M is standard, $s \llbracket x := c_a \rrbracket t$ implies $s(x/a)t$, and so $M \vDash_t \varphi$ by the semantic clause for ∀. Hence $M \vDash_s [x := c_a]\varphi$.

Conversely, if $M \nvDash_s \forall x\varphi$, then for some $a \in A_\mu$ and some t with $s(x/a)t$ we have $M \nvDash_t \varphi$. But then v_t is $v_s(x/a)$, so in M_A we have $v_s \llbracket x := c_a \rrbracket v_t$. By part (2) of Theorem 3.3.7 it follows that there is an M-state t' such that $s \llbracket x := c_a \rrbracket t'$ and $v_{t'} = v_t$. Hence by 3.3.8(2), $M \nvDash_{t'} \varphi$, which yields $M \nvDash_s [x := c_a]\varphi$.

(2) For the reader. ∎

Now in classical first-order logic an alternative approach to quantification that is often used is to put

$$A \models \forall x\varphi[s] \quad \text{iff} \quad \text{for all } a \in A,\ A \models \varphi^{x}_{c_a}[s],$$

where $\varphi^{x}_{c_a}$ is the formula obtained by replacing all free occurrences of x in φ by the constant c_a. To have adopted this approach for $Fma(L^A)$ would have required a prior notion of "free variable" for formulae containing modal operators. The present approach is simpler, and if anything is a more intuitive semantic analysis, but it ought still to be equivalent to the alternative for first-order formula. In view of 3.3.9(1) it seems that this equivalence will obtain if the formulae $[x := c_a]\varphi$ and $\varphi^{x}_{c_a}$ hold in exactly the same states in standard models, i.e. if the formula

$$(\dagger) \qquad [x := c_a]\varphi \leftrightarrow \varphi^{x}_{c_a}$$

is valid in standard models.

In order to establish the standard-validity of $(\dagger)$ we need some preliminary observations. Firstly, for any $s \in S_A$ it is readily proven that if σ and τ are L^A-expressions, and x is a variable of the same Boolean type, or the same sort, as σ, then the s-value of τ^{x}_{σ} is the same as the value assigned to τ by the A-valuation $s(x/s(\sigma))$. Here τ^{x}_{σ} is the expression obtained by replacing *every* occurrence of x in τ by σ (so that τ^{x}_{σ} is just τ if $x \notin Var\tau$). In symbols, we have

$$s(\tau^{x}_{\sigma}) = s(x/s(\sigma))(\tau).$$

From this it can be shown that for any first-order φ,

$$A^{+} \models \varphi^{x}_{\sigma}[s] \quad \text{iff} \quad A^{+} \models \varphi[s(x/s(\sigma))]$$

(cf. e.g. the Substitution Lemma of Enderton (1972), p.127, for a proof for total valuations s). Using the result of Exercise 3.3.5(1), we conclude that

(a) $\qquad M_A \models_s \varphi^{x}_{\sigma} \quad \text{iff} \quad M_A \models_{s(x/s(\sigma))} \varphi.$

But in the natural model M_A, the relation $[\![x := c_a]\!]$ determines a total function, with

$$s [\![x := c_a]\!] t \quad \text{iff} \quad t = s(x/a) = s(x/s(c_a)),$$

and so

(b) $$M_A \models_s [x := c_a]\varphi \quad \text{iff} \quad M_A \models_{s(x/s(c_a))} \varphi.$$

The equivalences (a) and (b) yield the validity of formula (†) in M_A and hence in any standard L^A-model.

However for a general expression σ the formula

$$[x := \sigma]\varphi \leftrightarrow \varphi^x_\sigma$$

need not be standardly-valid, because, unlike c_a, σ could be undefined. In a state having $v_s(\sigma) = \omega$, $[x := \sigma]\varphi$ will hold (since $(x := \sigma)$ does not terminate) but φ^x_σ may not hold (e.g. if φ is Dx).

3.3.10 EXERCISE.

For any first-order φ, the formulae

$$\varphi^x_\sigma \rightarrow [x := \sigma]\varphi, \qquad \text{and}$$

$$[x := \sigma]\varphi \leftrightarrow (D\sigma \rightarrow \varphi^x_\sigma)$$

are valid in all standard models. ∎

Our next concern is to prove that the meaning of any formula is unaffected by an assignment to a variable that does not occur in that formula. For first-order formulae we know the stronger fact that the meaning is unaffected if the assignment does not involve a *free* variable. This is the substance of the following result.

3.3.11 EXERCISE.

Let $s(x/\sigma)t$ in an A-based model M. Then:

(1) $v_s(\tau^x_\sigma) = v_t(\tau)$, for any L^A-expression τ;

(2) If M has enough states,

$$M \models_s \varphi^x_\sigma \quad \text{iff} \quad M \models_t \varphi,$$

for any first-order $\varphi \in Fma(L^A)$. ■

When x is not free in first-order φ then φ^x_σ is φ itself, so that if $s [\![x := \sigma]\!] t$ in a standard model M, this last Exercise implies that

$$M \models_s \varphi \quad \text{iff} \quad M \models_t \varphi.$$

3.3.12 THEOREM.

Suppose that the variable x does not occur in the L^A-command α. In the natural model M_A let $s,t \in S_A$ have $s(x/a)t$. Then we have

$$t [\![\alpha]\!] t' \quad \textit{iff} \quad \textit{there exists } s' \textit{ with } s [\![\alpha]\!] s' \textit{ and } s'(x/a)t'.$$

Proof.

The result is proven for all s and t in S_A, and proceeds by induction on the formation of α (the reader is encouraged to draw some diagrams of the relationships involved).

Recall that in M_A we have

$$s(x/a)t \quad \text{iff} \quad (s =_x t \text{ and } t(x) = a) \quad \text{iff} \quad t = s(x/a).$$

Note also from Exercise 3.3.11(1) that when $s(x/a)t$ we have

$$s(\tau^x_{c_a}) = t(\tau)$$

for any L^A-expression τ, and so if $x \notin Var\tau$,

$$s(\tau) = t(\tau).$$

a. If α is the assignment $(y := \tau)$, then by assumption $y \neq x$ and $x \notin Var\tau$.

If $t [\![\alpha]\!] t'$ then, by definition of M_A, $t =_y t'$ and $t'(y) = t(\tau) \neq \omega$. But then by the above note, $s(\tau) = t(\tau) \neq \omega$, and so $s [\![y := \tau]\!] s'$ where s' is the A-valuation $s(y/s(\tau))$. But since $s' =_y s =_x t =_y t'$ and $s'(y) = s(\tau) = t(\tau) = t'(y)$, we have $s' =_x t'$. Moreover $t'(x) = t(x) = a$, and so $s'(x/a)t'$ as desired.

Conversely, if $s [\![y := \tau]\!] s'$ for some s' having $s'(x/a)t'$, then $t' =_x s' =_y s =_x t$ and $t'(x) = a = t(x)$, so that $t' =_y t$. But $t'(y) = s'(y) = s(\tau) = t(\tau)$ and, since $s [\![y := \tau]\!] s'$, we have $s(\tau) \neq \omega$. Thus $t(\tau) \neq \omega$ and $t' = t(y/y(\tau))$, i.e. $t [\![y := \tau]\!] t'$ as desired.

b. Assume that the Theorem holds for β and for γ, and that α is $(\beta;\gamma)$. Then $x \notin Var\beta \cup Var\gamma$.

If $t [\![\alpha]\!] t'$ then for some u, $t [\![\beta]\!] u [\![\gamma]\!] t'$. Applying the hypothesis on β yields a state u' for which $s [\![\beta]\!] u'$ and $u'(x/a)u$. But then applying the hypothesis on γ to u' and u, since $u [\![\gamma]\!] t'$ there exists an s' with $u' [\![\gamma]\!] s'$ and $s'(x/a)t'$. Since $s [\![\beta]\!] u' [\![\gamma]\!] s'$, we have $s [\![\beta;\gamma]\!] s'$.

On the other hand, if $s [\![\beta;\gamma]\!] s'$ for some s' having $s'(x/a)t'$, then there exists u' with $s [\![\beta]\!] u' [\![\gamma]\!] s'$. Then if u is the valuation $u'(x/a)$, so that the relation $u'(x/a)u$ obtains, the hypothesis on β gives $t [\![\beta]\!] u$. But then applying the hypothesis on γ to u' and u (since $u'(x/a)u$), we have $u' [\![\gamma]\!] s'$ and $s'(x/a)t$, hence $u [\![\gamma]\!] t'$. But then $t [\![\beta]\!] u [\![\gamma]\!] t'$, giving $t [\![\beta;\gamma]\!] t'$. (Keep drawing those diagrams).

Hence the result holds for $(\beta;\gamma)$.

c. Assume the result for β and γ, and suppose that α is $(\varepsilon \Rightarrow \beta,\gamma)$.

If $t [\![\alpha]\!] t'$ then either $t(\varepsilon)=1$ and $t [\![\beta]\!] t'$, or else $t(not\text{-}\varepsilon) = 1$ and $t [\![\gamma]\!] t'$. Assume the latter (the former case is similar). Since $x \notin Var\alpha$, x does not occur in ε or in γ. The hypothesis on γ then implies that for some s', $s [\![\gamma]\!] s'$ and $s'(x/a)t'$. But also x does not occur in $not\text{-}\varepsilon$, and so $s(not\text{-}\varepsilon) = t(not\text{-}\varepsilon) = 1$. Thus $s [\![\varepsilon \Rightarrow \beta,\gamma]\!] s'$ as desired.

The rest of this case is left to the reader.

d. Let α be $(\varepsilon\#\beta)$, and assume the result for β.

If $t \llbracket \alpha \rrbracket t'$ then $t'(\mathit{not}\text{-}\varepsilon) = 1$ and for some n there exist $t_o, \ldots, t_n$ with $t_o = t$, $t_n = t'$, and $t_i(\varepsilon) = 1$ and $t_i \llbracket \beta \rrbracket t_{i+1}$ whenever $0 \leqslant i < n$. We then construct a sequence $s_o, \ldots, s_n$ such that $s_o = s$, and $s_i \llbracket \beta \rrbracket s_{i+1}$ and $s_{i+1}(x/a)t_{i+1}$ whenever $0 \leqslant i < n$. Since we then have $s_o(x/a)t_o$ by the main hypothesis this gives $s_i(x/a)t_i$ for $0 \leqslant i \leqslant n$. But x does not occur in β, nor in ε, hence not in $\mathit{not}\text{-}\varepsilon$, so this implies that $s_n(\mathit{not}\text{-}\varepsilon) = t_n(\mathit{not}\text{-}\varepsilon) = 1$, while for $0 \leqslant i < n$, $s_i(\varepsilon) = t_i(\varepsilon) = 1$. But then by putting $s' = s_n$ we get $s \llbracket \varepsilon\#\beta \rrbracket s'$ and $s'(x/a)t'$ as desired.

To define the sequence of s_i's, let $s_o = s$. But then $s_o(x/a)t_o$, so we may assume for the inductive step that $s_i(x/a)t_i$ for an i having $0 \leqslant i < n$. But since $t_i \llbracket \beta \rrbracket t_{i+1}$, by applying the Theorem for β to s_i and t_i in place of s and t, it follows that there exists some state u with $s_i \llbracket \beta \rrbracket u$ and $u(x/a)t_{i+1}$. We put $s_{i+1} = u$. This inductively generates the sequence $s_o, \ldots, s_n$ with the desired properties.

Conversely, if $s \llbracket \varepsilon\#\beta \rrbracket s'$ and $s'(x/a)t'$, then for some n there exist states $s_o, \ldots, s_n$ having $s_o = s$, $s_n = s'$, $s_n(\mathit{not}\text{-}\varepsilon) = 1$, and $s_i(\varepsilon) = 1$ and $s_i \llbracket \beta \rrbracket s_{i+1}$ whenever $0 \leqslant i < n$. For each i such that $0 \leqslant i \leqslant n$, let t_i be the valuation $s_i(x/a)$. Then for $0 \leqslant i < n$ we apply the hypothesis on β to s_i and t_i (since $s_i(x/a)t_i$) and conclude from the fact that $s_i \llbracket \beta \rrbracket s_{i+1}$ and $s_{i+1}(x/a)t_{i+1}$ that we have $t_i \llbracket \beta \rrbracket t_{i+1}$. Moreover $t_i(\varepsilon) = s_i(\varepsilon) = 1$ when $0 \leqslant i < n$, and $t_n(\mathit{not}\text{-}\varepsilon) = s_n(\mathit{not}\text{-}\varepsilon) = 0$, since in all cases $s_i(x/a)t_i$ and x does not occur in ε, hence not in $\mathit{not}\text{-}\varepsilon$. But this means that $t_o \llbracket \varepsilon\#\beta \rrbracket t_n$. Since $t_o = s(x/a) = t$, and $t_n = s'(x/a) = t'$, this completes the proof that the Theorem holds for $(\varepsilon\#\beta)$.

e. The case that α is $(\beta|\gamma)$ is left as an exercise. ∎

3.3.13 THEOREM.

Let $\varphi \in Fma(L^A)$ and suppose that x does not occur in φ. Then in M_A, if $s(x/a)t$ we have

$$M_A \models_s \varphi \quad \textit{iff} \quad M_A \models_t \varphi.$$

Proof.

We prove the result for all s and t, by induction on the formation of φ.

1. If $\varphi \in \mathit{Bexp}(L^A)$, then since $x \notin \mathit{Var}\varphi$ we have $\varphi^x_{c_a} = \varphi$, and so by Exercise 3.3.11(1), $v_s(\varphi) = v_t(\varphi)$. Hence $v_s(\varphi) = 1$ iff $v_t(\varphi) = 1$.

2. Suppose that φ is $(\psi \rightarrow \theta)$ and the result holds for ψ and θ. Then since $x \notin \mathit{Var}\varphi$, x does not occur in ψ or in θ, and it follows easily from the hypotheses on ψ and θ that the result holds for φ.

3. Let φ be $[\alpha]\psi$ and assume the result for ψ.

If $M_A \not\models_s \varphi$, then for some s' we have $s [\![\alpha]\!] s'$ and $M_A \not\models_{s'} \psi$. Let t' be the M_A-state $s'(x/a)$. Then $s'(x/a)t'$, so as $x \notin \mathit{Var}\psi$, the hypothesis on ψ gives $M_A \models_{t'} \psi$. But also, by 3.3.12, since $x \notin \mathit{Var}\alpha$, we have $t [\![\alpha]\!] t'$. Hence $M_A \not\models_t [\alpha]\psi$.

On the other hand, if $M_A \not\models_t \varphi$, then for some t' we have $t [\![\alpha]\!] t'$ and $M_A \not\models_{t'} \psi$. Then by 3.3.12 there exists a state s' for which $s [\![\alpha]\!] s'$ and $s'(x/a)t'$. The induction hypothesis on ψ then gives $M_A \not\models_{s'} \psi$, and thus $M_A \not\models_s [\alpha]\psi$.

Thus the result holds for φ.

4. Suppose that φ is $\forall y\psi$, with $y \in X_\mu$, and assume that the result holds for ψ. Since $x \notin \mathit{Var}\varphi$, we have $x \neq y$, and $x \notin \mathit{Var}\psi$. But then for each $b \in A_\mu$, by the case 3 just proven, the result then holds for the formula $[y := c_b]\psi$, a formula in which x still does not occur. From this, using Theorem 3.3.9(1), we conclude that

$$\begin{aligned} M_A \models_s \forall y\psi \quad &\text{iff} \quad \text{for all } b \in A_\mu \quad M_A \models_s [y := c_b]\psi \\ &\text{iff} \quad \text{for all } b \in A_\mu \quad M_A \models_t [y := c_b]\psi \\ &\text{iff} \quad M_A \models_t \forall y\psi . \end{aligned}$$

Hence the result holds for φ. ■

3.3.14 COROLLARY.

If $x \notin Var\varphi$, then in any standard A-based model M, if $s [\![x := \sigma]\!] t$ then

$$M \models_s \varphi \quad iff \quad M \models_t \varphi.$$

Proof.

If M is standard, then $s [\![x := \sigma]\!] t$ implies that $s(x/a)t$, where $a = v_s(\sigma) \neq \omega$. Then in M_A we have $v_s(x/a)v_t$. Hence

$$M \models_s \varphi \quad \text{iff} \quad M_A \models_{v_s} \varphi \qquad (3.3.8(1))$$

$$\text{iff} \quad M_A \models_{v_t} \varphi \qquad (3.3.13)$$

$$\text{iff} \quad M \models_t \varphi.$$

■

3.3.15 THEOREM.

In any standard model, all instances of the following formula-schemata are valid. (The variables that are unquantified may in each case be Boolean, or of sort μ).

(1) $\varphi \to \forall x\varphi$, if $x \notin Var\varphi$

(2) $\forall x\varphi \to [x := \sigma]\varphi$

(3) $\forall y[x := y]\varphi \to \forall x\varphi$, if $y{=}x$ or $y \notin Var\varphi$

(4) $[y := \tau][y := \sigma]\varphi \to (D\tau \to [y := \sigma^y_\tau]\varphi)$

(5) $\forall y\varphi \to [y := \tau]\forall y\varphi$

(6) $[y := \tau][x := \sigma]\varphi \to (D\tau \to [x := \sigma^y_\tau][y := \tau]\varphi$, if $x \notin Var(y := \tau)$

(7) $\forall x[y := \tau]\varphi \to [y := \tau]\forall x\varphi$, if $x \notin Var(y := \tau)$

(8) $(\tau = \sigma) \to ([y := \tau]\varphi \leftrightarrow [y := \sigma]\varphi)$.

Proof.

It suffices, by 3.3.8(3), to prove that these are valid in natural models. For the purpose of the proof we suppose we are working in a fixed natural model M_A.

(1) Suppose $\models_s \varphi$. If $x \notin Var\varphi$ then for each $a \in A_\mu$ (where μ is the sort of x), if $s(x/a)t$ then by 3.3.13 we have $\models_t \varphi$. Hence the semantic clause for $\forall$ gives $\models_s \forall x\varphi$.

(2) Let $\models_s \forall x\varphi$. If $s(\sigma) = \omega$, then $[\![x := \sigma]\!] = \emptyset$ and so $[x := \sigma]\varphi$ holds at s. Otherwise $s(\sigma) = a$ for some $a \in A_\mu$. Then if $s [\![x := \sigma]\!] t$, $s(x/a)t$ and so $\models_t \varphi$, since $\forall x\varphi$ holds s. Hence $\models_s [x := \sigma]\varphi$.

(3) Note that $(x := y)$ is only defined if x,y are of the same sort μ.

Suppose $\not\models_s \forall x\varphi$. Then for some $a \in A_\mu$ and some state t, $s(x/a)t$ and $\not\models_t \varphi$. If $y \neq x$, let $s' = s(y/a)$, so that $s [\![y := c_a]\!] s'$, and let $t' = s'(x/a)$, so that $s'(x/a)t'$. But x does not occur in $(y := c_a)$, since y is not equal to x, so 3.3.12 yields $t [\![y := c_a]\!] t'$. But $y \notin Var\varphi$, so then 3.3.14 gives $\not\models_{t'} \varphi$. Since $s'(x/a)t'$ and $a = s'(y)$, $s' [\![x := y]\!] t'$ and thus $\models_{s'} [x := y]\varphi$. But $s(y/a)s'$, and so $\not\models_s \forall y[x := y]\varphi$ as desired. Finally, if $y = x$, then $t [\![x := x]\!] t$, as $t(x) = a \neq \omega$, so $\not\models_t [x := x]\varphi$ and hence $\not\models_s \forall x[x := x]\varphi$.

(4) Suppose $[y := \tau][y := \sigma]\varphi$ and $D\tau$ both hold at s. Then $s(\tau) \neq \omega$, so that with $t = s(y/s(\tau))$ we have $s [\![y := \tau]\!] t$ and hence $\models_t [y := \sigma]\varphi$. Therefore if $s [\![y := \sigma^y_\tau]\!] s'$, then $s'(y) = s(\sigma^y_\tau) \neq \omega$ and $s' =_y s =_y t$. Thus $t =_y s'$ and, by 3.3.11(1), $t(\sigma) = s(\sigma^y_\tau) = s'(y)$. Hence $t [\![y := \sigma]\!] s'$. But $[y := \sigma]\varphi$ holds at t, and so φ holds at s'. This shows $\models_s [y := \sigma^y_\tau]\varphi$.

(5) Let $\models_s \forall y\varphi$. Then if $s [\![y := \tau]\!] t$ we have $s =_y t$. For any $b \in A_\mu$ (where $y \in X_\mu$), if $t(y/b)t'$ we then have $t =_y t'$, hence $s =_y t'$, and $t'(y) = b$, so that $s(y/b)t'$. But $\forall y\varphi$ holds at s, and so φ holds at t'. Therefore $\models_t \forall y\varphi$.

This shows that $\models_s [y := \tau]\forall y\varphi$.

(6) Let $[y := \tau][x := \sigma]\varphi$ and $D\tau$ hold at s. Then $s(\tau) \neq \omega$, so that with $t = s(y/s(\tau))$ we get $s [\![y := \tau]\!] t$ and so $\models_t [x := \sigma]\varphi$. Then to show that

$[x := \sigma^y_\tau][y := \tau]\varphi$ holds at s we have to show that if $s [\![x := \sigma^y_\tau]\!] s' [\![y := \tau]\!] t'$, then φ holds at t'. But given such s' and t', we have $s(\tau) = s'(\tau)$ as $x \notin Var\tau$. Hence $t(y) = t'(y)$. Because $t =_y s =_x s' =_y t'$, this implies that $t =_x t'$. But $y \neq x$, so $t'(x) = s'(x) = s(\sigma^y_\tau) \neq \omega$, and by 3.3.11(1), $s(\sigma^y_\tau) = t(\sigma)$. Altogether this establishes $t [\![x := \sigma]\!] t'$, which, since $[x := \sigma]\varphi$ holds at t, gives $\models_{t'} \varphi$ as desired.

(7) Let $\models_s \forall x[y := \tau]\varphi$ and suppose $s [\![y := \tau]\!] t$. We have to show that $\models_t \forall x \varphi$. So, let $b \in A_\mu$ and $t(x/b)t'$. Then if $s' = s(x/b)$ we have $s(x/b)s'$ and so $\models_{s'} [y := \tau]\varphi$. But $t'(y) = t(y)$, as $y \neq x$, and $t(y) = s(\tau) = s'(\tau)$, as $x \notin Var\tau$. Since $t'(x) = b = s'(x)$, and $t' =_x t =_y s =_x s'$, this altogether gives $t' =_y s'$ and $t'(y) = s'(\tau)$, so that $s' [\![y := \tau]\!] t'$. But $[y := \tau]\varphi$ holds at s', giving $\models_{t'} \varphi$. This shows that $\forall x \varphi$ holds at t as desired.

(8) If $\models_s (\tau = \sigma)$ then it follows that $s(\tau) = s(\sigma)$ (with neither in fact being ω). But then the definition of M_A implies that for any t, $s [\![y := \tau]\!] t$ if and only if $s [\![y := \sigma]\!] t$. But from this it follows that $[y := \tau]\varphi$ holds at s if and only if $[y := \sigma]\varphi$ does.

■

The restrictions on variables in the statement of Theorem 3.3.15 cannot be relaxed. For instance, in the case of (3), the formula

$$\forall y[x := y](x = y) \rightarrow \forall x(x = y)$$

is not valid, since the antecedent $\forall y[x := y](x = y)$ is valid in any standard model, while the consequent $\forall x(x = y)$ will hold only when A_μ is a one-element set.

The restriction on x in case (7) is violated by the formulae

$$\forall x[y := x+1](y = x+1) \rightarrow [y := x+1]\forall x(y = x+1)$$

$$\forall x[x := y+1](x \geqslant 1) \rightarrow [x := y+1]\forall x(x \geqslant 1)$$

But in the natural model over the data-type $\mathbb{N}$, $\forall x(y = x+1)$ and $\forall x(x \geqslant 1)$ fail in all states, so the two consequents do not hold in any state in which x, resp. y, is defined. However the antecedents are valid in $M_{\mathbb{N}}$.

3.3.16 EXERCISE.

Give examples to show that the formula 3.3.15(6) need not be valid if $x=y$ or if $x \in Var\tau$. ■

3.4 PROOF THEORY.

The axioms we need for a language L are, in addition to the schemata A1 - A18 of Chapter 2, the following, where in each case a variable without any associated quantifier may be Boolean, or of some sort μ.

Quantifiers

A19 $\forall x(\varphi \to \psi) \to (\forall x\varphi \to \forall x\psi)$

A20 $\forall x\varphi \to [x := \sigma]\varphi$

A21 $\varphi \to \forall x\varphi$, where $x \notin Var\varphi$

A22 $\forall y[x := y]\varphi \to \forall x\varphi$, where $y \notin \{x\} \cup Var\varphi$

A23 $\forall y\varphi \to [y := \tau]\forall y\varphi$

A24 $\forall x[y := \tau]\varphi \to [y := \tau]\forall x\varphi$, where $x \notin Var(y := \tau)$

Assignments

A25 $\neg[x := \sigma]\mathit{false} \leftrightarrow D\sigma$

A26 $[x := \sigma]\varphi \vee [x := \sigma]\neg\varphi$

A27 $[x := \sigma]\varepsilon \leftrightarrow (D\sigma \to \varepsilon^{x}_{\sigma})$, for ε a Boolean expression

A28 $[y := \tau][y := \sigma]\varphi \to (D\tau \to [y := \sigma^{y}_{\tau}]\varphi)$

A29 $[y := \tau][x := \sigma]\varphi \rightarrow (D\tau \rightarrow [x := \sigma^{y}_{\tau}][y := \tau]\varphi)$,

where $x \notin Var(y := \tau)$

A30 $(\tau = \sigma) \rightarrow ([y := \tau]\varphi \leftrightarrow [y := \sigma]\varphi)$

Algebraic Expressions

A31 $D(\sigma = \tau) \leftrightarrow D\sigma \wedge D\tau$

A32 $(\sigma = \tau) \rightarrow (\varepsilon \rightarrow \varepsilon')$, where the Boolean expression ε' differs from ε only in having τ in one or more places where ε has σ

A33 $D\delta(\sigma_1, \ldots, \sigma_n) \leftrightarrow (D\sigma_1 \wedge \ldots \wedge D\sigma_n)$

A34 $\sigma = \sigma$, where σ is a *constant* algebraic expression

A35 $D(\varepsilon \supset \sigma,\tau) \leftrightarrow (\varepsilon \wedge D\sigma) \vee (\textit{not-}\varepsilon \wedge D\tau)$

A36 $((\varepsilon \supset \sigma,\tau) = \rho) \leftrightarrow (\varepsilon \wedge (\sigma = \rho)) \vee (\textit{not-}\varepsilon \wedge (\tau = \rho))$

Notice that in view of the equivalence of ε and $(\varepsilon = \textit{true})$, we could construe A15 as a special case of A36. Also A35 is just a restatement of A16, but for algebraic instead of Boolean expressions. Similarly for A31 and A17.

We have one new rule of inference:

Universal Generalisation

UG: *From* φ *infer* $\forall x\varphi$.

However, for the rule OI of Omega-Iteration we expand the class *Afm* of admissible forms, as defined at the end of §2.3. For a given language L, the class *Afm*(L) of admissible forms for L is defined by adding to the three defining conditions given for *Afm* in 2.3 the condition if $\Phi \in Afm(L)$, then $\forall x\Phi \in Afm(L)$ for any non-Boolean variable x of L.

The result 2.3.8 that for any s

$$\models_s \Phi([\varepsilon\#\alpha]\varphi) \quad \text{iff} \quad \text{for all } n,\ \models_s \Phi(\varphi_n(\varepsilon,\alpha))$$

continues to hold in all standard models for the new notion of admissible form, as the reader may verify (use Exercise 3.3.3(5) for the new inductive case).

For the language of §2.1, a *logic* was defined as a subset of the set *Fma* of formulae. Since we are now concerned with many different languages L, a more abstract stance will be taken. A logic will be regarded as a pair (Λ_a, Λ_r), where Λ_a is a collection of axiom-schemata that includes at least A1 - A36, and Λ_r is a collection of rules of inference that includes at least MP, TR, OI, and UG. Then with respect to a particular language L, by "*the logic* Λ *in* L" we shall mean the *smallest* subset of $Fma(L)$ that contains all L-formulae that are instances of members of Λ_a, and is closed under all instances in L of the rules in Λ_r.

For such a notion of a "logic" it would not be appropriate to have axioms and rules that refer to particular variables that might belong to some languages and not to others. We can formalise this requirement by introducing the notion of a *relettering* as being a function f which maps the set of L-variables injectively into itself, with $f(x)$ being of the same sort as x. The *relettering of* φ *by* f is then the formula obtained by uniformly replacing each occurrence of each variable x in φ by $f(x)$. Similarly an instance of a rule of inference can be relettered by applying f to all of its premisses and its conclusion simultaneously. Using this notion, we can say that a logic Λ must be such that in any language the class of instances of each member of Λ_a is closed under all reletterings, and similarly for the class of instances of each rule in Λ_r.

A Λ-*theory in* L is a set $\Gamma \subseteq Fma(L)$ that contains Λ in L and is closed under the two rules MP and OI as before (although OI now encompasses a wider class of admissible forms). If $\Sigma \cup \{\varphi\} \subseteq Fma(L)$, then φ is Λ-*deducible from* Σ *in* L if φ belongs to every Λ-theory in L that contains Σ. This relationship will be symbolised by "$\Sigma \vdash_\Lambda \varphi$" as before. Σ is *Λ-consistent in L* if $\Sigma \nvdash_\Lambda$ *false* in L. A Λ-theory in L is *maximal in L* if it is Λ-consistent in L and contains one of φ and $\neg\varphi$ for each $\varphi \in Fma(L)$.

3.4.1 THEOREM.

(1) *If* $\vdash_\Lambda (\varphi \to \psi)$ *then* $\vdash_\Lambda (\forall x\varphi \to \forall x\psi)$

(2) $\vdash_\Lambda \sigma = \tau \to D\sigma \wedge D\tau$

(3) $\vdash_\Lambda not\text{-}(\sigma = \tau) \to D\sigma \wedge D\tau$

(4) $\vdash_\Lambda \sigma = \tau \to \tau = \sigma$

(5) $\vdash_\Lambda \sigma = \tau \to (\sigma = \rho \to \tau = \rho)$

(6) $\vdash_\Lambda \sigma = \tau \to (\tau = \rho \to \sigma = \rho)$

(7) $\vdash_\Lambda Dx_1 \wedge \ldots \wedge Dx_n \to D\sigma$, if $Var\sigma = \{x_1, \ldots, x_n\}$

(8) $\vdash_\Lambda \bigwedge_{1 \leqslant i \leqslant n} (\sigma_i = \tau_i) \to (f(\sigma_1, \ldots, \sigma_n) = f(\tau_1, \ldots, \tau_n))$

(9) $\vdash_\Lambda \varepsilon^x_\sigma \to [x := \sigma]\varepsilon$

(10) $\vdash_\Lambda \neg\varepsilon^x_\sigma \to [x := \sigma]\neg\varepsilon$

(11) $\vdash_\Lambda [x := \sigma]\neg\varepsilon \leftrightarrow (D\sigma \to \neg\varepsilon^x_\sigma)$

Proof.

(1) If $\vdash_\Lambda \varphi \to \psi$, then by UG, $\vdash_\Lambda \forall x(\varphi \to \psi)$ and so A19 and MP give $\vdash_\Lambda \forall x\varphi \to \forall x\psi$.

(2) From the Boolean axiom A13, as in 2.4.2(2), we get $\vdash_\Lambda (\sigma = \tau) \to D(\sigma = \tau)$, from which the formula $(\sigma = \tau) \to D\sigma \wedge D\tau$ follows by A31 and PC.

(3) Using part (2),

$$\vdash_\Lambda ((\sigma = \tau) = \mathit{false}) \to D(\sigma = \tau),$$

from which A31 again gives the desired result.

(4) - (6) Similar to parts (5) - (7) of 2.4.2, but using A32 in place of A11.

(7) By induction on the formation of σ. The result is trivial (by PC) if σ is a single variable. It holds inductively if σ is $\mathfrak{f}(\sigma_1,\ldots,\sigma_n)$ by A33, since then $Var\sigma = Var\sigma_1 \cup \ldots \cup Var\sigma_n$. When σ is $(\varepsilon \supset \sigma_1, \sigma_2)$ we have $Var\sigma = Var\varepsilon \cup Var\sigma_1 \cup Var\sigma_2$, so that if the result holds for ε, σ_1, and σ_2 we get $\vdash_\Lambda \varphi \to D\sigma_1$, $\vdash_\Lambda \varphi \to D\sigma_2$ and $\vdash_\Lambda \varphi \to D\varepsilon$, where φ is the conjunction of the Dx's for $x \in Var\sigma$. Hence by A13, $\vdash_\Lambda \varphi \to (\varepsilon \vee \textit{not}\text{-}\varepsilon)$. By PC and either A16 for Boolean σ_1, σ_2 or A35 for the algebraic case, this leads to $\vdash_\Lambda \varphi \to D\sigma$.

The inductive case of σ being $(\sigma_1 = \sigma_2)$ is similar, using A17 and A31. Details are left to the reader.

(8) "$\bigwedge_{1 \leqslant i \leqslant n} (\sigma_i = \tau_i)$" abbreviates the formula $(\sigma_1 = \tau_1) \wedge \ldots \wedge (\sigma_n = \tau_n)$. We give the derivation for the case n=2.

Using part (2) of this Theorem, we first observe that

$$\vdash_\Lambda (\sigma_1 = \tau_1) \wedge (\sigma_2 = \tau_2) \to D\sigma_1 \wedge D\sigma_2.$$

Hence by A33

$$\vdash_\Lambda (\sigma_1 = \tau_1) \wedge (\sigma_2 = \tau_2) \to D\mathfrak{f}(\sigma_1,\sigma_2).$$

But

$$(\sigma_1 = \tau_1) \to (D\mathfrak{f}(\sigma_1,\sigma_2) \to \mathfrak{f}(\sigma_1,\sigma_2) = \mathfrak{f}(\tau_1,\sigma_2))$$

and

$$(\sigma_2 = \tau_2) \to (\mathfrak{f}(\sigma_1,\sigma_2) = \mathfrak{f}(\tau_1,\sigma_2) \to \mathfrak{f}(\sigma_1,\sigma_2) = \mathfrak{f}(\tau_1,\tau_2))$$

are both instances of A32. Applying PC to these last three Λ-theorems yields

$$\vdash_\Lambda (\sigma_1 = \tau_1) \wedge (\sigma_2 = \tau_2) \to (\mathfrak{f}(\sigma_1,\sigma_2) = \mathfrak{f}(\tau_1,\tau_2)).$$

(9) Since $\vdash_{PC} \varepsilon^x_\sigma \to (D\sigma \to \varepsilon^x_\sigma)$, the result follows from A27.

(10) (Defining $(\neg\varepsilon)^x_\sigma$ as $\neg(\varepsilon^x_\sigma)$ obviates the need for bracketing in this formula).

Since $\vdash_{PC} D\sigma \wedge \neg\varepsilon^x_\sigma \rightarrow \neg(D\sigma \rightarrow \varepsilon^x_\sigma)$, by A27 and PC we get

$$\vdash_\Lambda D\sigma \wedge \neg\varepsilon^x_\sigma \rightarrow \neg[x := \sigma]\varepsilon.$$

Hence by the determinism axiom A26,

$$\vdash_\Lambda D\sigma \rightarrow (\neg\varepsilon^x_\sigma \rightarrow [x := \sigma]\neg\varepsilon). \qquad \text{(i)}$$

But using A25 we can show

$$\vdash_\Lambda \neg D\sigma \rightarrow [x := \sigma]\varphi$$

(with the help of 2.4.1(6)). If φ is taken here to be $\neg\varepsilon$, by PC we get

$$\vdash_\Lambda \neg D\sigma \rightarrow (\neg\varepsilon^x_\sigma \rightarrow [x := \sigma]\neg\varepsilon) \qquad \text{(ii)}$$

PC applied to (i) and (ii) gives, finally,

$$\vdash_\Lambda \neg\varepsilon^x_\sigma \rightarrow [x := \sigma]\neg\varepsilon.$$

(11) From 2.4.1(8), $\vdash_\Lambda \neg[x := \sigma]\mathit{false} \rightarrow ([x := \sigma]\neg\varepsilon \rightarrow \neg[x := \sigma]\varepsilon)$. Then by A15, part (9), and PC, $\vdash_\Lambda D\sigma \rightarrow ([x := \sigma]\neg\varepsilon \rightarrow \neg\varepsilon^x_\sigma)$. Whence by PC, $\vdash_\Lambda [x := \sigma]\neg\varepsilon \rightarrow (D\sigma \rightarrow \neg\varepsilon^x_\sigma)$. For the converse, we have

$$\vdash_\Lambda \neg D\sigma \rightarrow [x := \sigma]\neg\varepsilon,$$

as noted in the proof of (10), and

$$\vdash_\Lambda \neg\varepsilon^x_\sigma \rightarrow [x := \sigma]\neg\varepsilon,$$

as proven in (10), and these last two Λ-theorems yield

$$\vdash_\Lambda (D\sigma \rightarrow \neg\varepsilon^x_\sigma) \rightarrow [x := \sigma]\neg\varepsilon$$

by PC. ∎

Since a logic as now defined is, at least, a logic as defined in §2.4, and since the definition of "Λ-theory" is unchanged, a good many of the results of that section, and of §2.5, remain true with no alteration to their proofs. These include 2.4.1, 2.4.2, 2.4.4, 2.4.5, 2.4.6, 2.4.7 (the Deduction Theorem) and its corollary 2.4.8 about consistency, 2.4.9 (the α-Deduction Lemma) and its Corollary 2.4.10, and 2.5.1. As to 2.4.3, part (5), viz.

$$\vdash_\Lambda \Phi([\varepsilon\#\alpha]\varphi) \to \Phi(\varphi_n(\varepsilon,\alpha)),$$

remains true, but now for all $\Phi \in Afm(L)$: the new inductive case of $\forall x\Phi$ is taken care of by 3.4.1(1). The rest of 2.4.3 holds unchanged.

3.4.2 THEOREM.

If $\Sigma \vdash_\Lambda \varphi$ in L, and $x \in X_\mu$ is an L-variable that has no occurrence in Σ, then $\Sigma \vdash_\Lambda \forall x\varphi$ in L.

Proof.

Let Γ be any Λ-theory in L that contains Σ. Put $\Delta = \{\psi \in Fma(L) : \forall x\psi \in \Gamma\}$. Our aim is to show that $\forall x\varphi \in \Gamma$, i.e. that $\varphi \in \Delta$. Since $\Sigma \vdash_\Lambda \varphi$ it suffices then to show that Δ is a Λ-theory in L that contains Σ.

Now if $\psi \in \Sigma$, $x \notin Var\psi$ by hypothesis, and so by A21, since $\Lambda \subseteq \Gamma$ we have $(\psi \to \forall x\psi) \in \Gamma$. But $\Sigma \subseteq \Gamma$, so $\psi \in \Gamma$ and hence by MP $\forall x\psi \in \Gamma$, giving $\psi \in \Delta$. Thus $\Sigma \subseteq \Delta$.

If $\vdash_\Lambda \psi$, then by UG $\vdash_\Lambda \forall x\psi$, so $\forall x\psi$ belongs to the Λ-theory Γ, giving $\psi \in \Delta$. Hence Δ contains Λ, and we are left to show its closure under MP and OI.

MP: If $(\psi \to \theta)$, $\psi \in \Delta$, then $\forall x(\psi \to \theta)$, $\forall x\psi \in \Gamma$. But by A19, $\forall x(\psi \to \theta) \to (\forall x\psi \to \forall x\theta)$ belongs to Γ, hence by MP $\forall x\theta \in \Gamma$, giving $\theta \in \Delta$ as desired.

OI: If $\{\Phi(\psi_n(\varepsilon,\alpha)) : n \in \mathbb{N}\} \subseteq \Delta$, then $\{\forall x\Phi(\psi_n(\varepsilon,\alpha)) : n \in \mathbb{N}\} \subseteq \Gamma$. But then applying the OI-closure of Γ to the admissible form $(\forall x\Phi) \in Afm(L)$, we have $\forall x\Phi([\varepsilon\#\alpha]\psi) \in \Gamma$, and so $\Phi([\varepsilon\#\alpha]\psi) \in \Delta$.

∎

(Note the formal parallelism between the proof of 3.4.2, and that of the α-Deduction Lemma 2.4.9).

3.4.3 COROLLARY.

If $\Sigma \vdash_{\Lambda} [x := y]\varphi$ *in* L, *and* $y \notin Var(\Sigma \cup \{\forall x\varphi\})$, *then* $\Sigma \vdash_{\Lambda} \forall x\varphi$ *in* L.

Proof.

Since $y \notin Var\Sigma$, 3.4.2 gives $\Sigma \vdash_{\Lambda} \forall y[x := y]\varphi$. But since $y \notin Var\varphi \cup \{x\}$, A22 gives

$$\Sigma \vdash_{\Lambda} \forall y[x := y]\varphi \rightarrow \forall x\varphi.$$

Hence the result follows by MP. ∎

RICH THEORIES

Let $L' = (Z, O, Y)$ be a language, with $Y = \{Y_\mu : \mu \in Z\}$ a Z-sorted system of variables. For each μ, let $W_\mu \subseteq Axp_\mu(L')$ be a set of algebraic L'-expressions of sort μ, and put $W = \{W_\mu : \mu \in Z\}$. Then if Γ is a Λ-theory in L', we say that W is a *system of witnesses for* Γ *in* L' if for each $\varphi \in Fma(L')$ and each variable $x \in Y_\mu$ (any μ),

if $\forall x\varphi \notin \Gamma$ then there exist some $\sigma \in W_\mu$ such that
$[x := \sigma]\varphi \notin \Gamma$.

Γ is a W-*rich* Λ-*theory in* L' if

(i) W is a system of witnesses for Γ in L', and

(ii) Γ is a *maximal* Λ-theory in L'.

3.4.4 THEOREM.

If Γ *is a* $\mathcal{W}$*-rich* Λ*-theory in* L';

(1) $\forall x_\mu \varphi \in \Gamma$ *iff for all* $\sigma \in W_\mu$, $[x_\mu := \sigma]\varphi \in \Gamma$;

(2) *if* $[x := \sigma]\varphi \notin \Gamma$, *then* $D\sigma \in \Gamma$;

(3) *if* $D\tau \in \Gamma$, *where* $\tau \in Axp_\mu(L')$, *then* $D\sigma$, $(\tau = \sigma) \in \Gamma$ *for some* $\sigma \in W_\mu$;

(4) *if* $\neg D\tau \in \Gamma$, *then for all* $\sigma \in W_\mu$ *(where* τ *is of sort* μ*)*, $(\tau = \sigma) \notin \Gamma$.

Proof.

(1) Since, by A20, $(\forall x_\mu \varphi \rightarrow [x_\mu := \sigma]\varphi \in \Gamma$, and Γ is closed under MP, we have $\forall x_\mu \varphi \in \Gamma$ only if $[x_\mu := \sigma]\varphi \in \Gamma$ for all $\sigma \in W_\mu$. The converse holds by the definition of "$\mathcal{W}$-rich".

(2) Since $\vdash_\Lambda [x := \sigma]\mathit{false} \rightarrow [x := \sigma]\varphi$, by 2.4.1(6), if $[x := \sigma]\varphi \notin \Gamma$ we have $[x := \sigma]\mathit{false} \notin \Gamma$, and so $\neg[x := \sigma]\mathit{false} \in \Gamma$ as Γ is maximal. But then A25 gives $D\sigma \in \Gamma$.

(3) Since $D\tau \in \Gamma$, $\neg(\tau = \tau) \notin \Gamma$ and so $(D\tau \rightarrow \neg(\tau = \tau)) \notin \Gamma$. If x is an L'-variable of sort μ, it then follows from 3.4.1(11) that $[x := \tau]\neg(\tau = x) \notin \Gamma$. Hence by A20, $\forall x \neg(\tau = x) \notin \Gamma$. Since Γ is $\mathcal{W}$-rich, there must then be some $\sigma \in W_\mu$ such that $[x := \sigma]\neg(\tau = x) \notin \Gamma$. Therefore by 3.4.1(11), $(D\sigma \rightarrow \neg(\tau = \sigma)) \notin \Gamma$. By the property 2.5.1(3) of maximal sets, this requires that $D\sigma \in \Gamma$ and $\neg(\tau = \sigma) \notin \Gamma$, whence by maximality $(\tau = \sigma) \in \Gamma$.

(4) If we did have $(\tau = \sigma) \in \Gamma$, 3.4.1(2) would yield $D\tau \in \Gamma$, which is impossible if $\neg D\tau \in \Gamma$, since Γ is consistent.

■

Now let $L = (Z, O, X)$ be a fixed, but arbitrary, language. In order to develop a completeness theorem for Λ in L, we extend to a new language, to be called $L^{\mathcal{W}}$, by adding new variables that are ultimately to be used as witnesses. For each $\mu \in Z$, let W_μ be a new denumerably infinite set of variables that is disjoint from the set of all L-variables, and from $W_{\mu'}$, for $\mu' \neq \mu$. Put

$W = \{W_\mu : \mu \in Z\}$, $X{+}W = \{X_\mu \cup W_\mu : \mu \in Z\}$, and $L^W = (Z, O, X{+}W)$.

First we confirm that adding new variables to L does not allow any new L-formulae to become provable:

3.4.5 THEOREM.

For any $\varphi \in Fma(L)$,

$$\vdash_\Lambda \varphi \text{ in } L \quad \text{iff} \quad \vdash_\Lambda \varphi \text{ in } L^W.$$

Proof.

The set Γ of L-formulae that are Λ-theorems in L^W includes all L-formulae that are instances of schemata in Λ_a, and is closed under the rules of Λ_r. Hence Γ is a Λ-theory in L, so contains all the Λ-theorems in L. In other words, $\vdash_\Lambda \varphi$ in L implies $\vdash_\Lambda \varphi$ in L^W.

For the converse, suppose that $\nvdash_\Lambda \varphi$ in L. Let $y \mapsto y'$ be a mapping of variables in $X{+}W$ to variables in X that

(1) for each $\mu \in Z$ maps $X_\mu \cup W_\mu$ bijectively onto X_μ; and

(2) leaves all variables in φ fixed.

Since $X_\mu \cup W_\mu$ and X_μ are denumerably infinite, and $Var\varphi$ is finite, such a transformation is readily definable. Then for each L^W-formula ψ, let ψ' be the L-formula obtained by uniformly replacing each occurrence of each variable y in ψ by y'. The transformation $\psi \mapsto \psi'$ maps $Fma(L^W)$ bijectively onto $Fma(L)$, taking instances of axiom-schemata to instances of the same schemata, and instances of rules to instances of the same rules (indeed the transformation is a relettering in the sense defined earlier in our discussion of the notion of a logic). Thus the set

$$\Gamma = \{\psi \in Fma(L^W) : \vdash_\Lambda \psi' \text{ in } L\}$$

is a Λ-theory in L^W. But φ' is just φ, as all variables in φ have $y' = y$, and so $\varphi \notin \Gamma$. Hence φ cannot be a Λ-theorem in L^W.

∎

Our next result is an analogue of Theorem 2.5.2, and its proof will take advantage of the work already done in proving 2.5.2.

3.4.6 THEOREM.

If $\Sigma \cup \{\varphi\} \subseteq Fma(L)$, then $\Sigma \vdash_\Lambda \varphi$ in L^W iff φ belongs to every W-rich Λ-theory in L^W that contains Σ.

Proof.

The implication from left to right is immediate from the definition of "$\Sigma \vdash_\Lambda \varphi$ in L^W".

Conversely, if $\Sigma \nvdash_\Lambda \varphi$ in L^W, then

$$\Gamma_0 = \Sigma \cup \{\neg\varphi\}$$

is Λ-consistent in L^W, by 2.4.8(2). We then proceed to extend Γ_0 to a W-rich Λ-theory Γ in L^W. We will then have $\Sigma \subseteq \Gamma$ and $\neg\varphi \in \Gamma$, hence $\varphi \notin \Gamma$, which will establish the Theorem.

Let $\varphi_0, \varphi_1, \varphi_2, \ldots\ldots$ be an enumeration of the *denumerable* set $Fma(L^W)$. The definition of Γ follows very closely the construction in 2.5.2, and the reader is advised to have a finger inserted at that point of the text (page 73).

Assuming inductively that Γ_n has been defined, we construct Γ_{n+1} according to one of *four* possibilities

Case 1: If $\Gamma_n \vdash_\Lambda \varphi_n$ in L^W, put $\Gamma_{n+1} = \Gamma_n \cup \{\varphi_n\}$.

Otherwise, (i.e. if $\Gamma_n \nvdash_\Lambda \varphi_n$ in L^W)

Case 2: If φ_n is neither of the form $\Phi([\varepsilon\#\alpha]\psi)$, nor of the form $\forall x\psi$, put $\Gamma_{n+1} = \Gamma_n \cup \{\neg\varphi_n\}$; otherwise

Case 3: If φ_n is of the form $\Phi([\varepsilon\#\alpha]\psi)$, define Γ_{n+1} exactly as in Case 3 of the proof of 2.5.2; otherwise

Case 4: If φ_n is of the form $\forall x\psi$, with x of sort μ say, put

$$\Gamma_{n+1} = \Gamma_n \cup \{\neg[x := w]\psi, \neg\varphi_n\},$$

where w is some variable in W_μ that does not occur in Γ_n or in φ_n. It is apparent that in this construction only *finitely* many formulae are added to Γ_0 to get Γ_n (in fact at most $2n$ are added). But Γ_0 consists only of L-formulae, and so has no W-variables at all. Hence only finitely many members of W_μ appear in $\Gamma_n \cup \{\varphi_n\}$, leaving us infinitely many ways to choose the w needed for Case 4. To be specific we could take the least of them in some fixed enumeration of W_μ.

Notice that in any case, if $\varphi_n \notin \Gamma_{n+1}$ then $\neg\varphi_n \in \Gamma_{n+1}$. Moreover in Case 4, Γ_{n+1} is Λ-consistent in L^W. For if not, then, using the Deduction Theorem and 2.4.8(2), we would have

$$\Gamma_n \vdash_\Lambda \neg[x := w]\psi \rightarrow \varphi_n.$$

But by axiom A20,

$$\Gamma_n \vdash_\Lambda \varphi_n \rightarrow [x := w]\psi.$$

This is enough to show, using PC, that

$$\Gamma_n \vdash_\Lambda [x := w]\psi \quad \text{in} \quad L^W.$$

But, by definition, $w \notin Var(\Gamma_n \cup \{\forall x\psi\})$, and so by Corollary 3.4.3 this yields

$$\Gamma_n \vdash_\Lambda \forall x\psi \quad \text{in} \quad L^W,$$

which contradicts the definition of "Case 4".

If we now put

$$\Gamma = \bigcup\{\Gamma_n : n \in \mathbb{N}\}$$

then the proof of 2.5.2 carries over as is to show that Γ is a maximal Λ-theory in L^W. But now if $\forall x\psi \notin \Gamma$ for an L^W-formula ψ, with x of sort μ, then $\forall x\psi$ is φ_n for some n, and so $\varphi_n \notin \Gamma_{n+1}$, hence $\Gamma_n \nvdash_\Lambda \varphi_n$ in L^W and we are in Case 4. By construct of Γ_{n+1}, there is then some $w \in W_\mu$ with $\neg[x := w]\psi \in \Gamma$, and so $[x := w]\psi \notin \Gamma$.

Hence Γ is W-rich as desired. ∎

3.4.7 COROLLARY.

For any $\varphi \in Fma(L)$,

$$\vdash_\Lambda \varphi \text{ in } L \quad \text{iff} \quad \varphi \text{ belongs to every } W\text{-rich } \Lambda\text{-theory in } L^W.$$

Proof.

Taking $\Sigma = \emptyset$ in the Theorem, we have that φ belongs to every W-rich Λ-theory in L^W just in case $\vdash_\Lambda \varphi$ in L^W, which, by 3.4.5, holds just in case $\vdash_\Lambda \varphi$ in L. ∎

3.5 COMPLETENESS

Let Δ be a fixed W-rich Λ-theory in the language L^W defined in the last section. We use Δ to construct a Z-sorted data type A^Δ in which elements are named by certain witnesses from W. For each $\mu \in Z$, let

$$C_\mu = \{w \in W_\mu : Dw \in \Delta\},$$

and put $C = \{C_\mu : \mu \in Z\}$. Since $[x := w]\varphi \notin \Delta$ only if $Dw \in \Delta$, by 3.4.4(2), Δ in fact has C as a system of witnesses in L^W, and so is a C-rich Λ-theory in L^W.

For $w, z \in C_\mu$, define

$$w \sim z \quad \text{iff} \quad (w = z) \in \Delta.$$

Then $\sim$ is a reflexive relation on C_μ, by definition of the latter, which is shown by the Λ-theorems $(w = z \to z = w)$ (3.4.1(4)), and $(w = z \to (z = z' \to w = z'))$ (3.4.1(6)), to be symmetric and transitive as well. So $\sim$ is an equivalence relation on C_μ. For each $w \in C_\mu$ let

$$\tilde{w} = \{z \in C_\mu : w \sim z\}$$

be the $\sim$-equivalence class of w in C_μ, and let

$$A^\Delta_\mu = \{\tilde{w} : w \in C_\mu\}$$

The original signature O is extended to a new signature O^Δ, still Z-sorted, by putting

$$O^\Delta_{\lambda,\mu} = O_{\lambda,\mu} \cup C_\mu, \qquad \text{and}$$

$$O^\Delta_{\nu,\mu} = O_{\nu,\mu} \quad \text{if} \quad \nu \neq \lambda .$$

Then the collection

$$A^\Delta = \{A^\Delta_\mu : \mu \in Z\}$$

is made into a *minimal* O^Δ-algebra in which each A^Δ_μ-element is named by one of the new constants in C_μ. This done as follows.

(i) The constant $w \in C_\mu$ is interpreted as the element

$$w_\Delta = \tilde{w} \in A^\Delta_\mu .$$

(ii) The O-constant $c \in O_{\lambda,\mu}$ is interpreted as the element $c_\Delta \in A^\Delta_\mu$ defined by

$$c_\Delta = \tilde{w} \quad \text{iff} \quad (c = w) \in \Delta.$$

To see that this definition is appropriate, observe that by A34 we have $Dc \in \Delta$, and hence by 3.4.4(3) there is some $w \in W_\mu$ with $Dw \in \Delta$, so that indeed $w \in C_\mu$, and $(c = w) \in \Delta$. But if $(c = z) \in \Delta$ for any $z \in C_\mu$, then using 3.4.1(5) we get $(w = z) \in \Delta$, so that $w \sim z$ and $\tilde{w} = \tilde{z}$. This shows that a $w \in C_\mu$ needed for the above definition of c_Δ does exist, and c_Δ is uniquely determined as $\tilde{w}$.

(iii) The operation symbol $f \in O_{\mu_1 \ldots \mu_n,\mu}$ names the operation

$$f_\Delta : A^\Delta_{\mu_1} \times \ldots \times A^\Delta_{\mu_n} \to A^\Delta_\mu ,$$

that has

$$f_\Delta(\tilde{w}_1, \ldots, \tilde{w}_n) = \tilde{w} \quad \text{iff} \quad (f(w_1, \ldots, w_n) = w) \in \Delta$$

To see that this makes sense, if $w_1, \ldots, w_n \in C_\mu$ then, using 3.4.1(7), we get $Df(w_1, \ldots, w_n) \in \Delta$. Hence by 3.4.4(3) there exists a $w \in C_\mu$ with $(f(w_1, \ldots, w_n) = w) \in \Delta$. Then as in (ii), although w may not be uniquely determined, $\tilde{w}$ is. Moreover if $w_1 \sim z_1, \ldots, w_n \sim z_n$, then by 3.4.1(8), $(f(w_1, \ldots, w_n) = f(z_1, \ldots, z_n)) \in \Delta$, and so for any $w \in C_\mu$, by 3.4.1(5) and 3.4.1(6) we get

$$(f(w_1, \ldots, w_n) = w) \in \Delta \quad \text{iff} \quad (f(z_1, \ldots, z_n) = w) \in \Delta.$$

Hence f_Δ is a well-defined operation.

This completes the definition of the $\mathcal{O}^\Delta$-algebra A^Δ.

Our next step is to build a standard A^Δ-based model M_Δ for a language L^Δ that is intermediate between $L = (Z, \mathcal{O}, X)$ and $L^W = (Z, \mathcal{O}, X+W)$. We put

$$L^\Delta = (Z, \mathcal{O}^\Delta, X).$$

In effect L^Δ results from L^W by retaining the witnesses in C as constants and deleting W from the variable-system, thereby deleting all commands of the form $(w := \sigma)$ and all formula of the form $\forall w\varphi$ for w in W. Thus $Fma(L) \subseteq Fma(L^\Delta) \subseteq Fma(L^W)$, and $Cmd(L) \subseteq Cmd(L^\Delta) \subseteq Fma(L^W)$. Moreover since an expression is *formally* just a string of symbols we actually have $Axp(L^\Delta) = Axp(L^W)$, although interpretation of an expression may differ in models of the two languages.

To define M_Δ we need one more new concept. Let

$$Diag_\mu(\Delta) = \Delta \cap \{(\sigma = \tau), \neg(\sigma = \tau) : \sigma, \tau \in Con_\mu(\mathcal{O}^\Delta)\}$$

and

$$Diag(\Delta) = \bigcup \{Diag_\mu(\Delta) : \mu \in Z\}.$$

$Diag(\Delta)$, the "*diagram*" of A^{Δ}, is a subset of $Fma(L^{\Delta})$. It consists of all formulae in Δ that are equations, or negations of equations, between *constant* O^{Δ}-expressions. All of the L^{ω}-formulae in Δ that were used to define A^{Δ} are present in $Diag(\Delta)$. In fact all members of $Diag(\Delta)$ are true under their natural interpretation in A^{Δ}, and taken as a whole they constitute a complete description of the algebraic structure of that algebra (see Theorem 3.7.2 below for a result that is based on, and amplifies, this observation).

Now let S_{Δ} be the collection of all sets $\Gamma \subseteq Fma(L^{\Delta})$ such that

(i) Γ is a C-rich Λ-theory in L^{Δ}, and

(ii) $Diag(\Delta) \subseteq \Gamma$.

3.5.1 EXERCISE.

$$\Delta \cap Fma(L^{\Delta}) \in S_{\Delta}.$$

■

3.5.2 THEOREM.

If $\sigma, \tau \in Con_{\mu}(L^{\Delta})$, *then for all* $\Gamma \in S_{\Delta}$,

$$(\sigma = \tau) \in \Gamma \quad \textit{iff} \quad (\sigma = \tau) \in \Delta.$$

Proof.

If $(\sigma = \tau) \in \Delta$, then $(\sigma = \tau) \in Diag(\Delta) \subseteq \Gamma$. On the other hand, if $(\sigma = \tau) \notin \Delta$, then as Δ is maximal, $\neg(\sigma = \tau) \in \Delta$. Hence $\neg(\sigma = \tau) \in Diag(\Delta) \subseteq \Gamma$. Thus $\neg(\sigma = \tau) \in \Gamma$, so by consistency of Γ, $(\sigma = \tau) \notin \Gamma$.

■

The next result is central to our modelling of assignment commands. The variable y involved may be Boolean.

3.5.3 THEOREM.

Let $\Gamma \in S_\Delta$ *and* $(y := \tau) \in Cmd(L^\Delta)$. *Then if* $D\tau \in \Gamma$, *we have* $\Gamma(y := \tau) \in S_\Delta$, *where*

$$\Gamma(y := \tau) = \{\varphi \in Fma(L^\Delta) : [y := \tau]\varphi \in \Gamma\}.$$

Proof.

If $D\tau \in \Gamma$, then by A25 $\neg[y := \tau]\mathit{false} \in \Gamma$. Then for the reasons given in the analysis of $\Gamma(\alpha)$ in the section 2.6 on determinism, $\Gamma(y := \tau)$ is a Λ-consistent Λ-theory in L^Δ which, by axiom A26, is maximal.

Moreover, if $\varphi \in Diag(\Delta) \subseteq \Gamma$, then φ is either a Boolean expression or the negation of a Boolean expression, and so by Theorem 3.4.1, parts (9) and (10),

$$\vdash_\Lambda \varphi^y_\tau \rightarrow [y := \tau]\varphi.$$

But by definition of $Diag(\Delta)$, the variable y does not occur in φ, so φ^y_τ is just φ itself and so belongs to the Λ-theory Γ. But then $[y := \tau]\varphi \in \Gamma$, giving $\varphi \in \Gamma(y := \tau)$. This establishes that $Diag(\Delta) \subseteq \Gamma(y := \tau)$, and it remains to show that C is a system of witnesses for $\Gamma(y := \tau)$ in L^Δ.

Suppose then that $\forall x\varphi \notin \Gamma(y := \tau)$, where $\varphi \in Fma(L^\Delta)$ and $x \in X_\mu$. Then $[y := \tau]\forall x\varphi \notin \Gamma$.

Case 1: Suppose $x=y$. Then by A23, $\forall y\varphi \notin \Gamma$. Since Γ is C-rich, it follows that there is a witness $w \in C_\mu$ such that $[y := w]\varphi \notin \Gamma$. But $D\tau \in \Gamma$, and hence $(D\tau \rightarrow [y := w]\varphi) \notin \Gamma$.

Now $\vdash_\Lambda [y := \tau][y := w]\varphi \rightarrow (D\tau \rightarrow [y := w]\varphi)$, by A28, and from this we conclude that

$$[y := \tau][y := w]\varphi \notin \Gamma,$$

giving $[y := w]\varphi \notin \Gamma(y := \tau)$ as desired.

Case 2: We have $x \neq y$. Now since $D\tau \in \Gamma$, by 3.4.4(3) there is a constant $z \in C_\mu$ such that $(\tau = z) \in \Gamma$. By invoking A30 (with σ as z) we then deduce that $[y := z]\forall x\varphi \notin \Gamma$. But now x does not occur in $(y := z)$, and so we can apply A24 to get $\forall x[y := z]\varphi \notin \Gamma$. It follows that there is a witness $w \in C_\mu$ such that

$$[x := w][y := z]\varphi \notin \Gamma.$$

Then, reasoning as in Case 1, but using A29 in place of A28, we find that

$$[y := z][x := w]\varphi \notin \Gamma.$$

By A30 again, this leads to

$$[y := \tau][x := w]\varphi \notin \Gamma,$$

and hence

$$[x := w]\varphi \notin \Gamma(y := \tau).$$

This completes the proof that the set $\Gamma(y := \tau)$ is C-rich, and hence completes the proof that it belongs to S_Δ.

■

We now define the *canonical* L^Δ*-model* to be the structure

$$M_\Delta = (A^\Delta, S_\Delta, v, [\![\cdot]\!]),$$

where

(1) for each $\Gamma \in S_\Delta$ and $p \in Bvb$,

$$v_\Gamma(p) = \begin{cases} 1 & \text{if } p \in \Gamma \\ 0 & \text{if } not\text{-}p \in \Gamma \\ \omega & \text{if } \neg Dp \in \Gamma \end{cases}$$

(2) For each variable $x \in X_\mu$,

(i) if $\neg Dx \in \Gamma$, $v_\Gamma(x) = \omega$; while

(ii) if $Dx \in \Gamma$ then

$$v_\Gamma(x) = \tilde{w} \in A^\Delta_\mu \quad \text{iff} \quad (x = w) \in \Gamma.$$

(3) For an assignment command $(y := \tau)$,

$$\Gamma [\![y := \tau]\!] \Gamma' \quad \text{iff} \quad \Gamma' = \Gamma(y := \tau) \text{ and } \Gamma(y := \tau) \in S_\Delta,$$

while for a structured command $[\![\alpha]\!]$ is defined by the standard-model condition for α.

With regard to the definition of $v_\Gamma(x)$ in (2), we know that exactly one of $\neg Dx$ and Dx belongs to Γ. If $\neg Dx \in \Gamma$, then by 3.4.4(4) $(x = w) \notin \Gamma$ for all $w \in C_\mu$. On the other hand if $Dx \in \Gamma$ then by 3.4.4(3), $(x = w) \in \Gamma$ for some $w \in C_\mu$. Then, as in the construction of A^Δ, $\tilde{w}$ is uniquely determined. For if also $(x = z) \in \Gamma$, where $z \in C_\mu$, then by 3.4.1(5), $(w = z) \in \Gamma$. But $(w = z) \in Diag(\Delta)$ and hence from .5.2, $(w = z) \in \Delta$, giving $w \sim z$ and $\tilde{w} = \tilde{z}$. Thus $v_\Gamma(x)$ is well-defined as $\tilde{w}$.

The relation $[\![y := \tau]\!]$ determines a partial function on S_Δ which is defined at Γ just in case $\Gamma(y := \tau) \in S_\Delta$, i.e. just in case $\mathit{false} \notin \Gamma(y := \tau)$. This last condition holds if and only if $[y := \tau]\mathit{false} \notin \Gamma$. Hence by A25, $[\![y := \tau]\!]$ is defined at Γ just in case $D\tau \in \Gamma$.

.5.4 THEOREM.

In M_Δ,

1) *For any* $\varepsilon \in Bexp(L^\Delta)$,

$$v_\Gamma(\varepsilon) = \begin{cases} 1 & \mathit{if} \quad \varepsilon \in \Gamma \\ 0 & \mathit{if} \quad \mathit{not}\text{-}\varepsilon \in \Gamma \\ \omega & \mathit{if} \quad \neg D\varepsilon \in \Gamma \end{cases}$$

2) *For any* $\sigma \in Aexp_\mu(L^\Delta)$,

(i) *if* $\neg D\sigma \in \Gamma$, *then* $v_\Gamma(\sigma) = \omega$, *while*

(ii) *if* $D\sigma \in \Gamma$, *then* $v_\Gamma(\sigma) \in A^\Delta_\mu$, *and for* $w \in C_\mu$,

$$v_\Gamma(\sigma) = \tilde{w} \quad \mathit{iff} \quad (\sigma = w) \in \Gamma.$$

Proof.

The two statements are interrelated, since algebraic expressions can contain Boolean ones, and vice versa.

(1). The proof of (1) proceeds exactly as for its analogue Theorem 2.5.4, except for the one new case - when ε is $(\sigma = \tau)$ for some $\sigma, \tau \in Axp_\mu(L^\Delta)$. In this case we make the inductive assumption that part (2) of this Theorem holds for σ and for τ.

(a) If $(\sigma = \tau) \in \Gamma$, then by A31, $D\sigma$, $D\tau \in \Gamma$, and, by hypothesis on σ and τ, from 2(ii) we have $(\sigma = w)$, $(\tau = z) \in \Gamma$ for some $w, z \in C_\mu$. Then since $(\sigma = \tau) \in \Gamma$, using 3.4.1(5) we get $(\tau = w) \in \Gamma$ and then $(w = z) \in \Gamma$. Hence by 3.5.2, $(w = z) \in \Delta$, giving $w \sim z$. Thus $v_\Gamma(\sigma) = \tilde{w} = \tilde{z} = v_\Gamma(\tau)$, giving $v_\Gamma(\sigma = \tau) = 1$.

(b) If *not*-$(\sigma = \tau) \in \Gamma$, then by 3.4.1(3) $D\sigma$, $D\tau \in \Gamma$, so as in case (a), $v_\Gamma(\sigma) = \tilde{w}$ and $v_\Gamma(\tau) = \tilde{z}$ for some $w, z \in C_\mu$. But if $\tilde{w} = \tilde{z}$, then $(w = z) \in \Delta$, hence $(w = z) \in \Gamma$ by 3.5.2. However since $(\sigma = w)$, $(\tau = z) \in \Gamma$, this leads via 3.4.1 to $(\sigma = \tau) \in \Gamma$, which is incompatible with *not*-$(\sigma = \tau) \in \Gamma$. Hence we have $v_\Gamma(\sigma) \neq v_\Gamma(\tau)$ with σ and τ both defined at Γ, so $v_\Gamma(\sigma = \tau) = 0$.

(c) If $\neg D(\sigma = \tau) \in \Gamma$, then via A31, $D\sigma \wedge D\tau \notin \Gamma$, so either $D\sigma \notin \Gamma$ or $D\tau \notin \Gamma$. Hence by the inductive hypothesis either $v_\Gamma(\sigma)$ or $v_\Gamma(\tau)$ is ω. Thus $v_\Gamma(\sigma = \tau)$ is ω.

Hence (1) holds for $(\sigma = \tau)$.

(2). The proof proceeds by induction on the formation of σ.

(a) If σ is a variable, (2) holds by the definition of M_Δ and subsequent observations.

(b) Let σ be a constant $c \in O^\Delta_{\lambda,\mu}$.

If $c \in O_{\lambda,\mu}$, then $Dc \in \Gamma$ by A34, $v_\Gamma(c) = c_\Delta$, and the definition of c_Δ in A^Δ_μ gives that for any $w \in C_\mu$,

$$v_\Gamma(c) = \tilde{w} \quad \text{iff} \quad (c = w) \in \Delta.$$

But for such w, $(c = w) \in Diag(\Delta)$, so

$$(c = w) \in \Delta \quad \text{iff} \quad (c = w) \in \Gamma.$$

On the other hand, if $c \in C_\mu$, then $Dc \in Diag(\Delta)$, so $Dc \in \Gamma$, and $v_\Gamma(c) = \tilde{c}$. Then for $w \in C_\mu$,

$$v_\Gamma(c) = \tilde{w} \quad \text{iff} \quad \tilde{c} = \tilde{w} \quad \text{iff} \quad (c = w) \in \Delta \quad \text{iff} \quad (c = w) \in \Gamma.$$

Hence (2) holds for c.

(c) Suppose σ is $f(\sigma_1, \ldots, \sigma_n)$ where f belongs to $O_{\mu_1 \ldots \mu_n, \mu}$, and σ_i to $Axp_{\mu_i}(L^\Delta)$ for $1 \leqslant i \leqslant n$. Assume inductively that (2) holds for each of the σ_i's.

Now by A33 we have

$$D\sigma \in \Gamma \quad \text{iff} \quad D\sigma_1, \ldots, D\sigma_n \in \Gamma.$$

(i) If $\neg D\sigma \in \Gamma$, then $D\sigma \notin \Gamma$, hence $D\sigma_i \notin \Gamma$ for some i. The induction hypothesis on σ_i then gives $v_\Gamma(\sigma_i) = \omega$, which by definition yields $v_\Gamma(\sigma) = \omega$.

(ii) If $D\sigma \in \Gamma$, then, for each i, $D\sigma_i \in \Gamma$ and so by the hypothesis there exists a constant $w_i \in C_{\mu_i}$ with $v_\Gamma(\sigma_i) = \tilde{w}_i$ and $(\sigma_i = w_i) \in \Gamma$. Then by definition of $v_\Gamma(\sigma)$ we have, for $w \in C_\mu$

$$\begin{aligned} v_\Gamma(\sigma) = \tilde{w} \quad & \text{iff} \quad f_\Delta(\tilde{w}_1, \ldots, \tilde{w}_n) = \tilde{w} \\ & \text{iff} \quad (f(w_1, \ldots, w_n) = w) \in \Delta \qquad \text{(defn. } f_\Delta) \\ & \text{iff} \quad (f(w_1, \ldots, w_n) = w) \in \Gamma \qquad (3.5.2) \end{aligned}$$

But by 3.4.1(8), $(\sigma = f(w_1, \ldots, w_n)) \in \Gamma$, and this, similarly to previous cases, implies that

$$(f(w_1, \ldots, w_n) = w) \in \Gamma \quad \text{iff} \quad (\sigma = w) \in \Gamma.$$

Hence (2) holds for $f(\sigma_1, \ldots, \sigma_n)$.

(d) Suppose σ is $(\varepsilon \supset \rho,\tau)$, where $\varepsilon \in Bxp(L^{\Delta})$ and $\rho,\tau \in Axp_{\mu}(L^{\Delta})$. This time our induction hypothesis is that (2) holds for ρ and τ, while (1) holds for ε.

In view of A35, we have

$$D\sigma \in \Gamma \quad \text{iff} \quad (\varepsilon \wedge D\rho) \in \Gamma \quad \text{or} \quad (\textit{not-}\varepsilon \wedge D\tau) \in \Gamma$$

(i) If $\neg D\sigma \in \Gamma$, then neither $(\varepsilon \wedge D\rho)$ nor $(\textit{not-}\varepsilon \wedge D\tau)$ belong to Γ. But we know (2.5.1(6)) that exactly one of $\neg D\varepsilon$, $\textit{not-}\varepsilon$, and ε belongs to Γ.

If $\neg D\varepsilon \in \Gamma$, then the induction hypothesis on ε gives $v_{\Gamma}(\varepsilon) = \omega$, hence $v_{\Gamma}(\sigma) = \omega$.

If $\varepsilon \in \Gamma$, then as $(\varepsilon \wedge D\rho) \notin \Gamma$, we must have $\neg D\rho \in \Gamma$. Hence by the induction hypothesis on ε and ρ, $v_{\Gamma}(\varepsilon) = 1$ and $v_{\Gamma}(\rho) = \omega$, making $v_{\Gamma}(\sigma) = \omega$.

Finally, if $\textit{not-}\varepsilon \in \Gamma$ similarly reasoning yields $v_{\Gamma}(\varepsilon) = 0$ and $v_{\Gamma}(\tau) = \omega$, whence $v_{\Gamma}(\sigma) = \omega$.

Thus in any case, if $\neg D\sigma \in \Gamma$, then $v_{\Gamma}(\sigma) = \omega$.

(ii) If $D\sigma \in \Gamma$, then one of $(\varepsilon \wedge D\rho)$ and $(\textit{not-}\varepsilon \wedge D\tau)$ must belong to Γ. Suppose in fact that $(\varepsilon \wedge D\rho) \in \Gamma$, so ε, $D\rho \in \Gamma$. The hypothesis on ε then gives $v_{\Gamma}(\varepsilon) = 1$, whence $v_{\Gamma}(\sigma) = v_{\Gamma}(\rho)$, while the hypothesis on ρ implies that $v_{\Gamma}(\rho) = \tilde{z}$ for some $z \in C_{\mu}$ having $(\rho = z) \in \Gamma$. But then for any $w \in C_{\mu}$

$$\begin{aligned} v_{\Gamma}(\sigma) = \tilde{w} \quad & \text{iff} \quad \tilde{z} = \tilde{w} \\ & \text{iff} \quad (z = w) \in \Delta \\ & \text{iff} \quad (z = w) \in \Gamma \qquad (3.5.2) \\ & \text{iff} \quad (\rho = w) \in \Gamma \qquad (\text{as } (\rho = z) \in \Gamma). \end{aligned}$$

But since $\varepsilon \in \Gamma$, $(\rho = w) \in \Gamma$ iff $\varepsilon \wedge (\rho = w) \in \Gamma$. Moreover $\textit{not-}\varepsilon \notin \Gamma$ and so $\textit{not-}\varepsilon \wedge (\rho = w) \notin \Gamma$ for any w. It follows by A36 that $(\sigma = w) \in \Gamma$ iff $\varepsilon \wedge (\rho = w) \in$ and so altogether

$$v_{\Gamma}(\sigma) = \tilde{w} \quad \text{iff} \quad (\sigma = w) \in \Gamma.$$

The case of $(\textit{not-}\varepsilon \wedge D\tau) \in \Gamma$ follows similar lines, and it is left to the reader to fill in the details and thereby complete the proof that (2) holds for $(\varepsilon \supset \rho,\tau)$, and hence complete the inductive proof of the Theorem. ■

Theorem 3.5.4 is the first step in the derivation of a "Fundamental Theorem" for the model M_Δ. But for that we need to verify that we are dealing with the right kind of structure.

3.5.5 THEOREM.

M_Δ is a standard model for L^Δ.

Proof.

We have only to check the standard-model conditions for an assignment $(y := \tau) \in Cmd(L^\Delta)$.

(i) If $v_\Gamma(\tau) \neq \omega$, then by 3.5.4(2) $D\tau \in \Gamma$, which guarantees, as noted earlier, that $\Gamma(y := \tau) \in S_\Delta$. Then taking $\Gamma' = \Gamma(y := \tau)$ gives a Γ' with $\Gamma [\![y := \tau]\!] \Gamma'$ as desired.

(ii) Suppose $\Gamma [\![y := \tau]\!] \Gamma'$. We require that $v_\Gamma =_y v_{\Gamma'}$ and $v_{\Gamma'}(y) = v_\Gamma(\tau) \neq \omega$.

By definition of M_Δ we have $\Gamma(y := \tau) = \Gamma' \in S_\Delta$. Hence, as $false \notin \Gamma'$, $[y := \tau] false \notin \Gamma$, so by A25 $D\tau \in \Gamma$. 3.5.4(2) then gives $v_\Gamma(\tau) \neq \omega$.

Thus $v_\Gamma(\tau) = \tilde{w}$ for some constant w having $(\tau = w) \in \Gamma$. But by 3.4.1(9),

$$\vdash_\Lambda (\tau = w) \rightarrow [y := \tau](y = w)$$

and so $[y := \tau](y = w) \in \Gamma$, giving $(y = w) \in \Gamma'$, and so by 3.5.4(2) $v_{\Gamma'}(y) = \tilde{w} = v_\Gamma(\tau)$.

But if x is any variable of sort μ say, with x distinct from y, then 3.4.1(9) gives

$$\vdash_\Lambda (x = w) \rightarrow [y := \tau](x = w),$$

so that if $v_\Gamma(x) = \tilde{w} \in A^\Delta_\mu$, then, by similar reasoning, it follows that $v_{\Gamma'}(x) = \tilde{w}$. On the other hand if $v_\Gamma(x) = \omega$, then $\neg Dx \in \Gamma$, and, since 3.4.1(10) gives

$$\vdash_\Lambda \neg Dx \rightarrow [y := \tau]\neg Dx,$$

we deduce $\neg Dx \in \Gamma'$, and so $v_{\Gamma'}(x) = \omega$. Thus in either case $v_{\Gamma}(x) = v_{\Gamma'}(x)$.

Finally, if p is a Boolean variable then 3.4.1(9) and 3.4.1(10) give all of

$$p \rightarrow [y := \tau]p$$

$$not\text{-}p \rightarrow [y := \tau]not\text{-}p$$

$$\neg Dp \rightarrow [y := \tau]\neg Dp$$

as Λ-theorems. From these by similar arguments, and using 3.5.4(1), it follows that $v_{\Gamma}(p) = v_{\Gamma'}(p)$.

Hence $v_{\Gamma} =_y v_{\Gamma'}$. ∎

The case of the Fundamental Theorem for the formula $[\alpha]\varphi$ depends on the two "α-Lemmata", which in Chapter 2 were the results 2.5.6 and 2.5.7. The analogues for M_{Δ} now follow.

3.5.6 FIRST α-LEMMA.

In M_{Δ}, for all $\alpha \in Cmd(L^{\Delta})$,

$$\Gamma [\![\alpha]\!] \Gamma' \quad \textit{only if} \quad \{\varphi : [\alpha]\varphi \in \Gamma\} \subseteq \Gamma'$$

Proof.

If α is an assignment, the result holds by definition of $[\![\alpha]\!]$. The inductive cases for α a structured command then follow exactly as in the proof of 2.5.6, and as in §2.7 for alternations $(\alpha|\beta)$. ∎

3.5.7 SECOND α-LEMMA.

If $\alpha \in Cmd(L^{\Delta})$, *then for all* $\varphi \in Fma(L^{\Delta})$,

$$\text{if } M_{\Delta} \models_{\Gamma} \varphi \text{ implies } \varphi \in \Gamma \text{ for all } \Gamma \in S_{\Delta},$$

then

$$M_{\Delta} \models_{\Gamma} [\alpha]\varphi \quad \text{implies} \quad [\alpha]\varphi \in \Gamma \text{ for all } \Gamma \in S_{\Delta}.$$

Proof.

It suffices to prove the result for α an assignment $(y := \tau)$, since the inductive cases follow as in Chapter 2.

So, suppose $M_{\Delta} \models_{\Gamma} [y := \tau]\varphi$. Then if $D\tau \in \Gamma$, we know that $\Gamma(y := \tau) \in S_{\Delta}$ and $\Gamma [\![y := \tau]\!] \Gamma(y := \tau)$. But then φ holds at $\Gamma(y := \tau)$ in M_{Δ}, and so the hypothesis on φ gives $\varphi \in \Gamma(y := \tau)$. Hence $[y := \tau]\varphi \in \Gamma$. On the other hand if $D\tau \notin \Gamma$ we have $[y := \tau]\mathit{false} \in \Gamma$ via A25. But

$$\vdash_{\Lambda} [y := \tau]\mathit{false} \rightarrow [y := \tau]\varphi,$$

(cf. 2.4.1(6)), and so we reach $[y := \tau]\varphi \in \Gamma$ in any case. ■

3.5.8 FUNDAMENTAL THEOREM FOR M_{Δ}.

For any $\varphi \in Fma(L^{\Delta})$,

$$M_{\Delta} \models_{\Gamma} \varphi \quad \text{iff} \quad \varphi \in \Gamma.$$

Proof.

For $\varphi \in Bxp(L^{\Delta})$, the result follows from 3.5.4(1). The inductive case for $\rightarrow$ is unchanged, while that for $[\alpha]$ follows from the two α-Lemmata (3.5.6, 3.5.7) as in the Fundamental Theorem of §2.5.

We have one new case:- when φ is $\forall x\psi$ for some $x \in X_{\mu}$ and $\psi \in Fma(L^{\Delta})$. We make the inductive assumption that the result holds for ψ. But then, as just noted, the result holds for $[\alpha]\psi$ for all $\alpha \in Cmd(L^{\Delta})$, and so in particular holds for $[x := w]\psi$ whenever $w \in C_{\mu}$.

Recalling that in M_{Δ} each $\tilde{w} \in A^{\Delta}_{\mu}$ is "named" by the constant w, we then have

$$M_\Delta \models_\Gamma \forall x\psi \quad \text{iff} \quad \text{for all } \tilde{w} \in A^\Delta_\mu \quad M_\Delta \models_\Gamma [x := w]\psi$$

(by 3.3.9(1))

$$\text{iff} \quad \text{for all } w \in C_\mu, \ \ [x := w]\psi \in \Gamma$$

$$\text{iff} \quad \forall x\psi \in \Gamma \qquad (3.4.4(1))$$

Hence the result holds for $\forall x\psi$ as desired. ■

Let PL denote the smallest logical system for our present type of language - the system whose axioms are exactly A1 - A36 and whose rules are exactly MP, TR, OI, and UG.

3.5.9 THE COMPLETENESS THEOREM FOR PL.

Let $L = (Z,O,X)$ be any language. Then for $\varphi \in Fma(L)$ the following are equivalent:

(1) $\vdash_{PL} \varphi$ *in* L ;

(2) φ *is valid in all natural* L*-models* ;

(3) φ *is valid in all standard* L*-models.*

Proof.

(1) implies (2) : For any O-algebra A, the set $\{\varphi \in Fma(L) : M_A \models \varphi\}$ contains all instances of the PL-axioms and is closed under the PL-rules. Hence it is a PL-theory in L which contains all PL-theorems in L.

(2) implies (3) : By 3.3.8(3).

(3) implies (1) : Suppose that $\nvdash_{PL} \varphi$ in L. Then if W is a new Z-sorted system of variables disjoint from X, by 3.4.7 there exists a W-rich PL-theory Δ in the language L^W with $\varphi \notin \Delta$. Then if $\Delta_0 = \Delta \cap Fma(L^\Delta)$ we have $\varphi \notin \Delta_0$, while $\Delta_0 \in S_\Delta$ (Exercise 3.5. But $\varphi \in Fma(L^\Delta)$, and so by the Fundamental Theorem, φ fails to hold at state Δ_0 in the standard model M_Δ. ■

.5.10 EXERCISES.

Let φ be any first-order formula.

1) Show that if x is not free in φ, then

$$\varphi \to \forall x\varphi$$

; valid in all standard models, hence is PL-derivable. Give a proof-theoretic erivation of it.

2) Do the same for the formula

$$[x := \sigma]\varphi \leftrightarrow (D\sigma \to \varphi^x_\sigma). \qquad \blacksquare$$

TRONG COMPLETENESS

In §2.5 (cf. the remarks prior to Theorem 2.5.4) we derived a strong com- leteness theorem for the non-quantificational language based on Boolean variables d program letters. This took the form:

> every Λ-consistent subset of *Fma* is satisfied at some state of some standard Λ-model (viz. the model M_Λ).

To consider the analogous property for the languages of this chapter, ppose that Σ is Λ-consistent in L. If Σ is also Λ-consistent in L^W, then by .4.6 (with φ as *false*), there will be a W-rich Λ-theory Δ in L^W with $\Sigma \subseteq \Delta$. But en with $\Delta_o = \Delta \cap Fma(L^\Delta)$, it would follow from the Fundamental Theorem for M_Δ that is simultaneously satisfied at Δ_o in the standard model M_Δ.

Thus the kind of strong completeness theorem we may contemplate is:

> every Λ-consistent subset of $Fma(L)$ is satisfied at some state of some standard Λ-model.

it in order for the above argument to go through, we need to know, for $\Sigma \subseteq Fma(L)$, at

(1) if Σ is Λ-consistent in L, then Σ is Λ-consistent in L^W.

If $(X_\mu - Var\Sigma)$ is infinite, for each μ, a proof of (1) can be obtained by the method used to prove Theorem 3.4.5. For, the bijective mapping $y \longmapsto y'$ of variables in $X+W$ to variables in X can be arranged to leave all members of $Var\Sigma$ fixed. Then if $\Sigma \nvdash_\Lambda false$ in L, the set

$$\{\psi \in Fma(L^W) : \Sigma \vdash_\Lambda \psi' \text{ in } L\}$$

will be a consistent Λ-theory in L^W containing Σ, showing that $\Sigma \nvdash_\Lambda false$ in L^W.

A proof of (1) in the case that $Var\Sigma$ is cofinite in X_μ has thus far eluded the author, and the problem is offered as a challenge to the interested reader.

There is another notion of strong completeness, corresponding to stronger concepts of "consistency" and "realisability", that is already covered by the constructions of this section. This notion takes the form:

every consistent set of formulae has a model.

To say that Σ *has* M *as a model*, or that M *is a model of* Σ, means that all members of Σ are *valid* in M, i.e. hold at all states (which is how we have used the concept of "Λ-model" in relation to a logic Λ). This is stricter than requiring that Σ be satisfied at some state of M, and both properties have been widely discussed in the literature of first-order logic. In some studies (e.g. Chang and Keisler (1973)), the distinction does not really emerge, as the word "model" is applied only to sentences and a sentence is satisfied by one valuation if and only if it is satisfied by all (cf. Exercise 3.3.1(2)).

The set of formulae valid in a particular standard Λ-model is a Λ-theory, but in general it has additional properties to closure under MP and OI. In fact it is a *logic* in its own right, being closed under TR, UG, and reletterings of its members (reletterings were defined in the discussion of the definition of "logic" on page 139). This indicates that a more restricted kind of deducibility is appropriate to a notion of "consistent" that corresponds to "has a model". We will say that φ

is *strictly* Λ-deducible from Σ in L if φ belongs to every Λ-theory in L that contains Σ and is closed under TR, under UG, and under reletterings in L of its members. Then Σ will be called *strongly* Λ-consistent in L if *false* is not strictly Λ-deducible from Σ in L.

The strict-deducibility relation, in which the use of UG is allowed, corresponds to the deducibility relation discussed for first-order logic in, e.g., Shoenfield (1967) and Monk (1976), and for infinitary logic in Aczel (1973) and Barwise (1975, §III.4). These studies do not need to include closure under relettering in their definition, since that is a derivable property of the standard proof theory of first-order languages. This follows from the observation that if ψ is obtained by relettering a bound variable in the first-order formula φ, then φ and ψ are provably materially equivalent, i.e. $\vdash (\varphi \leftrightarrow \psi)$ (cf. e.g. Monk (1976), Theorem 10.59), while if ψ arises by relettering a free variable in φ then ψ is derivable from φ via UG and the universal instantiation axiom $\forall x\varphi \rightarrow \varphi^x_y$.

Now if Λ is a logic, and $\Sigma \subseteq Fma(L)$, we may define a new logic $\Lambda(\Sigma)$ by adding the members of Σ as new axioms to the axioms of Λ. In doing this we choose to treat the members of Σ as axiom *schemata*, so that with reference to any language L' (with possibly $L' = L$) we include as axioms of $\Lambda(\Sigma)$ in L' all L'-formulae obtainable as reletterings in L' of formulae from Σ.

If Σ is *strongly* Λ-consistent in L, then there must exist a Λ-theory Γ in L that is closed under TR, UG, and reletterings in L, but with *false* $\notin \Gamma$. But then Γ contains all axioms of $\Lambda(\Sigma)$ in L, so its closure properties ensure that it contains all $\Lambda(\Sigma)$-theorems in L. Hence $\nvdash_{\Lambda(\Sigma)}$ *false* in L. Corollary 3.4.7 then implies that there exists at least one $\mathcal{W}$-rich $\Lambda(\Sigma)$-theory Δ in the language $L^{\mathcal{W}}$. Therefore we can carry through the construction of the standard model M_Δ based on the set of $\mathcal{C}$-rich $\Lambda(\Sigma)$-theories in L^Δ that contain $Diag(\Delta)$. Since these theories contain all $\Lambda(\Sigma)$-theorems in L^Δ, it follows from the Fundamental Theorem for M_Δ that the latter is a model for Σ itself, as well as for Λ in L^Δ. Thus we have established that

> every strongly Λ-consistent subset of $Fma(L)$ has a standard Λ-model.

3.6 NON-ENUMERABILITY OF PL

The rule OI is an infinitary version of Hoare's Iteration Rule, each corresponding naturally to the semantic condition

$$[\![\varepsilon\#\alpha]\!] \subseteq [\![\varepsilon]\alpha]\!]^{\infty} \lceil \mathit{not}\text{-}\varepsilon .$$

However if OI is replaced by Hoare's Rule, the resulting system is weaker than PL and does not axiomatise the class of formulae valid in all natural (or standard) models. This follows from the fact, to be proven now, that the set of PL-theorems is not effectively enumerable. To show this we use the characterisation outlined in §1.10 of the data type $\mathbb{N}$.

Let $O^{\mathbb{N}}$ be a signature having a single sort, an individual constant c_o, a one-placed function letter $\mathfrak{f}$, and two two-placed function letters $\oplus$ and $\otimes$. In the language $L^{\mathbb{N}} = (O^{\mathbb{N}}, X)$, with X a single set of individual variables, let $\varphi_{\mathbb{N}}$ be the conjunction of the seven formulae

N1 $\quad \forall x \neg(\mathfrak{f}x = c_o)$

N2 $\quad \forall x \forall y(\mathfrak{f}x = \mathfrak{f}y \rightarrow x = y)$

N3 $\quad \forall x(x \oplus c_o = x)$

N4 $\quad \forall x \forall y(x \oplus \mathfrak{f}y = \mathfrak{f}(x \oplus y))$

N5 $\quad \forall x(x \otimes c_o = c_o)$

N6 $\quad \forall x \forall y(x \otimes \mathfrak{f}y = (x \otimes y) \oplus x)$

N7 $\quad [x := c_o]\forall y \neg[\alpha_{\mathbb{N}}]\,\mathit{false}$,

where $\alpha_{\mathbb{N}}$ is the command

$$(\mathit{not}\text{-}(x = y)\#(x := \mathfrak{f}x)),$$

i.e. *while not*-$(x = y)$ *do* $x := \mathfrak{f}x$, and x and y are two distinct variables.

The structure $(\mathbb{N}, 0, \mathfrak{f}_{\mathbb{N}}, +, \times)$ is an $O^{\mathbb{N}}$-algebra, wherein c_o is interpreted as the number 0, $\mathfrak{f}$ as the successor function $\mathfrak{f}_{\mathbb{N}} : n \longmapsto n+1$, and $\oplus$ and $\otimes$ as the operations + and × of addition and multiplication on $\mathbb{N}$. The first-order sentences

N1 - N6 are all true in $\mathbb{N}$, and hence are valid in the natural model $M_{\mathbb{N}}$ (3.3.5(1)). N7 is also valid in this model: when initiated in state $s \in S_{\mathbb{N}}$, $\alpha_{\mathbb{N}}$ halts, following execution of $(x := c_0)$, after n iterations of $(x := \delta x)$, given that $n = t(y)$, where t is the state $s(x/0)$.

3.6.1 THEOREM.

Let $(A, 0_A, \delta_A, +_A, \times_A)$ *be an* $0^{\mathbb{N}}$*-algebra, and* s *a state in the natural model* M_A. *Then* $\varphi_{\mathbb{N}}$ *holds at* s *in* M_A *if and only if* $\mathbb{N}$ *is isomorphic to* A.

Proof.

By "$\mathbb{N}$ is isomorphic to A" we mean that there exists a function $h : \mathbb{N} \to A$ mapping $\mathbb{N}$ *bijectively* onto A and preserving the $0^{\mathbb{N}}$-operations, i.e. having

(1) $h(0) = 0_A$,

(2) $h(n+1) = \delta_A(h(n))$,

(3) $h(m+n) = h(m) +_A h(n)$, and

(4) $h(m\times n) = h(m) \times_A h(n)$.

Now if such an *isomorphism* h exists, it establishes that A and $\mathbb{N}$ are identical copies of the same abstract structure: by identifying n with $h(n)$ we can identify the two algebras, thus associating each $s \in S_{\mathbb{N}}$ with a unique state in S_A, and thereby identifying the two models $M_{\mathbb{N}}$ and M_A. The argument that shows $\varphi_{\mathbb{N}}$ to be valid in $M_{\mathbb{N}}$ can then be transferred to establish $M_A \models \varphi_{\mathbb{N}}$, whence $M_A \models_s \varphi_{\mathbb{N}}$.

Conversely, suppose $M_A \models_s \varphi_{\mathbb{N}}$ (the point really is that since there are no "free" variables in $\varphi_{\mathbb{N}}$ to be interpreted in state s, $\varphi_{\mathbb{N}}$ will hold at one state if and only if it holds in all states). Then each of the first-order formulae N1 - N6 hold at s, and so is satisfied in A by the valuation s. Since each of them is a sentence, they are therefore all true of A (3.3.4(3)). Thus the operations 0_A, δ_A, $+_A$, $\times_A$ on A have all the properties expressed by N1 - N6.

A sequence $f^0(0_A)$, $f^1(0_A)$, $f^2(0_A)$, ... of A-elements is defined inductively by putting

$$f^0(0_A) = 0_A$$

and
$$f^{n+1}(0_A) = \delta_A(f^n(0_A)).$$

Then setting $h(n) = f^n(0_A)$ defines a map $h : \mathbb{N} \to A$ which is the desired isomorphism. Property (1) $(h(0) = 0_A)$ is immediate, and since $h(n+1) = \delta_A(f^n(0_A)) = \delta_A(h(n))$, property (2) follows readily. (3) is proved by induction on n, for fixed m, using the structure of A as expressed by N3 and N4. (4) has a similar proof using N5 and N6, while the role of N1 and N2 is to establish that

$$h(m) = h(n) \text{ only if } m=n,$$

i.e. that h is one-to-one.

These observations are all familiar from the axiomatic study of $\mathbb{N}$, and the details need not be repeated here. In fact it is known that the definition given for h is the only one we could have used: this is the only function from $\mathbb{N}$ to A that satisfies properties (1) and (2) (cf. Henkin (1960), Theorem 1). The only novelty here is that in the presence of N7, h maps $\mathbb{N}$ onto A, and so becomes an isomorphism. For, since N7 holds at s in M_A, we have

$$M_A \models_{s_o} \forall y \neg [\alpha_{\mathbb{N}}] \mathit{false},$$

where s_o is the state (A-valuation) $s(x/0_A)$ that has $s [\![x := c_o]\!] s_o$ and $s_o(x) = 0_A$. But then for any $b \in A$, by taking t to be $s_o(y/b)$ we get

$$M_A \models_t \neg [\alpha_{\mathbb{N}}] \mathit{false}.$$

Since M_A is standard it follows that for some $n \in \mathbb{N}$ there exist M_A-states $t_o, \ldots, t_n$ with $t_o = t$, $t_n(\mathit{not}\text{-}\mathit{not}\text{-}(x=y)) = 1$, whence $t_n(x=y) = 1$, with $t_i(\mathit{not}\text{-}(x=y)) = 1$ and $t_i [\![x := \delta x]\!] t_{i+1}$ whenever $0 \leq i < n$. This means that

$t_i =_x t_{i+1}$ and $t_{i+1}(x) = \delta_A(t_i(x))$ for $0 \leq i < n$. It follows that $t_0 =_x t_n$, and so as y is distinct from x,

$$t_n(y) = t_0(y) = b.$$

But it also follows, by a simple induction, that for $0 \leq i \leq n$, $t_i(x) = \delta_A^i(t_0(x))$. Now $t_0(x) = s_0(x) = 0_A$, and so these facts yield

$$t_n(x) = f^n(0_A) = h(n).$$

But $(x=y)$ holds at t_n, whence $t_n(x) = t_n(y)$, i.e. $h(n) = b$.

This proves that h is onto, as desired. ∎

3.6.2 COROLLARY.

For any $\psi \in Fma(L^{\mathbb{N}})$,

(1) $M_{\mathbb{N}} \models \psi$ *iff* $\vdash_{PL} (\varphi_{\mathbb{N}} \to \psi)$ *in* $L^{\mathbb{N}}$;

(2) *If* ψ *is a first-order sentence, then*

$$\mathbb{N} \models \psi \quad iff \quad \vdash_{PL} (\varphi_{\mathbb{N}} \to \psi) \text{ in } L^{\mathbb{N}}.$$

Proof.

(1) If $\vdash_{PL} (\varphi_{\mathbb{N}} \to \psi)$ then $M_{\mathbb{N}} \models (\varphi_{\mathbb{N}} \to \psi)$. But $M_{\mathbb{N}} \models \varphi_{\mathbb{N}}$, whence $M_{\mathbb{N}} \models \psi$.

Conversely, if $\nvdash_{PL} \varphi_{\mathbb{N}} \to \psi$, then by the Completeness Theorem 3.5.9 there exists a natural $L^{\mathbb{N}}$-model M_A having a state s with $M_A \models_s \varphi_{\mathbb{N}}$ but $M_A \not\models_s \psi$. Then by 3.6.1, $\mathbb{N}$ is isomorphic to A, so we may identify $M_{\mathbb{N}}$ with M_A. But $M_A \not\models \psi$, whence $M_{\mathbb{N}} \not\models \psi$.

(2) From (1), since 3.3.5(2) gives

$$\mathbb{N} \models \psi \quad \text{iff} \quad M_{\mathbb{N}} \models \psi.$$

∎

3.6.3 THEOREM.

The set of PL-*theorems in* $L^{\mathbb{N}}$ *is not effectively enumerable.*

Proof.

We can effectively determine by inspection whether any given $L^{\mathbb{N}}$-formula is of the form $\varphi_{\mathbb{N}} \rightarrow \psi$ for some first-order sentence ψ. Thus if there were an algorithm for enumerating the PL-theorems we could go through this enumeration picking out the ones of the form $\varphi_{\mathbb{N}} \rightarrow \psi$. By 3.6.2(2) this would give us an effective procedure for enumerating the first-order sentences that are true in the structure $\mathbb{N}$. However we know from Gödel's Incompleteness Theorem and Church's Thesis that no such effective procedure exists. ■

We can now explain properly why the infinitary rule OI cannot be replaced by Hoare's Rule, or indeed by any other finitary rule(s). The point is that in a proof theory in which all rules of inference take only finitely many premisses, the theorems can be characterised as those formulae that have a proof-sequence of finite length (cf. §2.4 for the definition of "proof-sequence"). Briefly, the argument is this: if Γ is the set of formulae having finite proof-sequences, then Γ (i) contains all axioms and (ii) is closed under the finitary rules of inference, but is a subset of any other set having these two properties, and so is the smallest such set.

Therefore, by enumerating the formula-sequences of finite length, which is always possible for a denumerable language, we could enumerate the set of theorems *if* we could decide of each sequence, as it appears, whether it is a proof-sequence or not. But to be able to do this we need only two very weak conditions: namely that

(1) the set of axioms be effectively enumerable, and

(2) the set of rules of inference be effectively enumerable, and each rule be effective (i.e. we can effectively decide whether something is an instance of that rule or not).

If (1) and (2) are satisfied, then given the enumerations of the axioms and rules, and an enumeration of the finite formula-sequences, the following algorithm will eventually (albeit inefficiently) generate all proof-sequences, and hence all theorems.

Stage n: Test each of the first n formula-sequences to see if it is a proof-sequence derived from amongst the first n axioms by using at most the first n rules.

Thus any finitary axiom system satisfying (1) and (2) has an effectively enumerable set of theorems, and so, by 3.6.3 and the Completeness Theorem for PL, cannot axiomatise the class of $L^{\mathbb{N}}$-formulae valid in all natural models.

3.7 AXIOMATISING THE THEORY OF A DATA TYPE.

In the language $L^{\mathbb{N}}$ for the model $\mathbb{N}$, let PLN denote the logic generated by adding the formula $\varphi_{\mathbb{N}}$ as an extra axiom to PL. Then PLN axiomatises the *theory of the* (natural) *model* $M_{\mathbb{N}}$, i.e. the set

$$\{\psi \in Fma(L^{\mathbb{N}}) \ : \ M_{\mathbb{N}} \models \psi\}.$$

We have

3.7.1 THEOREM.

For any $\psi \in Fma(L^{\mathbb{N}})$,

$$\vdash_{PLN} \psi \quad iff \quad M_{\mathbb{N}} \models \psi.$$

Proof.

The theory of $M_{\mathbb{N}}$ contains all the PLN-axioms and is closed under the PLN-rules (i.e. the PL-rules), and so includes all PLN-theorems.

Conversely, if $M_{\mathbb{N}} \models \psi$ then $\vdash_{PL} \varphi_{\mathbb{N}} \to \psi$ (3.6.2(1)), and so $\vdash_{PLN} \varphi_{\mathbb{N}} \to \psi$. But $\vdash_{PLN} \varphi_{\mathbb{N}}$, and hence by MP, $\vdash_{PLN} \psi$.

■

(It follows from this result that

$$\vdash_{PLN} \psi \quad \text{iff} \quad \mathbb{N} \models \psi$$

whenever ψ is a first-order sentence, and so there can be no algorithm for generating the PLN-theorems.)

In this section we consider ways of doing for a general data type A what we have just done for $\mathbb{N}$, i.e. ways of axiomatising the theory of the natural model M_A.

First of all, if the Z-sorted O-algebra is *finite*, i.e. if $\cup\{A_\mu : \mu \in Z\}$ is a finite set, then we can obtain a first-order sentence φ_A in the language L^A which (analogously to $\varphi_{\mathbb{N}}$) has the algebra A as its only model up to isomorphism. The idea is that in L^A we have a constant to name each of the finitely many A-elements and the structure of A can be completely described by a finite number of variable-free equations and inequalities involving these constants.

A simple example will convey the method of constructing φ_A: suppose A is a one-sorted algebra with only two elements, a and b, and a single operation δ_A having $\delta_A(a) = \delta_A(b) = a$. Then in L^A we have two constants c and d, with c_A being a and d_A being b. We take φ_A as the conjunction of the sentences

$$\neg(c = d)$$

$$(\delta c = c)$$

$$(\delta d = c)$$

$$\forall y((y = c) \vee (y = d)).$$

Then any algebra B having $B \models \varphi_A$ will be an isomorphic copy of A. To exhibit the underlying machinery quite explicitly, define $h : A \to B$ by putting $h(a) = c_B$ (the B-element named by c) and $h(b) = d_B$. Then the first sentence guarantees that h is one-to-one; the next two that h preserves the operation δ i.e. $h(\delta_A(z)) = \delta_B(h(z))$ for all $z \in A$; and the last sentence ensures that c_B and d_B are the only members of B, so that h is *onto*.

Thus for a finite algebra A we define PLA to be the logic generated in the language L^A by adding φ_A as an extra axiom to PL. Then the arguments we used for

$\mathbb{N}$ and $\mathbb{N}$ can be mimicked to show that

$$\vdash_{PLA} \psi \quad \text{iff} \quad M_A \models \psi.$$

This leaves us to deal with infinite algebras. Since we are concerned with omputationally significant data types we will assume, for reasons explained in §3.1, hat A is a *denumerably* infinite $\mathcal{O}$-minimal algebra. Thus each member of A is named y a constant $\mathcal{O}$-expression, and in view of the cardinality restriction we may presume he signature $\mathcal{O}$ to have only countably many symbols, so that the language $L = (Z,\mathcal{O},X)$ as denumerably many formulae.

However it is no longer possible to find a first-order sentence, or even et of such sentences, to characterise the infinite structure A. It is a basic fact f the metatheory of first-order logic, due to A. Tarski, that any set of sentences ith a denumerable model has models of arbitrarily large infinite cardinality. The est we can do is produce a set of sentences that gives a partial characterisation f A, in the sense that its models are just those algebras that include A as a sub- lgebra. This set of sentences is called the *diagram* of A, and is denoted $Diag(A)$. ts definition is similar to that of the set $Diag(\Delta)$ used earlier to construct the lgebra A^{Δ} (indeed we shall have $Diag(A^{\Delta}) = Diag(\Delta)$), and proceeds as follows.

A *constant $\mathcal{O}$-equation* of sort μ is a Boolean expression of the form $(\sigma = \tau)$, here $\sigma,\tau \in Con_{\mu}(\mathcal{O})$. Such an equation is *true in* A just in case σ_A and τ_A are the ame element of A_{μ}. By the *equational theory* of an $\mathcal{O}$-algebra A we shall mean the et of all constant equations (of all sorts) that are true in A. Then $Diag(A)$ is he union of the equational theory of A with the set of all negations $\neg(\sigma = \tau)$ of hose constant equations $(\sigma = \tau)$ that are *not* in the equational theory. Such negat- ons are true in A, since the constant equations that are not in the equational heory are precisely those that are false in A. Hence A is a model of $Diag(A)$.

.7.2 THEOREM.

An $\mathcal{O}$-algebra B is a model of $Diag(A)$ if and only if A is (isomorphic to) subalgebra of B.

Proof.

This is a well-known result from classical model theory (cf. e.g. Chang and Keisler (1973), Proposition 2.1.8). It is proven as follows.

Suppose every member of *Diag*(A) is true in $\mathcal{B}$. For each sort μ define a map $h_\mu : A_\mu \rightarrow B_\mu$, as follows. If $a \in A_\mu$, since A is $\mathcal{O}$-minimal there exists a $\sigma \in Con_\mu(\mathcal{O})$ such that a is σ_A: put $h_\mu(a) = \sigma_B$, the interpretation in $\mathcal{B}$ of σ. Now if a is also τ_A for some other expression τ, then A $\models (\sigma = \tau)$. Hence $(\sigma = \tau) \in$ *Diag*(A), so $\mathcal{B} \models (\sigma = \tau)$ and $\sigma_B = \tau_B$. This shows that h_μ is well-defined. Other members of *Diag*(A) establish, similarly, that h_μ is one-to-one and preserves all operations of the signature $\mathcal{O}$. Thus the h-image of A in $\mathcal{B}$ is a sub-algebra of $\mathcal{B}$ that is isomorphic to A.

Conversely, if A is a sub-algebra of $\mathcal{B}$, then σ_A and σ_B are the same element for each $\sigma \in Con_\mu(\mathcal{O})$, and so A and $\mathcal{B}$ satisfy the same constant equations and their negations. Hence $\mathcal{B}$ is a model of *Diag*(A). Finally then, if A is isomorphic to a sub-algebra A' of $\mathcal{B}$, we find that *Diag*(A) = *Diag*(A') and the same conclusion is reached.

∎

3.7.3 COROLLARY.

Let B *be a model of* Diag(A) *in which every element is named by some* $\sigma \in Con_\mu(\mathcal{O})$. *Then* A *and* B *are isomorphic.*

Proof.

In this case, each $b \in B_\mu$ is σ_B for some σ, so that $b = h_\mu(\sigma_A)$. Thus each map h_μ is also *onto*, hence bijective, which is enough to establish isomorphism.

∎

From Theorem 3.7.2 we can show that by adding *Diag*(A) as a set of new axioms to PL we obtain a logic that axiomatises the class of L-formulae valid in all models M_B, where A is a subalgebra of $\mathcal{B}$. For this system we cannot avoid in general having A as a *proper* subalgebra of $\mathcal{B}$: to build a countermodel for a non-theorem φ by the echniques of §3.5, we have first to expand $\{\neg\varphi\}$ to a rich theory, and for this we eed to introduce new witnesses which may in the constructed model denote new elenents that are not in A. In the language of the proof of 3.7.2 (cf. also 3.7.3), here are no first-order sentences that can be added to *Diag*(A) to force the map h_μ o be onto.

In the case of $\mathbb{N}$, we were able to find a modal formula that forced h_μ to e onto, but that depended on the particular nature of the structure involved. For general algebra A the problem can instead be solved by introducing a new infinitary ule:

he A-Rule.

From $\{[x_\mu := \sigma]\varphi : \sigma \in Con_\mu(0)\}$ *infer* $\forall x\varphi$.

he classical analogue of this, in the first-order language of $\mathbb{N}$, is the

mega-Rule.

From $\{\psi_n^x : n \in \mathbb{N}\}$ *infer* $\forall x\psi$, where n is the constant expression

$$\underbrace{s(s \ldots (s}_{n \text{ times}}\, c_0)\ldots)$$

hat names n in $\mathbb{N}$.

It is known that adjoining the Omega Rule to N1 - N6 and the usual machinery f first-order logic gives an axiomatisation of the first-order theory of $\mathbb{N}$. Why his is so may be seen from the following result and its consequences.

.7.4 THEOREM.

Let Λ *be any logic containing the* A-*rule. Then for all* $\varphi \in Fma(L)$,

$\vdash_\Lambda \varphi$ *in* L *iff* φ *belongs to every* $Con(0)$*-rich* Λ*-theory in* L.

Proof.

The proof follows the construction used for Theorem 3.4.6, taking $\Sigma = \emptyset$. If $\nvdash_\Lambda \varphi$ in L we extend $\Gamma_o = \{\neg\varphi\}$ to a $Con(O)$-rich Λ-theory, remaining within the language L. The only difficulty arises in Case 4 of the definition of Γ_{n+1}, where we have $\Gamma_n \nvdash_\Lambda \varphi_n$ and φ_n is of the form $\forall x_\mu \psi$. But this time the presence of the A-rule in Λ implies that for some $\sigma \in Con_\mu(O)$,

$$\Gamma_n \nvdash_\Lambda [x_\mu := \sigma]\psi.$$

Then putting $\Gamma_{n+1} = \Gamma_n \cup \{\neg[x_\mu := \sigma]\psi, \neg\varphi_n\}$, makes Γ_{n+1} Λ-consistent in L, just as in the proof of 3.4.6. But the rest of the latter then goes through unchanged to construct a Λ-theory Γ in L, with $\varphi \notin \Gamma$, and with $Con(O)$ as a system of witnesses for Γ in L. ■

To axiomatise the theory of M_A, we take PLA to be the logic generated in L by adding $Diag(A)$ to the set of PL-axioms, and the A-Rule to the PL-rules. In order finally to prove that

$$\vdash_{PLA} \varphi \quad \text{iff} \quad M_A \models \varphi$$

we argue as follows. If $\nvdash_{PLA} \varphi$ then there is a $Con(O)$-rich PLA-theory Δ in L with $\varphi \notin \Delta$. By following the method of §3.5 we then construct a standard model M_Δ, based on an algebra A^Δ, that rejects φ. Hence the natural model M_{A^Δ} rejects φ. But now A^Δ_μ is the quotient of the set $Con_\mu(O)$ itself by the equivalence relation "$(\sigma = \tau) \in \Delta$". This is because, by axiom A34, $D\sigma$ is in Δ for *every* witness $\sigma \in Con_\mu(O)$.

In A^Δ we define, as previously, the interpretation of an individual constant symbol $\sigma \in O_{\lambda,\mu}$ by putting

$$\sigma_\Delta = \tilde{\tau} \in A^\Delta_\mu \quad \text{iff} \quad (\sigma = \tau) \in \Delta.$$

But then we can prove inductively that this biconditional holds for any constant xpression $\sigma \in Con_{\mu}(\mathcal{O})$. But, as just noted, $(\sigma = \sigma) \in \Delta$, so that

$$\sigma_{\Delta} = \tilde{\sigma}.$$

his means that every A^{Δ}-element is named by a member of $Con(\mathcal{O})$, i.e. A^{Δ} is $\mathcal{O}$-minimal. t also implies that

$$\sigma_{\Delta} = \tau_{\Delta} \quad \text{iff} \quad (\sigma = \tau) \in \Delta.$$

ince, by definition of PLA, $Diag(A) \subseteq \Delta$, we then have that A^{Δ} is a model of $Diag(A)$, o that, by Corollary 3.7.4, A is isomorphic to A^{Δ}. Hence we can identify M_A with he falsifying model $M_{A^{\Delta}}$ for φ, and conclude that $M_A \not\models \varphi$.

Finally, to show that all PLA-theorems are M_A-valid the only new observation eeded is that, by the $\mathcal{O}$-minimality of A, the theory of M_A is closed under the A-Rule cf. 3.3.9(1)).

HE CONCEPT OF DATA TYPE REVISITED.

In order for an algebraic structure to be suitable for processing by a omputer, the basic relationships between its elements must be algorithmically eterminable. The machine must be capable of effectively evaluating a constant xpression (like $(37 \oplus ((4 \otimes 9) \oplus (62 \otimes 3)))$ in $L^{\mathbb{N}}$), and hence of deciding whether r not two such expressions have the same value. In other words it must be able to etermine whether any given constant equation belongs to the equational theory of he algebra.

Thus it seems reasonable to require of a data type A that its equational heory be a decidable set. But if we can decide which equations are in a set then e can decide which are not, and so if the equational theory is decidable, $Diag(A)$ ill be as well. In that case the logic PLA will have a decidable set of axioms.

The deliberations of this chapter lead us to the following proposal for an bstract definition of "data type":

a data type is a many-sorted algebra that is denumerable and minimal, and has a decidable equational theory.

If the operations of A are computable, then *Diag*(A) will indeed be decidable. For in that case we can effectively compute the values σ_A and τ_A of constant expressions σ,τ and compare them. This gives an effective procedure for deciding the truth of any constant equation in A. On the other hand, if *Diag*(A) is decidable, then we can show that the A-operations are computable *if* we can effectively list out the A-elements (of each sort). To see why this is so, assume *Diag*(A) is decidable and suppose, for instance, that we wish to find $f_A(a)$, where f_A is a one-placed operation taking values in A_μ. Given an effective listing of A_μ, we can systematically generate all constant equations $f(c_a) = c_b$, for $b \in A_\mu$, and test each of them in turn for membership of *Diag*(A), i.e. for truth. This gives an effective procedure for finding $f_A(a)$. In sum then we see that for an algebra A in which each carrier A_μ is effectively enumerable, decidability of *Diag*(A) is precisely equivalent to the requirement that the A-operations be computable.

3.8 FREEDOM AND SUBSTITUTION

Our whole approach to axiomatisation has been based on the replacement of the notion "φ^x_σ" by "$[x := \sigma]\varphi$". This has proven more tractable than dealing with the problem of defining freedom of variables and substitutability of free variables in modal formulae that contain commands α. However these concepts can be developed for some such formulae, and in this section the beginnings of this theory are sketched. The basic definitions are set out, and the main facts about them stated, but the proofs are left to the interested reader.

Rules for Freedom.

The notion of an occurrence of a variable x in a program α being *free in* α will be defined first. Such an occurrence is *bound* in α if it is not free in α.

x is *totally free* in α if it has no bound occurrence in α (possibly no occurrence at all).

The definition is by induction on the formation of α.

a. If α is the assignment $(x := \sigma)$, then every occurrence of a variable within σ is free in α, while the occurrence of x to the left of the symbol := is bound in α.

b. If α is the composite $(\beta;\gamma)$ then

(i) an occurrence of x in β is free in α iff it is free in β;

(ii) an occurrence of x in γ is free in α iff it is free in γ and also x is totally free in β.

c. If α is the conditional $(\varepsilon \Rightarrow \beta,\gamma)$ then each occurrence of x within ε is free in α, while an occurrence of x in β or γ respectively is free in α iff it is free in β or γ respectively.

d. If α is $(\varepsilon\#\beta)$ then an occurrence of x in α is free in α iff x is totally free in β.

e. If α is $(\beta|\gamma)$ then an occurrence of x in β, respectively γ, is free in α iff it is free in β, respectively γ.

Next we define the notion of a free occurrence in a *formula*.

1. If φ is a Boolean expression, every occurrence of a variable in φ is free in φ.

2. If φ is $(\psi \rightarrow \theta)$ then an occurrence of x in ψ, respectively θ, is free in φ iff it is free in ψ, respectively θ.

3. If φ is $[\alpha]\psi$, then

(i) an occurrence of x in α is free in φ iff it is free in α;

(ii) an occurrence of x in ψ is free in φ iff it is free in ψ and also x is totally free in α.

4. If φ is $\forall y\psi$, then

(i) if $y = x$, every occurrence of x in φ is bound;

(ii) if $y \neq x$, an occurrence of x is free in φ iff it is free in ψ.

Rules for Substitution.

To define φ^x_σ we first give a separate definition of α^x_σ. This is done by induction, first stating what it means for x to be *replaceable* by σ in φ, and then giving the definition of α^x_σ only when that condition is fulfilled.

a. If α is the assignment $(y := \tau)$ then x is replaceable by σ in α iff

either (i) $y = x$,

or (ii) $y \neq x$ and y does not occur in σ.

Then α^x_σ is $(y := \tau^x_\sigma)$.

b. If α is $(\beta;\gamma)$ then x is replaceable by σ in α iff

(i) x occurs bound in β and x is replaceable by σ in β, in which case

$$\alpha^x_\sigma \text{ is } (\beta^x_\sigma ; \gamma),$$

or else

(ii) x is totally free in β and replaceable by σ in both β and γ, in which case

$$\alpha^x_\sigma \text{ is } (\beta^x_\sigma ; \gamma^x_\sigma).$$

c. If α is $(\varepsilon \Rightarrow \beta,\gamma)$ then x is replaceable by σ in α iff it is replaceable by σ in both β and γ and also is either totally free in both or else occurs bound in both.

α^x_σ is $(\varepsilon^x_\sigma \Rightarrow \beta^x_\sigma, \gamma^x_\sigma)$.

d. If α is $(\varepsilon\#\beta)$ then x is replaceable by σ in α iff it is replaceable by σ in β and is also totally free in β.

Then α^x_σ is $(\varepsilon^x_\sigma \# \beta^x_\sigma)$.

e. If α is $(\beta|\gamma)$, x is replaceable by σ in α iff it is replaceable by σ in both β and γ and also is totally free in both, or else occurs bound in both. Then

$$\alpha^x_\sigma \text{ is } (\beta^x_\sigma \mid \gamma^x_\sigma).$$

Finally, for formulae we have the following rules.

1. If φ is a Boolean expression, then x is replaceable by σ in φ, and φ^x_σ, as defined previously, is the expression obtained by replacing every occurrence on x in φ by σ.

2. If φ is $(\psi \to \theta)$, x is replaceable by σ in φ iff it is replaceable by σ in both ψ and θ. Then

$$\varphi^x_\sigma \text{ is } (\psi^x_\sigma \to \theta^x_\sigma).$$

3. If φ is $[\alpha]\psi$, then x is replaceable by σ in φ iff

(i) x occurs bound in α and is replaceable by σ in α, in which case

$$\varphi^x_\sigma \text{ is } [\alpha^x_\sigma]\psi ;$$

or else

(ii) x is totally free in α and is replaceable by σ in both α and ψ, in which case

$$\varphi^x_\sigma \text{ is } [\alpha^x_\sigma]\psi^x_\sigma .$$

4. If φ is $\forall y\psi$, then x is replaceable by σ iff

(i) $x = y$, in which case

$$\varphi^x_\sigma \text{ is } \varphi,$$

or else

(ii) $x \neq y$ and x is replaceable by σ in ψ, and also y does not occur in σ. In this case

$$\varphi^x_\sigma \text{ is } \forall y\psi^x_\sigma .$$

3.8.1 THEOREM.

Suppose that x *is replaceable by* σ *in the* L^A*-command* α. *In the natural model* M_A *let* $s,t \in S_A$ *have* $s \llbracket x := \sigma \rrbracket t$. *Then*

(1) *if* x *occurs bound in* α, *we have*

$$t \llbracket \alpha \rrbracket t' \quad \textit{iff} \quad s \llbracket \alpha^x_\sigma \rrbracket t' ;$$

(2) *if* x *is totally free in* α, *we have*

$$t \llbracket \alpha \rrbracket t' \quad \textit{iff there exists } s' \textit{ with } s \llbracket \alpha^x_\sigma \rrbracket s' \quad \textit{and} \quad s' \llbracket x := \sigma \rrbracket t'$$

■

The second part of this theorem is somewhat reminiscent of Theorem 3.3.12, and its role in the next result is analogous to the use of 3.3.12 in proving Theorem 3.3.13.

3.8.2 THEOREM.

Suppose that x *is replaceable by* σ *in the* L^A*-formula* φ. *Then in* M_A, *if* $s \llbracket x := \sigma \rrbracket t$ *we have*

$$M_A \models_s \varphi^x_\sigma \quad \textit{iff} \quad M_A \models_t \varphi. \qquad ■$$

Of course in any model in which this Theorem holds,

$$\varphi^x_\sigma \rightarrow [x := \sigma]\varphi$$

will be valid. But in a natural model, where there are enough states, it gives also the validity of

$$[x := \sigma]\varphi \rightarrow (D\sigma \rightarrow \varphi^x_\sigma) .$$

Thus the formula

$$[x := \sigma]\varphi \leftrightarrow (D\sigma \rightarrow \varphi^x_\sigma)$$

is valid in all natural models, and therefore in all standard ones.

APPENDIX 1

SOME RELATED STUDIES

To conclude Part I we take a brief look at the work of other scholars in the field of programming logics. Our survey does not claim to be exhaustive, or even representative: for the most part it focuses on studies of the central problem that has motivated this book - the question of *completeness* of an axiomatisation.

ENGELER'S USE OF INFINITARY LANGUAGE

One of the first attempts to describe algorithmic properties in languages more powerful than those of first-order logic was made by Erwin Engeler (1967). He made use of the *infinitary* language $L_{\omega_1\omega}$, which is obtained by extending the formation rules for first-order L-formulae by allowing *countably long* disjunctions and conjunctions. These are formulae of the types

$$\bigvee_{i \in I} \varphi_i \quad \text{and} \quad \bigwedge_{i \in I} \varphi_i$$

respectively, where I is a countable (finite or denumerable) index set, that have the semantics

$$A \models \bigvee_{i \in I} \varphi_i[s] \quad \text{iff} \quad \text{for some } i \in I, \ A \models \varphi_i[s]$$

$$A \models \bigwedge_{i \in I} \varphi_i[s] \quad \text{iff} \quad \text{for all } i \in I, \ A \models \varphi_i[s] .$$

The typical program studied by Engeler is a finite sequence of *labelled* instructions of the forms

k: *if* ε *then go to* p *else go to* q

k: *do* α *then go to* p

The natural number k is the label of the instruction in each case, while p and q are labels of (possibly) other instructions. The operation α is typically an assignment to a variable. Termination is caused by an instruction to "*go to* j" when there is no instruction labelled j in the program.

With each program α of this type there is shown to correspond a formula φ_α of $L_{\omega_1\omega}$ that is true in A just in case α terminates in A for every input. In our notation,

$$A \models \varphi_\alpha \quad \text{iff} \quad M_A \models \neg[\alpha]\mathit{false}.$$

φ_α is said to *express an algorithmic property*. An example of such a property is "x_0 is a natural number", which is shown to correspond to termination of the number-theoretic program

1: *do* $x_1 := 0$ *then go to* 2

2: *if* $x_1 = x_0$ *then go to* 4 *else go to* 3

3: *do* $x_1 := x_1+1$ *then go to* 2

whose connection with the command $\alpha_{\mathbb{N}}$ of §3.6 should be apparent.

This theory is developed more fully in the book *Formal Languages : Automata and Structures* (Engeler, 1968). Proof theory is discussed via the notion of a "*sequent*" S, written

$$\Phi \rightarrow \Psi ,$$

which consists of two countable sets of quantifier-free formulae of $L_{\omega_1\omega}$. S is a *valid* sequent if a valuation that satisfies all of Φ in any given structure must satisfy at least one member of Ψ in that structure as well. Thus S is valid when the formula

$$\bigwedge\Phi \rightarrow \bigvee\Psi$$

is true in all structures.

An *axiom* is, essentially, a valid sequent having Φ and Ψ as finite sets of atomic formulae. A formal proof is presented as a "tree" of sequents, with axioms at the tips of the branches and the sequent to be "proved" at the root. The sequent at each node is to be thought of as being obtained from the ones immediately above it by applying a rule of inference. Engeler shows how to systematically generate a tree $T(S)$ of sequents with S as root, using syntactic operations that preserve validity of sequents. His Completeness Theorem then takes the form:

> *if* S *is valid then all branches of* $T(S)$ *are finite and terminate with axioms.*

In a later paper (Engeler 1975), other algorithmic properties are presented, including characterisations of the notions of "Archimedean ordered field" and "formally real field", and a study of geometrical operations for two-dimensional real affine geometry. The use of the standard complete proof-system for $L_{\omega_1\omega}$ is now advocated, and the termination concept is discussed as an n-ary predicate

$$Term_{\alpha}(x_1, \ldots, x_n)$$

where $x_1, \ldots, x_n$ (abbreviated to χ) are the variables of α. $Term_{\alpha}$ holds of an n-tuple $(a_1, \ldots, a_n)$ just in case α halts on input $a_1, \ldots, a_n$. $Term_{\alpha}(\chi)$ is shown to be definable as a disjunction of a sequence of quantifier-free first-order formulae in the variables χ. Thus the algorithmic property associated with α is expressed by the $L_{\omega_1\omega}$-sentence

$$\forall \chi Term_{\alpha}(\chi).$$

The problem of partial correctness of α is formulated in terms of a $2n$-ary predicate $Trans_{\alpha}(x_1, \ldots, x_n ; y_1, \ldots, y_n)$ which captures the computation performed by α. This predicate holds of $(a_1, \ldots, a_n ; b_1, \ldots, b_n)$ exactly when α with input $a_1, \ldots, a_n$ terminates with output $b_1, \ldots, b_n$. Thus a correctness assertion for α has the typical form

$$\forall \chi, y(\varphi(\chi) \wedge Trans_{\alpha}(\chi;y) \rightarrow \psi(y)).$$

But then the correctness problem reduces to the termination problem, for Engeler observes (p.241) that "$Trans_\alpha(\chi, y)$ can easily be expressed as $Term_\beta(\chi, y)$ for a new program β which arises from α by first storing away the values of y, then executing α and finally checking the actual outcome against the stored y values."

ALGORITHMIC LOGIC

Engeler's work was taken up and adapted by A. Salwicki (1970) who, in conjunction with a number of colleagues at Warsaw, developed the school of *Algorithmic Logic*. A comprehensive account of their work is given by Banachowski, Kreczmar, Mirkowska, Rasiowa, and Salwicki (1977), and a brief survey may be found also in Salwicki (1977).

Salwicki's "atomic" commands are "parallel" substitutions of the form

$$[x_1/\tau_1 \ \dots \ x_n/\tau_n]$$

which corresponds to a *simultaneous* performance of all the assignments $(x_1 := \tau_1), \dots, (x_n := \tau_n)$. (Included is the *empty* substitution [ ], corresponding to *skip*.) From these, further deterministic commands are generated by formation of $[\varepsilon]$, $\circ[\alpha\beta]$, $\underline{v}[\varepsilon\alpha\beta]$, $*[\varepsilon\alpha\beta]$, where ε is an open (quantifier-free) formula, and α,β are commands. These correspond, respectively, to ε? (cf. §2.6), (α;β), (*if* ε *then* α *else* β), and ((*while* $\neg\varepsilon$ *do* α);β). The latter was subsequently replaced by $*[\varepsilon\alpha]$, corresponding to (*while* ε *do* α), in a paper by Banachowski.

The rules for generation of formulae allow formation of

$$\alpha\varphi, \quad \bigcup\alpha\varphi, \quad \text{and} \quad \bigcap\alpha\varphi.$$

The first of these corresponds, in our notation, to $\neg[\alpha]\neg\varphi$, and the others are the existential and universal *iteration quantifiers*, with the informal interpretations

"after some finite number of iterations of α,φ", and

"every finite number of iterations of α terminates with φ true", respectively.

(This language was subsequently extended in a paper of Kreczmar to include the classical quantifiers $\forall x$, $\exists x$).

Using these concepts, the property "x_0 is a natural number", is expressed by the formula

$$[x_1/0] \cup [x_1/x_1+1](x_1 = x_0).$$

As an example of the use of $\cap$, consider the property "x is of infinite order" in a group with identity e (i.e. no power of x is equal to e). This can be expressed by

$$[y/e] \cap [y/yx](y \neq e)$$

The semantics of Salwicki's language, relative to an appropriate algebra A, assigns to each formula φ a function

$$\varphi_A : W \to \mathbb{B},$$

and to each command α a partial function

$$\alpha_A : W \to W,$$

where W is the set of totally-defined A-valuations. α_A is defined in the same manner as $[\![\alpha]\!]$ in the natural model over A (§3.6). The key clauses for φ_A are

$$(\alpha\varphi)_A(s) = \begin{cases} \varphi_A(\alpha_A(s)), & \text{if } \alpha_A(s) \text{ defined} \\ 0 & \text{otherwise} \end{cases}$$

$$(\cup\alpha\varphi)_A(s) = \sup_{n \in \mathbb{N}} (\alpha^n\varphi)_A(s)$$

$$(\cap\alpha\varphi)_A(s) = \inf_{n \in \mathbb{N}} (\alpha^n\varphi)_A(s),$$

where, inductively, $\alpha^0\varphi$ is φ, and $\alpha^{n+1}\varphi$ is $\alpha(\alpha^n\varphi)$.

A completeness theorem for this semantics was first given by G. Mirkowska, using the following infinitary rules for the iteration quantifiers:

From $(\psi \rightarrow \beta(\alpha^n \varphi))$ for all n, infer $(\psi \rightarrow \beta \cap \alpha\varphi)$;

From $(\beta(\alpha^n \varphi) \rightarrow \psi)$ for all n, infer $\beta \cup \alpha\varphi \rightarrow \psi$.

Iteration commands were handled by axioms that transformed $*[\varepsilon\alpha\beta]\varphi$ into an equivalent formula involving $\cup$. For the simpler *while*-commands this requires the single axiom

$$*[\varepsilon\alpha]\varphi \leftrightarrow \cup \ \underline{\mathrm{v}} \ [\varepsilon\alpha[\ ]](\neg\varepsilon \wedge \varphi).$$

The proof of completeness employed the Boolean algebraic techniques first introduced by Rasiowa and Sikorski (1950). The result was later extended by Banachowski to the language including $\forall$ and $\exists$.

More recently, Mirkowska (1979, 1980) has enlarged algorithmic logic to include non-deterministic programs by allowing formation of the command α *or* β. Two new types of assertion about programs are now added:

$\Delta\alpha\varphi$ - all computations of α are finite and end with φ true,

$\nabla\alpha\varphi$ - there exists a finite computation of α ending with φ true.

Here a "computation of α" means a sequence of states generated in executing α. This notion is formalised in a model in terms of sequences of "configurations" $\langle s, \alpha_1; \ldots; \alpha_n \rangle$, where s is a state, α_1 is the next command to be executed and $\alpha_2, \ldots, \alpha_n$ are those that remain to be dealt with.

The iteration quantifiers are now confined to non-deterministic commands, and appear in the forms $\nabla \cup \alpha\varphi$, $\Delta \cup \alpha\varphi$, $\nabla \cap \alpha\varphi$, $\Delta \cap \alpha\varphi$. Each of these requires its own infinitary rule for a complete axiomatisation.

There are many aspects to Algorithmic Logic, including sequent-style axiomatisations, an analysis of procedures, and the application by Rasiowa of many-valued logic to push-down algorithms. Information about these is provided in the survey of Banachowski et.al. cited above.

CONSTABLE'S PROGRAMMING LOGIC

The theory of Constable (1977) uses the notation $\alpha;\varphi$ for the statement "α halts (resulting) in φ". This is the same as Salwicki's $\alpha\varphi$ and the modal $\neg[\alpha]\neg\varphi$ (although developed independently). In addition, each command α may be asserted as a formula with the meaning "α halts". A propositional system of "monadic quantifier free" programming logic is developed in which conditionals, composites, and *while*-commands are formed from program letters. Commands are modelled deterministically, and the associated validity problem is proved decidable.

The full monadic logic is obtained by allowing quantification over states. For example, writing $s\varphi$ for "φ holds at s", the validity of "if ε then α halts with ψ true" is expressed by $\forall s(s\varepsilon \rightarrow s\alpha;\psi)$. This system is also decidable, and a completeness theorem is given using a "tableaux" method in which a proof is a finitely branching tree with formulae at the nodes, and the axioms are rules for extending the tree by adding nodes and branches.

Systems based on first-order assertion languages are discussed briefly as "polyadic" logics. It is observed that while the set of valid formulae is not enumerable, it would become so if the definition of "valid" was changed to admit non-standard models. No proof-system is given however.

A major feature of Constable's viewpoint is that in addition to a program's two functions as executed instruction and asserted formula, "an asserted program should play yet a third role and act like a *proof*. In its role as a proof, a program can be *verified*." This idea forms the basis of a logic of asserted programs, developed in detail in the book *A Programming Logic* by Constable and O'Donnell (1978). The authors argue (p.83) that "giving a command includes an implicit assertion that the command may be executed successfully. An impossible command is erroneous, and leads to nonsensical conclusions just as any erroneous assumption." They cite the compelling example of traditional forms of reasoning in geometry: a geometrical proof often contains instructions to perform operations. For example:

> "suppose A and B are on opposite sides of line CD. *Draw a line from* A *to* B. Then AB intersects CD...."

From this perspective, the basic rule of inference for assignments may be displayed simply as

$$\begin{array}{l} \psi^{r}_{\sigma} \\ r := \sigma \\ \hline \therefore\ \psi \end{array}$$

Constable and O'Donnell develop a formal semantics with proof-rules of this kind for assignments, conditionals, iteration and goto's, and treat also recursive procedures and functions, and arrays.

COMPLETENESS FOR HOARE-STYLE RULES

S.A. Cook (1975, 1978) gave the first general completeness result about derivation of correctness assertions $\varphi\{\alpha\}\psi$ by the kind of rules described in §1.4. In these assertions, φ and ψ are to be first-order L-formulae. Cook's idea was to take as given (i.e. as axioms) all first-order formulae that are valid in a particular model M and then derive all the M-valid correctness assertions by *finitary* rules in the style of Hoare. He observed that the desired completeness result could still be blocked if the language L failed to provide loop-invariants for *while*-commands. To obtain these we must assume that L is *expressive for* M, which means that for any first-order L-formula φ and L-command α there is a first-order L-formula φ_α such that for any state t,

$$M \models_t \varphi_\alpha \quad \text{iff} \quad \text{for some } s,\ M \models_s \varphi \ \text{ and } \ s [\![\alpha]\!] t.$$

φ_α is said to express the "strongest post-condition" for α relative to the precondition φ, for it is true at all and only those states reachable by starting (somewhere) with φ true and executing α. Thus we have

$$M \models \varphi\{\alpha\}\varphi_\alpha, \qquad \text{and}$$

$$M \models \varphi\{\alpha\}\psi \ \text{ only if } \ M \models \varphi_\alpha \rightarrow \psi.$$

The dual notion is that of a "weakest precondition" for α relative to a post-condition ψ. This is a first-order formula α_ψ such that

$$M \models_s \alpha_\psi \text{ iff for all } t,\ s [\![\alpha]\!] t \text{ implies } M \models_t \psi,$$

so that

$$M \models \alpha_\psi\{\alpha\}\psi, \qquad \text{and}$$

$$M \models \varphi\{\alpha\}\psi \text{ only if } M \models \varphi \to \alpha_\psi .$$

The programming language Cook considers is a simple deterministic fragment of Algol, including non-recursive procedures. He gives a set of finitary rules that suffice to derive all M-valid correctness assertions from the set of M-valid first-order L-formulae, provided that L is expressive for M. He notes also that the arithmetical language $L^{\mathbb{N}}$ of §3.6 is expressive for the natural model $M_{\mathbb{N}}$. Essentially this is because each deterministic program in this model describes a partial recursive function, and all such functions are definable by first-order $L^{\mathbb{N}}$-formulae.

The incompleteness result of Wand (1978) described in §1.6 is an instance of a language failing to be expressive for a certain model. A more general example is developed by Clarke (1979), who shows that the presence of a certain set of program constructs is sufficient to prevent any finitary completeness result. He defines a system H of Hoare-style rules to be *sound and complete in the sense of Cook* if it suffices to derive all and only the valid correctness assertions of any expressive model when augmented by the valid first-order formulae of that model. His incompleteness result is based on the *halting problem* for programs over finite models. For a finite M, the set of M-valid first-order formulae is recursive, so that if there exists a finitary H that is sound and complete in the sense of Cook, the set of M-valid correctness assertions will be effectively enumerable (for reasons explained in §3.6). Singling out those of the form $\mathit{true}\{\alpha\}\mathit{false}$ leads to an effective enumeration of the non-halting programs. From this it can be established that the halting problem for programs over M is decidable. The burden of Clarke's argument is then to show that for the language he considers, all finite models are expressive but have an undecidable halting problem.

This theme was taken up by Lipton and Snyder (1977), who gave a sufficient condition (viz. encodability of the halting problem for Turing machines with blank input tape) for a programming language to lack any sound and complete Hoare logic. The authors contend that "since any *reasonable* programming language is likely to be sufficiently powerful in the sense we require, our results show that complete and sound Hoare logics may only exist for very simple languages. Thus we feel that these results add mathematical reasons to further doubt the success of the verification of real programs".

The final outcome of the line of enquiry initiated by Clarke is the proof by Lipton (1977) that for any "acceptable" programming language the existence of a decidable halting problem for finite models is necessary *and sufficient* for the existence of a sound and complete Hoare logic. Again the author observes that "acceptability is a mild restriction that is satisfied by a wide class of programming languages."

The recent book *Mathematical Theory of Program Correctness* by Jaco de Bakker (1980) offers an encyclopaedic account of proof systems for partial correctness assertions. The program constructs for which proof-rules are provided include subscripted (array) variables, recursive procedures, blocks, procedures with parameters, and goto statements, with the Scott-Strachey denotational semantics being used to interpret the language studied. This language includes $L^{\mathbb{N}}$, and the completeness theorems presented depend on the fact that it is powerful enough to express weakest pre-conditions and strongest post conditions. The book includes a lucid appendix by J. Zucker that proves this fact in rigorous detail, using the Gödelian technique of recursive arithmetisation of syntax and semantics.

DYNAMIC LOGIC

As mentioned in §1.5, the application to programs of Kripke's modal logic semantics was initiated by Pratt (1976) and has become known as *dynamic* logic. *Propositional* dynamic logic was first studied in isolation by Fischer and Ladner (1977), using a language in which commands are generated from program letters by the constructs $(\alpha;\beta)$, $(\alpha|\beta)$, $\varphi?$, and α^*. The latter is the non-deterministic command "do α some finite number of times", and has the standard-model condition

$$s\,[\![\alpha^*]\!]\,t \quad \text{iff} \quad \text{for some } n \in \mathbb{N}, \quad s\,[\![\alpha]\!]^n\,t.$$

Thus the formula $[\alpha^*]\varphi$ would seem to be equivalent to $\neg\,\bigcup\,\alpha\,\neg\varphi$, where $\bigcup$ is Salwicki's existential iteration quantifier.

Using these primitives, the commands *if* ε *then* α *else* β and *while* ε *do* α are expressed, respectively, by

$$(\varepsilon?;\alpha)\,|\,((\neg\varepsilon)?;\beta) \quad \text{and} \quad (\varepsilon?;\alpha)^*;(\neg\varepsilon)?$$

Fischer and Ladner proved that the set of formulae true in all standard models is decidable, but left open the problem of providing a recursive axiomatisation for it. An explicit set of axioms was announced by Segerberg (1977), and the proof of completeness found by Parikh (1978), Gabbay (unpublished), and Segerberg (1978). The key axioms for α^* are

(1) $[\alpha^*]\varphi \to \varphi \wedge [\alpha][\alpha^*]\varphi,$ and

(2) $\varphi \wedge [\alpha^*](\varphi \to [\alpha]\varphi) \to [\alpha^*]\varphi,$

the latter being a kind of induction principle for the relation $[\![\alpha^*]\!]$ in standard models. Given (1), and the universal modal principle 2.4.1(3), the schema (2) is equivalent to the inference rule

If $\vdash \varphi \to [\alpha]\varphi$

then $\vdash \varphi \to [\alpha^*]\varphi,$

as the reader may care to verify. Note the analogy between this rule, and Hoare's

Iteration Rule. (1) itself plays a similar role to the combination of our A9 and A10. This similarity will be more apparent if the reader also verifies the fact that A9 and A10 together are equivalent to the single schema

$$[\varepsilon\#\alpha]\varphi \rightarrow (\mathit{not}\text{-}\varepsilon \rightarrow \varphi) \wedge (\varepsilon \rightarrow [\alpha][\varepsilon\#\alpha]\varphi)$$

(cf. 2.4.3(4)).

The latest, and perhaps most direct method of proving completeness using (1) and (2) is due to Kozen and Parikh (1980). A sequent-style axiomatisation has also been developed by Nishimura (1979).

Algebraic interpretations of propositional dynamic logic lead to the study of *dynamic algebra*, introduced by Kozen (1979), as a combination of Boolean algebra and *regular* (or Kleene) algebra (cf. Conway (1971)). Pratt (1979i) proves an algebraic version of the Parikh-Gabbay-Segerberg completeness theorem that yields a subdirect representation of certain free dynamic algebras in terms of finite algebras. Extensions of Stone's topological representation theory for Boolean algebras to dynamic algebras have been developed by Kozen (1979i, 1980). This work can be seen as providing algebraic analogues of the kind of canonical model construction developed in Chapter 2.

Quantificational dynamic logic, which replaces program letters by assignments and introduces $\forall$ and $\exists$, is studied in David Harel's doctoral thesis (1978). Amongst the many topics examined there, which include recursive programs and "the mathematics of diverging and failing", the most relevant to our present interests is *arithmetical completeness*. This is founded on the notion of an *arithmetical universe*, which (roughly) is a model whose base algebra A

(i) has the algebra $\mathbb{N}$ of natural-number arithmetic as a subalgebra;

(ii) has a predicate $\mathit{nat}(x)$ which holds only of the natural numbers in A; and

(iii) has an "encoding predicate", which allows finite sequences of A-elements to be encoded as single A-elements.

The significance of this notion is that for an arithmetical universe M all modal operators $[\alpha]$ can be eliminated: *any* formula φ is equivalent to some *first-order* formula ψ, in the sense that $M \models (\varphi \leftrightarrow \psi)$. We saw earlier that with the aid of appropriate axioms we could inductively eliminate assignments, composites, and conditionals, but that the same did not apply to *while*-commands. Similarly, $[\alpha^*]\varphi$ can in general only be reduced to the infinite set of formulae of the form $[\alpha]^n\varphi$. In an arithmetical universe however this obstacle can be overcome, essentially because of the ability of the encoding machinery to represent as single elements the finite sequences generated in executing α^*.

Harel defines a proof system to be *arithmetically complete* if it derives all and only the valid formulae of any given arithmetical universe when augmented by the *first-order* formulae that are valid in that universe. He proves that dynamic logic has a simple arithmetically complete axiomatisation in which α^* is characterised by the two inference rules

$$\vdash \varphi \to [\alpha]\varphi \quad \textit{implies} \quad \vdash \varphi \to [\alpha^*]\varphi,$$

and

$$\vdash nat(x) \wedge \psi(x+1) \to \neg[\alpha]\neg\psi(x) \quad \textit{implies} \quad \vdash nat(x) \wedge \psi(x) \to \neg[\alpha^*]\neg\psi(0).$$

In the second of these rules, ψ is any first-order formula having x as a free variable. Validity of the premiss requires that whenever ψ is true of a positive natural number, then by executing α it is possible to bring about a state in which ψ is true of the predecessor of that number. From this, the rule infers that whenever ψ is true of a natural number then by doing α some finite number of times we can make ψ true of 0. Patently this rule is based on the well-foundness of the predecessor relation on $\mathbb{N}$.

As to the generality of this completeness result, Harel states that any model can be extended to an arithmetical universe "by augmenting it, if necessary, with the natural numbers and additional apparatus for encoding finite sequences. Thus, reasoning about *any* kind of program, written over any domain, can in principle be carried out with a suitable arithmetical universe." He observes further that his notion is closely related to that of completeness in the sense of Cook. Some light is shed on this relationship by a result of DeMillo, Lipton, and Snyder, proven in Lipton (1977). This states that if L is expressive for M in Cook's sense, then either

(i) M contains the standard model of arithmetic, or

(ii) for each program α there is a number n such that α reaches at most n states in any computation (terminating or not) with any initial state.

This shows expressiveness to be a very strong restriction. As Lipton puts it, "it is almost equivalent to always having the assertion language contain all of arithmetic." Thus the difference between arithmetically complete and Cook-complete systems would seem to be that the latter, in addition to arithmetical universes, apply to the severely limited class of models described in (ii).

The degree of undecidability of the set of valid formulae of quantificational dynamic logic has been investigated by Pratt and Albert Meyer. They show that the set of valid formulae of the form $\neg[\alpha]\neg\psi$, where ψ is first-order, is recursively enumerable, but that this property is destroyed by prefixing modal operators $[\alpha]$ to first-order formulae. This means that the validity problem for total correctness assertions ("α halts with ψ true") is no more difficult than that for first-order formulae, but that the problem for *partial* correctness assertions ("if α halts, then ψ is true when it does") is harder. The set of valid formulae of the type $[\alpha]\psi$, for first-order ψ, is what is known as a Π^0_2 set. This means that, by Gödel-numbering, it can be represented in the standard model of arithmetic as a set defined by a first-order $L^{\mathbb{N}}$-formula that is *universal-existential*, i.e. of the form

$$\forall x \exists y \varphi$$

where φ is a quantifier-free formula defining a decidable relation on $\mathbb{N}$. Recursively enumerable sets on the other hand are definable by simpler existential formulae $\exists y\varphi$, where φ is quantifier-free.

The general validity problem for dynamic logic is however much more difficult than these special cases: the set of all valid formulae is not definable in first-order arithmetic at all! These and other related results are presented in Harel, Pratt, and Meyer (1977).

APPLICATIONS OF TEMPORAL LOGIC

The relation $[\![\alpha]\!]$ links an initial state s to a terminal state t obtained by executing α from s, but gives no information about any intermediate states generated in getting from s to t, or about what happens if α generates an infinite sequence of states by starting in s and never terminating (some programs are not supposed to terminate, e.g. one whose task is to print out an infinite sequence of numbers). To study such computation sequences, Pnueli (1977) suggested the use of *temporal logic*. This is a variant of modal logic (§1.5), which, as regards the future tense, interprets the formula $\Box\varphi$ to mean "φ will always be true", i.e. "φ is true now and at all future moments". This interpretation may also be rendered by the formula $\varphi \wedge G\varphi$, where $G\varphi$ means "φ is true at all future times" (excluding the present moment). Other connectives of temporal logic are

$F\varphi$ – φ will be true at some future time ;

$H\varphi$ – φ has always been true ;

$P\varphi$ – φ has been true at some past time ;

$X\varphi$ – φ will be true at the next moment of time ;

$\varphi U\psi$ – φ will be true *until* ψ is, i.e. there is a future moment at which ψ holds, with φ holding at all intervening times ;

$\varphi S\psi$ – φ has been true since ψ was.

The connective X is appropriate to models in which each point has an immediate successor - e.g. the natural ordering of the integers, or the sequence of states generated by a computation. The connectives U (until) and S (since) were studied by Hans Kamp (1968), who showed that they formed a *descriptively complete* set of operators, in the sense that for models in which time is an order-complete linear ordering, all tense-logical connectives can be defined in terms of U and S. Gabbay,

Pnueli, Shelah, and Stavi (1980) adapted this result to show that U alone plays a similar role for future-tense logic. To illustrate this expressive power, we observe that $F\varphi$ can be defined as $(true\ U\varphi)$ and then $G\varphi$ as $\neg F \neg \varphi$, while $X\varphi$ can be taken as an abbreviation for $(false\ U\varphi)$.

Gabbay et alia present a system DUX that gives a complete axiomatisation of the propositional logic of models that consist of an integer-like state-sequence $s_0, s_1, s_2, \ldots$. Amongst their more distinctive axioms are

$$X \neg \varphi \leftrightarrow \neg X\varphi$$

$$\varphi U \psi \leftrightarrow (X\psi \vee (X\varphi \wedge X(\varphi U \psi)))$$

$$\Box (\varphi \to X\varphi) \to (\varphi \to \Box \varphi)$$

The validity of the first two of these depends on the uniqueness of the next state and its relation to the other future states, while the third applies the principle of induction to the state-sequence.

A notable difference between Pnueli's approach and dynamic logic is that whereas the latter uses a formal language containing symbols for infinitely many commands, the former constructs a different logical system (extending DUX) for each program. Consider a fixed deterministic program α, consisting of a series of commands with labels $m_1, \ldots, m_e$ and containing variables $x_1, \ldots, x_n$. We assume m_1 is the unique entry point to α, and m_e the exit (Manna and Pnueli (1979), Pnueli (1981)). A *state* is defined as a pair $s = (m, a)$, where m is one of α's labels, and $a = (a_1, \ldots, a_n)$ an assignment of values to the program variables. For any input a, α generates a sequence $s_0, s_1, s_2, \ldots$ in an obvious way from $s_0 = (m_0, a)$.

The language for expressing assertions about the behaviour of α includes special formulae $atm_0, \ldots, atm_e$, corresponding to the labels, with atm_i being true at $s = (m, a)$ iff $m = m_i$. Using these, the Hoare-style partial correctness assertion $\varphi\{\alpha\}\psi$ is represented in the present formalism as the formula

$$atm_0 \wedge \varphi \to \Box (atm_e \to \psi).$$

Similarly, total correctness of α with respect to an input-output specification

(φ,ψ) is given by

$$atm_o \wedge \varphi \rightarrow \Diamond(atm_e \wedge \psi),$$

where $\Diamond = \neg\Box\neg$. This says "if φ is true on entry to α, then α will halt with ψ true on termination".

The real value of Pnueli's application of temporal logic would seem to be to the notion of a *concurrent* program. This involves a number of processors executing different programs in parallel using a shared memory environment, so that each can affect the values of variables used by others, making synchronisation necessary. Temporal logic can be used to formally express such desirable properties as *mutual exclusion* (no two processors can simultaneously perform a task that requires their cooperation), *fair merging* (no processor is delayed forever), and freedom from *deadlock* (when none can move). These are discussed by Manna and Pnueli (1979), and Pnueli (1981). Ben-Ari (1980) gives examples of formal temporal-logical proofs, using DUX, of some significant concurrent programs.

PROCESS LOGICS

The name "process logic" was given by Pratt (1979) to an interpretation in which the meaning $[\![\alpha]\!]$ of α is taken to be the set of state-sequences that can be generated by executing α. In addition to the now familiar $[\alpha]\varphi$ - i.e. *after* α,φ - he proposed the use of the following modalities

throughout α,φ	-	φ holds at every state of any sequence generated in executing α ;
sometime during α,φ	-	every α-computation has φ true at some point ;
α *preserves* φ	-	in every α-computation, once φ becomes true it remains true thereafter.

Pratt's paper contains some completeness results for various combinations of these modalities. Segerberg (1980, 1980i) presents a completeness theorem for *after* and *throughout* in models in which programs can always reach a terminal state. Parikh (1978i) devised a decidable system of *second-order* process logic, subsuming Pratt's, that included quantifiers ranging over states, and over paths (state-sequences). Harel (1979) established that Parikh's system is stronger than Pratt's, by showing that it, and not the latter, can express a connective $\Psi(\alpha,\varphi,\psi)$ (suggested by Pnueli) that has the following meaning:

> in any α-computation, if φ is true at some point then ψ is true at some later point

(cf. the DUX-formula $\Box(\varphi \rightarrow F\psi))$.

Nishimura (1980) carried out an amalgamation of dynamic logic with Pnueli's temporal connectives, to produce a language in which it is possible to interpret Parikh's second-order system, and hence Pratt's modalities *after*, *throughout*, *during*, and *preserves*, as well as Harel's Ψ. Indeed by extending the work of Gabbay, Pnueli, Shelah, and Stavi (1980) on descriptive completeness of DUX, Nishimura established that any potential language for process logic must be interpretable in his. But a drawback of his language is that it makes a cumbersome distinction between *state-formulae* (which are true or false at any given state) and *path-formulae* (which, rather, are true or false of a path). Finally, Harel, Kozen, and Parikh (1980) simplified matters by abandoning the state-formulae altogether to produce an elegant system, called PL, whose semantics and syntax we now outline.

A *path* is a finite or denumerable sequence of states (with repetitions allowed). The first and last states of path p are denoted $first(p)$ and $last(p)$, respectively, the latter being defined only when p is finite. Paths p and q may be concatenated just when $last(p) = first(q)$, with the concatenation being denoted pq (thus pq is always undefined for infinite p). q is a *suffix* of p if $p = rq$ for some r, in which case we write $p\,suf\,q$. If p has at least two elements, then it has a *longest* suffix, denoted $next(p)$. Hence the operation *next* will be undefined whenever p is a one-element path, i.e. a single state.

The language of PL extends that of propositional dynamic logic by the inclusion of two connectives, f and suf. The formula $f\varphi$ means intuitively that φ holds at the beginning of a path, while $(\varphi suf \psi)$ means "φ holds until ψ does" and corresponds to the connective *until* of temporal logic.

A PL-model consists of a set S of states, an assignment of truth-values to Boolean variables in each state, and an assignment to each program letter of a set of paths in S. Each command α is then inductively assigned a set $[\![\alpha]\!]$ of paths by putting

$$[\![\alpha;\beta]\!] = \{pq : p \in [\![\alpha]\!] \text{ and } q \in [\![\beta]\!]\}$$

$$[\![\alpha|\beta]\!] = [\![\alpha]\!] \cup [\![\beta]\!]$$

$$[\![\alpha^*]\!] = \{p_1 \dots p_n : n \in \mathbb{N} \text{ and } p_i \in [\![\alpha]\!] \text{ all } i\}$$

The satisfaction relation in a PL-model is taken to hold between formulae and *paths* rather than states. A Boolean variable holds of p iff it is true at $first(p)$. The Boolean connectives receive their usual meanings, viz.

$$\not\models_p false, \qquad \text{and}$$

$$\models_p \varphi \rightarrow \psi \quad \text{iff} \quad \models_p \varphi \text{ implies } \models_p \psi,$$

and the new clauses are

$\models_p [\alpha]\varphi$ iff for all $q \in [\![\alpha]\!]$, if pq is defined then $\models_{pq} \varphi$;

$\models_p f\varphi$ iff $\models_{first(p)} \varphi$;

$\models_p \varphi suf \psi$ iff for some q,

(i) $psufq$ and $\models_q \psi$, and

(ii) if $psufr$ and $rsufq$, then $\models_r \varphi$.

In this system many interesting connectives can be defined: write

$n\varphi$ for $\mathit{false}\,\mathit{suf}\,\varphi$,

L_0 for $\neg n\mathit{true}$,

$\mathit{some}\varphi$ for $\varphi \vee (\mathit{true}\,\mathit{suf}\,\varphi)$,

$\mathit{all}\varphi$ for $\neg\mathit{some}\neg\varphi$,

$\mathit{last}\varphi$ for $\mathit{some}(\varphi \wedge L_0)$,

fin for $\mathit{last}\,\mathit{true}$, and

inf for $\neg\mathit{fin}$.

Then $n\varphi$, corresponding to $X\varphi$ from temporal logic, says that the longest suffix exists and satisfies φ, i.e.

$$\models_p n\varphi \quad \text{iff} \quad \models_{next(p)} \varphi.$$

L_0 holds of a path iff it has no suffix, i.e. it consists of a single state. $\mathit{some}\varphi$ says that φ holds of some suffix or else of the state itself, while $\mathit{all}\varphi$ says that φ holds of all suffixes as well as the state itself (cf. $\Box\varphi$). $\mathit{last}\varphi$ expresses the existence of a last state in the path, with φ holding at that last state. Thus fin asserts that the path has a last state, i.e. is finite, and so inf asserts that it is infinite.

In these terms Pratt's connectives *throughout*, *during*, and *preserves*, are expressible as, respectively,

$[\alpha]\mathit{all}\varphi$,

$[\alpha]\mathit{some}\varphi$, and

$[\alpha](\mathit{some}\varphi \rightarrow (\mathit{all}\varphi \vee (\neg\varphi \wedge (\neg\varphi)\,\mathit{suf}\,\mathit{all}\varphi)))$,

while the original meaning of $[\alpha]\varphi$ (i.e. *after* α,φ), is now conveyed by

$$[\alpha](\mathit{fin} \rightarrow \mathit{last}\varphi).$$

Harel, Kozen, and Parikh present a finitary axiomatisation of this system of propositional process logic that includes the Segerberg axioms for dynamic logic. Perhaps the most interesting new axiom is

$$(n\varphi \rightarrow \varphi)\,\mathit{suf}\,\varphi \rightarrow n\varphi,$$

the *path induction axiom*, whose validity is based on the well-foundedness of the relation "*psufq*". As part of the completeness proof it is shown that adjunction of *fin* as an axiom gives a system characterised by models in which all paths are finite. Both systems are shown to have a decidable validity problem.

KRÖGER'S RULES FOR LOOPS

In a recent paper (that appeared after this manuscript was written), F. Kröger (1980) discusses infinitary rules for *while*-commands which are intimately related to our schema OI. He focuses on Hoare-style correctness assertions $\varphi\{\alpha\}\psi$, where φ and ψ are first-order, and uses commands *assume*ε which correspond to the test commands $\varepsilon?$ introduced in §2.6. He gives a completeness proof for correctness assertions that uses the following rule of inference (in our notation)

(1) *From* $\varphi\{(\varepsilon?;\alpha)^n;(\neg\varepsilon)?;\beta\}\psi$ *for all* n, *derive* $\varphi\{\varepsilon\#\alpha\}\psi$.

The idea here is that an execution of $(\varepsilon\#\alpha)$ is in fact an execution of $(\varepsilon?;\alpha)^n;(\neg\varepsilon)?$, for some n. This indeed is the basis of the dynamic logic definition of $(\varepsilon\#\alpha)$ as $(\varepsilon?;\alpha)^*;(\neg\varepsilon)?$. By invoking the composition axiom A7, and the Λ-theorem schema

$$[\varepsilon?]\varphi \leftrightarrow (\varepsilon \rightarrow \varphi),$$

it can be shown that in general

$$\vdash_\Lambda [(\varepsilon?;\alpha)^n;(\neg\varepsilon)?]\varphi \leftrightarrow \varphi_n(\varepsilon,\alpha),$$

which makes the connection between (1) and OI quite plain.

A variant of rule (1) considered by Kröger is

(2) *From* $\varphi\{(\varepsilon?;\alpha)^n\}\psi_n$, $\psi_n \wedge \neg\varepsilon \rightarrow \psi$ *for all* n,
derive $\varphi\{\varepsilon\#\alpha\}\psi$.

To derive the infinitely many premisses in (2) it is suggested that induction on n be used, as expressed in the further rule

(3) *From* $\varphi \rightarrow \psi_o$, $\psi_n \wedge \varepsilon\{\alpha\}\psi_{n+1}$, $\psi_n \wedge \neg\varepsilon \rightarrow \psi$ *for all* n,
derive $\varphi\{\varepsilon\#\alpha\}\psi$.

Each of the formulae ψ_n in rules (2) and (3) is intended to describe the state after n iterations of the loop involved in $(\varepsilon\#\alpha)$. By contrast, the loop invariants used in Hoare's Iteration Rule "describe all these states by one single formula". Kröger suggests that *"a proof of a loop by means of an invariant essentially corresponds to a proof by rule (2) using a set of formulas* ψ_n*, for which the premisses* $\varphi\{(\varepsilon?;\alpha)^n\}\psi_n$ *can be proved by straightforward mathematical induction on* n*. This mathematical induction, however, is only one method for proving the infinitely many premisses of (2) and this shows just the main difference between the two methods."* He then illustrates this point with some examples.

PART II APPLICATIONS

the main characteristic of intelligent thinking is that one is willing and able to study in depth an aspect of one's subject matter in isolation, for the sake of its own consistency, all the time knowing that one is occupying oneself with only one of the aspects. The other aspects have to wait their turn, because our heads are so small that we cannot deal with them simultaneously without getting confused.

Edsger Dijkstra.

We saw in Part I how to associate a language with a given data type, and how to axiomatise the class of valid formulae of this language. This has been the central core of our theory, the platform on which all subsequent developments and refinements are to be based. And thus far the techniques used have departed little from those found in the logical analysis of conventional mathematical structures. Indeed there has proven to be no substance to the early concern of some mathematicians, noted by Dijkstra (ADP, p.xvi) that 'the "dynamic" nature of the assignment statement did not seem to fit too well into the "static" nature of traditional mathematics'.

But if this is to be a significant approach to programming language semantics, it must be capable of analysing those concepts, and those methods of syntactic expression and manipulation, that are unique to programming languages, and which have emerged from programming practise and experience. In Part II we make a very modest beginning on such a project. The present chapter studies the notion of *function declaration* - a device that allows the programmer to write his own algorithm to compute the values of a certain function. Chapter 5 analyses *procedure* declarations - a device for invoking a subprogram by referring to an abbreviated name of it. Then in Chapter 6 we conclude with the beginnings of a theory of structured data types, by adding to our language *indexed variables* to denote components of *array* types. Throughout these studies we will adopt the practise of simplifying the framework as much as is consistent with a faithful presentation of the particular notion being studied.

CHAPTER 4

FUNCTION DECLARATIONS

4.1 USER-DEFINED FUNCTIONS

A function declaration has the syntactic form

$$\textit{function}\ F(x_1, \ldots, x_n);\alpha\ .$$

Here F is a *function variable*, in this case referring to an n-placed function. $x_1, \ldots, x_n$ are variables, known as *formal parameters*, whose role is to denote the argument (input) of the function denoted by F. α is a command in which $x_1, \ldots, x_n$ appear, and is known as the *body*; its role is to calculate the value (output) of the function F for argument $(x_1, \ldots, x_n)$.

For example, the following is a declaration designed to compute the remainder upon division of x by y.

$$
\begin{array}{l}
\textit{function}\ rem(x,y)\ ; \\
\qquad r := x\ ; \\
\qquad \textit{while}\ r \geqslant y\ \textit{do}\ r := r-y\ ; \\
\qquad rem := r
\end{array}
$$

Notice that included in the body is an assignment to the function variable itself (in this case *rem*). This is typical of function declarations, the idea being that the output of the function in question is to be the value that the variable F has when the body α terminates.

Here is another example of a function declaration (from Alagic and Arbib (1978), p.166), this one for an algorithm over $\mathbb{N}$ to compute the greatest natural number smaller than or equal to $\sqrt{a}$.

```
function root (a : integer) : integer ;
var x, y, z : integer ;
begin x := 0 ; y := 1 ; z := 1 ;
        while y ≤ a do
              begin x := x+1 ;
                    z := z+2 ;
                    y := y+z
              end ;
        root := x
end
```

(the algorithm is based on the fact that for $n > 0$, $n^2 = 1 + 3 + 5 + \ldots + (2n-1)$).

The words *begin* and *end* in this example play the role of the parentheses (and). The first occurrence of "*integer*" tells which data type the argument a comes from, while the second gives the data type of the values of the function. The symbol *var* is a device used in Pascal to declare that x,y,z are *local* variables to the function declaration. This means that they are referred to only within the function body itself, and have no wider significance in any larger program that has the function declaration as a component. On the other hand variables in the body that *are* referred to in such a larger context, i.e. in a program of which the declaration is a part, are said to be *non-local*, or *global* to that declaration.

The symbolism

var x, y, z

is called a *variable declaration.* A *block* is a variable declaration followed by a command. Thus in Pascal a function declaration consists of

(1) a heading that specifies the function variable and the formal parameters;

(2) a variable declaration specifying the variables that are local to the function declaration; and

(3) a command (the body), which generally includes an assignment to the function variable.

Now the declaration *function* $F(x_1, \ldots, x_n):\alpha$ is not itself a command. Rather, the body α of the declaration is executed whenever the computer encounters an expression of the syntactic form $F(\sigma_1, \ldots, \sigma_n)$. This is a *function designator*, within which the expressions σ_i are *actual parameters*. Examples are *root*(32), *root*(z+1), *rem*(9,z) etc. The function designator denotes the value that the function F gives to the argument denoted by $(\sigma_1, \ldots, \sigma_n)$.

CALL-BY-VALUE

An evaluation of a function designator by execution of the function body is known as a *function call*. There are a number of ways of making such a call, depending on how the formal parameters are treated. The one we shall concentrate on for now is *value substitution* or *call-by-value*. In this method each actual parameter σ_i is evaluated and its value is assigned to the corresponding formal parameter x_i. The body of F is then executed. When carrying out a function call by value the computer sets aside new memory for the formal parameters and then places the current value of each actual parameter in the memory location for the corresponding formal parameter. In executing the body, the formal parameters are taken as referring to the new locations assigned to them. What this amounts to is that the formal parameters become local to the function call.

In the Revised Algol 60 Report (Naur, 1963) there is a description of the calling of procedures - which we consider in the next chapter - that applies equally well to function calls as considered here. Execution of a call is described as being equivalent to processing a certain "fictitious block", in place of the original body, that is obtained by inserting assignment commands to represent the placement of actual-parameter values in the memory locations for formal parameters. Paragraph 4.7.3.1 of the Revised Report has "*these assignments being considered as being performed explicitly before entering the procedure body. The effect is as though an additional block embracing the procedure body were created in which these assignments were made to variables local to this fictitious block ... . As a consequence, variables called by value are to be considered as non-local to the body of the procedure but local to the fictitious block."* (read "function" for "procedure" in this quotation).

Thus evaluating $F(\sigma)$, given the declaration *function* $F(x):\alpha$, is equivalent to processing the "fictitious block"

$$\mathit{var}\ x\ ;$$
$$x := \sigma\ ;$$
$$\alpha$$

in which x has become a local variable.

In our formalisation of function declarations in the next section we will leave out the local variable declarations: there will be no *syntactic* indication that a formal parameter called by value is local to the function call. Instead we use the latter requirement to justify a syntactic restriction on the form of correctness assertions about function calls.

SIDE EFFECTS

In addition to computing the desired function-value, a function call can change the values of non-local variables occurring in its body. This is called a *side effect*. The following example of this phenomenon is adapted from Alagic and Arbib (1978), p.165.

```
function F(x) ;
begin a := x+1 ; F := a end
function G(x) ;
begin a := x+2 ; G := a end .
```

Here a is a non-local variable for both declarations. If we suppose that a initially has value 0, and attempt to evaluate $F(a)+G(a)$, we see that the answer depends on which of $F(a)$ and $G(a)$ are evaluated first. Taking $F(a)$ first, execution of the fictitious block

$$x := a \; ; \; a := x+1 \; ; \; F := a$$

results in a value of 1 to F, hence to $F(a)$, and a value to a itself of 1. Passing the latter to the body of G results in a value of 3 to $G(a)$. But doing it in the reverse order produces a value of 2 for $G(a)$ and 3 for $F(a)$.

It is apparent then that we must settle on a "preferred direction" in evaluating expressions if all expressions are to have determinate values (when defined). The convention we adopt is to always work from left to right. But then in the example, $F(a)+G(a)$ and $G(a)+F(a)$ will have different values, so that integer addition ceases to obey the commutative law. This is the sort of consequence that has lead many writers on the subject to advise the programmer against writing function declarations that allow side effects on non-local variables.

The accepted syntactic form of a function declaration can give the impression that a side effect on a formal parameter is present when in fact none occurs on implementation. Consider the following algorithm for multiplying two natural numbers x and y by adding x to itself y times.

```
function multiply (x,y : integer) : integer ;
var z ;
begin z := 0 ;
      while y ≠ 0 do
         begin z := z+x
               y := y-1
         end ;
      multiply := z
end
```

Now the body of this declaration contains an assignment to the formal parameter y. It is not precluded that y be a non-local variable for a program in which the declaration is embedded, and indeed such a program could contain the designator *multiply* (x,y), in which the actual parameters are the original formal ones. But, contrary to appearance, the corresponding function call does not change the value that y has as a non-local variable. For, as explained above, for the duration of the call y is treated as a local variable. A new memory area is set aside and assigned a separate copy of the value of the actual parameter (in this case y itself) Throughout the call "y" refers to this separate copy. When the body-execution is complete, this extra copy is deleted, and "y" goes back to its original role. What this all means is that (Alagic and Arbib, p.161) "any assignment to a parameter called by value is an assignment to the corresponding local variable, and it cannot affect the actual parameter". What changes is the value of the local variable created to correspond to the formal parameter.

Actually this last statement is a slight over-simplification. In a program containing a call of *multiply* (σ,τ) the value of σ or τ could change if they themselves contained a variable,other than a formal parameter,that happened to be non-local to the call. But that, according to Alagic and Arbib (p.160) would be "sloppy" and "an example of bad programming practise".

This whole situation can be readily circumvented by requiring declarations of functions to be written in such a way that only declared local variables receive assignments in the body. Thus *multiply* could be constructed as

```
function multiply (x,y) ;
var u, z ;
begin u := y ; z := 0 ;
     while u ≠ 0 do
          begin z := z+x
                u := u-1
          end ;
     multiply := z
end
```

Although this avoids ambiguities, it has to be recognised that the first version of *multiply* is a perfectly legitimate program, and this illustrates the fact that some conventions about the use of program variables at the writer level are different to those encountered in traditional mathematical logic. Perhaps the lessons we should then draw from this discussion are pragmatic ones about the desirability or otherwise of various conventions. Such discussions may suggest guidelines for "good" (e.g. comprehensible) program writing, such as avoiding the use of a non-local variable as a formal parameter, or a formal parameter as an actual one. These would be rather like rules for natural languages that declare certain constructions to be "bad grammar" or "bad style" even though syntactically well-formed.

Before moving to a formal analysis, there is one further conceptual matter to be explained. It is of the very essence of the mathematical meaning of "function" that each function value is uniquely determined by the argument that gave rise to it. But if the body of the declaration were non-deterministic, this principle could be violated: there might be many possible terminal values of the function variable, depending on how the body is in fact executed. Therefore we will require that function declarations involve only deterministic programs.

.2 ENVIRONMENTS AND FUNCTION CALLS

For simplicity of exposition we consider a one-sorted signature $\mathcal{O}$ with an associated denumerable set X of variables, for which we assume a fixed enumeration. This allows us to generate a language L along the lines of §3.2, but with one new aspect: we include the following new formation rule for expressions (where $Exp(L) = Axp(L) \cup Bxp(L)$);

for any $n \geqslant 1$, and any $\sigma_1, \ldots, \sigma_n \in Exp(L)$,

(i) if $x \in X$ then $x(\sigma_1, \ldots, \sigma_n) \in Axp(L)$,

and (ii) if $x \in Bvb$ then $x(\sigma_1, \ldots, \sigma_n) \in Bxp(L)$.

The new expressions $x(\sigma_1, \ldots, \sigma_n)$ are called *function designators*, with *actual parameters* σ_i. Notice that we have not introduced any new symbols to serve as function variables, but are using instead those variables that range over the data type of the intended function values. Generally the letter F will be used for a variable (Boolean or algebraic) to draw attention to its use as a function variable.

Any expression, command, or formula that contains *no* function designators will be called *simple*.

Each expression in a language has an associated *type*: a symbol indicating which data type its value comes from. In Chapter 6 we will consider a language that handles many data types at once, but for the present there are just $\mathbb{B}$ and some $\mathcal{O}$-algebra. Hence we can take $\{\mathbb{B},\mathcal{O}\}$ as our set of type symbols.

A function declaration is now formally defined as a symbolism

$$\mathit{function}\ F(x_1:\eta_1,\ \ldots,\ x_n:\eta_n):\eta\ ;\ \alpha$$

where

(1) F is a variable of type η, called the *function* variable or *main* variable of the declaration;

(2) for $1 \leqslant i \leqslant n$, x_i is a variable of type η_i, called a *formal parameter*;

(3) α is a command, the body of the declaration, that contains an assignment to F within it.

In order to give a meaning to expressions involving function designators $F(\sigma)$ we have to have a fixed declaration for F. An *environment* is defined to be a set E of function declarations that satisfies

(i) no two declarations in E have the same main variable; and

(ii) no declaration body appearing in E contains any alternative commands (i.e. those of the form $(\beta|\gamma)$).

An expression $\sigma \in \mathit{Exp}(L)$ is said to be *defined by* E if for every designator $F(\sigma_1,\ \ldots,\ \sigma_n)$ that occurs in σ there is a declaration in E that has formal parameters $x_1,\ \ldots,\ x_n$, with x_i being of the same type as σ_i for $1 \leqslant i \leqslant n$.

A given environment is like an extra set of axioms. It allows us to assign meanings to all expressions, commands, and formulae, and to develop an axiomatisation of the resulting class of valid formulae. Given a fixed environment E we now show how to associate with each expression σ a command *call*-σ and a *simple* expression σ^0. *call*-σ represents the algorithm executed by the computer in evaluating σ, and σ^0 denotes the value assigned to σ upon termination of *call*-σ. The inductive definition involves several cases, for which explanations are provided where appropriate.

(1) If σ is simple, *call*-σ is *skip* and σ^0 is σ.

(2) If σ is not defined by E, *call*-σ is *abort* and σ^0 is *false* (in fact any simple expression would do here for σ^0).

(3) Let σ be $f(\sigma_1, \ldots, \sigma_n)$, where f is an n-ary operation symbol of the signature O. In this case let $y_1, \ldots, y_n$ be the first n distinct variables in the enumeration of X that do not occur in any of *call*-σ_i or σ_i^0 for $1 \leqslant i \leqslant n$. Then *call*-$\sigma$ is

$$(\mathit{call}\text{-}\sigma_1 \; ; \; y_1 := \sigma_1^0 \; ; \; \ldots \; , \; \mathit{call}\text{-}\sigma_n \; ; \; y_n := \sigma_n^0)$$

and σ^0 is $f(y_1, \ldots, y_n)$.

The idea of this definition is that evaluation of $f(\sigma_1, \ldots, \sigma_n)$ proceeds by first evaluating $\sigma_1, \ldots, \sigma_n$, in that order, and then applying the operation f to the resulting n-tuple of values. However, having executed *call*-σ_1 and found σ_1 to then have the value of σ_1^0, subsequent execution of *call*-σ_2 may cause a change (side effect) in the value of σ_1^0. For this reason we introduce the new (local) variable y_1 to hold the value of σ_1^0 by the assignment $(y_1 := \sigma_1^0)$. Since y_1 does not occur in the rest of *call*-σ, its value is unaffected by the latter. In general, at the end of *call*-σ, y_i has the value that σ_i^0 had immediately after termination of *call*-σ_i. Since this may not be the same as the value of σ_i^0 after termination of *call*-σ itself, our analysis does not obviate side effects of the type discussed earlier. But it does reflect, we maintain, the intended meaning of "$f(\sigma_1, \ldots, \sigma_n)$" when processed from left to right.

(4) Suppose σ is a designator $F(\sigma_1, \ldots, \sigma_n)$ that is defined by E via the declaration

$$\textit{function}\ F(x_1, \ldots, x_n)\ ;\ \alpha.$$

Then $\textit{call}\text{-}\sigma$ is

$$(\textit{call}\text{-}\sigma_1\ ;\ x_1 := \sigma_1^0\ ;\ \ldots.,\ \textit{call}\text{-}\sigma_n\ ;\ x_n := \sigma_n^0\ ;\ \alpha),$$

while σ^0 is the main variable F.

(5) If σ is the conditional $(\varepsilon \supset \rho, \tau)$, let p be a Boolean variable not occurring in $\textit{call}\text{-}\rho$ or $\textit{call}\text{-}\tau$. Then $\textit{call}\text{-}\sigma$ is

$$(\textit{call}\text{-}\varepsilon\ ;\ p := \varepsilon^0\ ;\ (p \Rightarrow \textit{call}\text{-}\rho,\ \textit{call}\text{-}\tau))$$

and σ^0 is

$$(p \supset \rho^0, \tau^0).$$

In this case, at the end of execution of $\textit{call}\text{-}\sigma$, p has the value that ε^0 had after execution of $\textit{call}\text{-}\varepsilon$.

(6) Suppose σ is $(\rho = \tau)$. Let x be a variable of the same type as ρ and τ that does not occur in $\textit{call}\text{-}\tau$. Then $\textit{call}\text{-}\sigma$ is

$$(\textit{call}\text{-}\rho\ ;\ x := \rho^0\ ;\ \textit{call}\text{-}\tau)$$

and σ^0 is

$$(x = \tau^0).$$

This completes the definition of $\textit{call}\text{-}\sigma$ and σ^0. An important point to note in what follows is that since no body occurring in E has any alternative commands within it, the same holds of $\textit{call}\text{-}\sigma$ for every σ.

4.3 STANDARD MODELS

If $M = (A, S, v, [\![\cdot]\!])$ is a model of the kind developed in §3.3, then the operator v assigns a value in each state to each variable, and hence to each simple expression in the usual way. In order to extend v to expressions σ that are not simple we use the commands $call\text{-}\sigma$ and the simple expression σ^0, whose definition depends on a fixed environment E. M will be called an *E-model* if $[\![call\text{-}\sigma]\!]$ is a *functional* relation on S for every σ. In such a model we proceed as follows for non-simple σ:

(1) if σ is not defined by E, then $v_s(\sigma) = \omega$;

otherwise

(2) if there exists a state t with $s\,[\![call\text{-}\sigma]\!]\,t$ we put $v_s(\sigma) = v_t(\sigma^0)$. If there is no such t, then $v_s(\sigma) = \omega$.

The functionality of $[\![call\text{-}\sigma]\!]$ guarantees that $v_s(\sigma)$ is always unambiguously determined. σ will be *defined* (i.e. have a value other than ω) just in case $call\text{-}\sigma$ terminates with σ^0 defined on termination. Writing $halts(\alpha)$ for the formula $\neg[\alpha]false$, we thus have that

$$D\sigma \leftrightarrow halts(call\text{-}\sigma) \wedge [call\text{-}\sigma]D\sigma^0,$$

i.e.

$$D\sigma \leftrightarrow wp(call\text{-}\sigma,\ D\sigma^0),$$

is valid when non-simple σ is defined by E. It is valid also for non-simple σ that is not defined by E provided that M assigns to *abort* its standard meaning of $\emptyset$; and for simple σ provided that M assigns *skip* its standard meaning.

A Boolean expression ε will hold, i.e. have value 1, in state s just in case $call\text{-}\varepsilon$ halts when initiated in s, with ε^0 holding on termination. This gives the validity of

$$\varepsilon \leftrightarrow halts(call\text{-}\varepsilon) \wedge [call\text{-}\varepsilon]\varepsilon^0,$$

i.e.

$$\varepsilon \leftrightarrow wp(call\text{-}\varepsilon,\ \varepsilon^0).$$

Having defined the values of all expressions, the satisfaction relation in M is then determined for all formulae in the usual way. But notice that the value $v_s(\sigma)$ of some expressions is no longer given in terms of the values of their sub-expressions, but depends instead on the meanings in M of $call$-σ and σ^0. Whether or not σ gets its intuitively intended value will thus depend on whether M is a *standard* model that gives the commands $call$-σ their intended meanings. Standard-model conditions for general commands are developed according to the following considerations.

(a) An assignment $(x := \sigma)$ is executed by first evaluating σ and then assigning to x the resulting value (i.e. the value of σ^0). Hence the standard-model condition for general assignments is

$$[\![x := \sigma]\!] = [\![call\text{-}\sigma \ ; \ x := \sigma^0]\!] .$$

In a model that fulfills the standard-model conditions for *skip* and ; , this condition already holds for *simple* σ.

(b) The conditional $(\varepsilon \Rightarrow \alpha,\beta)$ is implemented by first evaluating ε and then using the resulting value (ε^0) to decide which of α and β to perform. Hence we require that

$$[\![\varepsilon \Rightarrow \alpha,\beta]\!] = [\![call\text{-}\varepsilon \ ; \ (\varepsilon^0 \Rightarrow \alpha,\beta)]\!] .$$

(c) To perform the iteration $(\varepsilon\#\alpha)$, ε is first evaluated. If the result (ε^0) is 1, α is executed, and then ε evaluated again. If the result is 1, α is executed ..... and so on. Hence the standard-model condition is

$$[\![\varepsilon\#\alpha]\!] = [\![call\text{-}\varepsilon \ ; \ \varepsilon^0 \ \# \ (\alpha \ ; \ call\text{-}\varepsilon)]\!] .$$

(d) The standard-model conditions for general composites $(\alpha;\beta)$ and alternatives $(\alpha|\beta)$ are as before.

An E-model will be called *standard* if in addition to the usual standard-model conditions for simple commands it satisfies the conditions listed in (a) to (d) above.

In §4.5 we shall need to know the effect of the command $call\text{-}F(\sigma)$ on a standard model, given the declaration $function\ F(x);\alpha$. Since $call\text{-}F(\sigma)$ is $(call\text{-}\sigma\ ;\ x := \sigma^0\ ;\ \alpha)$, $F(\sigma)$ will be defined at state s only if there are s_1, s_2, t with $s [\![call\text{-}\sigma]\!] s_1 [\![x := \sigma^0]\!] s_2 [\![\alpha]\!] t$ and F defined at t (since then $v_s(F(\sigma)) = v_t(F))$. But then the standard model condition on simple assignment requires that σ^0 be defined at s_1, and so, as $[\![call\text{-}\sigma]\!]$ is functional, $[call\text{-}\sigma]D\sigma^0$ holds at s. Moreover $call\text{-}F(\sigma^0)$ is equivalent to $(x := \sigma^0\ ;\ \alpha)$, since $call\text{-}\sigma^0$ is $skip$, and so the value of $F(\sigma^0)$ at s_1 is then $v_t(F) = v_s(F(\sigma)) \neq \omega$.

These arguments establish the following results, which we record for later reference.

4.3.1 THEOREM.

If the declaration $function\ F(x);\alpha$ *belongs to* E, *then in a standard* E*-model:*

(1) *if* $s [\![call\text{-}\sigma]\!] s'$ *then* $v_s(F(\sigma)) = v_{s'}(F(\sigma^0))$, *and*

(2) *the formulae*

$$DF(\sigma) \rightarrow halts(call\text{-}\sigma)$$

$$DF(\sigma) \rightarrow [call\text{-}\sigma](D\sigma^0 \wedge DF(\sigma^0))$$

are valid. ■

4.4 COMPLETENESS FOR SIMPLE CALLS

A function declaration is *simple* if its body contains no function designators. The functions *rem*, *root*, and *multiply* are all of this kind. An environment E will be called simple if every declaration in E is itself simple. For such an environment it is demonstrable (inductively) that the command $call\text{-}\sigma$ is simple for every expression σ, and this yields a systematic method of constructing standard

E-models, as follows.

Let (A,S,v) be a structure in which $v_s(x)$ has been defined for all variable x, and in which $[\![x := \sigma]\!]$ has been given as a *functional* relation on S for all *simple* expressions σ. Then $[\![\alpha]\!]$ may be defined by the usual standard-model conditions on α for all simple commands α. This ensures that $[\![\alpha]\!]$ thus defined is functional whenever it contains only ;, $\Rightarrow$, and # (cf. Ex. 2.6.4(6)). Since E is simple, $[\![\mathit{call}\text{-}\sigma]\!]$ is defined at this stage for all σ, and, as required by the definition of "E-model", is always functional. General assignments may now be defined by the standard-model condition

$$[\![x := \sigma]\!] = [\![\mathit{call}\text{-}\sigma \;;\; x := \sigma^0]\!] ,$$

while the interpretation of general composites and alternatives is defined inductivel by the usual standard conditions for ; and $|$. For conditionals $(\varepsilon \Rightarrow \alpha,\beta)$ and iterations $(\varepsilon\#\alpha)$, the usual standard-model conditions may be used, assuming that $[\![\alpha]\!]$ and $[\![\beta]\!]$ have been defined, provided that the test condition ε is itself simple. This leaves the way open finally to inductively put

$$[\![\varepsilon \Rightarrow \alpha,\beta]\!] = [\![\varepsilon^0 \Rightarrow \alpha,\beta]\!] \circ [\![\mathit{call}\text{-}\varepsilon]\!]$$

and

$$[\![\varepsilon\#\alpha]\!] = [\![\varepsilon^0 \# (\alpha \;;\; \mathit{call}\text{-}\varepsilon)]\!] \circ [\![\mathit{call}\text{-}\varepsilon]\!] ,$$

for general ε (since ε^0 is always simple) thereby completing the definition of a standard model for our current language.

Now the definitions of the natural model M_A over an O-algebra A (§3.3), and the canonical model M_Δ for a rich theory Δ (§3.5) both begin by interpreting simple assignments as functional relations. Therefore the construction given just now applies to these structures, to produce natural and canonical standard E-models for our new language with function designators. Moreover the new versions of M_A and M_Δ are identical to the original ones when restricted to simple commands. This allows us to reduce the Completeness problem for our new models to the results of §3.5, for the case of a simple environment. The way this is done will now be outlined.

A logic Λ now includes the rules MP, TR and UG as before, and the rule OI under a restriction: in $\Phi(\varphi_n(\varepsilon,\alpha))$, ε is required to be simple. The axioms for Λ include

(i) the axioms A1 - A7, and A18 for tautologies, termination, *skip*, *abort*, composites, and alternations;

(ii) the axioms A8, A9, A10 for conditions and iterations that have *simple* test expressions;

(iii) the Boolean expression axioms A11 - A17 and algebraic expression axioms A31 - A36 restricted to simple expressions;

(iv) the assignment axioms A25 - A30 for simple assignments;

(v) the quantifier axioms A19 - A24 restricted to simple assignments;

(vi) the new general Boolean expression axiom

A37 $\varepsilon \leftrightarrow halts(call\text{-}\varepsilon) \wedge [call\text{-}\varepsilon]\varepsilon^0$;

(vii) the new general command axioms

A38 $[x := \sigma]\varphi \leftrightarrow [call\text{-}\sigma\ ;\ x := \sigma^0]\varphi$

A39 $[\varepsilon \Rightarrow \alpha,\beta]\varphi \leftrightarrow [call\text{-}\varepsilon\ ;\ \varepsilon^0 \Rightarrow \alpha,\beta]\varphi$

A40 $[\varepsilon\#\alpha]\varphi \leftrightarrow [call\text{-}\varepsilon\ ;\ \varepsilon^0\ \#\ (\alpha\ ;\ call\text{-}\varepsilon)]\varphi$

Now let M_Δ be a standard canonical model constructed as in §§3.4 and 3.5, with the extensions described in this section. Then the Fundamental Theorem, viz.

$$M_\Delta \models_\Gamma \varphi \quad \text{iff} \quad \varphi \in \Gamma,$$

holds for simple φ as before. But if φ is a general Boolean expression ε, then, as observed in the previous section, we have

$$M_\Delta \models_\Gamma \varepsilon \quad \text{iff} \quad M_\Delta \models_\Gamma halts(call\text{-}\varepsilon) \wedge [call\text{-}\varepsilon]\varepsilon^0 .$$

Moreover, since the ambient environment E is simple, $halts(call\text{-}\varepsilon) \wedge [call\text{-}\varepsilon]\varepsilon^0$ is a simple formula, and so the Fundamental Theorem holds for it. With the aid of A37 we can then conclude that it holds for ε as well. In order to extend it to all formulae, it then suffices to establish the two α-Lemmata of 3.5.6 and 3.5.7. But the proofs given already for these results continue to hold for all simple commands, and, inductively, in the cases of general composites, general alternatives, and conditionals and iterations that have simple test expressions. In view of the presence of the M_Δ-valid axioms A38 - A40, this is enough to yield the α-Lemmata for all commands whatsoever.

The full details of this development are left to the reader.

4.5 A PROOF RULE FOR FUNCTIONS

In Clint and Hoare (1972) an inference rule is given for correctness assertions about function calls. Given the declaration

$$\textit{function}\ F(\chi);\alpha,$$

with parameter list χ and body α, the rule takes the form

$$\vdash \varphi \rightarrow [\alpha]\psi$$

only if

$$\vdash \forall\chi(\varphi \rightarrow \psi^F_{F(\chi)}),$$

but is to be applied only when α makes no assignments to any formal parameters or non-local variables (i.e. causes no side effects). We presume here that φ and ψ are first-order formulae, and note also that in the presence of the rule UG it suffices to derive $\varphi \rightarrow \psi^F_{F(\chi)}$ to then obtain the conclusion of the rule. Indeed (cf. Ex. 3.3.3(4)) it suffices to derive the ostensibly weaker assertion

$$D\chi \rightarrow (\varphi \rightarrow \psi^F_{F(\chi)}).$$

In Hoare and Wirth (1973), further prerequisites to the application of the rule are given, including that F is not free in φ, and none of the parameters in the list χ is free in ψ. Ashcroft, Clint and Hoare (1976) subsequently observed the need for more restrictions, relating to termination of the body. They considered the declaration *function* $F(x)$;

F := 0 ; *while true do skip*.

n a standard model the body of this declaration never terminates, and hence

$$true \rightarrow [F := 0 \ ;\ true\#skip](false \wedge F = 0)$$

s valid. But the proposed rule would allow us to then deduce the absurdity

$$\forall x(true \rightarrow false \wedge F(x) = 0).$$

The authors suggest that the contradiction could be avoided if the concl-sion of the rule were modified to read "*if* $F(x)$ *is defined then* $\varphi \rightarrow \psi^F_{F(x)}$" and onclude by observing that "*the successful use of functions in programming will epend on a proper treatment of termination, which is not possible within the calculus f conditional correctness*".

In order to consider the new proof rule in our present context, we need ome preliminary facts, which are recorded as exercises. The first is a refinement f the result (3.3.1) that satisfaction depends only on the values of *free* variables n formulae. The second fact is that the value of a variable is unaltered by any imple command whose execution involves no assignment to that variable.

.5.1 EXERCISES.

In a standard model:

1) Let $v_s(\sigma) = v_t(\rho)$. Then

(i) $v_s(\tau^x_\sigma) = v_t(\tau^x_\rho)$ if v_s and v_t assign the same values to all non-simple expressions occurring in τ and to all variables in τ other than x;

(ii) $\models_s \psi^x_\sigma$ iff $\models_t \psi^x_\rho$, if v_s and v_t agree on all non-simple expressions in ψ and all free variables of ψ other than x.

2) If α is a simple program having no assignment of the form $(y := \sigma)$, and $s [\![\alpha]\!] t$, then $v_s(y) = v_t(y)$. ■

It follows from the last exercise that if $s [\![\alpha]\!] t$ in a standard model, then v_s and v_t agree on any *simple* expression σ whose variables all have no assignment within α. But what if σ is a non-simple expression? In that case the value of σ is found by executing $call$-σ and evaluating σ^0. Intuitively then we would expect α to leave the result of this process unchanged if it made no assignments to variable in $call$ σ or σ^0. To formalise that intuition we need the following technical fact.

4.5.2 THEOREM.

Let Y be a fixed set of variables, and let β be a simple command such that all variables within expressions occurring in β are included in Y. Suppose that in a standard model there are states s, t such that v_s and v_t agree on all members of Y. Then if $s [\![\beta]\!] s'$, there exists a state t' such that $t [\![\beta]\!] t'$ and $v_{s'}$ and $v_{t'}$ agree on all members of Y.

Proof.

The proof is carried out for all states s and t, by induction on the formation of the simple command β.

a. Suppose β is the simple assignment $(y := \tau)$. Since then $s [\![y := \tau]\!] s'$, we must have $v_s(\tau) \neq \omega$. But by hypothesis $Var\tau \subseteq Y$, so v_s and v_t agree on all variables in the simple expression τ, which is enough to ensure that $v_t(\tau) = v_s(\tau) \neq \omega$. Since the model is standard, there must then be a state t' with $t [\![y := \tau]\!] t'$ as desired. For such a t' we have $v_t =_y v_{t'}$ and $v_{t'}(y) = v_t(\tau)$. But $v_s =_y v_{s'}$ and $v_{s'}(y) = v_{t'}(y)$, and so as v_s and v_t agree on Y, so too will $v_{s'}$ and $v_{t'}$.

b. Suppose β is $(\alpha;\gamma)$, and assume the result for α and γ. Then if $s [\![\beta]\!] s'$, there exists s'' with $s [\![\alpha]\!] s'' [\![\gamma]\!] s'$. By hypothesis on α, there then must be a state t'' with $t [\![\alpha]\!] t''$ and $v_{s''}$ and $v_{t''}$ agreeing on Y. Applying the assumed result for γ to s'' and t'', it follows that there is a t' with $v_{s'}$ agreeing with $v_{t'}$ on Y, and $t'' [\![\gamma]\!] t'$, hence $t [\![\alpha;\gamma]\!] t'$ as desired.

c. Suppose β is $(\varepsilon \Rightarrow \alpha,\gamma)$, and assume the result for α and γ. If $s [\![\beta]\!] t'$

then either $v_s(\varepsilon) = 1$ and s [[α]] s', or $v_s(\varepsilon) = 0$ and s [[γ]] s'. Assume the former (the latter is similar). Then by the induction hypothesis on α, there exists t' such that $v_{s'}$ and $v_{t'}$ agree on Y, and t [[α]] t'. But $Var\varepsilon \subseteq Y$, by hypothesis on β, and so v_s and v_t assign the same value to the simple expression ε. Hence $v_t(\varepsilon) = 1$, making t [[β]] t', and the result hold for β.

These cases indicate how the remaining ones work, and the rest of the proof is left to the reader (who may consult the proof of 3.3.12 for further guidance as to proof-strategy). ■

If a command α contains an assignment to a variable that occurs either in σ^0 or in an expression within the command *call*-σ, we will say that α *causes a side effect* on the expression σ. In the case that the expression in question is a simple variable x, α will thus cause a side effect on x just in case it contains an assignment of the form $(x := \tau)$. Armed with this notion, our above intuitive observation becomes the formal statement

4.5.3 THEOREM.

Assuming a simple environment, let α be a simple command that causes no side effect on σ. Then in a standard model, if s [[α]] t then $v_s(\sigma) = v_t(\sigma)$.

Proof.

Let Y be the set of all variables occurring in σ^0 and in expressions within *call*-σ. Then α makes no assignments to members of Y, and so by Exercise 4.5.1(2), v_s and v_t agree on Y.

Now suppose $v_s(\sigma) \neq \omega$. Then there exists a state s' with s [[*call*-σ]] s' and $v_s(\sigma) = v_{s'}(\sigma^0)$. Since the environment is simple, *call*-σ is a simple command so we can take it as β in 4.5.2 to obtain a t' with t [[*call*-σ]] t' and $v_{s'}$ and $v_{t'}$ agreeing on Y. But then $v_t(\sigma) = v_{t'}(\sigma^0)$, and, since $Var\sigma^0 \subseteq Y$, $v_{s'}(\sigma^0) = v_{t'}(\sigma^0)$, which gives the result that $v_t(\sigma) = v_s(\sigma) \neq \omega$. But Theorem 4.5.2 is symmetrical in s and t, so we can interchange their roles to show that if $v_t(\sigma) \neq \omega$ then

$v_s(\sigma) = v_t(\sigma) \neq \omega$. Altogether this is enough to make $v_s(\sigma) = v_t(\sigma)$ in general.

■

For the purposes of the following discussion let

$$\mathit{function}\ F(\chi)\,;\alpha$$

be a fixed declaration in a fixed simple environment E, with χ a list $(x_1, \ldots, x_n)$ of formal parameters. The body α is thus a simple command that in general contains an assignment to the main variable F. Let ψ be a fixed first-order formula with the property that α causes no side effect on any expression occurring in ψ *other than* F.

4.5.4 THEOREM.

In a natural E-model, the following are valid.

(1) $[\alpha]\psi \wedge \mathit{halts}(\alpha) \rightarrow (D\chi \rightarrow \psi^F_{F(\chi)})$

(2) $[\alpha]\psi \rightarrow (DF(\chi) \rightarrow \psi^F_{F(\chi)})$.

Proof.

(1) "$D\chi$" here abbreviates "$Dx_1 \wedge \ldots \wedge Dx_n$". The command $\mathit{call}\text{-}F(\chi)$ is, by definition

$$(\mathit{call}\text{-}x_1\ ;\ x_1 := x_1^0\ ;\ \ldots\ ;\ \mathit{call}\text{-}x_n\ ;\ x_n^0 := x_n\ ;\ \alpha)$$

which is equivalent, since the model is standard and each x_i is simple, to

$$(x_1 := x_1\ ;\ x_2 := x_2\ ;\ \ldots\ ;\ x_n := x_n\ ;\ \alpha)$$

But in a natural model we have

$$s\,[\![\,x := x\,]\!]\,t \quad \text{iff} \quad s(x) \neq \omega \text{ and } s = t,$$

and so

$$\models_s Dx \quad \text{iff} \quad s\,[\![\,x := x\,]\!]\,s.$$

Now suppose $[\alpha]\psi$, *halts* (α), and $D\chi$ all hold at s. Then there exists a state t with $s [\![\alpha]\!] t$ and $\models_t \psi$. Moreover Dx_i holds at s for $1 \leqslant i \leqslant n$, and so the above observation yields

$$s [\![x_1 := x_1]\!] s \ldots . \; s [\![x_n := x_n]\!] s [\![\alpha]\!] t \; .$$

This in turn entails

$$s [\![\mathit{call}\text{-}F(\chi)]\!] t,$$

so that

$$v_s(F(\chi)) = v_t(F) .$$

Since α causes no side effects to expressions of ψ other than F, it follows by 4.5.1(2) and 4.5.3 that v_s and v_t agree on all such expressions. Hence by 4.5.1(1ii),

$$\models_s \psi^F_{F(\chi)} \quad \text{iff} \quad \models_t \psi^F_F$$

But ψ^F_F is just ψ, which does hold at t, and so $\psi^F_{F(\chi)}$ holds at s as desired.

(2) Suppose $[\alpha]\psi$ and $DF(\chi)$ hold at s. Then $v_s(F(\chi)) \neq \omega$ and so there exists a t with $s [\![\mathit{call}\text{-}F(\chi)]\!] t$ and $v_s(F(\chi)) = v_t(F)$. By the analysis that began the proof of (1), we conclude that $s [\![\alpha]\!] t$. Hence ψ holds at t. From this, as in (1), it follows that $\psi^F_{F(\chi)}$ holds at s.

■

Part (1) of this Theorem yields the validity in natural (and hence standard) models of

$$wp(\alpha,\psi) \rightarrow (D\chi \rightarrow \psi^F_{F(\chi)}) .$$

Thus if $\varphi \rightarrow wp(\alpha,\psi)$ is valid, so too will be

$$D\chi \rightarrow (\varphi \rightarrow \psi^F_{F(\chi)}) .$$

But if the latter is valid, so too is

$$\forall x_1 \ldots \forall x_n (\varphi \rightarrow \psi^F_{F(\chi)}) .$$

Hence we obtain the standard-validity of the following version of the Clint-Hoare rule:

If $\vdash \varphi \rightarrow wp(\alpha, \psi)$

then $\vdash \forall \chi(\varphi \rightarrow \psi^{F}_{F(\chi)})$.

The essential modification here is an hypothesis ($halts(\alpha)$) about termination of the function body that overcomes the difficulty cited by Ashcroft, Clint, and Hoare (1976). The modification suggested by those authors is also accommodated here, for by part (2) of the last Theorem we get the validity of the rule

If $\vdash \varphi \rightarrow [\alpha]\psi$

then $\vdash DF(\chi) \rightarrow (\varphi \rightarrow \psi^{F}_{F(\chi)})$.

The restrictions imposed on ψ in this analysis relate naturally to the Clint-Hoare requirement that α makes no assignments to non-local variables. The role of φ and ψ in the correctness assertion $\varphi \rightarrow [\alpha]\psi$ is to describe the situation before and after execution of α. Typically then φ and ψ will make assertions about the values of variables that are not local to α. If α makes no assignments to such variables, then in any proposed application of the proof rule we can indeed expect that α causes no side effects on expressions within ψ other than F. In fact, as we saw in the second version of *multiply*, it is very easy to write any function declaration in such a way that its body α makes assignments only to local variables. Since the latter are used just to facilitate execution of the function call, and cease to have any significance once termination occurs, we would not expect them to figure in the "post-condition" ψ at all.

Next we consider calls of the function F that involve actual parameters other than the original formal ones. To simplify the notation, suppose that the declaration for F has a single formal parameter x. Suppose also that we are working in a fixed standard $\mathcal{E}$-model and that "$\models$" refers to validity in this model.

For any expression σ, *call*-$F(\sigma)$ is the command

$$(\mathit{call}\text{-}\sigma \ ; \ x := \sigma^0 \ ; \ \alpha),$$

where α is the body of the F-declaration. We continue to assume that α causes no side effect on any expression in ψ other than F.

4.5.5 THEOREM.

Suppose that x is not free in ψ, and that

$$\models \varphi \rightarrow [\mathit{call}\text{-}F(\sigma)]\psi.$$

Then

(1) $\models DF(\sigma) \rightarrow (\varphi \rightarrow [\mathit{call}\text{-}\sigma]\psi^F_{F(\sigma^0)})$,

and (2) *if σ is simple,*

$$\models DF(\sigma) \rightarrow (\varphi \rightarrow \psi^F_{F(\sigma)}).$$

Proof.

By validity of the composition axiom A7,

$$\models [\mathit{call}\text{-}F(\sigma)]\psi \rightarrow [\mathit{call}\text{-}\sigma][x := \sigma^0][\alpha]\psi.$$

But the formula of 4.5.4(2) is valid in standard models if it is valid in natural ones, and it leads us to conclude that

$$\models [\mathit{call}\text{-}\sigma][x := \sigma^0][\alpha]\psi \rightarrow [\mathit{call}\text{-}\sigma][x := \sigma^0](DF(x) \rightarrow \psi^F_{F(x)}).$$

But we know (from Ex. 3.5.10) that

$$[x := \sigma^0](DF(x) \rightarrow \psi^F_{F(x)})$$

holds at a state only if

$$D\sigma^0 \rightarrow (DF(x) \rightarrow \psi^F_{F(x)})^x_{\sigma^0}$$

does. Moreover the consequent of the formula just given is equal to

$$DF(\sigma^0) \rightarrow (\psi^F_{F(x)})^x_{\sigma^0} ,$$

and, *since x is not free in ψ*, the consequent of this last formula is equal to $\psi^F_{F(\sigma^0)}$.

Putting all of these pieces together we arrive at a demonstration that

$$\models [\mathit{call}\text{-}F(\sigma)]\psi \rightarrow [\mathit{call}\text{-}\sigma](D\sigma^0 \rightarrow (DF(\sigma^0) \rightarrow \psi^F_{F(\sigma^0)})).$$

But we saw in Theorem 4.3.1 that

$$\models DF(\sigma) \rightarrow [\mathit{call}\text{-}\sigma](D\sigma^0 \wedge DF(\sigma^0)).$$

These last two valid formulae entail that

$$\models DF(\sigma) \rightarrow ([\mathit{call}\text{-}F(\sigma)]\psi \rightarrow [\mathit{call}\text{-}\sigma]\psi^F_{F(\sigma^0)}),$$

from which (1) follows readily if $\varphi \rightarrow [\mathit{call}\text{-}F(\sigma)]\psi$ is valid.

(2) By (1), since $\mathit{call}\text{-}\sigma$ is *skip* and σ^0 is σ when σ is simple.

■

The requirement that the formal parameter x not be free in ψ, which is stated explicitly in Hoare and Wirth (1973), p.344, is appropriate to the role of x in executing the command $\mathit{call}\text{-}F(\sigma)$. As we saw in discussing *multiply*, $F(\sigma)$ is evaluated by passing the value of σ to a new local variable referred to by "x". That is, by paragraph 4.7.3.1 of the Revised Algol 60 Report, x is treated as local to the fictitious block $(x := \sigma^0 \ ; \ \alpha)$. Thus in execution of $\mathit{call}\text{-}F(\sigma)$ when the actual parameter σ is not x itself, we may regard x as a local variable whose role is simply to facilitate evaluation of $F(\sigma)$. Hence x would not feature in any post-condition ψ to a correctness assertion about $\mathit{call}\text{-}F(\sigma)$.

The result of 4.5.5(1) can be refined if we eliminate side effects, not just from the declaration body α, but from the whole of the evaluation of $F(\sigma)$. Alternatively, we confine ourselves to post-conditions that receive no side effects rom this evaluation.

.5.6 THEOREM.

If call-σ causes no side effect on any expression in ψ other than F, then

$$\models [call\text{-}\sigma]\psi^{F}_{F(\sigma^0)} \to (halts(call\text{-}\sigma) \to \psi^{F}_{F(\sigma)}).$$

roof.

Suppose $[call\text{-}\sigma]\psi^{F}_{F(\sigma^0)}$ and $halts(call\text{-}\sigma)$ hold at s. Then for some t we ave s ⟦ $call\text{-}\sigma$ ⟧ t and $\models_t \psi^{F}_{F(\sigma^0)}$. But by 4.3.1(1), $v_s(F(\sigma)) = v_t(F(\sigma^0))$, and by .5.1(2) and 4.5.3, v_s and v_t agree on all expressions in ψ other than F. Hence y 4.5.1(1ii), $\models_s \psi^{F}_{F(\sigma)}$ as desired.

■

.5.7 COROLLARY.

Suppose x is not free in ψ, call-F(σ) causes no side effect on any expres-ion occurring in ψ other than F, and

$$\models \varphi \to [call\text{-}F(\sigma)]\psi.$$

hen

$$\models DF(\sigma) \to (\varphi \to \psi^{F}_{F(\sigma)}).$$

roof.

Since $call\text{-}F(\sigma)$ is $(call\text{-}\sigma\ ;\ x := \sigma^0\ ;\ \alpha)$ it follows that $call\text{-}\sigma$ also auses no side effects in ψ except to F. Hence by applying 4.5.5(1) and 4.5.6 to he hypothesis we obtain

$$\models DF(\sigma) \to (\varphi \to (halts(call\text{-}\sigma) \to \psi^{F}_{F(\sigma)}).$$

ince, by 4.3.1(2), we have

$$\models DF(\sigma) \to halts(call\text{-}\sigma),$$

he desired conclusion follows.

■

With regard to assignments involving function designators, we have the following result.

4.5.8 THEOREM.

If F is not free in ψ, and α causes no side effects on expressions in ψ, then the formula

$$[y := F(x)]\psi \leftrightarrow (DF(x) \rightarrow \psi^{y}_{F(x)})$$

is valid in standard models.

Proof.

It suffices to show validity in natural models. Suppose then that $[y := F(x)]\psi$ holds at state s in a natural model. If $DF(x)$ holds at s, then there exists t with $s \llbracket \mathit{call}\text{-}F(x) \rrbracket t$ and $v_s(F(x)) = v_t(F) \neq \omega$. Since $\mathit{call}\text{-}F(x)$ is $(x := x;\alpha)$, it follows as in the proof of 4.5.4(1) that $v_s(x) \neq \omega$ and $s \llbracket \alpha \rrbracket t$. But since F is defined at t, and the model is standard, there exists t' with $t \llbracket y := F \rrbracket t'$. Hence we have $s \llbracket \mathit{call}\text{-}F(x) \; ; \; y := F \rrbracket t'$ and so $s \llbracket y := F(x) \rrbracket t'$ (by validity of A38). It follows that ψ holds at t', and hence as $t(y/F)t'$, ψ^{y}_{F} holds at t (3.3.11).

Now as α causes no side effects on expressions in ψ, it causes none on expressions of ψ^{y}_{F} other than F. As $v_s(F(x)) = v_t(F)$ and $s \llbracket \alpha \rrbracket t$, it follows that since ψ^{y}_{F} holds at t, $(\psi^{y}_{F})^{F}_{F(x)}$ holds at s. But this last formula is just $\psi^{y}_{F(x)}$, as F is not free in ψ. This shows that $(DF(x) \rightarrow \psi^{y}_{F(x)})$ holds at s.

The converse is left to the reader since it involves very similar reasoning

■

4.5.9 EXERCISE.

If x and F are not free in ψ, and $\mathit{call}\text{-}F(\sigma)$ causes no side effects on expressions in ψ, then

$$\models [y := F(\sigma)]\psi \leftrightarrow (DF(\sigma) \rightarrow \psi^{y}_{F(\sigma)}).$$

■

4.6 CALL-BY-NAME

Instead of evaluating $F(\sigma)$, given the declaration *function* $F(x);\alpha$, by assigning the value of σ to x and then executing α, we could proceed to execute the command that is obtained from α by literally replacing each occurrence of the formal variable x by σ. This method of dealing with an actual parameter is known as "name replacement", or "call by name". It requires that σ itself be a variable of the same type as x. Variables treated in this way are known as *variable parameters*, while those called by value are *value parameters*. Algol 60 identifies the latter by prefixing the word *value* to them in the declaration, and leaves variable parameters undesignated. Pascal adopts the opposite convention of prefixing *var* to variable parameters and leaving value parameters undesignated.

Paragraph 4.7.3.2 of the Revised Report on Algol 60 describes the effect of the call-by-name method as follows. "*Any formal parameter not quoted in the value list is replaced, throughout the body, by the corresponding actual parameter ... . Possible conflicts between identifiers inserted through this process and other identifiers already present within the body will be avoided by suitable systematic changes of the formal or local identifiers involved.*"

The point about conflicts between identifiers is illustrated by the declaration

function $F(x)$;

$y := sin\ x\ ;\ F := y/x.$

Here y is serving as a local variable to facilitate computation of the function $sin\ x/x$. Were we to call y itself by name, to evaluate $F(y)$, we would however find ourselves executing

$$y := sin\ y\ ;\ F := y/y$$

and returning the value 1 no matter what (non-zero) value y had. To avoid this situation we would have to replace y by some other local variable. According to Alagic and Arbib (p.159), "this is performed by the compiler, and so the programmer does not have to be concerned with that".

We will follow the Pascal conventions and write declarations in the form

$$\mathit{function}\ F(x_1,\ \dots,\ x_n\ ;\ \mathit{var}\ y_1,\ \dots,\ y_m)\ ;\ \alpha$$

to indicate that $x_1, \dots, x_n$ are formal value parameters and $y_1, \dots, y_m$ are formal variable parameters. We write $\alpha(y|z)$ to denote the command obtained by replacing *every* occurrence of the variable y by the variable z in α.

For simplicity of exposition, suppose $n = m = 1$, and we have one value parameter x and one variable parameter y. This allows us to consider function designators of the form $F(\sigma,z)$, where the actual parameter σ is an expression, and z is a variable. We extend the definition of call-σ given in §4.2 to such designators by defining call-$F(\sigma,z)$ to be the command

$$(\mathit{call}\text{-}\sigma\ ;\ x := \sigma^0\ ;\ \alpha(y|z)).$$

The theory then proceeds as before.

4.6.1 EXERCISES.

(1) If $\models \varphi \to [\mathit{call}\text{-}F(\sigma,z)]\psi$

then $\vdash DF(\sigma,z) \to (\varphi \to \psi^F_{F(\sigma,z)})$,

provided that x is not free in the first-order formula ψ, and call-$F(\sigma,z)$ causes no side effect on any expression in ψ other than F.

(2) If x, ψ and call-$F(\sigma,z)$ are constrained as in (1), then

$$\models [w := F(\sigma,z)]\psi \leftrightarrow (DF(\sigma,z) \to \psi^w_{F(\sigma,z)}).$$

■

4.7 NON-RECURSIVE FUNCTIONS

A declaration *function* $F(x);\alpha$ that fails to be simple has some function designator, say $G(\tau)$, within its body α. For instance α may contain the assignment $(y := G(\tau))$. But if G is given by a declaration *function* $G(z);\beta$, we could replace this assignment by the equivalent command (call-$G(\tau)$; $y := G(\tau)^0$), i.e.

$$(\mathit{call}\text{-}\tau \ ; \ z := \tau^0 \ ; \ \beta \ ; \ y := G).$$

If call-τ and β are simple, this equivalent command is simple, and the replacement may well reduce α to a simple command. Alternatively, call-τ and/or β could contain new function designators, which we then subject to the same analysis. If after a finite number of repetitions of this process we reach a stage where only simple commands are produced, then the original α has been replaced by an equivalent sequence of simple commands, and our theory can be adapted to cater for designators involving F.

However there are some algorithms, the so-called *recursive* ones, for which this strategy cannot work. The extreme case is where a designator of the form $F(\sigma)$ appears in the body of F itself. The most celebrated example of this involves the *factorial* function

$$x! = 1 \times 2 \times \ldots \times x.$$

Since $0! = 1$, and otherwise $x! = x \times (x-1)!$, we can compute factorials in $\mathbb{N}$ by the algorithm

```
function Fact(x) ;
   var z ;
   begin if x = 0 then Fact := 1
         else begin z := Fact (x-1) ;
                    Fact := x × z
              end
   end.
```

(Actually we could have avoided the local variable z and directly put $Fact := x \times Fact(x-1)$, but the formulation given makes it easier to bring out the following point).

Let α be the body of *Fact*. According to the above recipe we replace $(z := Fact(x-1))$ in α by $(\mathit{call}\text{-}Fact(x-1)\ ;\ z := Fact)$, i.e.

$$(\mathit{call}\text{-}(x-1)\ ;\ x := x-1\ ;\ \alpha\ ;\ z := Fact).$$

(Note that $(x-1)$ is not a variable, so it has to be treated as a value parameter). However this introduces a *new* copy of α containing the assignment we were trying to eliminate!

To avoid this situation we must bar any designators involving F from α, and more generally from the body of any function that has to be called in order to complete the execution of α. To achieve this we introduce some new terminology. Given an environment E, we write $F_1(E)F_2$ to mean that there exists a function declaration in E that has F_1 as its main variable and a designator of the form $F_2(\sigma)$ occurring in its body. An *E-sequence* is a finite list $F_1, \ldots, F_n$ of variables, not necessarily distinct, having $F_1(E)F_2 \ \ldots.\ (E)F_n$. In these terms we can define E to be a *non-recursive* environment if for every main variable F of a declaration in E there are only finitely many different E-sequences that start with F. In particular every simple environment is non-recursive: the number of E-sequences is 0.

To see how this concept eliminates recursive algorithms like *Fact*, observe that if E contains the above declaration for this function we have $Fact(E)Fact$, and hence $Fact(E)Fact(E)\ \ldots.\ (E)Fact$ for any number of repetitions. In other words there are infinitely many E-sequences that start with *Fact*. In general if any E-sequence has a repetition anywhere in it we can construct infinitely many E-sequence that start from the repeated variable.

Now in a non-recursive environment the number of function designators encountered in processing a function body is finite. This number can be used as a measure of complexity in showing inductively that every command α is equivalent to a simple command α^0. The definition proceeds simultaneously with the inductive definition of the simple command *call*-σ, and has

$$(x := \sigma)^0 = (\mathit{call}\text{-}\sigma \;;\; x := \sigma^0)$$

$$(\alpha;\beta)^0 = (\alpha^0 \;;\; \beta^0)$$

$$(\varepsilon \Rightarrow \alpha,\beta)^0 = (\mathit{call}\text{-}\varepsilon \;;\; \varepsilon^0 \Rightarrow \alpha^0,\beta^0)$$

$$(\varepsilon\#\alpha)^0 = (\mathit{call}\text{-}\varepsilon \;;\; \varepsilon^0 \;\#\; (\alpha^0 \;;\; \mathit{call}\text{-}\varepsilon))$$

$$(\alpha|\beta)^0 = (\alpha^0|\beta^0)\,.$$

In the definition of *call*-σ we make one modification - when σ is the expression $F(\tau,z)$, given the E-declaration

$$\mathit{function}\ F(x \;;\; \mathit{var}\ y) \;;\; \alpha.$$

Here, since F cannot occur in α, we can make the inductive assumption that α^0 has already been defined. (In fact since the number of E-sequences beginning with F is finite, we can use the relation $F_1(E)F_2$ to impose a finite-tree structure on the collection of function calls involved in executing α and construct α^0 by induction over the formation of this tree). *call*-$F(\tau,z)$. is then defined as

$$(\mathit{call}\text{-}\tau \;;\; x := \tau^0 \;;\; \alpha^0(y|z))\,.$$

With these definitions it can be shown that in a standard model, as defined in §4.3, the relations $[\![\,\alpha\,]\!]$ and $[\![\,\alpha^0\,]\!]$ are identical, and hence the schema

$$[\alpha]\varphi \leftrightarrow [\alpha^0]\varphi$$

is valid. By adopting it as an axiom we reduce the proof of the Fundamental Theorem to the simple case.

CHAPTER 5

PROCEDURES

5.1 DECLARATIONS

A *procedure declaration* gives a name to a command α in such a way that α can be invoked as a subroutine of some longer program simply by inserting its name at the desired point, rather than writing out the whole of α itself. The advantages to the programmer of such a facility are obvious when α is a lengthy command that is to be used several times.

As an example, the following declaration assigns the name "*swap*" to an algorithm for interchanging the values of the variables x and y.

procedure swap ;
var u ;
begin u := x ; x := y ; y := u end.

An example of an actual command that used this declaration would be

begin $x := 1 \; ; \; y := 2$; *swap end*

The variable u here is *local* to the declaration block, and its role is to facilitate the interchange of the values of the non-local variables x and y. The example shows that, unlike a function declaration, it is desirable, and sometimes essential, that a procedure body be allowed to make assignments to non-local variables.

As written, *swap* can only process the two particular variables x and y. But this limitation can be overcome by allowing procedure declarations to have formal parameters, just as for functions. Thus we form

```
procedure swap (x,y) ;
   var u ;
   begin u := x ; x := y ; y := u end.
```

Then a program may include commands of the form *swap* (z,w), where z and w are variables (actual parameters) of the same types as the formal parameters x and y respectively. Such commands are known as *procedure calls*.

The same notation as before is used to distinguish value and variable parameters. Consider, for example, the declaration

```
procedure mult (x,y ; var z) ;
   var u ;
   begin u := y ; z := 0 ;
        while u ≠ 0 do
              begin z := z + x ;
                    u := u - 1 ;
              end
   end
```

The effect of the call $mult(\sigma,\tau,r)$ is to assign to the variable r the product of the values of the expressions σ and τ. Thus this call corresponds to the assignment

$$r := multiply(\sigma,\tau),$$

where *multiply* is the function whose declaration was given in §4.1.

Value parameters generally serve to supply the procedure with values, i.e. data to work on, while variable parameters often serve to communicate the results of the procedure call. This is sometimes described in terms of value parameters *supplying input* and variable parameters *recording output*.

A procedure declaration can be recursive, i.e. involve a call of itself, as in *procedure* $Fact(x\ ;\ var\ y)$

  var u ;

  begin if $x = 0$ *then* $y := 1$

    else begin $Fact(x-1,\ u)$;

      $y := x \times u$

    end

  end

5.2 CALLING A PROCEDURE

To simplify our formal discussion of procedure declarations we return to a one-sorted language $(\mathcal{O}, X)$ and add to it a set Pid of symbols to be called *procedure identifiers*. The rules for command formation are then augmented by

(1) $Pid \subseteq Cmd$, and

(2) if $P \in Pid$ then $P(\sigma_1, \ldots, \sigma_n\ ;\ z_1, \ldots, z_m) \in Cmd$

for any $\sigma_1, \ldots, \sigma_n \in Exp$ and $z_1, \ldots, z_m \in X \cup Bvb$.

These two new types of commands are *procedure calls*.

A *procedure declaration* is, formally, a symbolism either of the "parameter-less" form

(I) *procedure* $P\ ;\ \alpha$,

or else of the form

(II) *procedure* $P(x_1, \ldots, x_n\ ;\ var\ y_1, \ldots, y_m)\ ;\ \alpha$,

where

(i) $P \in Pid$,

(ii) the variables $x_1, \ldots, x_n$ are formal value parameters,

(iii) the variables $y_1, \ldots, y_m$ are formal variable parameters,

(iv) α is a command, the procedure *body*.

An *environment* is a set E of procedure declarations, no two of which have the same procedure identifier. A procedure call γ is *defined by* E if either

(i) γ is a single identifier P and there is a declaration of the form (I) in E with P as its identifier; or else

(ii) γ is of the form $P(\sigma_1, \ldots, \sigma_n ; z_1, \ldots, z_m)$ and there is a declaration for P in E of the form (II) for which each σ_i and z_j is of the same type as the corresponding x_i and y_j respectively.

A command is *simple* if it contains no subcommands that are procedure calls, and an environment E is simple if every procedure body in E is simple. For such an environment, each procedure call γ has the same effect as a certain simple command *call*-γ. To define this we introduce the notation

$$\alpha(y \;, \ldots, y_m | z_1, \ldots, z_m)$$

to denote the command obtained by uniformly replacing the variable y_i by z_i in α, for $1 \leqslant i \leqslant m$. The construction of *call*-γ is by cases, as follows.

(1) *call*-γ is *abort* if γ is not defined by E.

(2) if γ is P, and E has the declaration

$$\textit{procedure } P \;;\; \alpha \;,$$

then *call*-γ is α.

(3) if γ is $P(\sigma_1, \ldots, \sigma_n ; z_1, \ldots, z_m)$, and E has the declaration

$$\textit{procedure } P(x_1, \ldots, x_n ; y_1, \ldots, y_m) \;;\; \alpha \;,$$

then *call*-γ is

$$(x_1 := \sigma_1 \;;\; \ldots . \;;\; x_n := \sigma_n \;;\; \alpha(y_1, \ldots, y_m | z_1, \ldots, z_m) .$$

Each command α can now be turned into an equivalent simple command α^0 by replacing each procedure call γ in α by the simple command *call*-γ. In particular,

γ^0 is just $call\text{-}\gamma$ itself. In a standard model we would require that α and α^0 have the same meaning. For this it suffices that each procedure call have

$$[\![\gamma]\!] = [\![call\text{-}\gamma]\!] ,$$

since if the model satisfies the appropriate standard-model conditions for all other command-constructs it follows inductively that

$$[\![\alpha]\!] = [\![\alpha^0]\!]$$

for all commands α.

Thus in constructing a standard model, such as the natural M_A or canonical M_Δ, we may proceed as usual with assignments, composites, conditionals, iterations, and alternations, and *define* $[\![\gamma]\!]$ to be $[\![call\text{-}\gamma]\!]$. If the environment E is simple, then $call\text{-}\gamma$ will be simple and the definition well-founded.

As to completeness, the discussion just given indicates that the additional axiom schema

$$[\gamma]\varphi \leftrightarrow [call\text{-}\gamma]\varphi$$

allows us to reduce the proof of the Fundamental Theorem to the simple case.

5.2.1 EXERCISE.

Extend the theory just outlined to encompass non-recursive procedures whose bodies contain calls of other procedures.

■

5.3 HOARE'S RULE OF SUBSTITUTION

In Hoare (1971) a proof rule for non-recursive procedures with parameters is given in which parameter passing is modelled logically by substitution for variables. A declaration is written in the form

$$\textit{procedure}\ P(\chi\ ;\ y)\ ;\ \alpha\ ,$$

with the formal parameter list divided into a list y of all those which are subject to assignment in the body α, and a list χ of those which do not appear on the left of any assignment command in α. It is assumed that all non-local variables of α appear among the formal parameters. Hoare states (p.105) that "these decisions merely simplify the discussion; they do not involve any loss of generality, since any program can fairly readily be transformed to one which observes the conventions."

In any call of P, the variables in χ may be replaced by expressions as actual parameters, while members of y are to be replaced by other variables. This treatment of the members of χ and y respectively is close to the distinction between value and variable parameters, and indeed some expositions define the variable parameters of a procedure as being those that receive assignment in its body. Accordingly, in what follows we shall call members of χ by value and members of y by name.

Hoare's *Rule of Invocation* is that

$$\vdash \varphi \to [\alpha]\psi$$

implies $$\vdash \varphi \to [P(\chi,y)]\psi\ ,$$

while for actual parameters other than the original formal ones, the *Rule of Substitution* states that

$$\vdash \varphi \to [P(\chi;y)]\psi$$

implies $$\vdash \varphi^{\chi\,y}_{\underline{\sigma}\,z} \to [P(\underline{\sigma};z)]\psi^{\chi\,y}_{\underline{\sigma}\,z}\ .$$

Here it will be assumed that φ and ψ are first-order formulae. $\varphi^{\chi\,y}_{\underline{\sigma}\,z}$ is the formula obtained from φ by substituting each expression in the list $\underline{\sigma}$ for (all free occurrences of) the corresponding variable in the list χ, and each variable in the list z for the corresponding member of y.

Notice that in general, $\varphi^{x'\,x}_{\sigma'\,\sigma}$ need not be the same formula as $(\varphi^{x'}_{\sigma'})^{x}_{\sigma}$, unless x does not occur freely in φ. Notice also that the argument for the validity of

$$\varphi^x_\sigma \to [x := \sigma]\varphi$$

in any standard model (cf. 3.3.10) extends to give the standard-validity of

$$(\varphi^{x'}_{\sigma'})^x_\sigma \to [x := \sigma \ ; \ x' := \sigma']\varphi.$$

These observations will be employed below.

The reason why the Rule of Invocation is validated by our present theory can be adequately conveyed under the simplification that χ consists of a single variable x. For, if

$$\varphi \to [\alpha]\psi$$

is valid in a standard model, then so too is

$$[x := x]\varphi \to [x := x][\alpha]\psi.$$

But the command $(x := x)$ terminates only if x is defined, and in that case is equivalent to *skip*. Indeed

$$\theta \to [x := x]\theta$$

is standardly-valid for any θ at all, so the standard validity of the previous formula leads to that of

$$\varphi \to [x := x \ ; \ \alpha]\psi.$$

Since $(x := x \ ; \ \alpha)$ is in this case *call*-$P(\chi;y)$, and a standard model validates

$$[\gamma]\theta \leftrightarrow [\mathit{call}\text{-}\gamma]\theta,$$

this leads to the validity of

$$\varphi \to [P(\chi,y)]\psi$$

as desired.

For the Rule of Substitution a limitation is necessary, as indicated by Hoare's example (p.107)

procedure $P(x;y)$;

$y := x+1$.

Since $\mathit{true} \to [y := x+1](y = x+1)$

is valid, the Invocation and Substitution rules as given would lead from it to the invalid

$$\mathit{true} \to [P(z,z)](z = z+1).$$

To avoid this situation, Hoare imposes the restriction (p.106) that in the call $P(\underline{\sigma},\mathrm{z})$, all variables in the list z must be distinct and none of them may be contained in the list of expressions $\underline{\sigma}$. Thus in the example, the substitution rule does not apply to the call $P(z,z)$.

In order to investigate the semantic mechanisms underlying the Rule of Substitution we study the meaning of the command $\alpha(y|z)$, assuming that the variable z does not occur in α, so that no conflict of identifiers arises. We assume also that we are working in a fixed standard model, and write

$$s(y : z)t$$

to mean that states s and t assign the same values to all variables other than y and z, and y gets the same value in t that z gets in s. Thus $s(y : z)t$ means that

(i) $v_t(y) = v_s(z)$, and

(ii) $v_t(w) = v_s(w)$ if $y \neq w \neq z$

(no commitment is made about $v_t(z)$).

Notice that $s[\![y := z]\!]t$ implies $s(y : z)t$.

5.3.1 LEMMA.

If $s(y : z)t$, *then*

(1) $v_t(\sigma) = v_s(\sigma^y_z)$ *for any expression* σ *that does not contain* z; *and*

(2) $\models_s \varphi^y_z$ *iff* $\models_t \varphi$ *for any first-order formula* φ *in which* z *has no free occurrence.*

Proof.

For the reader. ∎

5.3.2 THEOREM.

Suppose that α *is simple (i.e. contains no procedure calls) and* $z \notin Var\alpha$. *Then if* $s(y : z)t$ *and* $s [\![\alpha(y|z)]\!] s'$, *there exists a state* t' *with* $t [\![\alpha]\!] t'$ *and* $s'(y : z)t'$.

Proof.

The result is proven for all s, t, and s', by induction on the formation of α.

a. Suppose α is the assignment $(w := \sigma)$.

Case 1. If w is y, then α is $(y := \sigma)$ and $\alpha(y|z)$ is $(z := \sigma^y_z)$. Hence, as the model is standard, $v_{s'}(z) = v_s(\sigma^y_z) \neq \omega$. But by hypothesis z does not occur in σ, and so the Lemma 5.3.1(1) gives $v_t(\sigma) = v_s(\sigma^y_z)$, implying that σ is defined at t. Hence there exists a t' with $t [\![y := \sigma]\!] t'$. Then $v_{t'}(y) = v_t(\sigma) = v_{s'}(z)$, and, since $s' =_z s(y : z)t =_y t'$, no alterations to variables other than y and z have been involved here. This yields $s'(y : z)t'$ as desired.

Case 2. w is not y. Then $\alpha(y|z)$ is $(w := \sigma^y_z)$. As in Case 1, standardness of the model implies that σ is defined at t, and so there must be a t' with $t [\![w := \sigma]\!] t'$. Then as $y \neq w$, $v_{t'}(y) = v_t(y) = v_s(z)$. But as z does not occur in α, $z \neq w$, so $v_s(z) = v_{s'}(z)$. Also $v_{t'}(w) = v_t(\sigma) = v_s(\sigma^y_z) = v_{s'}(w)$. And for any other variable r, except z, $v_{t'}(r) = v_{s'}(r)$. Hence, again we get $s'(y : z)t'$.

b. If α is *abort*, so is $\alpha(y|z)$, and the result is vacuously true.

If α is *skip*, so is $\alpha(y|z)$, giving $s = s'$. The result then follows by putting $t' = t$.

c. Suppose α is $(\beta;\gamma)$ and the result, for any s, t, and s', holds for β and for γ.

Then $\alpha(y|z)$ is $(\beta(y|z)\ ;\ \gamma(y|z))$ and so the main hypothesis on α implies the existence of a state u such that $s [\![\beta(y|z)]\!] u [\![\gamma(y|z)]\!] s'$. Applying the induction hypothesis on β to s, t, and u yields a state u' with $t [\![\beta]\!] u'$ and $u(y : z)u'$. Then applying the hypothesis on γ to u, u', and s' yields a state t' with $u' [\![\gamma]\!] t'$, making $t [\![\beta;\gamma]\!] t'$, and $s'(y : z)t'$.

d. Suppose α is $(\varepsilon \Rightarrow \beta,\gamma)$, and the result holds for β and γ. Then $\alpha(y|z)$ is $(\varepsilon^y_z \Rightarrow \beta(y|z),\ \gamma(y|z))$. The main hypothesis on α and the standard-model condition for $\Rightarrow$ imply that either $\models_s \varepsilon^y_z$ and $s [\![\beta]\!] s'$, or else $\models_s not\text{-}\varepsilon^y_z$ and $s [\![\gamma]\!] s'$. Assume the latter (the former case is similar). Then by Lemma 5.3.1(1) we have $\models_t not\text{-}\varepsilon$, and by the induction hypothesis on γ there exists a t' with $t [\![\gamma]\!] t'$, hence $t [\![\varepsilon \Rightarrow \beta,\gamma]\!] t'$, and $s'(y : z)t'$.

e. Suppose α is $\varepsilon\#\beta$, and the result holds for β. Then $\alpha(y|z)$ is $\varepsilon^y_z \# \beta(y|z)$, and z does not occur in ε or β.

Case 1. We have $\models_s not\text{-}\varepsilon^y_z$ and $s = s'$. Then, as in (d) we have $\models_t not\text{-}\varepsilon$, so with $t = t'$ we get the desired result.

Case 2. We have $s_0 [\![\beta(y|z)]\!] s_1 \ldots [\![\beta(y|z)]\!] s_n$ for some states $s_0, \ldots, s_n$ such that $s_0 = s$, $s_n = s'$, $\models_{s_n} not\text{-}\varepsilon^y_z$, and for $0 \leqslant i < n$, $\models_{s_i} \varepsilon^y_z$. Then by an inductive construction, using Lemma 5.3.1(1) and the method for the case of $(\beta;\gamma)$, we obtain a sequence $t_0, \ldots, t_n$ with $t_0 = t$, $s_i(y : z)t_i$ for $0 \leqslant i \leqslant n$, $\models_{t_i} \varepsilon$ and $t_i [\![\beta]\!] t_{i+1}$ for $0 \leqslant i < n$, and $\models_{t_n} not\text{-}\varepsilon$. By putting $t' = t_n$ we then get $t [\![\varepsilon\#\beta]\!] t'$ and $s'(y : z)t'$ as desired.

f. The case that α is $(\beta|\gamma)$ is similar to $(\varepsilon \Rightarrow \beta,\gamma)$, and is left to the reader.

∎

5.3.3 COROLLARY.

If z does not occur in α and is not free in ψ, then in a natural model

$$\models \varphi \rightarrow [\alpha]\psi$$

implies $$\models \varphi^y_z \rightarrow [\alpha(y|z)]\psi^y_z \ .$$

Proof.

Suppose that $\models_s \varphi^y_z$ and $s [\![\alpha(y|z)]\!] s'$. We have to show that ψ^y_z holds at s'. Let t be the valuation $s(y/s(z))$. Then φ holds at t (cf. 3.3.11(2)), and so if $\varphi \rightarrow [\alpha]\psi$ is valid in the model, then $[\alpha]\psi$ holds at t. But $s(y : z)t$, and so Theorem 5.3.3 yields a t' such that $s'(y : z)t'$ and $t [\![\alpha]\!] t'$, whence $\models_{t'} \psi$. But then $t'(y) = s'(z)$ and, since z does not occur freely in ψ, s' and t' agree on all other free variables of ψ. Hence ψ^y_z holds at s' (cf. 4.5.1(lii)).

■

The last result will now be applied to show validity for a version of the substitution rule for a call $P(\underline{\sigma},\mathrm{z})$ of a simple procedure declaration

$$\textit{procedure}\ P(\mathrm{x}\ ;\ y)\ ;\ \alpha.$$

The derivation of the validity of

$$\varphi^{\mathrm{x}\,y}_{\underline{\sigma}\,\mathrm{z}} \rightarrow [P(\underline{\sigma},\mathrm{z})]\psi^{\mathrm{x}\,y}_{\underline{\sigma}\,\mathrm{z}}$$

from that of

$$\varphi \rightarrow [P(\mathrm{x},y)]\psi$$

requires a number of restrictions. First we have Hoare's requirement that all variable parameters be distinct, with none of them occurring among the value parameters. Next we suppose that the actual parameter list is distinct from the formal parameter list, and in fact that none of the variables in x, y occur in $\underline{\sigma}$, z. Finally we require that none of the z-variables occur in α or are free in ψ. For α, this accords with the call-by-name requirement of avoidance of conflicts of identifiers in substitution of variables. For ψ it corresponds to another of the requirements of Hoare (1971) which stipulates (p.107) that if any of the variables in $\underline{\sigma}$ or z occur in ψ (or φ in fact) then they must be systematically replaced by fresh variables before applying the substitution rule. The requirement also relates naturally to the intuitive situation: since our intention is to literally use z in place of y, the post-condition $\psi^{\chi\, y}_{\underline{\sigma}\, \mathrm{z}}$ to $P(\underline{\sigma};\mathbf{z})$ should make exactly the same assertion about the values of z that the post-condition ψ to $P(\chi;y)$ makes about the values of y. Hence $\psi^{\chi\, y}_{\underline{\sigma}\, \mathrm{z}}$ should have free z-variables exactly where ψ has the corresponding y-variables free - a requirement that would fail if any z-variables were already free in ψ.

To simplify the demonstration, suppose χ is (x,x'), y is (y,y'), $\underline{\sigma}$ is (σ,σ') and z is (z,z'). Our restrictions entail that each of these four lists is disjoint from the others.

Now suppose that in a natural model

$$\models \varphi \rightarrow [P(\chi;y)]\psi .$$

Then

$$\models \varphi \rightarrow [\mathit{call}\text{-}P(\chi;y)]\psi .$$

But $\mathit{call}\text{-}P(\chi;y)$ is

$$(x := x \ ; \ x' := x' \ ; \ \alpha),$$

and $(x := x)$ is equivalent to skip if x is defined. Hence we infer that

$$\models Dx \wedge Dx' \wedge \varphi \rightarrow [\alpha]\psi.$$

Applying 5.3.3, noting that χ and y are disjoint, we then get

$$\models Dx \wedge Dx' \wedge \varphi^{y}_{z} \rightarrow [\alpha(y|z)]\psi^{y}_{z} .$$

But if z and z' are distinct, and do not occur in y, then z' does not occur in $\alpha(y|z)$ and is not free in ψ^{y}_{z}. Hence we can apply 5.3.3 again to get

$$\models Dx \wedge Dx' \wedge (\varphi^{y}_{z})^{y'}_{z'} \rightarrow [\alpha(y|z)(y'|z')](\psi^{y}_{z})^{y'}_{z'} .$$

In view of the disjointness of z and y, $(\varphi^{y}_{z})^{y'}_{z'}$ is just $\varphi^{y\,y'}_{z\,z'}$, i.e. φ^{y}_{z}, and similarly for ψ, while $\alpha(y|z)(y'|z')$ is $\alpha(y|\mathrm{z})$. We thus find that

$$\models [x := \sigma \; ; \; x' := \sigma'](Dx \wedge Dx' \wedge \varphi^{y}_{z}) \rightarrow [x := \sigma \; ; \; x' := \sigma'][\alpha(y|z)]\psi^{y}_{z} \; .$$

But in a standard model, x and x' are always defined on termination of $(x := \sigma \; ; \; x' := \sigma')$, i.e.

$$[x := \sigma \; ; \; x' := \sigma'](Dx \wedge Dx')$$

is valid. Moreover, as noted earlier,

$$(\theta^{x'}_{\sigma'})^{x}_{\sigma} \rightarrow [x := \sigma \; ; \; x' := \sigma']\theta$$

is valid for first-order θ. Putting these facts together, we reach

$$\models ((\varphi^{y}_{z})^{x'}_{\sigma'})^{x}_{\sigma} \rightarrow [x := \sigma \; ; \; x' := \sigma' \; ; \; \alpha(y|z)]\psi^{y}_{z} \; .$$

The antecedent of this last formula is $\varphi^{\chi\, y}_{\underline{\sigma}\, z}$, in view of our parameter-restrictions. Also, $(x := \sigma \; ; \; x' := \sigma' \; ; \; \alpha(y|z))$ is $\mathit{call}\text{-}P(\underline{\sigma};z)$. Since $[\![\mathit{call}\text{-}\gamma]\!] = [\![\gamma]\!]$ in a standard model, we finally have

$$\models \varphi^{\chi\, y}_{\underline{\sigma}\, z} \rightarrow [P(\underline{\sigma};z)]\psi^{y}_{z}.$$

Now the Rule of Substitution actually has $\psi^{\chi\, y}_{\underline{\sigma}\, z}$ in place of ψ^{y}_{z} here, but these two formulae will be identical if the value parameters χ are not free in ψ. This last restriction is explicitly imposed in the version of the rule presented by Alagic and Arbib (1978, p.282) (cf. also Hoare and Wirth (1973), p.345).

Whether the restrictions we have employed render the Substitution rule impractical, or whether, alternatively, assertions involved in a genuine correctness proof can be made to conform to them, is a matter of pragmatics, i.e. of language use rather than of syntax or semantics. The analysis given here helps to expose and clarify the deep structure of the situation, so that the ramifications of such issues are better understood, and standards of language use can be established. That, perhaps, is the real value of the present kind of study.

CHAPTER 6

ARRAYS

6.1 ARRAY TYPES

A practically useful programming language will have at least three data types: *integer* (i.e. $\mathbb{N}$, or an implementation-defined subset of $\mathbb{N}$), *Boolean* (i.e. $\mathbb{B}$), and *real* (some set of real numbers). But languages like Pascal have techniques for building new structures out of such *ground types*. In this final chapter we study one of them: the *array*.

An array is a function from one data type to another. If $a : A_1 \to A_2$ is such a function, then A_1 is called the *index* type, and A_2 the *base* or *component* type. An element i of A_1 is an *index* of the array a; its corresponding function-value in A_2 is denoted $a[i]$ and is called a *component* of a. If A_1 is the finite subset $\{1, \ldots, n\}$ of $\mathbb{N}$, then the array a can be presented by displaying its values in a list $\langle a[1], a[2], \ldots, a[n] \rangle$. In this way an array is often viewed as an indexed list, or vector, of components.

We use the symbol $(A_1 \to A_2)$ to denote the set of functions from A_1 to A_2. Members of $(A_1 \to A_2)$ are said to be "of type $A_1 \to A_2$" or "of type *array*$[A_1]$*of* A_2".

As we introduce data types we will need to extend our formal language to apply to them. Each structure will have its own associated variables, and variable-systems of different structures will not overlap. To keep the notation manageable we will assume for expository purposes that our data types are *one*-sorted, so that we distinguish variables of different types, but do not worry about different sorts within a given type. The notation $\sigma{:}A$ may be employed to indicate that the expression

σ is *of type* A, i.e. that the value $v_s(\sigma)$ of σ is always a member of A^+.

The index of an array component may be obtained by evaluating some algebraic expression: if x is a variable of type *array*$[A_1]$*of* A_2, denoting an array $a : A_1 \to A_2$, and $\sigma{:}A_1$ is an expression denoting the element $i \in A_1$, then the component $a[i]$ will be denoted by $x[\sigma]$. The latter is a new kind of expression which is generally called an *indexed variable*. It produces a new kind of assignment command, of the form

$$x[\sigma] := \tau,$$

where τ has the same type as $x[\sigma]$ (in this case A_2). The effect of this command is to change $a[i]$, the component of a indexed by i, to the A_2-element that is denoted by τ.

If A_1 and A_2 are the same data type, it may well be that in the expression $x[\sigma]$, x itself appears within σ. The following example of this, where the data type is $\mathbb{N}$, is taken from page 26 of Burstall (1972).

$$a[(a[i] + 1) \times a[i+1]] := 0.$$

Consider the two assertions

$$(\varphi_1) \quad (1 \leqslant i \leqslant 9) \wedge \forall y(1 \leqslant y < 100 \to a[y] = y),$$

and

$$(\varphi_2) \quad a[i \times i + 2 \times i + 1] \neq a[i].$$

Burstall observes that if the first assertion holds, then after execution of the assignment the second assertion is true. However, "*attempts to substitute* 0 *for* $a[(a[i] + 1) \times a[i+1]]$ in $a[i \times i + 2 \times i + 1] \neq a[i]$ *merely leave it unchanged, but the unchanged assertion does not follow from the first assertion.*"

Burstall's response to this apparent failure of Hoare's Rule of Assignment is to deal with the whole new *array* a' that is created by the assignment, rather than just the new component. On the other hand Brady (1977) states (p.202) that "the problem is that logical substitution fails to capture the idea of evaluating an expression ... to yield the component of the data structure a to be assigned a new value", and claims that in Burstall's solution "a clear distinction is made between 'simple' assignment and assignment to data structures, which is intuitively unsatisfactory since *all* assignment statements invoke the same process." But the latter point of view appears to be based on a misconception about the syntactic category of the variable being assigned a new value. This is perhaps caused by the practise of calling $x[\sigma]$ an indexed *variable* when it is not a variable in the conventional sense but is rather a compound expression created by a syntactic operation involving a variable and other expressions. The variable whose value is altered by the assignment $(x[\sigma] := \tau)$ is the array variable x, and since an *expression* is the syntactic entity conventionally used to denote an object obtained by operating on the value of a variable, we need a new expression of type $(A_1 \to A_2)$ to denote the array produced by executing $(x[\sigma] := \tau)$. This is clearly recognised by Burstall, Hoare (1972, p.117) and Hoare and Wirth (1973, pp.341,345) and we will adopt the notational conventions of the last two references in using the symbolism $(x, \sigma{:}\tau)$ for this desired new expression. If x denotes the array $a : A_1 \to A_2$, σ the index $i \in A_1$, and τ the A_2-element j, then in the substitution notation of §3.3, $(x, \sigma{:}\tau)$ denotes the function $a(i/j)$, i.e. the unique function $a' : A_1 \to A_2$ that has $a =_i a'$ and $a'(i) = j$.

Thus the assignment $(x[\sigma] := \tau)$ has the same effect as

$$x := (x, \sigma{:}\tau)$$

(Hoare (1972), p.117), so that for an Axiom of Assignment we contemplate

$$[x[\sigma] := \tau]\psi \leftrightarrow (D\tau \to \psi')$$

where ψ' results from ψ by the replacement of the free variable x by the expression $(x, \sigma{:}\tau)$ (Hoare and Wirth (1973), p.345). This replacement applies to occurrences of x at the front of an indexed variable $x[\rho]$, to form expressions of the kind $(x, \sigma{:}\tau)[\rho]$. In this way our new kind of assignment does after all invoke the same process as the kind originally studied in Chapter 3.

Applying this theory to Burstall's example, if σ denotes $(a[i]+1) \times a[i+1]$ then since

$$\varphi_1 \to [a[\sigma] := 0]\varphi_2$$

holds, so too should

$$\varphi_1 \rightarrow a'[i\times i + 2\times i + 1] \neq a'[i],$$

where a' is $(a, \sigma{:}0)$. In proving this we may avail ourselves of such elementary truths about the data structures involved as

$$\forall y(y \neq \sigma \rightarrow a'[y] = a[y]),$$

and $$a'[\sigma] = 0.$$

But then the proof is straightforward, since these last two assertions in combination with φ_1 yield $\sigma = (i\times i + 2\times i + 1) = (i+1)^2 \neq i$, and so $a'[i\times i + 2\times i + 1] = 0$, while $a'[i] = a[i] = i \geqslant 1$. As Burstall observes, "*the distinction between a and a' and the condition that all elements which are not assigned to are unchanged reduce the problem to elementary algebra.*"

INDEX TYPES

The indices of an array form a data type in their own right, and in Pascal it is required that this be a *scalar* type, which means a finite linearly ordered set of explicitly named entities. A definition of A as a scalar type takes the form

type $A = (c_1, \ldots, c_n)$

where $c_1, \ldots, c_n$ are constants. Examples are

type days = (*mon, tue, wed, thur, fri, sat, sun*)

type sex = (*male, female*)

type Boolean = (*true, false*)

Thus an array variable x whose index type is A as declared above has its value completely specified by the values of the vector $\langle x[c_1], \ldots, x[c_n]\rangle$ of associated component variables.

Because the indices of an array are linearly ordered, a convenient notation can be introduced for operations that process the components in sequential order.

The symbolism

$$\textit{for } z := c_i \textit{ to } c_j \textit{ do } \alpha,$$

where $i \leqslant j$, is an abbreviation for the command

$$(z := c_i \ ; \ \alpha \ ; \ z := c_{i+1} \ ; \ \alpha \ ; \ \ldots . \ ; \ z := c_j \ ; \ \alpha).$$

Now in Pascal it is possible to make a direct assignment of the value of one array variable y to another x by the command $x := y$ (cf. Welch and Elder (1979), p.140). If x and y have the index type $(c_1, \ldots, c_n)$, this command is equivalent to

$$\textit{for } z := c_1 \textit{ to } c_n \textit{ do } x[z] := y[z].$$

In other words a direct assignment to an array variable can always be presented as a sequence of assignments to its indexed component variables. Such a presentation is closer to what the computer actually does than a description of the assignment as an atomic action.

THE VALUES OF INDEXED VARIABLES

Having observed that $x[\sigma]$ is more like a compound expression than a conventional variable, we must recognise that it is not a compound expression in the conventional sense either. If it were, then its value would be determined, via some fixed operation, by the values of x and σ. But although this will be the case when x and σ are both defined, $x[\sigma]$ may have a value independently when x has none. To see how this can be, let x be a variable of type $\textit{array}\{1,2\}$ of $\{0, \ldots, 9\}$, and let α be

$$(x[1] := 3 \ ; \ x[2] := 9).$$

After termination of α, x will denote the array represented by the sequence $<3,9>$. But if x is undefined before execution of α then it will still be undefined at the point of termination of $(x[1] := 3)$, before initiation of $(x[2] := 9)$, even though at that point $x[1]$ does have a value, viz. 3. An array variable is only defined if *all* of its associated components are defined, and it is possible for some components to be defined while others are not. In that sense the value of x may depend on that of $x[\sigma]$, rather than conversely.

The way we formalise this situation is to make the attachment of values to indexed variables part of the definition of "model" in the case of variables $x[c]$ whose index is one of the constants that *defines* the relevant index type. Such a constant c will be called a *scalar*, and the associated $x[c]$ a *scalar-indexed* variable The given values of these scalar-indexed variables will then be used to inductively define the values of array-denoting expressions, as well as variables with more complex indices.

This approach is based on the recognition that an individual in a data type may have many different names - e.g. the constant expressions 2+2+2, 2×3, 3×2, 5+1, 2+4 all denote the same number. But in setting up our index types we will select one canonical name (e.g. 6) for each individual and use it to define the scalar types in which this individual is to appear. These canonical names are our scalars, and so although different expressions may in general refer to the same individual, different scalars denote different individuals.

6.2 SYNTAX AND SEMANTICS OF ARRAYS

LANGUAGE

Let L be a one-sorted language, consisting of a signature O and a denumerable set X of algebraic variables. Let C be a set of constant O-expressions (i.e. $C \subseteq Con(O)$, where the latter was defined in §3.1). The members of C are called *scalars*. C^* denotes the set of finite sequences $\langle c_1, \ldots, c_n\rangle$ of scalars c_i. The set $T(C)$ of types over C is defined as follows

(1) $C^* \cup \{O\} \subseteq T(C)$; and

(2) If $T \in C^* \cup \{O\}$ and $T' \in C^*$, then $(T' \to T) \in T(C)$.

Members of $C^* \cup \{O\}$ will be called *base* types while members of C^* will be called *scalar* or *index* types. A type of the form $(T' \to T)$ is an *array type*, with associated *index* type T' and *component type* T. If T' is $<c_1, \ldots, c_n>$, then the scalars c_i are indices of the type $(T' \to T)$.

Now if A is an O-algebra, we can associate with each $T \in T(C)$ a data type A_T as follows

(i) If T is O, A_T is A.

(ii) If T is $<c_1, \ldots, c_n>$, A_T is the finite set $\{(c_1)_A, \ldots, (c_n)_A\}$ consisting of the A-elements named by the constant expressions $c_1, \ldots, c_n$ (cf. §3.1).

(iii) If T is the array type $(T_1 \to T_2)$ then A_T is the set $(A_{T_1} \to A_{T_2})$ of functions from A_{T_1} to A_{T_2}. Given that $A_{T_1} = \{b_1, \ldots, b_n\}$, we may present such a function (array) $a : A_{T_1} \to A_{T_2}$ as the n-tuple $<a(b_1), \ldots, a(b_n)>$.

In order to describe *data structures* of the form $\{A_T : T \in T(C)\}$ we expand L to a new language L_C by adding, for each *array* type T, a new set X_T of *array variables*. Assuming as usual a set Bvb of Boolean variables we then proceed to define the set $Bxp(L_C)$ of Boolean L_C-expressions and the set $Axp_T(L_C)$ of algebraic L_C-expressions of type T for every $T \in T(C)$. The definitions of these syntactic categories are developed simultaneously by induction on the lengths of expressions.

(I) For Boolean expressions, we have

(1) $Bvb \subseteq Bxp(L_C)$ and $\mathit{false} \in Bxp(L_C)$.

(2) If $\varepsilon, \delta, \partial \in Bxp(L_C)$, then $(\varepsilon \supset \delta, \partial) \in Bxp(L_C)$.

(3) If $\sigma, \tau \in Bxp(L_C)$, or $\sigma, \tau \in Axp_T(L_C)$ for some base type T, then $(\sigma = \tau) \in Bxp(L_C)$.

(II) If T is a base type, then:

(1) $X \subseteq Axp_T(L_C)$, where X is the set of algebraic variables of L.

(2) $O_\lambda \subseteq Axp_T(L_C)$, where O_λ is the set of individual constant symbols of O.

(3) If $\mathfrak{f}$ is an n-ary operation symbol of O, and $\sigma_1, \ldots, \sigma_n \in Axp_T(L_C)$, then $\mathfrak{f}(\sigma_1, \ldots, \sigma_n) \in Axp_T(L_C)$.

(4) If $\varepsilon \in Bxp(L_C)$ and $\sigma, \tau \in Axp_T(L_C)$, then $(\varepsilon \supset \sigma,\tau) \in Axp_T(L_C)$.

(5) If T' is a scalar type, $\rho \in Axp_{(T' \to T)}(L_C)$, and $\sigma \in Axp_{T'}(L_C)$, then $\rho[\sigma] \in Axp_T(L_C)$.

(III) If T is the array type $(T_1 \to T_2)$, then:

(1) $X_T \subseteq Axp_T(L_C)$.

(2) If $\rho \in Axp_T(L_C)$, $\sigma \in Axp_{T_1}(L_C)$, and $\tau \in Axp_{T_2}(L_C)$, then $(\rho,\ \sigma{:}\tau) \in Axp_T(L_C)$.

We will sometimes write "$\sigma{:}T$" to indicate that σ is an expression of type T, i.e. $\sigma \in Axp_T$.

The expression $\rho[\sigma]$ introduced in (II5) is called an *indexed variable* when ρ is an array variable. If x is an array variable of type $(\langle c_1, \ldots, c_n\rangle \to T)$, then the n scalar-indexed variables $x[c_1], \ldots, x[c_n]$ are called the *components* of x. Each array variable x thus has a fixed number of associated components and in the semantical theory to follow these will determine the value of x.

Notice that in (II) we allow any constant to appear in an expression of scalar type T, even when the constant does not denote any member of A_T. This is because an expression like $y+2$ could denote a member of A_T even if "2" does not - e.g. if $A_T = \{4,5,6\}$ and y denotes any of 2,3,4.

The definition of the set of L_C-commands requires one new formation rule:

if $x[\sigma], \tau \in Axp_T(L_C)$ for some base type T,
then $(x[\sigma] := \tau) \in Cmd(L_C)$.

In defining L_C-formulae we allow formation of $(\forall x\varphi)$ when x is an *array* variable, and otherwise proceed as before.

MODELS

An A-*valuation* of L_C, for a data type A, is a function s that assigns

(1) to each $p \in Bvb$ a value $s(p) \in \mathbb{B}^+$;

(2) to each $x \in X$ a value $s(x) \in A^+$;

(3) to each component $x[c]:T$ of an array variable $x:(T' \to T)$ a value $s(x[c]) \in A_T^+$.

Any such valuation can be extended to give a value $s(\sigma)$ to any expression σ. To our previous rules for calculating this value we add rules for expressions $\rho:(T_1 \to T_2)$ of array type and associated expressions $\rho[\sigma]:T_2$, where $\sigma:T_1$. Suppose that T_1 is $<c_1, \ldots, c_n>$, with $(c_i)_A = b_i$ for $1 \leqslant i \leqslant n$, so that $A_{T_1} = \{b_1, \ldots, b_n\}$.

We consider $s(\rho[\sigma])$ first, under the inductive assumption that $s(\sigma)$ has been defined. We then proceed by induction on the formation of ρ.

(1) Suppose ρ is the array variable x. Then if $s(\sigma) \notin A_{T_1}$, put $s(x[\sigma]) = \omega$. Otherwise, if $s(\sigma) = b_i$, say, put $s(x[\sigma]) = s(x[c_i])$.

(2) Let ρ be $(\rho_0, \sigma_0:\tau)$, and suppose $s(\rho_0[\sigma])$ has been defined. We may suppose also that $s(\sigma_0)$ and $s(\tau)$ have been defined. Then if $s(\sigma) \neq s(\sigma_0)$, put $s(\rho[\sigma]) = s(\rho_0[\sigma])$. If $s(\sigma) = s(\sigma_0) \in A_{T_1}$,

$$s(\rho[\sigma]) = \begin{cases} s(\tau) & \text{if } s(\tau) \in A_{T_2} \\ \omega & \text{if } s(\tau) \notin A_{T_2}. \end{cases}$$

Otherwise $s(\rho[\sigma]) = \omega$.

This defines $s(\rho[\sigma])$ for all ρ and σ, and allows us to turn to the definition of $s(\rho)$ itself.

(1) Let ρ be the array variable x. Then if $s(x[c_i]) = \omega$ for some component $x[c_i]$ of x, put $s(x) = \omega$. Otherwise, $s(x)$ is the array represented by the n-tuple $<s(x[c_1], \ldots, s(x[c_n])>$.

(2) Let ρ be $(\rho_0, \sigma_0 : \tau)$.

If $s(\sigma_0) \in A_{T_1}$ and $s(\tau) \in A_{T_2}$, with $s(\sigma_0) = b_i$ say, and moreover $s(\rho_0[c_j]) \neq \omega$ for $j \neq i$, then $s(\rho)$ is that array $a : A_{T_1} \to A_{T_2}$ having

$$a(b_j) = \begin{cases} s(\tau) & \text{if } j = i \\ s(\rho_0[c_j]) & \text{if } j \neq i. \end{cases}$$

Otherwise $s(\rho) = \omega$.

6.2.1 EXERCISES.

(1) If $s(\sigma) = \omega$, $s(\rho[\sigma]) = \omega$.

(2) If $s(\rho[\sigma]) \neq \omega$ and $s(\rho) \neq \omega$, then $s(\rho[\sigma]) = s(\rho)(s(\sigma))$.

(3) If $s(\sigma) = s(\tau)$, then $s(\rho[\sigma]) = s(\rho[\tau])$.

(4) If $s(x[c_j]) = t(x[c_j])$ for $j \neq i$, while $s(\tau) = t(x[c_i])$, then $s(x, c_i : \tau) = t(x)$. ∎

An L_C-*model* is a structure

$$M = (A, S, v, [\![\cdot]\!]),$$

where A is an O-algebra in which different scalars from C name different elements, and v assigns to each $s \in S$ an A-valuation v_s of L_C, while $[\![\cdot]\!]$ assigns a binary relation on S to each L_C command.

Given states $s, t \in S$ we will write $s(z/\sigma)t$ to mean that $v_t(z) = v_s(\sigma)$ and otherwise v_s and v_t agree on all Boolean, algebraic, and component variables.

Let L_C^A be the language of the present type founded on the signature O^A that has names for all members of A. An A-based L_C^A-model is *standard* if in addition to our previous standard-model conditions it satisfies, for $x : (T_1 \to T_2)$ with $T_1 = \langle c_1, \ldots, c_n \rangle$,

(1) if $v_s(\sigma) \in A_{T_1}$ and $v_s(\tau) \in A_{T_2}$, there exists a state t with $s\,[\![\, x[\sigma] := \tau \,]\!]\, t$; and

(2) if $s\,[\![\, x[\sigma] := \tau \,]\!]\, t$, then $v_s(\tau) \in A_{T_2}$ and for some i $v_s(\sigma) = v_s(c_i) \in A_{T_1}$ and $s(x[c_i]/\tau)t$.

To erect a standard-model structure on (A, S, v) it suffices to have the correct interpretations of assignments to Boolean, algebraic, and component variables. For, given the relation $[\![\, x[c] := \tau \,]\!]$ satisfying (1) and (2) for each scalar index c of x, then for general σ we can put

$$s\,[\![\, x[\sigma] := \tau \,]\!]\, t \quad \text{iff} \quad v_s(\sigma) = v_s(c) \text{ for some index } c \text{ such that } s\,[\![\, x[c] := \tau \,]\!]\, t.$$

The meanings of all other programs are then given by their usual standard-model conditions. This procedure provides the definition of the *natural* L_C^A-model M_A as a standard model having the set S_A of A-valuations of L_C^A as its states. We put, for $x[c]$ a component of $x : (T_1 \rightarrow T_2)$,

$$s\,[\![\, x[c] := \tau \,]\!]\, t \quad \text{iff} \quad s(\tau) \in A_{T_2} \quad \text{and} \quad s(x[c]/\tau)t.$$

6.2.2 EXERCISES.

In a standard model:

(1) If $s\,[\![\, x[\sigma] := \tau \,]\!]\, t$, then $v_t(x) = v_s(x, \sigma{:}\tau)$.

(2) If $v_s(\sigma) = v_s(\rho)$, then $s\,[\![\, x[\sigma] := \tau \,]\!]\, t$ iff $s\,[\![\, x[\rho] := \tau \,]\!]\, t$, and so $\models_s [x[\sigma] := \tau]\varphi$ iff $\models_s [x[\rho] := \tau]\varphi$.

(3) If $v_s(\sigma) = v_s(\tau)$, then $s\,[\![\, x[\rho] := \sigma \,]\!]\, t$ iff $s\,[\![\, x[\rho] := \tau \,]\!]\, t$, and so $\models_s [x[\rho] := \sigma]\varphi$ iff $\models_s [x[\rho] := \tau]\varphi$.

(4) If $x[c]$ is a component of x and τ is of type O^A, then

$$[x[c] := \tau]\varphi \leftrightarrow (D\tau \rightarrow \varphi^x_{(x,c:\tau)}),$$

is valid for first-order φ. ∎

The result of the last exercise requires some modification if τ is of scalar type or if c is to be replaced by some more general σ having the index type of x. If σ is an expression and T a base type, we define the Boolean expression $D_T\sigma$ as follows.

(i) if T is 0^A, $D_T\sigma$ is $D\sigma$.

(ii) if T is $<c_1, \ldots, c_n>$, then $D_T\sigma$ is

$$(\sigma = c_1) \vee (\sigma = c_2) \vee \ldots \vee (\sigma = c_n).$$

Then we have, in either case,

$$v_s(D_T\sigma) = 1 \quad \text{iff} \quad v_s(\sigma) \in A_T.$$

From this we obtain the validity in standard models of

$$[x[c] := \tau]\varphi \leftrightarrow (D_{T_1}\tau \rightarrow \varphi^x_{(x,c:\tau)})$$

and more generally

$$[x[\sigma] := \tau]\varphi \leftrightarrow (D_{T_1}\sigma \wedge D_{T_2}\tau \rightarrow \varphi^x_{(x,\sigma:\tau)})$$

(where $x[c]$ is a component of $x : (T_1 \rightarrow T_2)$, and φ is first-order).

In defining the satisfaction relation in the case of the quantifier $\forall x$, we adopt the approach of §3.3 when $x \in X$. When x is an array variable of type $T = (T_1 \rightarrow T_2)$ we contemplate the condition

$$M \models_s \forall x\varphi \quad \text{iff} \quad \text{for all } a \in A_T, \text{ if } s(x/a)t \text{ then } M \models_t \varphi.$$

Now when $x \in X$, $s(x/a)t$ means that v_s and v_t agree on all variables except x, while $v_t(x) = a$. But when x is an array variable a different definition is appropriate. For, in order for v_t to assign the array $a : A_{T_1} \rightarrow A_{T_2}$ to x it must make appropriate assignments to all of the component variables of x. Thus, assuming that T_1 is $<c_1, \ldots, c_n>$, in this case we take $s(x/a)t$ to mean that

(i) $v_t(x[c_i]) = a((c_i)_A)$ for $1 \leqslant i \leqslant n$, and

(ii) v_s agrees with v_t on all algebraic and Boolean variables, and all components of array variables other than x.

If the quantifier $\forall x$ is to receive its intended meaning, then the model M must *have enough states*. If x is an array variable of type T, this means that

for all $s \in S$ and all $a \in A_T$ there exists a state t with $s(x/a)t$.

Now for algebraic variables, the corresponding requirement was seen to be a consequence of the standard-model conditions on assignments. But that argument does not work for array variables, since we have introduced neither direct assignments to them, nor constants to name whole arrays. Nonetheless the requirement *is* satisfied in a standard model, as we shall now show.

Suppose, as above, that T is $(T_1 \to T_2)$, with $T_1 = \langle c_1, \ldots, c_n \rangle$ and $A_{T_1} = \{b_1, \ldots, b_n\}$ where $b_i = (c_i)_A$. Then given an array $a \in A_T$, let $d_1, \ldots, d_n$ be 0^A-constants that name the A-elements $a(b_1), \ldots, a(b_n)$ that define a. Then we take α to be the command

$$(x[c_1] := d_1 \ ; \ \ldots \ ; \ x[c_n] := d_n).$$

Since the model is standard, for a given s there will be a state t_1 with $s \llbracket x[c_1] := d_1 \rrbracket t_1$. But then there will be a t_2 with $t_1 \llbracket x[c_2] := d_2 \rrbracket t_2$. We continue this process inductively to obtain t_i for all $i \leqslant n$ with $t_i \llbracket x[c_{i+1}] := d_{i+1} \rrbracket t_{i+1}$. The standard-model conditions on assignment to component variables then guarantee that $s(x/a)t_n$.

Hence in a standard model a quantifier for an array variable ranges over the set of *all* arrays of that type. Moreover, in such a model satisfaction for $\forall$ is characterised by assignments to the variable in question. We already know (3.3.9) that if $x \in X$ then

$$M \models_s \forall x\varphi \quad \text{iff} \quad \text{for all } b \in A, \ M \models_s [x := c_b]\varphi.$$

To adapt this to the case of an array variable x of index type $<c_1, \ldots, c_n>$ we introduce the notation

$$x := <\sigma_1, \ldots, \sigma_n>$$

as an abbreviation for the command

$$(x[c_1] := \sigma_1 ; \ldots ; x[c_n] := \sigma_n).$$

Thus the command α above is $(x := <d_1, \ldots, d_n>)$, while the assignment $(x := y)$, where y is a variable of the same type as x, could be defined to be $(x := <y[c_1], \ldots, y[c_n]>)$.

It is left to the reader to prove the following result.

6.2.3 THEOREM.

Let x be a variable of type $(<c_1, \ldots, c_n> \to T)$. Then if M is standard

$$M \models_s \forall x\varphi \quad \textit{iff} \quad \textit{for all } b_1, \ldots, b_n \in A_T,$$
$$M \models_s [x := <c_{b_1}, \ldots, c_{b_n}>]\varphi. \qquad \blacksquare$$

In this formal theory we have not introduced quantification over scalar types, since the assertion "for all x of type $<c_1, \ldots, c_n>$, φ" can be readily formalised as

$$[x := c_1]\varphi \wedge [x := c_2]\varphi \wedge \ldots \wedge [x := c_n]\varphi.$$

6.3 AXIOMS FOR ARRAYS

In this section we outline a completeness theorem for the standard semantics of languages of the form L_C. First we list the new axioms we need.

In this list $x[c]$ and $y[c]$ are scalar-indexed components of the array variables x and y. The types of expressions should be clear from the context and will in any case be made clear as we come to use each axiom in what follows.

A41 $\forall x\varphi \rightarrow [x := \langle w_1, \ldots, w_n\rangle]\varphi$

A42 $\neg[x := \langle w_1, \ldots, w_n\rangle]\mathit{false} \rightarrow D_T w_1 \wedge \ldots \wedge D_T w_n$ where $w_i : T$

A43 $(\forall w_1 \ldots \forall w_n [x := \langle w_1, \ldots, w_n\rangle]\varphi) \rightarrow \forall x\varphi$ where $w_i \notin Var\varphi$

A44 $Dx[c] \rightarrow D_T x[c]$ where $x[c]:T$

A45 $(\sigma = \tau) \rightarrow (x[\sigma] = x[\tau])$

A46 $Dx[\sigma] \rightarrow D_T\sigma$ where $\sigma : T$

A47 $D(\rho_0,\sigma_0:\tau)[\sigma] \leftrightarrow ((\sigma = \sigma_0) \wedge D_{T_1}\sigma_0 \wedge D_{T_2}\tau) \vee (\neg(\sigma = \sigma_0) \wedge D\rho_0[\sigma])$

where $\rho_0 : (T_1 \rightarrow T_2)$

A48 $(\sigma = \sigma_0) \wedge D_{T_1}\sigma_0 \wedge D_{T_2}\tau \rightarrow ((\rho_0,\sigma_0:\tau)[\sigma] = \tau)$

A49 $\neg(\sigma = \sigma_0) \wedge D\rho_0[\sigma] \rightarrow ((\rho_0,\sigma_0:\tau)[\sigma] = \rho_0[\sigma])$

A50 $Dx \leftrightarrow Dx[c_1] \wedge \ldots \wedge Dx[c_n]$

A51 $D(\rho_0,\sigma_0:\tau) \leftrightarrow D_{T_1}\sigma_0 \wedge D_{T_2}\tau \wedge \bigwedge_{1 \leq j \leq n} (\neg(c_j = \sigma) \rightarrow D\rho_0[c_j])$

A52 $\neg[x[c] := \tau]\mathit{false} \leftrightarrow D_T\tau$ where $\tau : T$

A53 $\neg[x[\sigma] := \tau]\mathit{false} \rightarrow D_T\sigma$ where $\sigma : T$

A54 $[x[c] := \tau]\varphi \vee [x[c] := \tau]\neg\varphi$

A55 $[x[c] := \tau]\varepsilon \leftrightarrow (D_T\tau \rightarrow \varepsilon^{x}_{(x,c:\tau)})$ where $\varepsilon \in Bxp$, $\tau : T$

A56 $\forall y\varphi \rightarrow [y[c] := \tau]\forall y\varphi$

A57 $[y[c] := \tau][y := \langle w_1, \ldots, w_n\rangle]\varphi \rightarrow (D_T\tau \rightarrow [y := \langle w_1, \ldots, w_n\rangle]\varphi)$

A58 $(\tau = \sigma) \rightarrow ([y[c] := \tau]\varphi \leftrightarrow [y[c] := \sigma]\varphi)$

A59 $\forall x[y[c] := \tau]\varphi \rightarrow [y[c] := \tau]\forall x\varphi$ where $x \notin \{y\} \cup Var\tau$

A60 $[y[c] := \tau][x := w]\varphi \rightarrow (D_T\tau \rightarrow [x := w][y[c] := \tau]\varphi)$
where $x \notin \{y\} \cup Var\tau$

A61 $[y[c] := \tau][x := \langle w_1, \ldots, w_n\rangle]\varphi \rightarrow (D_T\tau \rightarrow [x := \langle w_1, \ldots, w_n\rangle][y[c] := \tau]\varphi)$
where $x \notin \{y\} \cup Var\tau$

A62 $\neg(c = d)$ where $c,d \in C$ and $c \neq d$

A63 $(\sigma = \rho) \rightarrow ([x[\sigma] := \tau]\varphi \leftrightarrow [x[\rho] := \tau]\varphi)$.

By a logic Λ we shall now mean a system that has at least

(1) the axioms A1 - A36, with all algebraic expressions restricted to *base* types;

(2) the axioms A41 - A63;

(3) the rules MP and TR;

(4) the rule OI for the same definition of admissible form as in §3.4, i.e. we include the form $\forall x\Phi$ only for *algebraic* x;

(5) the rule UG: From φ infer $\forall x\varphi$, for *algebraic* variables x.

Given L_C, we form a new language L_C^W by adding a new set W of algebraic variables to serve as witnesses, and ultimately as constants out of which canonical models are built. A set Γ of L_C^W-formulae is a W-rich Λ-theory in L_C^W if it is a maximal Λ-theory in L_C^W such that whenever $\forall x\varphi \notin \Gamma$ then

(i) if $x \in X$, then $[x := w]\varphi \notin \Gamma$ for some $w \in W$; and

(ii) if x is of type $(\langle c_1, \ldots, c_n\rangle \rightarrow T)$, then
$[x := \langle w_1, \ldots, w_n\rangle]\varphi \notin \Gamma$ for some $w_1, \ldots, w_n \in W$.

6.3.1 THEOREM.

If Γ is a W-rich Λ-theory in L_C^W, and $x:(<c_1, \ldots, c_n> \to T)$, then

$$\forall x\varphi \in \Gamma \quad \textit{iff} \quad \text{for all } w_1, \ldots, w_n \in W \text{ such that } D_T w_1, \ldots, D_T w_n \in \Gamma,$$
$$[x := <w_1, \ldots, w_n>]\varphi \in \Gamma.$$

Proof.

The implication from left to right follows readily from A41. Conversely, if $\forall x\varphi \notin \Gamma$ then $[x := <w_1, \ldots, w_n>]\varphi \notin \Gamma$ for some w_i by W-richness, and it remains only to show that $D_T w_i \in \Gamma$. But since it follows that

$$[x := <w_1, \ldots, w_n>]\mathit{false} \notin \Gamma \qquad \text{(cf. 2.4.1(6))},$$

the desired result is provided by A42. ∎

The proof of Theorem 3.4.6 adapts in the present context to show that any set Γ_0 of L_C-formulae that is Λ-consistent in L_C^W extends to a W-rich Λ-theory in L_C^W. The one new step comes in the construction of Γ_{n+1}, when $\Gamma_n \nvdash_\Lambda \varphi_n$ and φ_n is of the form $\forall x\psi$, with x an array variable of index type $<c_1, \ldots, c_n>$. Here, by taking $w_1, \ldots, w_n$ as the first n distinct members of W that do not occur in Γ_n or φ_n, we can Λ-consistently put

$$\Gamma_{n+1} = \Gamma_n \cup \{\neg[x := <w_1, \ldots, w_n>]\psi, \neg\varphi_n\}.$$

For it not, then reasoning as in 3.4.6, with A41 in place of A20, we would get

$$\Gamma_n \vdash_\Lambda [x := <w_1, \ldots, w_n>]\psi.$$

By n applications of 3.4.2 this would give

$$\Gamma_n \vdash_\Lambda \forall w_1 \ldots \forall w_n\ [x := <w_1, \ldots, w_n>]\psi,$$

and hence the contradiction $\Gamma_n \vdash_\Lambda \varphi_n$ by A43. The rest of the construction is unchanged.

Now, given a W-rich Λ-theory Δ in L_C^W, the definition of the data type A^Δ carries through just as in §3.5. A^Δ is based on the set

$$\{\tilde{w} : w \in C\},$$

where
$$C = \{w \in W : Dw \in \Delta\},$$

and
$$\tilde{w} = \{z \in C : (w \doteq z) \in \Delta\}.$$

The canonical model

$$M^C_\Delta = (A^\Delta, S_\Delta, v, [\![\cdot]\!])$$

is then defined for the language L^Δ_C in which the members of C are treated as constants and the algebraic variables are the original members of X. The definition of v_Γ proceeds as before for Boolean and algebraic variables, and treats component variables $x[c]$ like algebraic ones in having

(1) If $\neg Dx[c] \in \Gamma$ then $v_\Gamma(x[c]) = \omega$; and

(2) If $Dx[c] \in \Gamma$, then for $w \in C$

$$v_\Gamma(x[c]) = \tilde{w} \quad \text{iff} \quad (x[c] = w) \in \Gamma.$$

Now if $x[c]$ is of (base) type T, then $v_\Gamma(x[c])$ is required to be a member of $A^\Delta_T \cup \{\omega\}$. For $T = O$, there is nothing more to be said, while for T the scalar type $<d_1, \ldots, d_n>$ we appeal to A44. For if $v_\Gamma(x[c]) \neq \omega$ then we must have $Dx[c] \in \Gamma$, whence by A44 $D_T x[c] \in \Gamma$. The definition of the latter then leads to $(x[c] = d_i) \in \Gamma$ for some i. But then $v_\Gamma(x[c]) = \tilde{d}_i = (d_i)_{A^\Delta} \in A^\Delta_T$ as required.

To define $[\![\alpha]\!]$ in M^C_Δ we first put

$$\Gamma [\![z := \tau]\!] \Gamma' \quad \text{iff} \quad \Gamma' = \Gamma(z := \tau)$$

if z is a Boolean, algebraic, or component variable. This allows us to define $[\![\alpha]\!]$ in all other cases by the appropriate standard-model condition, as explained above.

To establish the Fundamental Theorem for M^C_Δ we first need an analogue of Theorem 3.5.4. That result now becomes the following.

6.3.2 THEOREM.

(1) *If* $\varepsilon \in Bxp(L_C^{\Delta})$,

$$v_{\Gamma}(\varepsilon) = \begin{cases} 1 & \textit{if} \quad \varepsilon \in \Gamma \\ 0 & \textit{if} \quad \textit{not-}\varepsilon \in \Gamma \\ \omega & \textit{if} \quad \neg D\varepsilon \in \Gamma. \end{cases}$$

(2) *If* $\sigma \in Axp_T(L_C^{\Delta})$, *then*

(i) *if* $\neg D\sigma \in \Gamma$, $v_{\Gamma}(\sigma) = \omega$;

(ii) *if* $D\sigma \in \Gamma$ *and* T *is a base type, then* $v_{\Gamma}(\sigma) \neq \omega$, *and*

$$v_{\Gamma}(\sigma) = \tilde{w} \ \textit{iff} \ (\sigma = w) \in \Gamma \ ;$$

(iii) *if* $D\sigma \in \Gamma$ *and* T *is an array type with associated index type* $<c_1, \ldots, c_n>$, *then* $v_{\Gamma}(\sigma) \neq \omega$, *and*

$$v_{\Gamma}(\sigma) = <\tilde{w}_1, \ldots, \tilde{w}_n> \ \textit{iff} \ (\sigma[c_1] = w_1 \wedge \ldots \wedge (\sigma[c_n] = w_n) \in \Gamma.$$

Proof.

The only essential new part of the proof is in part (2), where the algebraic expression is either of the form $\rho:(T_1 \to T_2)$ or $\rho[\sigma]:T_2$. For this, suppose that T_1 is $<c_1, \ldots, c_n>$, and so $A_{T_1}^{\Delta}$ is $\{\tilde{c}_1, \ldots, \tilde{c}_n\}$.

To establish (2) for $\rho[\sigma]$ we make the inductive assumption that it holds for σ. Then we proceed by induction on ρ.

(i) Let ρ be the array variable x. Suppose $\neg Dx[\sigma] \in \Gamma$. Then if $v_{\Gamma}(\sigma) = \omega$, immediately $v_{\Gamma}(x[\sigma]) = \omega$. Otherwise $v_{\Gamma}(\sigma) = \tilde{c}_i$ for some i, and so $(\sigma = c_i) \in \Gamma$ by the hypothesis on σ. Then by A45, $(x[\sigma] = x[c]) \in \Gamma$, from which, by A32, $(\neg Dx[\sigma] \to \neg Dx[c]) \in \Gamma$. Hence $\neg Dx[c] \in \Gamma$, giving $v_{\Gamma}(x[c]) = \omega$. But $v_{\Gamma}(x[\sigma]) = v_{\Gamma}(x[c])$.

On the other hand, if $Dx[\sigma] \in \Gamma$, then using A46 we have $D_{T_1}\sigma \in \Gamma$. Hence by similar reasoning we get $(\sigma = c_i) \in \Gamma$ for some i. Hence by A45, $(x[\sigma] = x[c_i]) \in \Gamma$. It follows that for $w \in C$, $(x[c_i] = w) \in \Gamma$ iff $(x[\sigma] = w) \in \Gamma$. But $v_{\Gamma}(\sigma) = v_{\Gamma}(c_i)$, and so $v_\Gamma(x[\sigma]) = v_\Gamma(x[c_i])$. Since the Theorem holds for $x[c_i]$ we then deduce that

$$v_\Gamma(x[\sigma]) = \tilde{w} \quad \text{iff} \quad (x[\sigma] = w) \in \Gamma,$$

and so the result holds for $x[\sigma]$.

(ii) Let ρ be $(\rho_0, \sigma_0 : \tau)$, and assume the result holds for $\rho_0[\sigma]$. We may inductively suppose also that it holds for σ_0 and τ.

Then by similar reasoning to (i) we have

$$D_{T_1}\sigma_0 \in \Gamma \quad \text{iff} \quad v_\Gamma(\sigma_0) \in A^{\Delta}_{T_1},$$

and also

$$D_{T_2}\tau \in \Gamma \quad \text{iff} \quad v_\Gamma(\tau) \in A^{\Delta}_{T_2}.$$

Now if $\neg D\rho[\sigma] \in \Gamma$, then by A47 neither $(\sigma = \sigma_0) \wedge D_{T_1}\sigma_0 \wedge D_{T_2}\tau$ nor $\neg(\sigma = \sigma_0) \wedge D\rho_0[\sigma]$ can belong to Γ. Invoking our induction hypothesis, it follows then that neither (a) $v_\Gamma(\sigma) = v_\Gamma(\sigma_0) \in A^{\Delta}_{T_1}$ and $v_\Gamma(\tau) \in A^{\Delta}_{T_2}$, nor (b) $v_\Gamma(\sigma) \neq v_\Gamma(\sigma_0)$ and $v_\Gamma(\rho_0[\sigma]) \neq \omega$ can obtain. Hence $v_\Gamma(\rho[\sigma])$ must be ω.

On the other hand if $D\rho[\sigma] \in \Gamma$, then by A47, A48, and A49, either (a) $(\rho[\sigma] = \tau) \in \Gamma$, or (b) $(\rho[\sigma] = \rho_0[\sigma]) \in \Gamma$, and moreover in case (a) $v_\Gamma(\sigma) = v_\Gamma(\sigma_0) \in A^{\Delta}_{T_1}$ and $v_\Gamma(\tau) \in A^{\Delta}_{T_2}$, whence $v_\Gamma(\rho[\sigma]) = v_\Gamma(\tau)$, while in case (b) $v_\Gamma(\sigma) \neq v_\Gamma(\sigma_0)$ and $v_\Gamma(\rho[\sigma]) = v_\Gamma(\rho_0[\sigma]) \neq \omega$. Using the inductive hypotheses on τ and $\rho_0[\sigma]$ we can then establish, in either case,

$$v_\Gamma(\rho[\sigma]) = \tilde{w} \quad \text{iff} \quad (\rho[\sigma] = w) \in \Gamma.$$

Hence the result holds for $\rho[\sigma]$.

This leaves us with the case of the array expression ρ.

(i) Suppose ρ is the array-variable x. Then if $\neg Dx \in \Gamma$, by A50 we have $Dx[c_i] \notin \Gamma$ for some i, whence $v_\Gamma(x[c_i]) = \omega$, making $v_\Gamma(x) = \omega$. But if $Dx \in \Gamma$, then A50 yields $Dx[c_i] \in \Gamma$ and hence $v_\Gamma(x[c_i]) \neq \omega$ for $1 \leqslant i \leqslant n$. But then $v_\Gamma(x)$ is the array $<v_\Gamma(x[c_1]), \ldots, v_\Gamma(x[c_n])>$. Thus

$$v_\Gamma(x) = <\tilde{w}_1, \ldots, \tilde{w}_n> \text{ iff } v_\Gamma(x[c_i]) = \tilde{w}_i \text{ for } 1 \leqslant i \leqslant n$$

$$\text{iff } (x[c_i] = w_i) \in \Gamma \text{ for } 1 \leqslant i \leqslant n$$

$$\text{iff } (x[c_1] = w_1) \wedge \ldots \wedge (x[c_n] = w_n) \in \Gamma.$$

Hence the result holds for x.

(ii) Let ρ be $(\rho_0, \sigma_0 : \tau)$ and assume the desired result holds for ρ_0, σ_0 and τ.

Then by A51 we find that $D\rho \in \Gamma$ just in case $v_\Gamma(\sigma_0) \in A^\Delta_{T_1}$, $v_\Gamma(\tau) \in A^\Delta_{T_2}$, and $v_\Gamma(\rho_0[c_j]) \neq \omega$ whenever $v_\Gamma(\sigma_0) \neq \tilde{c}_j$. In other words $D\rho \in \Gamma$ just in case $v_\Gamma(\rho) \neq \omega$.

Thus if $\neg D\rho \in \Gamma$, $v_\Gamma(\rho) = \omega$. On the other hand if $D\rho \in \Gamma$, with $v_\Gamma(\sigma_0) = \tilde{c}_i$ say, we have $(\sigma_0 = c_i) \in \Gamma$, which leads via A48 (with c_i as σ) to $(\rho[c_i] = \tau) \in \Gamma$. Also from A49 we find that $(\rho[c_j] = \rho_0[c_j]) \in \Gamma$ for $j \neq i$. Using the definition of $v_\Gamma(\rho)$ and the fact that the result holds for τ and for $\rho_0[c_j]$, we can then show that part (2ii) of the Theorem holds for ρ. These final details are left to the reader.

■

6.3.3 COROLLARY.

If σ is of base type T,

$$D_T\sigma \in \Gamma \quad \textit{iff} \quad v_\Gamma(\sigma) \in A^\Delta_T .$$ ■

Our next concern is to verify that M^C_Δ is a standard model, which means that we have to verify the standard-model condition for an L^Δ_C-assignment $(y[c] := \tau)$ to a component variable. First we need the following analogue of Theorem 3.5.3.

6.3.4 THEOREM.

Suppose $y[c]$ and τ are of base type T. Let $\Gamma \in S_\Delta$. Then if $D_T\tau \in \Gamma$, $\Gamma(y[c] := \tau) \in S_\Delta$.

Proof.

The proof is similar to 3.5.3 and we indicate how to adapt the latter.

First, A52 and A54 are used in place of A25 and A26 to show that $\Gamma(y[c] := \tau)$ is a maximal Λ-theory.

Next in a similar way to the derivation of 3.4.1(9) and 3.4.1(10) from A25 and A27, we can use A52 and A55 to establish

$$\vdash_\Lambda \varphi^y_{(y,c:\tau)} \rightarrow [y[c] := \tau]\varphi$$

where φ is any Boolean expression or the *negation* ($\neg$) of any Boolean expression. In particular,

$$\vdash_\Lambda \varphi \rightarrow [y[c] := \tau]\varphi$$

for $\varphi \in Diag(\Delta)$, and this establishes that $Diag(\Delta) \subseteq \Gamma(y[c] := \tau)$ as in 3.5.3.

It remains to show that $\Gamma(y[c] := \tau)$ is C-rich. Suppose then that $\forall x\varphi \notin \Gamma(y[c] := \tau)$, i.e. $[y[c] := \tau]\forall x\varphi \notin \Gamma$.

Case 1: If x is the array variable y, then by A56 $\forall y\varphi \notin \Gamma$, so the C-richness of Γ implies that $[y := \langle w_1, \ldots, w_n\rangle]\varphi \notin \Gamma$ for some witnesses $w_1, \ldots, w_n \in C$. But then using A57 and similar reasoning to 3.5.3 we find that $[y := \langle w_1, \ldots, w_n\rangle]\varphi$ is not in $\Gamma(y := \tau)$ either, as desired.

Case 2: We have x distinct from y. In the event that x is an algebraic variable we may proceed as in 3.5.3 using A58 in place of A30, A59 in place of A24, and A60 in place of A29 to get $[x := w]\varphi \notin \Gamma(y[c] := \tau)$, for some $w \in C$.

Finally, if x is an array variable other than y, we follow a similar argument using A58, A59, and A61 in place of A60, to get $[x := \langle w_1, \ldots, w_n\rangle]\varphi \notin \Gamma$ for some $w_1, \ldots, w_n \in C$.

■

We come now to our most central use of the array-assignment axiom A55.

6.3.5 THEOREM.

M^C_Δ *is a standard model.*

Proof.

A point to be checked here is that different scalars $c, d \in C$ name different elements of A^Δ. But A62 ensures that $\neg(c = d) \in \Delta$, and this is enough to make $(c)_{A^\Delta} \neq (d)_{A^\Delta}$.

To show that M^C_Δ is standard we have to establish the two standard-model conditions for an assignment $(y[c] := \tau)$ to a component $y[c]$ of an array variable $y:(T' \rightarrow T)$.

(1) If $v_\Gamma(\tau) \in A^\Delta_T$ then by 6.3.3 $D_T\tau \in \Gamma$. Hence by putting $\Gamma' = \Gamma(y[c] := \tau)$ it follows from 6.3.4 that there exist Γ' with $\Gamma [\![y[c] := \tau]\!] \Gamma'$.

(2) Suppose that $\Gamma [\![y[c] := \tau]\!] \Gamma'$. We require that $v_\Gamma(\tau) \in A^\Delta_T$ and $\Gamma(y[c]/\tau)\Gamma'$. The proof is an adaptation of that of 3.5.5. By definition of M^C_Δ, Γ' is $\Gamma(y[c] := \tau)$. Then since $\mathit{false} \notin \Gamma'$, $[y[c] := \tau]\mathit{false} \notin \Gamma$, so by A52, $D_T\tau \in \Gamma$, making $v_\Gamma(\tau) \in A^\Delta_T$.

Now as noted in the proof of 6.3.4, from A55 we can derive

$$\vdash_\Lambda \varphi^y_{(y,c:\tau)} \rightarrow [y[c] := \tau]\varphi$$

where φ is any Boolean expression or its negation. In particular

$$p \rightarrow [y[c] := \tau]p$$

$$\mathit{not}\text{-}p \rightarrow [y[c] := \tau]\mathit{not}\text{-}p$$

$$\neg Dp \rightarrow [y[c] := \tau]\neg Dp$$

$$(z = w) \rightarrow [y[c] := \tau](z = w)$$

$$\neg Dz \rightarrow [y[c] := \tau]\neg Dz$$

are all Λ-theorems, where p is any Boolean variable, w any member of C, and z any algebraic variable or any component variable that is not of the form $y[d]$. Hence by the reasoning given in 3.5.5, v_Γ and $v_{\Gamma'}$ agree on all such p and z.

Next we show that $v_{\Gamma'}(y[c]) = v_{\Gamma}(\tau)$. By the above theorem schema we have

$$\vdash_{\Lambda} ((y,c{:}\tau)[c] = w) \rightarrow [y[c] := \tau](y[c] = w).$$

But since c is a constant, by A34 $(c = c) \in \Gamma$. As c is one of the scalars defining the index type T' of y, it follows that $D_{T'}c \in \Gamma$. Hence by A48 we conclude that

$$((y,\ c{:}\tau)[c] = \tau) \in \Gamma.$$

Thus if $v_{\Gamma}(\tau) = \tilde{w}$, then $(\tau = w) \in \Gamma$ (6.3.2(2)), and so $((y,\ c{:}\tau)[c] = w) \in \Gamma$ (3.4.1(6)). Then using the last mentioned Λ-theorem we conclude that $(y[c] = w) \in \Gamma'$ so that $v_{\Gamma'}(y[c]) = \tilde{w}$ as desired.

All that remains is to show that v_{Γ} and $v_{\Gamma'}$ agree on $y[d]$ where d is any scalar index of y other than c. This time we have $\neg(c = d) \in \Gamma$ by A62, and hence $(c = d) \notin \Gamma$. Thus if $v_{\Gamma}(y[d]) = \omega$, $Dy[d] \notin \Gamma$, and so neither $(c = d) \wedge D_{T'}c \wedge D_{T}\tau$ nor $\neg(c = d) \wedge Dy[d]$ can belong to Γ. Using A47 we can conclude that

$$\neg D(y,\ c{:}\tau)[d] \in \Gamma.$$

But from A55 we have

$$\vdash_{\Lambda} \neg D(y,\ c{:}\tau)[d] \rightarrow [y[c] := \tau]\neg Dy[d].$$

This leads to $\neg Dy[d] \in \Gamma'$, hence $v_{\Gamma'}(y[d]) = \omega$.

On the other hand, if $v_{\Gamma}(y[d]) = \tilde{w}$, where $w \in C$, then

$$(y[d] = w) \in \Gamma.$$

But also $Dy[d] \in \Gamma$, so we can apply A49 to obtain

$$((y,\ c{:}\tau)[d] = y[d]) \in \Gamma.$$

Hence we have

$$(y,\ c{:}\tau)[d] = w) \in \Gamma.$$

Since

$$\vdash_{\Lambda} ((y,\ c{:}\tau)[d] = w) \rightarrow [y[c] := \tau](y[d] = w),$$

we find that $(y[d] = w) \in \Gamma'$, and so $v_{\Gamma'}(y[d]) = \widetilde{w}$.

Thus in any case $v_{\Gamma}(y[d]) = v_{\Gamma'}(y[d])$. ∎

The final preparation we need for the Fundamental Theorem is the extensions of the α-Lemmata 3.5.6 and 3.5.7 to L_C^{Δ}-commands.

6.3.6 FIRST α-LEMMA.

In M_{Δ}^{C},

$$\Gamma \llbracket \alpha \rrbracket \Gamma' \quad \textit{implies} \quad \{\varphi : [\alpha]\varphi \in \Gamma\} \subseteq \Gamma'.$$

Proof.

The result holds by definition of $\llbracket \alpha \rrbracket$ when α is an assignment $(y[c] := \tau)$ to a component variable. The only other new case is when α is $(y[\sigma] := \tau)$ for a general indexing expression σ. But then if $\Gamma \llbracket \alpha \rrbracket \Gamma'$, there is a scalar index c with $v_{\Gamma}(\sigma) = v_{\Gamma}(c)$ and $\Gamma \llbracket y[c] := \tau \rrbracket \Gamma'$. It follows that $(\sigma = c) \in \Gamma$, so that if $[y[\sigma] := \tau]\varphi \in \Gamma$, by A63 we get $[y[c] := \tau]\varphi \in \Gamma$, whence, as the result holds for $(y[c] := \tau)$, we have $\varphi \in \Gamma'$ as desired.

∎

6.3.7 SECOND α-LEMMA.

If $M_{\Delta} \models_{\Gamma} \varphi$ *implies* $\varphi \in \Gamma$ *for all* $\Gamma \in S_{\Delta}$,

then $M_{\Delta} \models_{\Gamma} [\alpha]\varphi$ *implies* $[\alpha]\varphi \in \Gamma$ *for all* $\Gamma \in S_{\Delta}$.

Proof.

The proof when α is an assignment $(y[c] := \tau)$ to a component variable is essentially the same as that given in 3.5.7 for an assignment to an algebraic variable. The other new case is when α is an assignment $(y[\sigma] := \tau)$ to a general indexed variable. Suppose then that $\models_\Gamma [y[\sigma] := \tau]\varphi$. If $D_T\sigma \in \Gamma$, where T is the type of σ, then $v_\Gamma(\sigma) = v_\Gamma(c) \in A_T^\Delta$ where c is some scalar index of y. But then $\models_\Gamma [y[c] := \tau]\varphi$ (Ex. 6.2.2(2)), and so $[y[c] := \tau]\varphi \in \Gamma$ as the Theorem holds for $(y[c] := \tau)$. Howeve $(\sigma = c) \in \Gamma$, and so by A63 we obtain $[x[\sigma] := \tau]\varphi \in \Gamma$ as desired.

On the other hand, if $D_T\sigma \notin \Gamma$ then we invoke A53 to conclude $[x[\sigma] := \tau]\mathit{false} \in \Gamma$. From this $[x[\sigma] := \tau]\varphi \in \Gamma$ follows in any case. ∎

6.3.8 FUNDAMENTAL THEOREM FOR M_Δ^C

For any $\varphi \in Fma(L_C^\Delta)$,

$$M_\Delta^C \models_\Gamma \varphi \quad \textit{iff} \quad \varphi \in \Gamma.$$

Proof.

In view of the two α-Lemmata we know that if the result holds for φ it holds for $[\alpha]\varphi$, whatever L_C^Δ-command α is. But this is enough to carry through the proof that it holds for all formulae whatsoever. The one new case is the inductive step for $\forall x\varphi$ when x is an array variable, of type $(\langle c_1, \ldots, c_n\rangle \to T)$, say.

Now given any witnesses $w_1, \ldots, w_n \in C$, we observe that if the result holds for φ, it holds for $[x[c_n] := w_n]\varphi$. But then it holds for $[x[c_{n-1}] := w_{n-1}][x[c_n] := w_n]\varphi$, and so on, leading to the conclusion that it holds for

$$[x[c_1] := w_1] \ldots\ldots [x[c_n] := w_n]\varphi.$$

Hence, via the composition axiom A7, it holds for

$$[x := \langle w_1, \ldots, w_n\rangle]\varphi.$$

But by Theorem 6.2.3,

$$M_\Delta^C \models_\Gamma \forall x\varphi \quad \text{iff} \quad \text{for all } \tilde{w}_1, \ldots, \tilde{w}_n \in A_T^\Delta$$

$$M_\Delta^C \models_\Gamma [x := \langle w_1, \ldots, w_n\rangle]\varphi,$$

while by Theorem 6.3.1

$$\forall x\varphi \in \Gamma \quad \text{iff} \quad D_T w_1, \ldots, D_T w_n \in \Gamma \text{ implies}$$

$$[x := \langle w_1, \ldots, w_n \rangle]\varphi \in \Gamma.$$

Since $D_T w_i \in \Gamma$ iff $\tilde{w}_i = v_\Gamma(w_i) \in A_T^\Delta$, we put all of these observations together to show that if the Fundamental Theorem holds for φ it holds for $\forall x\varphi$.

■

This completes our outline of a completeness theorem for the model theory of array types. An array is a "higher order" construct, which is notable in view of the fact that axiomatisation in higher order logic is usually only possible in relation to models in which the range of a higher-order variable is restricted to a subset of its possible values. Here we have allowed an array variable to denote *any* array of the appropriate type. The reason why this has not blocked the Completeness Theorem is that the arrays have been characterised by the properties of their components, and the latter are essentially first-order entities. This is underlined by the fact that we have not needed the rule of Universal Generalisation for quantification of array variables. It is left to the reader to verify *proof theoretically* that the inference of $\forall x\varphi$ from φ, when x is an array variable, is a derived rule of the logics defined in this section.

6.3.9 PROJECT.

Do for Pascal's *record* and *set* types what this chapter has done for arrays.

6.4 CALL-BY-REFERENCE

In a procedure call, an indexed variable $x[\sigma]$ may be used as an actual *variable* parameter. The call-by-name method discussed in §4.6 would then require us to substitute $x[\sigma]$ for the formal parameter throughout the declaration body. Alternatively, we may first evaluate the index σ to determine which component of the array x is designated by $x[\sigma]$, and then regard the formal parameter as referring to this particular component throughout the execution of the call. This interpretation is known as *call by reference*, and it can lead to a different result to call by name, as illustrated by the following example, taken from Wirth (1973), p.95.

procedure $P(y)$;

begin $i = i+1$; $y := y+2$ *end*

Here i is a variable of type *integer*. Suppose that x is a variable of type

array [1,2] *of integer*

and that initially i has value 1 and x has value <10,20>, i.e. $x[1]$ is 10 and $x[2]$ is 20.

Consider the call $P(x[i])$.

(1) If $x[i]$ is called by name, the procedure call is equivalent to execution of

$$(i := i+1 \ ; \ x[i] := x[i] + 2).$$

The effect of this is to increase $x[2]$ by 2, so that on termination i has value 2 and x has value <10,22>.

(2) In calling $x[i]$ by reference, the index i is first evaluated, thereby identifying $x[i]$ as $x[1]$. The latter then becomes the variable parameter, so the procedure call $P(x[i])$ is equivalent to $(i = i+1 \ ; \ x[1] := x[1] + 2)$, after which x has value <12,20>.

The essential point here is that execution of the procedure may alter the value of the index σ, and the alteration can occur before $x[\sigma]$ is itself processed. In call-by-name we consider the value of $x[\sigma]$ at the point of its processing in executing the body, while in call-by-reference "$x[\sigma]$" refers to the meaning of this indexed variable before execution starts.

It appears then that call-by-reference involves a combination of call-by-value and call-by-name (the three are also known, respectively, as variable substitution, value substitution, and substitution-by-name). In the above example of calling $x[\sigma]$ by reference, the index σ is first called by value, and then the formal parameter is replaced in the declaration body by the component $x[\mathrm{c}]$ of x that is indexed by the scalar c that denotes the value of σ. Since c is not determined by σ alone, but depends also on the initial state, this description cannot be directly modelled syntactically. What we propose to do then is use the "fictitious block" notion, introduced in §4.1, to model the prior evaluation of σ. The value of σ is assigned to a local variable z, and then $x[z]$ is substituted for $x[\sigma]$. By taking z as a new variable we ensure that its value remains fixed throughout the call at the initial value of σ.

Formally then, given a declaration

$$\mathit{procedure}\ P(\mathit{var}\ y)\ ;\ \alpha\ ,$$

we define call_r-$P(x[\sigma])$ to be the command

$$(z := \sigma)\ ;\ \alpha(y|x[z]),$$

where z is the first variable that does not occur in σ or α.

To model call-by-name for an indexed variable we take call_n-$P(x[\sigma])$ as $\alpha(y|x[\sigma])$.

Applying this approach to Wirth's example above, call_r-$(P(x[i]))$ is

$$(z := i\ ;\ i := i{+}1\ ;\ x[z] := x[z] + 2),$$

which does indeed terminate with x assigned $\langle 12,20\rangle$ when initiated with i as 1.

As another example, whose analysis is suggested as a research problem by Brady (1977), p.206, consider

$$\mathit{swap}\ (i,\ a[i]),$$

where *swap* was given in §5.1 by the declaration

procedure $swap(x,y)$;

var u ;

begin $u := x \; ; \; x := y \; ; \; y := u$ *end.*

Let us take a as a variable of type *array* [1,2] *of integer* here, and suppose that initially i has value 1 and a denotes <2,3>, i.e. $a[1]$ is 2 and $a[2]$ is 3. If $a[i]$ is called by reference, $swap(i,\ x[i])$ will assign the value of $x[1]$ to i, making $i = 2$, and then the original value of i to $x[1]$, ending with $i = 2$ and $a = \langle 1,3\rangle$. But in a call by name, *swap* will first assign the value of $x[1]$ to i as before, and then assign the original value of i to $x[i]$ - which now means to $x[2]$! The end result is that $i = 2$ and $a = \langle 2,1\rangle$. These two outcomes are precisely those produced by the commands $call_r\text{-}swap(i,\ a[i])$ and $call_n\text{-}swap(i,\ a[i])$, which are, respectively,

$$(z := i \; ; \; u := i \; ; \; i := x[z] \; ; \; x[z] := u),$$

and

$$(u := i \; ; \; i := x[i] \; ; \; x[i] := u).$$

With regard to Hoare's Rule of Substitution for procedure declarations, the theorem 5.3.2 holds also for commands of the form $\alpha(y|x[z])$, given that α is a simple command in which the variables x and z do not occur. From this we can deduce, as in 5.3.3, that

$$\models \varphi \to [\alpha]\psi$$

implies
$$\models \varphi^{y}_{x[z]} \to [\alpha(y|x[z])]\psi^{y}_{x[z]},$$

when φ and ψ are first-order formulae and x and z do not occur in α and are not free in ψ. But from the latter conclusion we further obtain

$$\models [z := \sigma]\varphi^{y}_{x[z]} \to [z := \sigma \; ; \; \alpha(y|x[z])]\psi^{y}_{x[z]}.$$

Now the formula

$$(\varphi^{y}_{x[z]})^{z}_{\sigma} \to [z := \sigma]\varphi^{y}_{x[z]}$$

is valid in standard models, and moreover its antecedent will just be $\varphi^y_{x[\sigma]}$ if z is not free in φ. Also, since the variable z is not in α its value will be unaltered by the command $\alpha(y|x[z])$. If this holds also for the variables in σ, so that $\alpha(y|x[z])$ does not change the value of σ, it follows that after execution of the command $(z := \sigma \; ; \; \alpha(y|x[z]))$, z and σ will have the same value, and hence $\psi^y_{x[z]}$ will hold just in case $(\psi^y_{x[z]})^z_\sigma$, i.e. $\psi^y_{x[\sigma]}$, does. Noting finally that the last-mentioned command is $\mathit{call}_r\text{-}P(x[\sigma])$, we put all of these pieces together to obtain the validity of the following rule of inference:

If $\vdash \varphi \rightarrow [\mathit{call}\text{-}P(y)]\psi$,

then $\vdash \varphi^y_{x[\sigma]} \rightarrow [\mathit{call}_r\text{-}P(x[\sigma])]\psi^y_{x[\sigma]}$,

provided that no variable in $x[\sigma]$ *nor any variable that is local to* $\mathit{call}_r\text{-}P(x[\sigma])$ *occurs in the body of* P *or is free in* φ *or* ψ.

FUNCTIONS

The call-by-reference technique can also be used for a function declaration

$$\mathit{function}\ F(\mathit{var}\ y)\ ;\ \alpha.$$

The evaluation of a designator $F(x[\sigma])$ when $x[\sigma]$ is to be called by reference is done by executing the command $\mathit{call}_r\text{-}F(x[\sigma])$, which is defined in a given environment (cf. §4.2) to be

$$(\mathit{call}\text{-}\sigma \; ; \; z := \sigma^0 \; ; \; \alpha(y|x[z])).$$

Here it is assumed that $\mathit{call}\text{-}\sigma$ has been defined according to some chosen parameter passing convention, and that z is a variable not occurring in σ^0 or α.

The value of $F(x[\sigma])$ in state s can then be defined to be the value of F in the terminal state (if it exists) resulting from initiation of $\mathit{call}_r\text{-}F(x[\sigma])$ in s.

In these terms, $\alpha(y|x[z])$ may be taken as the command executed to evaluate $F(x[z])$ (cf. the discussion of call-by-name in §4.6). Hence

$$[\alpha(y|x[z])]\psi \rightarrow (DF(x[z]) \rightarrow \psi^F_{F(x[z])})$$

will be valid in standard models, provided that $\alpha(y|x[z])$ causes no side effect on any expression in the first-order formula ψ other than F (cf. Theorem 4.5.4(2)).

Then applying the arguments used in the proof of Theorem 4.5.5 we infer

$$\models [call_r\text{-}F(x[\sigma])]\psi \rightarrow [call\text{-}\sigma](D\sigma^0 \rightarrow (DF(x[\sigma^0]) \rightarrow \psi^F_{F(x[\sigma^0])})$$

and then

$$\models DF(x[\sigma]) \rightarrow ([call_r\text{-}F(x[\sigma])]\psi \rightarrow [call\text{-}\sigma]\psi^F_{F(x[\sigma^0])}) \ ,$$

provided that z does not occur freely in ψ.

From this we obtain the validity of the following proof rule:

If $\alpha(y|x[z])$ *causes no side effect on any expression in* ψ *other than* F, z *does not occur freely in* ψ, *and*

$$\vdash \varphi \rightarrow [call_r\text{-}F(x[\sigma])]\psi \ ,$$

then

(1) $\vdash DF(x[\sigma]) \rightarrow (\varphi \rightarrow [call\text{-}\sigma]\psi^F_{F(x[\sigma^0])})$;

and

(2) *if* σ *is simple (i.e. has no designators),*

$\vdash DF(x[\sigma]) \rightarrow (\varphi \rightarrow \psi^F_{F(x[\sigma])})$.

As in Theorem 4.5.7 the conclusion of (2) can also be inferred for non-simple σ provided that $call_r\text{-}F(x[\sigma])$ itself causes no side effects on expressions within ψ other than F.

APPENDIX 2

SYNTAX IN BNF

The following is a presentation in Backus-Naur form of the language of assertions about programs for a data type (Ch. 3).

Boolean variables	p
Boolean expressions	ε
Algebraic variables	x
Operation symbols	f
Individual constants	c
Algebraic expressions	σ
Commands	α
Formulae	φ

$$\varepsilon ::= p \mid \mathit{false} \mid \mathit{if}\ \varepsilon_1\ \mathit{then}\ \varepsilon_2\ \mathit{else}\ \varepsilon_3 \mid \varepsilon_1 = \varepsilon_2 \mid \sigma_1 = \sigma_2$$

$$\sigma ::= x \mid c \mid f(\sigma_1, \ldots, \sigma_n) \mid \mathit{if}\ \varepsilon\ \mathit{then}\ \sigma_1\ \mathit{else}\ \sigma_2$$

$$\alpha ::= \mathit{skip} \mid \mathit{abort} \mid x := \sigma \mid \alpha_1;\alpha_2 \mid \mathit{if}\ \varepsilon\ \mathit{then}\ \alpha_1\ \mathit{else}\ \alpha_2 \mid$$
$$\mathit{while}\ \varepsilon\ \mathit{do}\ \alpha \mid \alpha\ \mathit{or}\ \beta$$

$$\varphi ::= \varepsilon \mid \varphi_1 \rightarrow \varphi_2 \mid [\alpha]\varphi \mid \forall x\varphi$$

Internal Logic	External Logic
$D\varepsilon$ is $(\varepsilon=\varepsilon)$	
not-ε is $(\varepsilon = \mathit{false})$	$\neg\varphi$ is $(\varphi \rightarrow \mathit{false})$
true is *not-false*, i.e. *Dfalse*	$\varphi \vee \psi$ is $(\neg\varphi \rightarrow \psi)$
ε *implies* δ is *if*-ε-*then*-δ-*else-true*	$\varphi \wedge \psi$ is $\neg(\varphi \rightarrow \neg\psi)$
ε *or* δ is *if*-ε-*then-true-else*-δ	$\varphi \leftrightarrow \psi$ is $(\varphi \rightarrow \psi) \wedge (\psi \rightarrow \varphi)$
ε *and* δ is *if*-ε-*then*-δ-*else-false*	$\exists x\varphi$ is $\neg\forall x\neg\varphi$
ε *iff* δ is $(\varepsilon = \delta)$	

APPENDIX 3

AXIOMS

§2.4 TAUTOLOGIES

A1 $\varphi \to (\psi \to \varphi)$

A2 $(\varphi \to (\psi \to \theta)) \to ((\varphi \to \psi) \to (\varphi \to \theta))$

A3 $\neg\neg\varphi \to \varphi$

TERMINATION

A4 $[\alpha](\varphi \to \psi) \to ([\alpha]\varphi \to [\alpha]\psi)$

STRUCTURED COMMANDS

A5 $[\mathit{skip}]\varphi \leftrightarrow \varphi$

A6 $[\mathit{abort}]\mathit{false}$

A7 $[\alpha;\beta]\varphi \leftrightarrow [\alpha][\beta]\varphi$

A8 $[\mathit{if}\ \varepsilon\ \mathit{then}\ \alpha\ \mathit{else}\ \beta]\varphi \leftrightarrow (\varepsilon \to [\alpha]\varphi) \wedge (\mathit{not}\text{-}\varepsilon \to [\beta]\varphi)$

A9 $\mathit{not}\text{-}\varepsilon \to \neg[\mathit{while}\ \varepsilon\ \mathit{do}\ \alpha]\mathit{false}$

A10 $[\mathit{while}\ \varepsilon\ \mathit{do}\ \alpha]\varphi \to (\varepsilon \to [\alpha][\mathit{while}\ \varepsilon\ \mathit{do}\ \alpha]\varphi)$

BOOLEAN EXPRESSIONS

A11 $\varepsilon = \delta \to (\partial \to \partial')$, where $\partial' = \partial$ with δ replacing some occurrences of ε.

A12 true

A13 $D\varepsilon \leftrightarrow (\varepsilon \vee \mathit{not}\text{-}\varepsilon)$

A14 $\varepsilon \to (\varepsilon = \mathit{true})$

A15 $(\varepsilon \supset \delta, \partial) \leftrightarrow (\varepsilon \wedge \delta) \vee (\mathit{not}\text{-}\varepsilon \wedge \partial)$

A16 $D(\varepsilon \supset \delta, \partial) \leftrightarrow (\varepsilon \wedge D\delta) \vee (\mathit{not}\text{-}\varepsilon \wedge D\partial)$

A17 $D(\varepsilon = \delta) \leftrightarrow D\varepsilon \wedge D\delta$

§2.7 ALTERNATION

A18 $[\alpha \ \mathit{or} \ \beta]\varphi \leftrightarrow [\alpha]\varphi \wedge [\beta]\varphi$

§3.4 QUANTIFIERS

A19 $\forall x(\varphi \to \psi) \to (\forall x\varphi \to \forall x\psi)$

A20 $\forall x\varphi \to [x := \sigma]\varphi$

A21 $\varphi \to \forall x\varphi$ $\quad x \notin Var\varphi$

A22 $\forall y[x := y]\varphi \to \forall x\varphi$ $\quad y \notin \{x\} \cup Var\varphi$

A23 $\forall y\varphi \to [y := \tau]\forall y\varphi$

A24 $\forall x[y := \tau]\varphi \to [y := \tau]\forall x\varphi$ where $x \notin Var(y := \tau)$

ASSIGNMENTS

A25 $\neg[x := \sigma]\mathit{false} \leftrightarrow D\sigma$

A26 $[x := \sigma]\varphi \vee [x := \sigma]\neg\varphi$

A27 $[x := \sigma]\varepsilon \leftrightarrow (D\sigma \to \varepsilon^{x}_{\sigma})$ where $\varepsilon \in Bxp$

A28 $[y := \tau][y := \sigma]\varphi \to (D\tau \to [y := \sigma^{y}_{\tau}]\varphi)$

A29 $[y := \tau][x := \sigma]\varphi \to (D\tau \to [x := \sigma^{y}_{\tau}][y := \tau]\varphi)$

where $x \notin Var(y := \tau)$

A30 $(\tau = \sigma) \to ([y := \tau]\varphi \leftrightarrow [y := \sigma]\varphi)$

ALGEBRAIC EXPRESSIONS

A31 $D(\sigma = \tau) \leftrightarrow D\sigma \wedge D\tau$

A32 $(\sigma = \tau) \to (\varepsilon \to \varepsilon')$, where ε' is ε with some replacement of σ by τ.

A33 $D\mathit{f}(\sigma_1, \ldots, \sigma_n) \leftrightarrow (D\sigma_1 \wedge \ldots \wedge D\sigma_n)$

A34 $\sigma = \sigma$ where σ is constant

A35 $D(\varepsilon \supset \sigma,\tau) \leftrightarrow (\varepsilon \wedge D\sigma) \vee (\mathit{not}\text{-}\varepsilon \wedge D\tau)$

A36 $((\varepsilon \supset \sigma,\tau) = \rho) \leftrightarrow (\varepsilon \wedge (\sigma = \rho)) \vee (\mathit{not}\text{-}\varepsilon \wedge (\tau = \rho))$

§4.4 COMMANDS WITH FUNCTION CALLS

A37 $\varepsilon \leftrightarrow \mathit{halts}(\mathit{call}\text{-}\varepsilon) \land [\mathit{call}\text{-}\varepsilon]\varepsilon^0$

A38 $[x := \sigma]\varphi \leftrightarrow [\mathit{call}\text{-}\sigma ; x := \sigma^0]\varphi$

A39 $[\mathit{if}\ \varepsilon\ \mathit{then}\ \alpha\ \mathit{else}\ \beta]\varphi \leftrightarrow [\mathit{call}\text{-}\varepsilon ; \mathit{if}\ \varepsilon^0\ \mathit{then}\ \alpha\ \mathit{else}\ \beta]\varphi$

A40 $[\mathit{while}\ \varepsilon\ \mathit{do}\ \alpha]\varphi \leftrightarrow [\mathit{call}\text{-}\varepsilon ; \mathit{while}\ \varepsilon^0\ \mathit{do}\ (\alpha;\mathit{call}\text{-}\varepsilon)]\varphi$

§6.3 ARRAY EXPRESSIONS AND INDEXED VARIABLES

A41 $\forall x\varphi \rightarrow [x := \langle w_1, \ldots, w_n\rangle]\varphi$

A42 $\neg[x := \langle w_1, \ldots, w_n\rangle]\mathit{false} \rightarrow D_T w_1 \land \ldots \land D_T w_n$ where $w_i : T$

A43 $(\forall w_1 \ldots \forall w_n [x := \langle w_1, \ldots, w_n\rangle]\varphi) \rightarrow \forall x\varphi$ where $w_i \notin \mathit{Var}\varphi$

A44 $Dx[c] \rightarrow D_T x[c]$ where $x[c]:T$

A45 $(\sigma = \tau) \rightarrow (x[\sigma] = x[\tau])$

A46 $Dx[\sigma] \rightarrow D_T\sigma$ where $\sigma:T$

A47 $D(\rho_0,\sigma_0:\tau)[\sigma] \leftrightarrow ((\sigma = \sigma_0) \land D_{T_1}\sigma_0 \land D_{T_2}\tau) \lor (\neg(\sigma = \sigma_0) \land D\rho_0[\sigma])$

where $\rho_0 : (T_1 \rightarrow T_2)$

A48 $(\sigma = \sigma_0) \land D_{T_1}\sigma_0 \land D_{T_2}\tau \rightarrow ((\rho_0,\sigma_0:\tau)[\sigma] = \tau)$

A49 $\neg(\sigma = \sigma_0) \land D\rho_0[\sigma] \rightarrow ((\rho_0,\sigma_0,\tau)[\sigma] = \rho_0[\sigma])$

A50 $Dx \leftrightarrow Dx[c_1] \land \ldots \land Dx[c_n]$

A51 $D(\rho_0,\sigma_0:\tau) \leftrightarrow D_{T_1}\sigma_0 \land D_{T_2}\tau \land \bigwedge_{1\leq j\leq n} (\neg(c_j = \sigma) \rightarrow D\rho_0[c_j])$

A52 $\neg[x[c] := \tau]\mathit{false} \leftrightarrow D_T\tau$ where $\tau:T$

A53 $\neg[x[\sigma] := \tau]\mathit{false} \rightarrow D_T\sigma$ where $\sigma:T$

A54 $[x[c] := \tau]\varphi \lor [x[c] := \tau]\neg\varphi$

A55 $[x[c] := \tau]\varepsilon \leftrightarrow (D_T\tau \rightarrow \varepsilon^{x}_{(x,c:\tau)})$ where $\varepsilon \in \mathit{Bxp}$, $\tau:T$

A56 $\forall y\varphi \rightarrow [y[c] := \tau]\forall y\varphi$

A57 $[y[c] := \tau][y := \langle w_1, \ldots, w_n\rangle]\varphi \rightarrow (D_T\tau \rightarrow [y := \langle w_1, \ldots, w_n\rangle]\varphi$

A58 $(\tau = \sigma) \rightarrow ([y[c] := \tau]\varphi \leftrightarrow [y[c] := \sigma]\varphi)$

A59 $\forall x[y[c] := \tau]\varphi \rightarrow [y[c] := \tau]\forall x\varphi$ where $x \notin \{y\} \cup \mathit{Var}\tau$

A60 $[y[c] := \tau][x := w]\varphi \rightarrow (D_T\tau \rightarrow [x := w][y[c] := \tau]\varphi)$

where $x \notin \{y\} \cup \mathit{Var}\tau$

A61 $$[y[c] := \tau][x := \langle w_1, \ldots, w_n\rangle]\varphi \rightarrow (D_T\tau \rightarrow [x := \langle w_1, \ldots, w_n\rangle][y[c] := \tau]$$

where $x \notin \{y\} \cup Var\tau$

A62 $$\neg(c = d)$$ where $c, d \in C$ and $c \neq d$

A63 $$(\sigma = \rho) \rightarrow ([x[\sigma] := \tau]\varphi \leftrightarrow [x[\rho] := \tau]\varphi) .$$

APPENDIX 4

STANDARD-MODEL CONDITIONS

STRUCTURED COMMANDS

§2.3 $[\![\mathit{skip}]\!]$ = the identity relation

$[\![\mathit{abort}]\!]$ = the empty relation

$[\![\alpha;\beta]\!] = [\![\beta]\!] \circ [\![\alpha]\!]$

$[\![\mathit{if}\ \varepsilon\ \mathit{then}\ \alpha\ \mathit{else}\ \beta]\!] = [\![\varepsilon\rceil\alpha]\!] \cup [\![\mathit{not}\text{-}\varepsilon\rceil\beta]\!]$

$[\![\mathit{while}\ \varepsilon\ \mathit{do}\ \alpha]\!] = [\![\varepsilon\rceil\alpha]\!]^{\infty}\lceil \mathit{not}\text{-}\varepsilon$

§2.7 $[\![\alpha\ \mathit{or}\ \beta]\!] = [\![\alpha]\!] \cup [\![\beta]\!]$

ASSIGNMENTS

§3.3 (1) If $v_s(\sigma) \neq \omega$, there exists t with $s\,[\![x := \sigma]\!]\,t$.

(2) $s\,[\![x := \sigma]\!]\,t$ implies $v_t(x) = v_s(\sigma) \neq \omega$ and $v_s =_x v_t$.

COMMANDS WITH FUNCTION CALLS

§4.3 $[\![x := \sigma]\!] = [\![\mathit{call}\text{-}\sigma\ ;\ x := \sigma^0]\!]$

$[\![\mathit{if}\ \varepsilon\ \mathit{then}\ \alpha\ \mathit{else}\ \beta]\!] = [\![\mathit{call}\text{-}\varepsilon\ ;\ \mathit{if}\ \varepsilon^0\ \mathit{then}\ \alpha\ \mathit{else}\ \beta]\!]$

$[\![\mathit{while}\ \varepsilon\ \mathit{do}\ \alpha]\!] = [\![\mathit{call}\text{-}\varepsilon\ ;\ \mathit{while}\ \varepsilon^0\ \mathit{do}\ (\alpha;\mathit{call}\text{-}\varepsilon)]\!]$

PROCEDURE CALLS

§5.1 $[\![\gamma]\!] = [\![\mathit{call}\text{-}\gamma]\!]$

ASSIGNMENTS TO INDEXED VARIABLES

§6.2 For $x:(T_1 \rightarrow T_2)$, where $T_1 = \langle c_1, \ldots, c_n \rangle$,

(1) if $v_s(\sigma) \in A_{T_1}$ and $v_s(\tau) \in A_{T_2}$, there exists t with $s ⟦ x[\sigma] := \tau ⟧ t$

(2) $s ⟦ x[\sigma] := \tau ⟧ t$ implies $v_s(\tau) \in A_{T_2}$ and for some i,

$$v_s(\sigma) = v_s(c_i) \quad \text{and} \quad s(x[c_i]/\tau)t.$$

REFERENCES

Aczel, Peter
(1973) *Infinitary logic and the Barwise compactness theorem*, in *Proceedings of the Bertrand Russell Memorial Logic Conference, Denmark 1971*, (published by School of Mathematics, University of Leeds), 234-277.

ADJ (Gougen, J.A., Thatcher, J.W., Wagner, E.G., and Wright, J.B.)
(1977) *Initial algebra semantics and continuous algebras*, *J.A.C.M.*, vol. 24, 68-95.

Alagic, Saud, and Arbib, Michael A.
(1978) *The Design of Well-Structured and Correct Programs*. Springer-Verlag.

Ashcroft, E.A., Clint, M., and Hoare, C.A.R.
(1976) *Remarks on "Program proving: jumps and functions", by M. Clint and C.A.R. Hoare*, *Acta Informatica*, vol. 6, 317-318.

de Bakker, Jaco
(1980) *Mathematical Theory of Program Correctness*. Prentice-Hall.

Banachowski, L., Kreczmar, A., Mirkowska, G., Rasiowa, H., and Salwicki, A.
(1977) *An introduction to algorithmic logic. Metamathematical investigations in the theory of programs*, in *Mathematical Foundations of Computer Science*, ed. by A. Mazurkiewicz and Z. Pawlak. Banach Centre Publications. Polish Scientific Publishers, Warsaw.

Barwise, Jon
(1975) *Admissible Sets and Structures*, Springer-Verlag.

Ben Ari, Mordechai
(1980) *Temporal logic proofs of concurrent programs*. Technical report 80-44, Tel Aviv.

Boolos, George
(1979) *The Unprovability of Consistency*. Cambridge University Press.

Bowen, Kenneth A.
(1979) *Model Theory for Modal Logic*. Reidel.

Brady, J.M.
(1977) *The Theory of Computer Science*. Chapman and Hall.

Burstall, R.M.
(1972) *Some techniques for proving correctness of programs which alter data structures.* *Machine Intelligence, vol. 7*, Edinburgh University Press, 23-50.

Chang, C.C., and Keisler, H.J.
(1973) *Model Theory.* North-Holland.

Clark, K.L., and Cowell, D.F.
(1976) *Programs, Machines, and Computation.* McGraw-Hill.

Clarke, E.M.
(1979) *Programming language constructs for which it is impossible to obtain good Hoare axiom systems*, J.A.C.M., vol. 26, 129-147.

Constable, R.L.
(1977) *On the theory of programming logics*, *Proc. 9th Annual A.C.M. Symposium on Theory of Computing*, Boulder, Colorado, May 1977, 269-285.

Constable, R.L. and O'Donnell, M.J.
(1978) *A Programming Logic.* Winthrop, Cambridge, Mass.

Conway, J.H.
(1971) *Regular Algebra and Finite Machines.* Chapman and Hall.

Cook, S.A.
(1975) *Axiomatic and interpretive semantics for an Algol fragment.* Tech. Report 79, Dept. of Computer Science, University of Toronto.

(1978) *Soundness and completeness of an axiom system for program verification*, *Siam J. Computing*, vol. 7, 70-90.

Clint, M., and Hoare, C.A.R.
(1972) *Program proving: jumps and functions*, *Acta Informatica*, vol. 1, 214-224.

Dijkstra, Edsger W.
(1976) *A Discipline of Programming.* Prentice-Hall.

Enderton, H.B.
(1972) *A Mathematical Introduction to Logic.* Academic Press.

Engeler, Erwin
(1967) *Algorithmic properties of structures*, *Mathematical Systems Theory*, vol. 1, 183-195.

(1968) *Formal Languages : Automata and Structures.* Markham, Chicago.

(1975) *On the solvability of algorithmic problems*, in *Logic Colloquium '73*, ed. by H.E. Rose and J.C. Shepherdson, Studies in Logic vol. 80, North-Holland, 231-251.

Fischer, M.J. and Ladner, R.E.
(1977) *Propositional modal logic of programs*, *Proc. 9th Annual A.C.M. Symposium on Theory of Computing*, Boulder, Colorado, 286-294. Revised version published as *Propositional dynamic logic of regular programs*, *J.Comp.Syst.Sci.*, vol. 18, 1979, 194-211.

Floyd, R.W.
(1967) *Assigning meanings to programs*, *Proc. Symp. Applied Math.*, vol 19, J.T. Schwartz (ed.), American Math. Soc., Providence, 19-32.

Gabbay, Dov M.
(1976) *Investigations in Modal and Tense Logics with Applications to Problems in Philosophy and Linguistics*. Reidel.

Gabbay, D., Pnueli, A., Shelah, S., and Stavi, Y.
(1980) *On the temporal analysis of fairness*. *Proc. 7th A.C.M. Symp. on Principles of Programming Languages*, 163-173.

Goldblatt, Robert
(1976) *Metamathematics of modal logic*, *Reports on Mathematical Logic*, Polish Scientific Publishers, Warsaw-Cracow, no. 6 (Part I), 41-78, and no. 7 (Part II), 21-52.

(1979) *Topoi*. Studies in Logic vol 98, North-Holland.

(1979i) *On the incompleteness of Hoare's rule for while commands*, *Notices of the A.M.S.*, vol 26, no. 6, p.A-524.

(1981) *The semantics of Hoare's Iteration Rule*, *Studia Logica*, to appear.

Goguen, J.A., Thatcher, J.W., and Wagner, E.G.
(1978) *An initial algebra approach to the specification, correctness, and implementation of abstract data types*, in *Current Trends in Programming Methodology, vol IV, Data Structuring*, ed. by Raymond T. Yeh, Prentice Hall, 80-149.

Harel, David
(1978) *Logics of Programs : Axiomatics and Descriptive Power*. Ph.D. thesis, Dept. of Electrical Engineering and Computer Science, M.I.T. Revised and published as *First-Order Dynamic Logic*, *Lecture Notes in Computer Science*, vol 68, Springer-Verlag, 1979.

(1979) *Two results on process logic*, *Information Processing Letters*, vol 8, no. 4, 195-198.

Harel, David; Kozen, Dexter; and Parikh, Rohit
(1980) *Process logic : expressiveness, decidability, completeness*. Research report, April 1980. *J.Comp.Syst.Sci.* to appear.

Harel, David, Meyer, Albert R., and Pratt, Vaughan R.
(1977) *Computability and completeness in logics of programs*, *Proc. 9th Annual A.C.M. Symposium on Theory of Computing*, Boulder, Colorado, 261-268. Also Report TM-97, Laboratory for Computer Science, M.I.T., February 1978.

Henkin, Leon
(1960) *On mathematical induction*, *American Math. Monthly*, vol 67, 323-338.

Hoare, C.A.R.
(1969) *An axiomatic basis for computer programming*, *C.A.C.M.*, vol 12, 576-580, 583.

(1971) *Procedures and parameters: an axiomatic approach*, in *Symposium on Semantics of Algorithmic Languages*, ed. by E. Engeler, Lecture Notes in Mathematics, vol 188, Springer-Verlag, 102-116.

(1972) *Notes on data structuring*, in *Structured Programming*, by O-J. Dahl, E.W. Dijkstra, and C.A.R. Hoare. Academic Press.

Hoare, C.A.R. and Wirth, N.
(1973) *An axiomatic definition of the programming language Pascal*, *Acta Informatica*, vol 2, 335-355.

Hoare, C.A.R. and Lauer, P.
(1974) *Consistent and complimentary formal theories of the semantics of programming languages*, *Acta Informatica*, vol 3, 135-153.

Hughes, G.E. and Cresswell, M.J.
(1968) *An Introduction to Modal Logic*. Methuen.

Kamp, J.A.W.
(1968) *Tense Logic and the Theory of Linear Order*, to be published as part of *Since and Until*, a volume in the series *Indices*, Bibliopolis, Naples.

Kozen, Dexter
(1979) *A representation theorem for models of *-free PDL*. Report RC7864, IBM Research Centre, Yorktown Heights, N.Y. Published in Lecture Notes in Computer Science vol 85, Springer-Verlag, 1980.

(1979i) *On the representation of dynamic algebras*, Report RC7898, IBM Research Centre, Yorktown Heights, N.Y.

(1980) *On the representation of dynamic algebras II*, Report RC8290, IBM Research Centre, Yorktown Heights, N.Y.

Kozen, Dexter, and Parikh, Rohit
(1980) *An elementary proof of the completeness of PDL*, Report RC8097, IBM Research Centre. Published in *Theoretical Computer Science*, vol. 14, 1981, 113-118.

Kreisel, Georg
(1970) *Principles of proof and ordinals implicit in given concepts*, in *Intuitionism and Proof Theory*, ed. by A. Kino, J. Myhill, and R.E. Vesley, North-Holland, 489-516.

Kripke, S.A.
(1963a) *Semantical analysis of modal logic I : normal propositional calculi*, *Zeitschr. f. Math. Logik und Grundlagen d. Math.*, vol 9, 67-96.

(1963b) *Semantical considerations on modal logics*, *Acta Philosophica Fennica, Modal and Many-valued Logics*, 83-94.

Kröger, F.
(1980) *Infinite proof rules for loops*, *Acta Informatica*, vol 14, 371-389.

Lemmon, E.J.
(1977) *An Introduction to Modal Logic : The "Lemmon Notes"* (in collaboration with Dana Scott). American Philosophical Quarterly, monograph series, vol 11, Basil Blackwell, Oxford.

Lipton, R.J.
(1977) *A necessary and sufficient condition for the existence of Hoare logics*, *Proc. 18th I.E.E.E. Annual Symposium on Foundations of Computer Science*, Providence, Rhode Island, Oct. 1977.

Lipton, R.J., and Snyder, L.
(1977) *Completeness and incompleteness of Hoare-like axiom systems*, unpublished manuscript, Dept. of Computer Science, Yale University.

Machtey, M., and Young, P.
(1978) *An Introduction to the General Theory of Algorithms*. North-Holland.

Manna, Z. and McCarthy, J.
(1970) *Properties of programs and partial function logic*, *Machine Intelligence, vol 5*, Edinburgh University Press, 27-37.

Manna, Z. and Pnueli, A.
(1979) *The modal logic of programs*, Computer Science Dept. Report no. STAN-CS-79-751, Stanford University.

Manna, Z. and Vuillemin, J.
(1973) *Fixed point approach to the theory of computation*, in *Automata, Languages, and Programming*, ed. by M. Nivat, North-Holland, 273-291.

Manna, Z. and Waldinger, R.
(1978) *The logic of computer programming*, *I.E.E.E. Transactions on Software Engineering*, vol SE-4, 199-229.

McCarthy, John
(1973) *A basis for a mathematical theory of computation*, in *Computer Programming and Formal Systems*, ed. by P. Braffort and D. Hirschberg, North-Holland, 33-70.

Mirkowska, Grazyna
(1979) *Model existence theorem in algorithmic logic with non-deterministic programs*, *Fundamenta Informaticae*, series IV, vol III.2, 157-170.

(1980) *Algorithmic logic with non-deterministic programs*, *Fundamenta Informaticae*, series IV, vol III.1, 45-64.

Monk, J. Donald
(1976) *Mathematical Logic*. Springer-Verlag.

Naur, P.
(1963) *Revised report on the algorithmic language Algol 60* (ed.), reprinted in *Description of Algol 60*, by H. Rutishauser, Springer-Verlag, 1967.

(1966) *Proof of algorithms by general snapshots*, *BIT*, vol 6, 310-316.

Nishimura, Hirokazu
(1979) *Sequential method in propositional dynamic logic*, *Acta Informatica*, vol 12, 377-400.

(1980) *Descriptively complete process logic*, *Acta Informatica*, vol 14, 359-369.

Parikh, Rohit
(1978) *The completeness of propositional dynamic logic*, in *Mathematical Foundations of Computer Science 1978*, Lecture Notes in Computer Science vol 64, 403-415.

(1978i) *A decidability result for second order process logic*, *Proc. 19th Annual I.E.E.E. Symposium on Foundations of Computer Science*, Ann Arbor, Michigan, 177-183.

Plotkin, G.D.
(1976) *A powerdomain construction*, *S.I.A.M. J. of Computing*, vol 5, 452-487.

Pnueli, A.
(1977) *The temporal logic of programs*, *Proc. 18th I.E.E.E. Annual Symposium on Foundations of Computer Science*, Providence, R.I., 46-57.

(1981) *The temporal semantics of concurrent programs*, *Theoretical Computer Science*, vol 13, 45-60.

Pratt, Vaughan R.
(1976) *Semantical considerations on Floyd-Hoare logic*. *Proc. 17th Annual I.E.E.E. Symposium on Foundations of Computer Science*, 109-121.

(1979) *Process logic*, *Proc. 6th Annual A.C.M. Symposium on Principles of Programming Languages*, San Antonio, Texas, 93-100.

(1979i) *Dynamic algebras: examples, constructions, applications*. Report TM-138, Laboratory for Computer Science, M.I.T.

Rasiowa, H., and Sikorski, R.
(1950) *A proof of the completeness theorem of Gödel*, *Fundamenta Mathematicae*, vol 37, 193-200.

Salwicki, A.
(1970) *Formalised algorithmic languages*, *Bull. Acad. Pol. Sci., Ser. Sci. Math. Astron. Phy.*, vol 18, 227-232.

(1977) *Algorithmic logic. A tool for investigations of programs*, in *Logic, Foundations of Mathematics, and Computability Theory*, ed. by Butts and Hintikka, Reidel, 281-295.

Scott, Dana
(1967) *Existence and description in formal logic*, in *Bertrand Russell: Philosopher of the Century*, ed. by Ralph Schoenman, George Allen and Unwin.

Scott, Dana, and Strachey, Christopher
(1971) *Towards a mathematical semantics for computer languages*, *Proc. Symposium on Computers and Automata*, ed. by J. Fox, Polytechnic Institute of Brooklyn Press, New York, 19-46. Also, Technical Monograph PRG-6, Programming Research Group, Oxford University.

Segerberg, Krister
(1971) *An essay in Classical Modal Logic*, Filosofiska studier 13, Uppsala Universitet.

(1977) *A completeness theorem in the modal logic of programs*, *Notices of the A.M.S.*, vol 24, p.A-552.

(1978) *A completeness theorem in the modal logic of programs*, to appear in the Banach Centre publications series, Warsaw.

(1980) *Applying modal logic*, *Studia Logica*, vol 39, 275-295.

(1980i) *"After" and "during" in dynamic logic*, *Acta Philosophica Fennica*, to appear.

Shoenfield, Joseph R.
(1967) *Mathematical Logic*. Addison-Wesley.

Stoy, Joseph E.
(1977) *Denotational Semantics*. M.I.T. Press.

Thomason, R.H.
(1970) *Some completeness results for modal predicate calculi*, in *Philosophical Problems in Logic*, ed. by K. Lambert, Reidel, 56-76.

Turing, A.M.
(1949) *Checking a large routine*, Report of a Conference on High Speed Automatic Calculating Machines, University Mathematical Laboratory, Cambridge, England, June 1949, 67-69.

von Neumann, John
(1963) *Collected Works, vol 5*, pp.91-99 (MacMillan).

Wand, Mitchell
(1978) *A new incompleteness result for Hoare's system*, *J.A.C.M.*, vol 25, 168-175.

Welch, John, and Elder, Jim
(1979) *Introduction to Pascal.* Prentice-Hall.

Wirth, N.
(1973) *Systematic Programming: An Introduction.* Prentice-Hall.

LIST OF SYMBOLS

$x := \sigma$	(vi),114
$\rightarrow$	5,38
$\wedge$	5,39
$\vee$	5,39
$\neg$	5,39
$\leftrightarrow$	5,39
$\forall$	5,114
$\exists$	5,114
$\varphi\{\alpha\}\psi$	15
$\vdash$	15
ψ_σ^r	15
$\alpha;\beta$	16
$[\alpha]$	17
true	17,36
$\Box\psi$	18,197
$\mathbb{N}$	20
skip	22
α^n	22
false	25,36
A^+	31
ω	31
$\models$	31,50
Dy	32
Bvb	36
Bxp	36
p	36
$\supset$	36
$=$	36
$\mathbb{B}$	37
$\equiv$	37,44
π	37
Cmd	37
abort	38
$\Rightarrow$	38
#	38
Fma	38
M	39,115
S	39
$[\![\;\;]\!]$	39
v	39,115
v_s	39,115
not	40
implies	40
or	40
and	40
iff	40
E_A	41 (47)
$M \models_s \varphi$	42
$\neq$	44
$\leqslant$	44
$<$	44
$\varphi]R$	47
$[\![\varphi]\alpha]\!]$	47
$R\lceil\varphi$	47

$[\![\alpha \lceil \varphi]\!]$	47
PoR	47
R^n	48
R^∞	48
$\varphi_n(\varepsilon,\alpha)$	54
Afm	55
$\vdash_\Lambda \varphi$	57
MP	58
TR	58
OI	58
PC	59
TI	60
PL	65
$\Sigma \vdash_\Lambda \varphi$	66
S_Λ	71
M_Λ	76
AD_α	87
AT_α	88
$wp(\alpha,\varphi)$	90
$wlp(\alpha,\varphi)$	91
$\varepsilon?$	93
$\alpha \mid \beta$	95
$\varepsilon \rightarrow \alpha$	96
if ... fi	97
IF, DIF	99
$t(\alpha)$	101
$wp_t(\alpha,\varphi)$	101
do ... od	104
DO	104
$P(A)$	109
λ	109
$O_{\lambda,\mu}$	109
$O_{\nu,\mu}$	109
A_ν	110
f_A	110
c_A	110
$Con(O)$	111
$L = (Z,O,X)$	113
$Bxp(L)$	113
$Axp(L)$	113
$Cmd(L)$	113
$Fma(L)$	113
S_A	117
$A^+ \models \varphi[s]$	117
$s(x/a)$	118
$g =_b h$	119
$s(x/a)t$	120
$s(x/\sigma)t$	121(260)
M_A	122
$\varphi^x_\sigma,\ \tau^x_\sigma$	128,178ff.
$Afm(L)$	138
L^W	146
A^Δ	150
L^Δ	151
$Diag(\Delta)$	151
M_Δ	154
$L^{\mathbb{N}}$	166
$\varphi_{\mathbb{N}}$	166
$\alpha_{\mathbb{N}}$	166
$Diag(A)$	173
$\alpha\varphi$	186
$\cup\alpha\varphi,\ \cap\alpha\varphi$	186

α^*	193
$Exp(L)$	213
$x(\sigma_1, \ldots, \sigma_n)$	213
E	214
$call\text{-}\sigma$	215
σ^0	215
$halts(\alpha)$	217
var	234(208)
$\alpha(y\|z)$	234
Pid	240
$call\text{-}\gamma$	241
$s(y:z)t$	245
$a[i]$	251
$(A_1 \to A_2)$	251
$\sigma:A$	251
$x[\sigma]$	252
C^*	256
$T(C)$	256
A_T	257
X_T	258
L_C	258
$Axp_T(L_C)$	258
$\rho[\sigma]$	258
$Cmd(L_C)$	258
$s(z/\sigma)t$	260
$D_T(\sigma)$	262
$x := \langle\sigma_1, \ldots, \sigma_n\rangle$	264
L_C^W	266
M_Δ^C	268
$call_r\text{-}$	279
$call_n\text{-}$	279

INDEX

actual parameter, 209,213
admissible form, 55,138
algebra, 108,110
algebraic expression, 113
algorithmic property, 184
α-Deduction Lemma, 70
α-Lemma
  First -, 82,96,160,275
  Second -, 84,96,161,275
alternative command, 95
arithmetical completeness, 194
arithmetical universe, 194
array, 251
assignment
  - command, 114
  rule of -, 6,26
axioms, 57,58,87,88,95,137,220,265, 285
axiom schema, 58

base, 115
base type, 251
block, 208,240
body, 207,240
Boolean
  - expression, 36
  - value, 39
  - variable, 36

call-by-name, 233
call-by-reference, 277ff.
call-by-value, 209
canonical model, 76,154,220,242,268
carrier, 110
characteristic function, 41
command, 37

Completeness Theorem, 77,162
component type, 251,257
composition, 16,47
  rule of -, 11
conditional connective, 37
conditional rule, 16
consequence (rule of), 7,14
consistent
  Λ -, 67
  Λ - in *L*, 139
  strongly -, 165
constant, 108,110
  - equation, 173
  - expression, 111
correct interpretation, 6
correctness, 3ff.
  partial -, 15
  total -, 15

data type, 108ff.,176f.
deducible, 58ff.
  Λ -, 66
  Λ - in *L*, 139
  strictly -, 165

Deduction Lemma
  α -, 70
Deduction Theorem, 68
deductively closed, 67
Detachment, 58
determinism, 29,87ff.
diagram, 152,173
Dummy Rule, 22
dynamic logic, 193

empty command, 22

E-model, 217
standard -, 218
environment, 214,241
equality relation, 41
equational theory, 173
equivalence of programs, 28
E-sequence, 236
expression, 36
algebraic -, 113
expressive, 190
external logic, 2

First α-Lemma, 82,96,160,275
first-order logic, 5
first-order formula, 114
fixed point, 53
formal parameter, 207
formula, 38
first-order -, 114
free occurrence, 26,178ff.
function call, 209
function declaration, 207
function designator, 209,213
functional relation, 43
Fundamental Theorem, 77
- for M_Δ, 161
- for M_Δ^C, 276

global variable, 208
guarded command, 96

Hoare's Iteration Rule, 9,63
has enough states, 120,263
holds, 31,42

implication connective, 38
incomplete system, 19
index (type), 251,254,257
indexed variable, 252,258
infinitary rule, 22
internal logic, 2,40

interpretation, 6
invariant, 9
isomorphic, 167
Iteration Rule, 9,58

Λ-consistent, 67
- in L, 140
Λ-deducible, 66
- in L, 139
Λ-model, 71
Λ-theory, 65
- in L, 139
maximal -, 71
language, 113
L_C-model, 260
local variable, 208,238
logical system (logic), 57,59,139,
266

main variable, 214
maximal Λ-theory, 71
- in L, 140
metalanguage, 3
meta-variable, 58
minimal subalgebra, 112
modal logic, 17
model, 39,43,115,164
canonical -, 76,154,220,242,268
E -, 217
Λ -, 71
natural -, 122,220,242
standard -, 47,48,121,218,260,273

natural model, 122,220,242
non-determinism, 95ff.
non-recursive, 236

Omega-Iteration Rule, 58
Omega Rule, 23,175

powerset, 109

procedure declaration, 238
procedure identifier, 240
process logic, 200
program letter, 37
propositional calculus, 59

recursive, 235
relettering, 139
rich theory, 144,266
rigid designator, 116
rule
  A -, 175
  assignment -, 6,26
  composition -, 11
  consequence -, 7
  detachment -, 58
  infinitary -, 22
  invocation -, 243
  iteration -, 9,58
  omega -, 23,175
  omega-iteration -, 58
  substitution -, 243
  terminal implication -, 60
  termination -, 58
  universal generalisation -, 138

satisfaction, 42
  simultaneous -, 79
scalar, 254,256,257
Second α-Lemma, 84,96,161,275
sentence, 118
sequent, 184
sequential connectives, 40
side effect, 210,225
signature, 109
simple, 214,219,241
sort, 109
standard model, 47,48,95,121,218,
  260,273,289
state, 30,39
step-wise refinement, 17
strictly deducible, 165
string, 109
strong completeness, 78,163
strongest post-condition, 190
strongly consistent, 165
subalgebra, 21

tautology, 60
temporal logic, 197
terminal implication rule, 58
termination, 13,25
  - rule, 58
test command, 93
theory
  Λ -, 65
  Λ - in L, 139
  maximal -, 71
  maximal - in L, 140
  rich -, 144,266
top-down design, 17
type, 214

undefined expression, 30
universal generalisation, 138

valid, 43
valuation, 39,115,259
  total -, 118
value parameter, 233,240
value substitution, 209
variable declaration, 208
variable parameter, 233,240

weakest liberal pre-condition, 91
weakest pre-condition, 90,191
witnesses, 144

/ol. 77: G. V. Bochmann, Architecture of Distributed Computer ;ystems. VIII, 238 pages. 1979.

/ol. 78: M. Gordon, R. Milner and C. Wadsworth, Edinburgh LCF. /III, 159 pages. 1979.

/ol. 79: Language Design and Programming Methodology. Pro- :eedings, 1979. Edited by J. Tobias. IX, 255 pages. 1980.

'ol. 80: Pictorial Information Systems. Edited by S. K. Chang and :. S. Fu. IX, 445 pages. 1980.

'ol. 81: Data Base Techniques for Pictorial Applications. Proceed- ıgs, 1979. Edited by A. Blaser. XI, 599 pages. 1980.

'ol. 82: J. G. Sanderson, A Relational Theory of Computing. VI, 47 pages. 1980.

'ol. 83: International Symposium Programming. Proceedings, 1980. :dited by B. Robinet. VII, 341 pages. 1980.

'ol. 84: Net Theory and Applications. Proceedings, 1979. Edited y W. Brauer. XIII, 537 Seiten. 1980.

ol. 85: Automata, Languages and Programming. Proceedings, 1980. dited by J. de Bakker and J. van Leeuwen. VIII, 671 pages. 1980.

'ol. 86: Abstract Software Specifications. Proceedings, 1979. Edited y D. Bjørner. XIII, 567 pages. 1980

'ol. 87: 5th Conference on Automated Deduction. Proceedings, 980. Edited by W. Bibel and R. Kowalski. VII, 385 pages. 1980.

'ol. 88: Mathematical Foundations of Computer Science 1980. 'roceedings, 1980. Edited by P. Dembiński. VIII, 723 pages. 1980.

'ol. 89: Computer Aided Design - Modelling, Systems Engineering, :AD-Systems. Proceedings, 1980. Edited by J. Encarnacao. XIV, 61 pages. 1980.

'ol. 90: D. M. Sandford, Using Sophisticated Models in Reso- ıtion Theorem Proving.
(I, 239 pages. 1980

ol. 91: D. Wood, Grammar and L Forms: An Introduction. IX, 314 ages. 1980.

'ol. 92: R. Milner, A Calculus of Communication Systems. VI, 171 ages. 1980.

'ol. 93: A. Nijholt, Context-Free Grammars: Covers, Normal Forms, nd Parsing. VII, 253 pages. 1980.

ol. 94: Semantics-Directed Compiler Generation. Proceedings, 980. Edited by N. D. Jones. V, 489 pages. 1980.

'ol. 95: Ch. D. Marlin, Coroutines. XII, 246 pages. 1980.

'ol. 96: J. L. Peterson, Computer Programs for Spelling Correction: 'I, 213 pages. 1980.

ol. 97: S. Osaki and T. Nishio, Reliability Evaluation of Some Fault- olerant Computer Architectures. VI, 129 pages. 1980.

'ol. 98: Towards a Formal Description of Ada. Edited by D. Bjørner nd O. N. Oest. XIV, 630 pages. 1980.

'ol. 99: I. Guessarian, Algebraic Semantics. XI, 158 pages. 1981.

ol. 100: Graphtheoretic Concepts in Computer Science. Edited by I. Noltemeier. X, 403 pages. 1981.

'ol. 101: A. Thayse, Boolean Calculus of Differences. VII, 144 pages. 981.

ol. 102: J. H. Davenport, On the Integration of Algebraic Functions. -197 pages. 1981.

'ol. 103: H. Ledgard, A. Singer, J. Whiteside, Directions in Human actors of Interactive Systems. VI, 190 pages. 1981.

'ol. 104: Theoretical Computer Science. Ed. by P. Deussen. VII, 61 pages. 1981.

ol. 105: B. W. Lampson, M. Paul, H. J. Siegert, Distributed Systems – rchitecture and Implementation. XIII, 510 pages. 1981.

'ol. 106: The Programming Language Ada. Reference Manual. X, 43 pages. 1981.

Vol. 107: International Colloquium on Formalization of Programming Concepts. Proceedings. Edited by J. Diaz and I. Ramos. VII, 478 pages. 1981.

Vol. 108: Graph Theory and Algorithms. Edited by N. Saito and T. Nishizeki. VI, 216 pages. 1981.

Vol. 109: Digital Image Processing Systems. Edited by L. Bolc and Zenon Kulpa. V, 353 pages. 1981.

Vol. 110: W. Dehning, H. Essig, S. Maass, The Adaptation of Virtual Man-Computer Interfaces to User Requirements in Dialogs. X, 142 pages. 1981.

Vol. 111: CONPAR 81. Edited by W. Händler. XI, 508 pages. 1981.

Vol. 112: CAAP '81. Proceedings. Edited by G. Astesiano and C. Böhm. VI, 364 pages. 1981.

Vol. 113: E.-E. Doberkat, Stochastic Automata: Stability, Nondeterminism, and Prediction. IX, 135 pages. 1981.

Vol. 114: B. Liskov, CLU, Reference Manual. VIII, 190 pages. 1981.

Vol. 115: Automata, Languages and Programming. Edited by S. Even and O. Kariv. VIII, 552 pages. 1981.

Vol. 116: M. A. Casanova, The Concurrency Control Problem for Database Systems. VII, 175 pages. 1981.

Vol. 117: Fundamentals of Computation Theory. Proceedings, 1981. Edited by F. Gécseg. XI, 471 pages. 1981.

Vol. 118: Mathematical Foundations of Computer Science 1981. Proceedings, 1981. Edited by J. Gruska and M. Chytil. XI, 589 pages. 1981.

Vol. 119: G. Hirst, Anaphora in Natural Language Understanding: A Survey. XIII, 128 pages. 1981.

Vol. 120: L. B. Rall, Automatic Differentiation: Techniques and Applications. VIII, 165 pages. 1981.

Vol. 121: Z. Zlatev, J. Wasniewski, and K. Schaumburg, Y12M Solution of Large and Sparse Systems of Linear Algebraic Equations. IX, 128 pages. 1981.

Vol. 122: Algorithms in Modern Mathematics and Computer Science. Proceedings, 1979. Edited by A. P. Ershov and D. E. Knuth. XI, 487 pages. 1981.

Vol. 123: Trends in Information Processing Systems. Proceedings, 1981. Edited by A. J. W. Duijvestijn and P. C. Lockemann. XI, 349 pages. 1981.

Vol. 124: W. Polak, Compiler Specification and Verification. XIII, 269 pages. 1981.

Vol. 125: Logic of Programs. Proceedings, 1979. Edited by E. Engeler. V, 245 pages. 1981.

Vol. 126: Microcomputer System Design. Proceedings, 1981. Edited by M. J. Flynn, N. R. Harris, and D. P. McCarthy. VII, 397 pages. 1982.

Voll. 127: Y.Wallach, Alternating Sequential/Parallel Processing. X, 329 pages. 1982.

Vol. 128: P. Branquart, G. Louis, P. Wodon, An Analytical Description of CHILL, the CCITT High Level Language. VI, 277 pages. 1982.

Vol. 129: B. T. Hailpern, Verifying Concurrent Processes Using Temporal Logic. VIII, 208 pages. 1982.

Vol. 130: R. Goldblatt, Axiomatising the Logic of Computer Programming. XI, 304 pages. 1982.